Pathways and Crime Prevention

Pathways and Crime Prevention
Theory, policy and practice

Edited by

Alan France and Ross Homel

WILLAN
PUBLISHING

Published by

Willan Publishing
Culmcott House
Mill Street, Uffculme
Cullompton, Devon
EX15 3AT, UK
Tel: +44(0)1884 840337
Fax: +44(0)1884 840251
e-mail: info@willanpublishing.co.uk
website: www.willanpublishing.co.uk

Published simultaneously in the USA and Canada by

Willan Publishing
c/o ISBS, 920 NE 58th Ave, Suite 300,
Portland, Oregon 97213-3786, USA
Tel: +001(0)503 287 3093
Fax: +001(0)503 280 8832
e-mail: info@isbs.com
website: www.isbs.com

First published 2007

Hardback
ISBN: 978 1 84392 202 5

Paperback
ISBN: 978 1 84392 201 8

British Library Cataloguing-in-Publication Data

A catalogue record for this book is available from the British Library

Project managed by Deer Park Productions, Tavistock, Devon
Typeset by GCS, Leighton Buzzard, Bedfordshire, LU7 1EU
Printed and bound by T.J. International Ltd, Padstow, Cornwall

Contents

Figures and tables

Figures

Tables

Acknowledgements

The chapters in this book were presented originally at the Pathways and Prevention International Symposium held in Brisbane on 29 and 30 September 2005. The symposium was a joint initiative of the Key Centre for Ethics, Law, Justice and Governance at Griffith University and the UK Economic and Social Science Research Council Research Network, Pathways Into and Out of Crime (www.shef.ac.uk/pathways-into-and-out-of-crime). We would like to acknowledge the financial support of both bodies, as well as the financial sponsorship of Mission Australia and of the Queensland government through the Department of Communities. We would also like to thank Australian Academic Press, publishers of the *Australian and New Zealand Journal of Criminology*, for their permission to publish the papers from Volume 39, No. 3 (2006), a special issue on Pathways and Prevention. We would particularly like to acknowledge the support and considerable practical assistance provided by the journal editor, Professor Paul Mazerolle, in the preparation of those papers.

Contributors

Caryn Anderson is lecturer and programme co-ordinator, Graduate School of Library and Information Science, Simmons College, USA.

Thilo Boeck is a senior research fellow working on the ESRC Pathways Project based at De Montfort University, Leicester, UK.

Linda Caldwell is Professor of Recreation, Park and Tourism Management at the Pennsylvania State University, USA, and secretary of the Children and Youth working group of the World Leisure Association.

Rebecca Denning completed her PhD at Griffith University on juvenile justice policies and programmes in 2005, and currently manages the Criminal Justice Research Unit in the Queensland Department of the Premier and Cabinet.

Leigh Dunkerton worked as a research fellow at the University of Sheffield on the Pathways Into and Out of Crime ESRC research project. She is currently based at the University of Salford as the co-ordinator for Greater Manchester Making Research Count Initiative.

David Evans is Associate Professor of Special Education in the Faculty of Education and Social Work at the University of Sydney.

Alan France is Professor of Social Policy Research and Director of the Centre for Research in Social Policy at Loughborough University, UK.

Kate Freiberg is a developmental psychologist and senior research fellow on the Pathways to Prevention Project in the Key Centre for Ethics, Law, Justice and Governance at Griffith University, Brisbane.

Jacqueline Goodnow AC is Emeritus Professor of Psychology and Professorial Research Fellow at the Institute of Child Development Macquarie University in Sydney.

Kaye Haw is Principal Research Fellow at the University of Nottingham in the UK and principal fundholder of the Nottingham ESRC Pathways Into and Out of Crime Project.

Alan Hayes is Director of the Australian Institute of Family Studies. He is also Chair of the Australian Council for Children and Parenting (ACCAP) and Deputy Chair of the Stronger Families and Communities Partnership.

Jacqueline Homel is a psychologist working on her PhD in the Regulatory Institutions Network at the Australian National University.

Ross Homel is Professor of Criminology and Criminal Justice and Director of the Key Centre for Ethics, Law, Justice and Governance at Griffith University, Brisbane. He is also Director of Research and Development for the Pathways to Prevention Project.

Karin Ishimine is undertaking her PhD in the Faculty of Education and Social Work at the University of Sydney.

Hazel Kemshall is Professor of Community and Criminal Justice at De Montfort University, UK.

Cherie Lamb is the manager of the Mission Australia Pathways to Prevention Service.

Jeanette Lawrence is Associate Professor in Developmental Psychology in the School of Behavioural Science at the University of Melbourne.

Marie Leech is general manager, community services, at Mission Australia. She is a member of the board of directors of the Australian Institute of Families and the Stronger Families and Communities Strategy Partnership.

Margot Legosz is an epidemiologist and acting deputy director of the Research and Prevention Unit of the Queensland Crime and Misconduct Commission.

Bronwyn Lind is Deputy Director of the New South Wales Bureau of Crime Statistics and Research in Australia.

Robert MacDonald is Professor of Sociology and Youth Studies in the School of Social Sciences and Law at the University of Teesside in the UK.

Catherine Mahoney is Senior Researcher, Research and Social Policy Unit, Mission Australia.

Louise Marsland is Chief Research Officer in the Department of Health and Human Sciences at the University of Essex in the UK.

Paul Mazerolle is Research Professor in the Key Centre for Ethics, Law, Justice and Governance at Griffith University and is editor of the *Australian and New Zealand Journal of Criminology*.

Elena Miceski, formerly a research officer at the Queensland Crime and Misconduct Commission, is pursuing a PhD in criminology.

Gillian Pugh DBE recently retired as chief executive of Coram Family in 2005. She is an adviser to the Children, Young People and Families Directorate at the Department for Education and Skills and a visiting professor at London University Institute of Education.

Jennifer Sanderson is a developmental psychologist and research officer at the Queensland Crime and Misconduct Commission.

Edward Smith is Director of Evaluation Research in the Prevention Centre at the Pennsylvania State University, USA.

Don Weatherburn is the Director of the New South Wales Bureau of Crime Statistics and Research.

Introduction

Pathways and crime prevention: a difficult marriage?

Alan France and Ross Homel

For at least a quarter of a century the study of the developmental origins of crime and delinquency has been, in the words of Nagin and Tremblay (2005: 873), 'both an important and contentious topic in criminology'. Indeed, as these researchers note, the contemporary international wave of research within this genre is 'testimony to the central position of what has come to be called developmental criminology' (2005: 874). We estimate that since 1990 the journal *Criminology* has devoted at least one third of its articles to some aspect of developmental criminology. Many other journals, broader perhaps in their theoretical and methodological orientations than *Criminology*, are also now devoting considerable space to themes such as the effects of child abuse and family violence on children and young people's personal development, or the influence of poverty and social exclusion on pathways towards adulthood and perhaps towards crime.

Our aim with this book is to add to this growing body of knowledge, particularly from an Australian and United Kingdom perspective, and to highlight some important theoretical, methodological and policy debates. Drafts of all the chapters were delivered at an international symposium we organised in Brisbane in September 2005. The symposium had the title *Pathways and Prevention*, and had as a primary aim the creation of a dialogue between prevention researchers and developmental and life-course criminologists and others who do research relevant to the understanding of pathways into and out of crime. We wanted to know how prevention research informs pathways research, and to explore the implications of pathways research for prevention policies and planning.

Woven throughout the book are six core themes that emerged from the symposium papers and the discussions about them:

- improving the *conceptual foundations of pathways research*;
- deepening and widening our thinking about the *methods* that are used in pathways and prevention research;
- exploring new *empirical research into pathways and social contexts*;
- applying the insights of pathways thinking to the *design and implementation of preventive interventions*;
- exploring new *evidence from evaluations of preventive interventions*;
- reflecting on the *intersections between research, practice and policy*.

Reflecting these themes, the book is divided into two parts. Part 1 concentrates mainly on the first four themes, drawing on seven symposium papers first published in the *Australian and New Zealand Journal of Criminology* (2006: Volume 39 No. 3), and two other symposium papers that explore continuities in specific problems (sexual victimisation and bullying) across the life course. Part 2 of the book consists of seven symposium papers that focus on the last three themes that are all related to the theory, policy and practice of prevention from a life-course or developmental perspective. The authors of these chapters are united by an interest in improving prevention strategies by drawing upon a contextualised understanding of pathways and of the institutional and political forces that determine the sustainability of initiatives and that shape the policies that inform practice.

An interdisciplinary emphasis: the Brisbane international symposium

The symposium brought together approximately 60 scholars from a number of countries and from many disciplines, ranging through anthropology, criminology, early childhood studies, education, paediatrics, psychology, political science, public health, social work and social policy, sociology, and statistics. This interdisciplinary mix was quite deliberate, since, as we note in Chapter 1, pathways research draws broadly on 'theoretical and empirical work in the field of life-course studies and the developmental sciences, including developmental psychology, life-span sociology and psychology, life-history research, and studies of the life cycle' (see p. 12).

Criminology in the past two decades has made important contributions to these fields, and indeed is perhaps coming to be viewed as a model for how some of these disciplines could implement important innovations in life-course theory and methods of inquiry. For example, it is argued that literacy scholars should be looking to longitudinal research in criminology and the health sciences in order to expand the breadth of topics engaged within reading research (Vanderstaay 2006). Nevertheless the criminological corpus overall is small in comparison with that of other disciplines, reflecting criminology's specialised focus. We wanted to explore what light might be thrown by cognate research on problems that currently preoccupy criminologists, such as the role of life events in influencing the life course, the theorisation of social context and of human agency, the extent of and predictability of continuity or discontinuity in antisocial behaviour from childhood to adulthood, and the origins and consequences of crime and violence and other problem behaviours (Farrington 2005; Sampson and Laub 2005).

Some of the funding for the symposium came from the interdisciplinary UK research network Pathways Into and Out of Crime that is funded by the Economic and Social Research Council (http://www.pcrrd.group.shef.ac.uk) and a number of speakers spoke about their research through this network. Other speakers were members of the Australian Developmental Crime Prevention Consortium, an interdisciplinary group that wrote the 1999 federal government report *Pathways to Prevention: Developmental and Early Intervention Approaches to Crime in Australia*. Some speakers were not members of either of these groups and presented papers from the perspectives of their own or in some cases other disciplines. This interdisciplinarity has been expressed throughout this book in discussions on both pathways and on prevention.

For example, criminology has always been strongly influenced by psychology (Garland 2002), but the influence has tended to come from a kind of psychology that accords a central place to individual development at the expense of external influences. In their chapters Jacqueline Goodnow and Jeanette Lawrence, both developmental psychologists, contest this view of development, raising important questions about the social contexts that help shape individual biographies and the nature of person–environment interactions across the life course. In our own paper we approach the question of pathways by drawing more upon the sociological literature, especially the works of writers such as Bourdieu (1991), arguing that much debate in this area could benefit from theories that offer explanations of the cultural practices of young people in disadvantaged communities. From a different angle Don Weatherburn, trained as an experimental psychologist, questions our ability to explain juvenile crime rates at the aggregate level using sociological constructs of informal social control such as collective efficacy. He and Bronwyn Lind argue that the overwhelming weight of evidence supports an individual-level explanation, with the key process being the corrosive effects of poverty on the capacities of families and parents to provide loving, nurturing environments for their children.

New insights at the symposium did not only arise from debates between psychologists and sociologists. Linda Caldwell and Ed Smith come from a leisure studies background and draw not only upon recent debates within their own discipline but also on their own data to show how leisure and its theorisation is critical to the developmental perspective on youth crime. A major emphasis in the papers from the ESRC Network is the relevance of social anthropology and cultural studies to enhancing our understanding of pathways into and out of crime. Hazel Kemshall and her colleagues, for example, draw upon the work of Lupton (1999) while Kaye Haw uses the work of Douglas (1966) and Barthes (2000) to show how understanding cultural practice can add significant knowledge to our understanding of social processes. As a final example, Marie Leech, a social worker by training, draws with her colleagues on such diverse fields or 'lenses' as organisational learning, knowledge management and integration and implementation sciences to analyse how the learnings from a community-based developmental project can be captured and translated into routine practices.

Creating dialogue between pathways and prevention research

As we have already stated, we very much wanted at the Brisbane symposium to create a dialogue between those researching pathways and those researching prevention. However, it is striking how little attention pathways researchers (including developmental criminologists) seem to pay to prevention. In the voluminous literature on longitudinal studies in criminology the implications for prevention are often reduced (at best) to a listing of risk factors that may be 'both causal and modifiable' (Farrington 2003: 175). As one example of many, only in the very last sentence of their chapter on the development of male offending in the Pittsburgh Youth Study do

Loeber and his colleagues (2003: 131) observe that 'One of the greatest challenges for us in the future is to translate research findings into practice ... challenges include the generation of information relevant for preventive interventions'.

Similarly, in the larger life-course literature little attention is paid, at least explicitly, to prevention or early intervention. For example, the 728-page *Handbook of the Life Course* (Mortimer and Shanahan 2004) has no references to these terms in its index, and none of the 34 chapters appears to mention them. In fact there is plenty of material in the book that provides food for prevention thinking, particularly the discussions of desistance from crime (Sampson and Laub 2004; Uggen and Massoglia 2004), and the discussion of social capital as a unifying concept for understanding the links between socio-economic status and health over the life course (Frytak *et al.* 2004). However, the lessons must be drawn out by the assiduous reader.

While we did our best to get pathways authors presenting at the symposium to write about the implications of their work for prevention, few realistically managed to 'cross the divide'. Most papers in Part 1 of this book focus to a large extent on theoretical or empirical issues to do with pathways into and out of crime. This being said, all the papers give us valuable insights into issues that we might need to consider when constructing future prevention programmes. By way of illustration, the ideas that Jacqueline Goodnow proposes for describing social contexts have important preventive implications, for example by drawing our attention to *when* in the life course we might intervene. Limiting the focus to the early years leads to a limited view of contextual influences across the life-span, a theme amplified within an historical and policy context by Alan Hayes in Part 2. Similarly, Jacqueline's discussion of context as routes or opportunities is critically important because it points to such preventive strategies as making routes available for disadvantaged young people and keeping them open, a point we explore at some length in our own chapter.

The difficulties in bridging the gap between pathways and prevention research are not all one-way. If pathways researchers tend to treat prevention problems as an afterthought, prevention researchers have not generally been very energetic in absorbing the pathways literature and theorising the prevention process in the light of new findings about life-course development. Much prevention work is very 'mission-oriented' and focused on technical processes that take a set of problems to be tackled as unproblematic. When prevention has been informed by evidence what tends to emerge is simple models that link social problems to 'risk and protection', giving limited attention to the complex processes that underlie these apparently straightforward statistical relationships (Homel 2005).

Conclusion

Developmental criminology and life-course themes, including developmental prevention, have not been as prominent in the writings of criminologists from Australia and New Zealand in the past two decades as they have been in work in North America. In the UK 'pathways research' is more entrenched and certainly there seems to be no end to government funded prevention initiatives, but the dominant risk-prevention paradigm has created deep divisions. We offer this book as a contribution to the field that draws especially (but not solely) on work being done in Australia and the UK. Our hope is that the theoretical, methodological and policy issues raised will heighten interest in pathways and prevention research and lead to fruitful interdisciplinary collaborations that help to create better models for theory and practice.

References

Barthes, R. (2000) *Mythologies*. New York: Vintage.

Bourdieu, P. (1991) *The Logic of Practice*. Cambridge: Polity Press.

Douglas, M. (1966) *Purity and Danger: An Analysis of Concepts of Purity and Taboo*. London: Routledge and Kegan Paul.

Farrington, D.P. (2003) 'Key Results from the First Forty Years of the Cambridge Study in Delinquent Development', in T.P. Thornberry and M. Krohn (eds) *Taking Stock of Delinquency: An Overview of Findings from Contemporary Longitudinal Studies*. New York: Kluwer, pp. 137–84.

Farrington, D.P. (2005) 'Conclusions about Developmental and Life-course Theories', in D.P. Farrington (ed.) *Integrated Developmental and Life-course Theories of Offending*. Advances in Criminological Theory, Vol. 14. New Brunswick, NJ: Transaction Publishers, pp. 247–56.

Frytak, J., Harley, C. and Finch, M. (2004) 'Socioeconomic Status and Health over the Life Course: Capital as a Unifying Concept', in J.T. Mortimer and M.J. Shanahan (eds) *Handbook of the Life Course*. New York: Springer, pp. 623–43.

Garland, D. (2002) 'Of Crimes and Criminals: The Development of Criminology in Britain', in M. Maguire, R. Morgan and R. Reiner (eds)

The Oxford Handbook of Criminology, 3rd edn. Oxford: Oxford University Press, pp. 7–50.

Homel, R. (2005) 'Developmental Crime Prevention', in N. Tilley (ed.) *Handbook of Crime Prevention and Community Safety.* Cullompton: Willan Publishing, pp. 71–106.

Loeber, R., Farrington, D., Stouthamer-Loeber, M., Moffitt, T.E., Caspi, A., White, H.R., Wei, E.H. and Beyers, J.M. (2003) 'The Development of Male Offending: Key Findings from Fourteen Years of the Pittsburgh Youth Study', in T.P. Thornberry and M. Krohn (eds) *Taking Stock of Delinquency: An Overview of Findings from Contemporary Longitudinal Studies.* New York: Kluwer, pp. 93–130.

Lupton, D. (1999) *Risk.* London: Routledge.

Mortimer, J. and Shanahan, M. (2004) 'Preface', in J.T. Mortimer and M.J. Shanahan (eds) *Handbook of the Life Course.* New York: Springer, pp. xi–xvi.

Nagin, D.S. and Tremblay, R.E. (2005) 'Developmental Trajectory Groups: Fact or a Useful Statistical Fiction?', *Criminology*, 43: 873–904.

Sampson, R. and Laub, J. (2004) 'Desistance from Crime over the Life Course', in J.T. Mortimer and M.J. Shanahan (eds) *Handbook of the Life Course.* New York: Springer, pp. 295–310.

Sampson, R.J. and Laub, J.H. (2005) 'A life-course view of the development of crime', *The Annals of the American Academy of Political and Social Science*, 602: 12–45.

Uggen, C. and Massoglia, M. (2004) 'Desistance from Crime and Deviance as a Turning Point in the Life Course', in J.T. Mortimer and M.J. Shanahan (eds) *Handbook of the Life Course.* New York: Springer, pp. 311–30.

Vanderstaay, S.L. (2006) 'Learning from longitudinal research in criminology and the health sciences', *Reading Research Quarterly*, 41: 328–50.

Part I

Understanding pathways into and out of crime

Introduction

Alan France and Ross Homel

All the authors in this section have a common interest in pathways research and in its implications for prevention policy and practice, but there are widely divergent interpretations of what a 'pathway' is and differing views on the kind of theoretical lens through which the concept should be viewed. Probably all authors, regardless of their theoretical stance, would agree with Jeanette Lawrence when she states in Chapter 2 (p. 30): 'The pathway is a useful metaphor for prevention strategists, because it assists social scientists to organise information about individual lives into coherent and interpretable patterns.' However, not all would accept the term 'developmental pathway' despite the non-deterministic, whole-of-life and socially embedded notion of pathways that Lawrence (consistent with thinking in contemporary developmental psychology) outlines in her chapter. Indeed the terms 'development' and 'developmental' are highly controversial in some quarters (e.g. Hil 1999).

Perhaps Sampson and Laub (2005a) in their recent critique of the developmental criminology paradigm best express the main concerns of the critics. Their paper is published in special volume 602 of the *Annals of the American Academy of Political and Social Sciences*, November 2005, which consists entirely of papers presenting different sides of the debate on how we should think about and do research on 'development' in criminology. Sampson and Laub question the notion of developmentally distinct groups that have unique causes, a central feature of the famous typology introduced by Terrie Moffitt (1993) that distinguishes *life-course persistent* from *adolescent-limited* offenders. As they state in a related paper, developmental accounts tend to assume 'pre-programming' that leads to a view of the life course as 'an unwinding, an unfolding, or an unrolling of what is fundamentally "already there"' (Sampson and Laub 2005b: 178). Sampson and Laub acknowledge that some developmentalists emphasise social interactions, but they argue that developmental models nevertheless remain limited because they accord insufficient weight to human agency and to 'random developmental noise', as well as to the turning points embedded in institutional transitions that so characterised the pathways of the sample of Glueck men that they studied (Sampson and Laub 1993).

A number of the chapters in this book add to the North American debate, first by addressing the relationship between individual pathways and social context or social structure. Jacqueline Goodnow explores the 'available paths/routes/opportunities/maps' that help structure and influence pathways into and out of crime, a theme that we also develop in our chapter by distinguishing societal access routes from individual developmental pathways. We argue for greater awareness of social structure, political action and localised cultural influence, while Jacqueline highlights additional ways of theorising context as 'activities/routines/cultural practices'. Jeanette Lawrence, on the other hand, argues for recognition of a life-course perspective that explores the intra-individual and inter-individual aspects of 'experience' as critical to understanding the different pathways into and out of crime.

A second way the present set of chapters contributes to current debates relates to the relationship between risk factors and offending. Pathways research and developmental criminology in particular have, over the previous 20 years, been much influenced by the risk-factor paradigm (Farrington 1994). Three chapters directly challenge the dominance of this approach, raising questions about the ways it has come to construct the 'problem' in particular ways that limit our thinking. Kaye Haw, for example, is interested in how the concept of 'risk factor' has become a 'generative metaphor' which has lifted the concept to mythological status in the UK, especially among policy-makers and practitioners with power to intervene in the lives of children.

Robert MacDonald and Hazel Kemshall and her colleagues take a different approach. MacDonald draws upon data from his qualitative longitudinal study in the UK to show how risk-factor analysis has been unable to explain the complexity of pathways for young people with difficult lives. He argues, similar to Sampson and Laub, that even though many young people may well have signs of risk, the future is far less predictable than claimed in the risk-factor model. As he says, 'stuff happens, sometimes for the better, sometimes for the worse and sometimes with unclear, equivocal outcomes' (p. 123), leaving the question of predictability uncertain. Hazel Kemshall and her colleagues explore the conceptualisation of risk in late modern society, arguing that the dominance of 'artefact' approaches to risk analysis is limited and that social constructionist approaches have much to offer in trying to make sense of how young people defined as 'at risk' become involved in offending.

Don Weatherburn and Bronwyn Lind engage with the North American debate in an entirely different way, by taking the fight directly onto territory carved out by Robert Sampson in an influential series of papers on the concept of collective efficacy (e.g. Sampson 2004; Sampson *et al.* 1997). Weatherburn and Lind argue in contrast to Sampson that the crucial link between structural factors like poverty and crime is the capacity of parents to parent effectively, and not the collective efficacy of residents in an area to intervene to maintain order. If this argument is correct then neighbourhood-level interventions should be accorded a lower priority than approaches that strengthen families and support parents. The policy choice is a real one but as the authors emphasise, it needs to be informed by research that more rigorously compares the explanatory power of both proposed pathways.

Methods

The methods we use as scholars to do pathways or prevention research are a core theme of this book. In many respects the debates in the special volume of the *Annals of the American Academy of Political and Social Sciences* revolve around issues of method, particularly the appropriateness of the search for typologies of offender trajectories using the semi-parametric group-based methods developed by Nagin (1999). While not always focused on statistical methods, the chapters in this book also aim to provide alternative perspectives on how we might explore pathways.

Kemshall and her colleagues, drawing upon a wide range of work within the ESRC research network, argue for a synthesis of epistemological positions within social science. They suggest that such a synthesis should be based on the recognition of the importance of using diverse methods to investigate the complex social processes underpinning pathways. They summarise the results of three research projects that explored the influence of some classic risk factors from a strong constructionist position (school exclusion), a moderate constructionist position (social capital and risk-taking), and a weak constructionist position (substance use). The issue for these authors is one of 'fit' across differing levels of analysis rather than 'grand explanatory theory' (p. 105).

We also argue in our own chapter for a form of methodological pluralism, one that values and centralises the voice of young people. Previous research in this field has paid limited attention to what the young themselves have to say about pathways, and such a research strategy could provide valuable insights into the access routes they perceive as available to them as well as the barriers to moving forward in their lives. Rob MacDonald goes further in arguing for the return to ethnography as a tool for achieving a more qualitative, biographical and historically informed understanding of the diversity of social processes that influence the choices young people make. He emphasises, for example, the value of interviewees' retrospective biographical accounts in exploring the impact of events on transitions, as well as the crucial importance of understanding risks presented by the historical and spatial contexts, such as the historically unprecedented influx of cheap heroin in the mid-1990s.

Jacqueline Homel's study of bullying at school and in post-school settings, especially the workplace, illustrates the value of listening to the voices of young people and the value of the biographical and qualitative approach to pathways research advocated by MacDonald. Using extensive qualitative data from focus groups with young adults, Jacqueline explores at some depth the relationships between different forms of bullying at different ages, and the complex nature of the interactions between developmental transitions and social settings (school, home, workplace and the larger economic and political contexts). She also highlights some specific methodological problems that arise when measuring social contexts and when comparing behaviours in different settings at different life phases.

Implications for prevention

Across these first seven chapters there are a range of implications for prevention work. Don Weatherburn and Bronwyn Lind explore the links between poverty and violence, illustrating the potential of pathways research to influence prevention practice by, in this case, contrasting a 'collective efficacy pathway' with a 'family support pathway'. Other chapters in this part of the book have equally important implications for prevention thinking. We have already noted that the ideas Jacqueline Goodnow proposes for describing social contexts have important preventive implications by drawing attention to when in the life course we might intervene and how we might adopt preventive strategies to make access routes available for disadvantaged young people and keep them open.

Jeanette Lawrence's theoretical analysis of developmental pathways similarly links development with prevention by taking as a starting point observations and analyses of typical and atypical patterns of experience in people's lives. While accepting the main elements of Sampson and Laub's (2005a) critique of developmental criminology, she recommends that prevention planning be based on the kind of fine-grained analysis of trajectories carried out by Nagin and Tremblay (2005), with careful attention to the distinctive strategies required for dealing with beginnings, middles and ends of patterns.

From a different perspective, an implication of the work of Hazel Kemshall and her colleagues in exploring at some depth the *meaning* of school exclusion to the young people involved could be to question the preventive benefits of a simple-minded programme that focused on exclusion without attending both to how schools construct the phenomenon of 'exclusion' and to the mismatch between students' needs and the school experience.

Paul Mazerolle and Jacqueline Homel use contrasting methodologies to explore continuities in *victimisation* across the life course, thus adding to the more common emphasis on continuities in offending. Paul and his colleagues from the Queensland Crime and Misconduct Commission explore continuities in sexual victimisation from childhood to adulthood in a sample of offenders, finding both high levels of victimisation and high levels of continuity. Their multivariate analyses of risk factors include a range of personal, lifestyle and relationship variables. Their results favour a 'heterogeneity model' over a 'state dependent or experiential model', which means that stable characteristics of individuals or their environments are more important in promoting continuity than more ephemeral lifestyle-related contingencies. Long-term developmental rather than situational prevention approaches therefore seem to be called for.

Jacqueline Homel's study of bullying is relevant to both victimisation and offending in a range of contexts across childhood and early adulthood. On the basis of her research Jacqueline proposes a number of specific prevention strategies, including timing interventions to take maximum advantage of the potential of life transitions (such

7

as leaving school) to also be *turning points* for victims or offenders, and focusing prevention programmes on the *norms* that operate in workplaces and other settings, not just on individual bullies and victims.

It is clear from these examples that pathways research has plenty to say about prevention. What is needed now is a new generation of preventive initiatives using innovative methodologies that explicitly build on previously unexplored insights from pathways studies.

References

Farrington, D.P. (1994) 'Early developmental prevention of juvenile delinquency', *Criminal Behaviour and Mental Health*, 4: 209–27.

Hil, R. (1999) 'Beating the developmental path: Critical notes on the "Pathways to Prevention Report" ', *Youth Studies Australia*, 18(4): 49–50.

Moffitt, T. (1993) 'Adolescent-limited and life-course-persistent antisocial behavior: A developmental taxonomy', *Psychological Review*, 100: 674–701.

Nagin, D.S. (1999) 'Analyzing developmental trajectories: Semi-parametric, group-based approach', *Psychological Methods*, 4: 39–177.

Nagin, D.S. and Tremblay, R.E. (2005) 'Developmental trajectory groups: Fact or a useful statistical fiction?', *Criminology*, 43: 873–904.

Sampson, R. (2004) 'Neighborhood and community: Collective efficacy and community action', *New Economy*, 11: 106–13.

Sampson, R.J. and Laub, J.H. (1993) *Crime in the Making: Pathways and Turning Points Through Life*. Cambridge, MA: Harvard University Press.

Sampson, R.J. and Laub, J.H. (2005a) 'A life-course view of the development of crime', *Annals of the American Academy of Political and Social Science*, 602: 12–45.

Sampson, R.J. and Laub, J.H. (2005b) 'A General Age-graded Theory of Crime: Lessons Learned and the Future of Life-course Criminology', in David P. Farrington (ed.), *Integrated Developmental and Life-course Theories of Offending*. Advances in Criminological Theory, Vol. 14. New Brunswick, NJ: Transaction Publishers, pp. 165–181.

Sampson, R., Raudenbush, S. and Earls, F. (1997) 'Neighborhoods and violent crime: A multilevel study of collective efficacy,' *Science*, 277: 918–24.

Chapter 1

Societal access routes and developmental pathways: Putting social structure and young people's voice into the analysis of pathways into and out of crime

Alan France and Ross Homel

Abstract

Central to pathways research is the analysis of the social processes involved in human action and the influences that have shaping qualities. At the heart of these social processes are human beings who exercise agency and help construct themselves and their environments. Shaping influences include changing social structures; political ideologies and policy innovations; and changes taking place in the cultural sphere of social life. In studying the actions of individuals within changing social environments it is important to make a distinction between *individual developmental pathways* and *societal access routes*. Access routes appear in different forms to different people in terms of accessibility and attractiveness. Understanding this perceptual dimension requires listening to the voices of children and young people. This is illustrated by reference to the work of the UK ESRC research network, Pathways Into and Out of Crime, which shows how culture, structure and policy influence young people's everyday lives and decisions. It also shows that what young people really value is not programmes but a supportive relationship with a non-judgemental adult who is able to help them negotiate their way through difficult circumstances. The focus of prevention efforts should be on changing social arrangements to create opportunities and systems that facilitate the formation of such supportive structures.

Introduction

The starting point for this chapter is our belief that western societies could do better in improving the developmental pathways of children and young people if more attention were paid to understanding and changing social arrangements that limit opportunities for participation in mainstream institutions. We propose as a tool for thinking about how this might be done the development of a sharper analytical distinction between the concepts of *individual developmental pathways* and *social pathways* or *societal access routes*. (These concepts are also discussed by Jacqueline Goodnow and Jeanette Lawrence in this volume.) They tend to intertwine in the literature, and it is often unclear whether change at the individual or at some structural level is being referred to (or whether both are meant in some sense). While the two concepts are indeed closely related, our contention is that longitudinal and prevention research has emphasised the study of individual pathways and behaviours to the detriment of research on social, cultural and political processes and the concomitant changes in social contexts that bear so directly on the lives of children and young people. Improvement in the well-being of individuals is always the bottom line, but sustainable individual change is underpinned by structural or cultural change that opens up new routes to social participation and hence new possibilities for individual development.

We also propose that our understanding of these processes could be greatly improved if we listened more to what children and young people have to tell us about their experiences of developmental pathways. Such an approach is not new to social science (James and Prout 1997) or to certain areas of criminology (France 2006), but within research on pathways and prevention the voices and perspectives of children and young people have not been prominent. An approach that values their contribution would help us understand more about those broader societal access routes and the influences they have on the choices of young people and the opportunities open to them.

David Farrington (2005) has summarised some current theoretical debates in developmental and life-course criminology. These include the extent to which antisocial behaviour exhibits continuity from childhood into adulthood, or is characterised by change and unpredictability; the usefulness of underlying constructs like antisocial propensity; the extent to which it is useful to attempt to distinguish types of offenders; and the importance of life events in influencing the life course, including offending behaviours. All these questions are of fundamental importance, and have their counterparts in other areas of life-course and developmental research. However, they are very much focused on individual factors and processes. One way of broadening the agenda is to ask about social contexts and processes of change (Goodnow, this volume; Homel 2005). Beyond this level of analysis, however, are larger questions about social and political processes, such as the reproduction and intensification over generations of the 'social gradient' in health and developmental outcomes (Keating and Hertzman 1999); and the failure of mainstream institutions such as schools to engage successfully with many socially disadvantaged children, young people and families (Connell 1982).

Risk-factor approaches, and longitudinal studies more broadly, have not been especially helpful in addressing these larger issues, or even the questions about immediate social contexts. This is partly because individuals' social environments, including how these environments change or stay the same, are much more difficult to study than intra-individual changes (Developmental Crime Prevention Consortium 1999; Homel 2005). This limitation is in turn partly a reflection of the narrow disciplinary focus of many who have worked in the field. For example, much pathways research has conceptualised childhood either in terms of a biological experience that is developmental, linear and relatively deterministic, with behaviour understood as being linked to stages of cognitive and social development, or in terms of socialisation, where the environment imposes constraints and channels children's and young people's behaviour (France 2006). Both approaches construct children and young people as passive, and are characterised by a tendency to fall into either a biological or cultural reductionism.

Recent research has shown that childhood is far more complex than these approaches suggest, being greatly influenced by historical trends, political processes and social contexts, as well as by biological or psychological processes (James and Prout 1997). Within these processes children themselves are active contributors to their own childhood. They are competent social actors who have to manage and negotiate their ways through the institutionalised processes that construct childhood in particular ways. Children and young people express their own agency through social action.

We therefore propose a life-course theoretical perspective (Elder *et al.* 2004) that draws more fully than in the past on sociology and on research in human services, as well as on psychology and the health sciences, and which recognises both the social processes involved in human action and the influences that have shaping qualities. At the heart of these social processes are human beings who exercise agency and have a hand in constructing themselves and their environments. Shaping influences include those forces to which we have already alluded: changing social structures; political ideologies and policy innovations; and changes taking place in the cultural sphere of social life. We argue in addition for a methodological pluralism that accords equal value to positivist and interpretive approaches, blending qualitative and quantitative data to study (for example), 'developmental changes in parallel with sociological and demographic shifts in situation and context' (Furstenberg 2004: 667). A critical methodological step, we propose, is to take seriously the voices of children and young people in understanding contexts and planning prevention (Prout 2000). Some of the problems posed above by Farrington (2005) might take on new hues if viewed within this enlarged multidisciplinary framework.

In this chapter we address these challenges, drawing on our experiences in doing research on pathways and on prevention policy and practice. In the next section we amplify our remarks on developmental pathways and societal access routes, highlighting the role that societal access routes and social contexts play in how children and young people negotiate and manage their relationship with crime. In the second part we explain why listening to children and young people is important to our understanding of pathways, showing how their voices can give us greater insight into their lives. In the third and major section we widen the questions to explore some of the theoretical issues around processes and changing social contexts, and ways of incorporating different methods and voices into the research process. Within this we illustrate how structure, politics and culture can influence the everyday lives and social contexts of children's and young people's pathways. We draw on examples from recent research carried out through the ESRC research network, Pathways Into and Out of Crime, that prioritised young people's explanations (www.pcrrd.group.sheffield.ac.uk).

Developmental pathways and societal access routes

By *pathways research* we mean both theoretical and empirical work in the field of life-course studies and the developmental sciences, including developmental psychology, life-span sociology and psychology, life-history research, and studies of the life cycle (Elder *et al.* 2004). Numerous methodologies are used in these fields, including biographical, historical and demographic analyses, and quantitative longitudinal methods. Distinguishing features of these broad fields are a focus that goes beyond age-specific studies on childhood or early adulthood (still the overwhelming bulk of the longitudinal research in criminology), and a concern with 'social pathways, their developmental effects, and their relation to personal and social-historical conditions' (Elder *et al*. 2004: 7). So the *life course* refers to 'the age-graded, socially-embedded sequence of roles that connect the phases of life' (Mortimer and Shanahan 2004: xi), while Elder *et al*. define *social pathways* as 'the trajectories of education and work, family and residences that are followed by individuals and groups through society ... individuals generally work out their own life course and trajectories in relation to institutionalised pathways and normative patterns' (Elder *et al*. 2004: 8).

These are useful concepts that have guided our thinking, although as we have already argued it is important to make a sharper distinction between individual developmental pathways and societal access routes. We define developmental pathways as sequences and chains of events and experiences over time involving changes both within and around the person (Lawrence, this volume), while by societal access routes we mean the routes, opportunities, open doors, or ways forward that are available within a society to individuals at different points in their lives. The concept of a societal access route is by no means new, although a number of terms are used in the literature to capture the general idea. Elder *et al*. (2004) use 'institutionalised pathways and normative patterns', as in the quote above, but they also talk about 'social pathways' or simply 'opportunities', while Jacqueline Goodnow (this volume) refers to 'available routes/opportunities/options'.

Societal access routes are shaped by social arrangements and institutional practices and so are features of the society rather than the individual. This makes social arrangements as important as individuals in prevention research and planning. However, access routes do not exist in some kind of platonic realm of unchanging forms. On the contrary, they are constantly changing as society changes, and they have a strong perceptual dimension and so appear in different forms to different people. It is not just a matter of 'what is', it is also a question of 'what is perceived to be' at any particular time, both in terms of the accessibility of opportunities and their attractiveness. Understanding the perceptual dimension therefore becomes fundamental both to studying pathways and developing effective prevention policies, reinforcing the importance of the voices of children and young people.

The key challenge, then, is how to conceptualise social context and opportunity structures, whether at the level of impact on individual behaviour or at the level of social programmes or professional practices that aim to bring about social change in communities. With respect to the question of behaviour, we propose that the developmental pathways and societal accesses routes of children and young people should be understood in relation to structural, political and cultural forces that operate at global, national and local levels. Most pathways research would recognise the influence of a range of external factors such as those within the local community or neighbourhood or peer groups (e.g. Farrington 2003; Wikström 2004), yet such concepts tend to be narrowly understood, reduced in many cases to individual and family interactions within small-scale geographical spaces. While we do not deny the importance of small-scale influences, we should also recognise the complex ways in which global and national economic and political forces influence community life and how informal and formal forms of social control within community spaces operate to include and exclude. Wider social and economic structures are usually given a limited role to play in any explanation, and the potential of government policies and programmes to make problems worse is too rarely recognised (Armstrong 2004; Bessant *et al.* 2002).

Putting the voices of young people into pathways research

How might research methods that help us understand the multidimensional aspects of social context be strengthened? Recent debates within developmental criminology have focused on using new advanced quantitative research methods as ways of understanding criminal careers, especially at the group level (Blumstein 2005; Maughan 2005; Nagin and Tremblay 2005; Raudenbush 2005). While such an approach has much to offer, it fails to fully comprehend the complexity of pathways or to provide insights into the meaning of life events (Sampson and Laub 2005). It also throws little light on the way children and young people make choices about their lives.

Social science research has traditionally been shaped by a dominant orthodoxy that sees children and young people as either unable to explain their lives or as passive social actors (James and Prout 1997). For example, in the 1970s the Birmingham Centre for Cultural Studies theorised the newly emerging 'youth culture', arguing it was a new form of political resistance to structural changes (Hall and Jefferson 1975). Their analysis was based upon their own observation and interpretation of events, and little credence was given to the voice and explanations of the young themselves (France 2006). As a result we were left with a partial and uncertain interpretation of events. There was no certainty that the young people involved saw their actions in the ways portrayed by the researchers. More recently, research has shown that if we do prioritise children's and young people's voices we can gain valuable insights about the meaning they give to their everyday lives and actions (James and Prout 1997). For example, Smith *et al.* (2005) explored young people's understanding of citizenship. By talking to the young they were able to show how they defined their citizenship and how they acted upon it.

Such an approach to understanding children's and young people's lives does not privilege one epistemological position over another. There is much value in a form of methodological pluralism that rejects epistemological positioning and is pragmatic, recognising the important contributions of different approaches to accessing the social world (Payne *et al.* 2004). Qvortrup (1997), for example, shows how quantitative data can provide a valuable mechanism for giving voice to children and young people. Historically, the gathering and analysis of large data sets has marginalised their voices, and academic surveys tend to be developed around adult questions and assumptions. Approaches that actively engage children and young people can help identify the types of issues that are important to them and help us create tools that are 'child and youth friendly' (France *et al.* 1999). Recent developments in childhood studies have also seen the emergence of a wide range of new qualitative techniques that assist in accessing their voices and perspectives (Lewis *et al.* 2004). For example, childhood and youth researchers have been developing methods that are less dependent on either the written or spoken word. These include 'write and draw' techniques, vignettes that use storyboards taken from popular culture, and multimedia technologies such as computers, cameras and video cameras. There has also been much discussion over the use of traditional methods such as the interview and focus groups. Of course, like all research methods these new developments have methodological challenges related to ethics, interpretation and validity.

The incorporation of some of these new methods into studies of criminal careers and developmental pathways would be valuable. Not only would they provide an understanding of what types of societal access routes might be open to children and young people in different contexts, they would illuminate how young people see themselves and their own futures in relation to societal opportunities or barriers. As Sampson and Laub (2005) argue, disciplines such as developmental criminology have not given much credence to the role of agency in notions of onset of or desistance from criminal careers. Yet by listening to the voices of children and young people we can gain a better understanding of the social processes and institutional interactions that shape their pathways. Such an approach can also throw light on how agency is expressed in social action.

Widening the question: processes, opportunities and changing social contexts

In this section we discuss the social context of opportunities and developmental pathways by exploring the interplay between the structural, the political and the cultural. It is within these intersecting processes that children and young people make their choices, especially in relation to criminal activity. To enhance the argument we illustrate these processes by drawing on the work of the ESRC research network. Examples are taken from a project researching the pathways of young people with early evidence of problem behaviours (Armstrong et al. 2006). This project followed 110 children and young people aged between 11 and 18 with a mean age of 14 who had been either excluded from school, identified as having an emotional behavioural difficulty (EBD) or had just entered the criminal justice system. Of these, 81 were boys and 29 girls with 26 being from Asian and African Caribbean descent. The research was conducted over three years and was located in four geographical areas in the UK. The examples that follow come from a sample of 13 case studies. These young people were interviewed three times; with their consent, significant others such as mothers, brothers, friends and professional workers were also interviewed.

The influence of social structure

The choices available to us, and the structures around us are influential in shaping our lives. Human action is not purely an intra-individual psychological phenomenon. As individuals we are reflexive on who we are (including how we become who we are) and how others perceive us. Selfhood becomes a dialectical synthesis of internal and external definitions. 'Self-identity is not something that is just given ... but something that has to be routinely created and sustained in reflexive activities of the individual' (Giddens 1991: 52). The influence of modern structures and institutions is critical in this process and raises questions about freewill. Individuals negotiate and navigate their relationships with 'society' and therefore the notion of 'choice' must always be recognised as taking place within a particular context. So we are products of social and psychological forces, but we are also causal agents in the construction of our environments and ourselves (Gecas 2004).

The influence of social structure on human action is critical in shaping our social context. External economic factors are particularly important (Devine *et al.* 2005). Developmental criminology has a tendency to rehearse the view that economic factors are low predictors of future offending (Farrington 2002). Structural factors are understood as only one part of a jigsaw in identifying the relationships between parenting and offending (Farrington 1996), neglect and offending (Weatherburn and Lind, this volume), or the decline of informal social control in disorganised communities (Sampson and Laub 1993). The broader economic context of social life and its relationship to offending is missing in this form of analysis. Developmental criminologists also tend to theorise economic structures and restructuring at the simple level of neighbourhood or community. Notions of changes to 'place' or 'locality' in a broader context that recognises other social spaces in cities or towns that are critical to the lives of the young, is not usually included in this analysis.

Major changes have been taking place in how cities are responding to global deindustrialisation (Taylor *et al.* 1996). This is having a significant impact not only on shaping neighbourhoods and community life but also on both the opportunity structures in and around local areas (MacDonald, this volume) and young people's self-perception of their own social futures (Connelly and Neil 2001; MacDonald and Marsh 2005). While contemporary evidence shows that long-term involvement in criminal careers can be greatly affected by employment patterns and opportunities in later life (Sampson and Laub 2005), evidence also shows how young people's present-day understandings of local labour markets and their emerging social futures can greatly influence their sense of inclusion, willingness and ability to take non-criminal pathways in adolescence (Craine 1997). 'Turning points' linked to young people's experience of work but also perceptions of their own future employment chances may well be influential in shaping criminal careers in late adolescence (Sampson and Laub 1993). Life in such environments is challenging and difficult.

Managing the limited opportunities and illegal pathways are a part of everyday life.

Economic restructuring is also influencing how local spaces and environments are used, policed and managed (Loader 1996). Major changes are taking place in the ordering of social space in cities and towns as a result of economic restructuring (Taylor *et al.* 1996). This is having an effect on the everyday lives of the young and their engagement with law enforcement and criminal justice. For example, within new out-of-town shopping malls and private housing estates young people are consistently seen as 'the problems' to be removed (McCahill 2002). These malls and estates are related to a range of changes taking place in the reconstruction of public space, where young people are 'designed out' of certain spaces, especially those designated as 'family friendly' (Malone 1999). This can have major implications for the young. Evidence shows that they are monitored more intensely through CCTV, being seen as potential problems, leading to increased arrests for minor offences (Norris and Armstrong 1999). They are also being given more attention by the police, which is leading to many entering the criminal justice system before they have committed offences that warrant such a response (McAra and McVie 2005). Such understandings of the impact of economic change are invisible within much developmental criminology.

Examples from the ESRC project show how these structural contexts can be influential in shaping access routes and opportunities. On leaving school one research participant, Jake, got a job with his uncle in the building trade. He did not really like the job, finding it 'boring' and offering little for the future, but he wanted to have all the things we take for granted as adults: a car, a home, nice clothes and a good life. He already had a girlfriend who was pregnant but was going to have an abortion. They were trying to make a go of it but were having difficulties. He also felt that working for £175 per week for his uncle was secondary to the possibilities of making £1,000 a day selling heroin, although he was torn between the legal route and the illegal route: 'There's two of me really, there's like me when I go on to work and me when I come home from work and I'm different.'

In the end Jake quit his job and college placement to spend more time with his friends (the 'other self') and to concentrate on dealing drugs. Six months later he was arrested for dealing. The choice for Jake was hard because he was keen to try and make it legally, yet this route offered limited financial benefits while criminal pathways offered hope of a 'better' life.

Criminal activity can also offer a respite from boring lives, bringing pleasure into lives that are sometimes difficult. Yet getting pleasure for many was restricted to things that did not cost money. As a result, finding fun was a major part of everyday life in the neighbourhood. Yet how the police (and the community) viewed this type of activity could be very different. For example, James lived in an area where the dumping of stolen cars was a normal practice. He had a record of petty offences. One of these was an incident when he and a few of his friends pushed an engineless car to a place where they could use it for a 'bit of fun.' To not be involved was unthinkable for James, since it would have created problems for him in the form of exclusion and derision from his friends. But the movement of the car was not a 'big deal' to James: it was not a criminal act, just a bit of fun that brightened up their day. This was not how the local police saw it; they accused them of stealing the car. With the increased forms of surveillance and policing this incident was defined as serious, leading to James and his friends being arrested.

Changing cultural patterns

So far we have considered the influence of the structural in terms of societal pathways but we must also recognise that human action is greatly influenced by culture. Pierre Bourdieu (1991) has introduced the idea of *habitus* and the importance of cultural and social capital as a way of understanding cultural life. He argues that our way of life, our values and our dispositions are inherited from our own individual and collective histories and traditions. These guide us in responding to cultural rules, contexts and events. The habitus is set by the social and historical conditions of its production. It gives rise to and serves as the classifying basis for individual collective practices. It helps shape our world-view and locates our practices in certain social environments, producing and reproducing existing cultural practices. In this context habitus produces a predisposed yet seemingly normalised way of seeing the world and acting within it. The everyday routine and habits of individuals become critical to our daily lived lives (Giddens 1991). Habitus not only provides a framework for 'bracketing' or 'answering' the experiences we encounter in our lives but also for creating feelings and emotions that underpin our sense of ontological security. This then helps shape our feelings of 'taking life for granted', 'habit', 'routine' and the 'everyday'.

Meanings of childhood, youth and their developmental pathways can therefore be structured in particular ways dependent upon the local cultural context. Local ways of doing things shape the everyday experience of being a child or young person. But we also need to recognise the importance of children's and young people's own cultures in this process (James and Prout 1997). Historically this has been constructed around notions of 'deviant youth subcultures', yet these are not always good representations of the everyday, being focused on minority groups of young men who are defined as problematic (France 2006). Most young people live ordinary lives that have strong connections to the 'normal way that things are done' in their communities. This can have significant influences on choices and opportunities and be important in how they perceive and understand crime. There is a growing body of work that recognises the importance of this cultural context of criminal behaviour (Bottoms *et al.* 2004; MacDonald and Marsh 2005; Sampson and Laub 2005) and its relationship to everyday lives in deprived communities.

Young people in the ESRC research project lived in areas of high deprivation where opportunities were limited; they also tended to live in areas of high crime. Crime was clearly a part of their everyday lives and historically it has shaped community life. Most young people had been involved in some form of low-level offending, but more importantly the majority encountered crime on a regular basis either as victims or as witnesses to crime. As a result they had to find ways, on a daily basis, of managing their relationships with crime in their own neighbourhoods. In this context crime in the locality of place was normalised and what would seem to us as extraordinary was for most young people a normal part of the everyday. In this context pathways into and out of crime were not about choice, they were fluid and unpredictable and ever-changing.

Jake's story is about drifting into crime with groups of friends in the area in which he lives. Here it is quite normal and ordinary to be involved in such activities. It is what generations have done before him. Jake explains it as wanting to feel 'included', to be seen as 'one of the boys'. But it is also about having a 'laff' and having something to do. This interplay between crime and fun has always been how young people have managed the boredom of the everyday. But it is also about survival on the streets and the need to maintain status in a tough world. Jake believes that being on the street requires him to be tough: 'You can't be weak … and … you can't let no one treat you like an idiot …you can't in that game.'

Being strong and not showing weakness are critical for how Jake survives on 'his' streets. These are culturally specific terms that can be historically located, forming a part of his habitus and guiding him on how 'to be' in 'this place.' Doing crime therefore is not about the act itself but about the way it helps him manage his everyday life.

Political forces and changing social policies

Politics is a further powerful influence. Social policies can have a significant impact on shaping the institutional response to crime (Muncie 2004). Recently children's policy in the UK has become more co-ordinated and holistic, aiming to increase children's rights and participation (Department for Education and Skills 2004). At its heart is the laudable desire to tackle child poverty and need among families and to protect children from abuse and neglect. Massive resources have been provided to create child-friendly policies and practices, one consequence of which has been the expansion of childcare opportunities outside the family structure. However, the policies have also led to increased forms of negative surveillance, especially of those defined as 'troublesome' (Muncie 2004). Mechanisms have been created for monitoring risk across the life course and new forms of regulation and control have been installed in community structures (Brown 2004). Within this we have also seen a separation of youth justice from the holistic approach to children's policy. This has increased the use of punishment and especially imprisonment for those children and young people who are seen not to conform (Muncie 2004; Pugh, this volume).

While New Labour champions 'evidence-based policy' (Department for Education and Employment 2000), many policy developments in this area have been driven not by evidence but ideology. Crime policies in particular are not always based on scientific evidence, being constructed more by a desire to be seen by the electorate to be 'tough on crime' (Newburn 2002). But this is not just about policies of youth justice it is also about prevention and early intervention. Risk reduction and early intervention programmes such as Sure Start and the Children's Fund have consistently been restructured away from their original goals to meet political objectives around issues of employability (France and Utting 2005). A recent example in the UK is Tony Blair's threat to stop funding Sure Start (the Labour Party's flagship early intervention initiative). He is highly critical of its 'failure' to deliver on its promises and suggests the reason is poor multi-agency co-operation (*Guardian*, 24 May 2006). His argument is not informed by evidence but more by a desire to shift policy and cut national spending at a time when the national evaluation of Sure Start is unable to report on impact.

Research from the ESRC project also suggests that the risk-factor analysis of young people's lives is having negative impacts on those who are defined as 'troubled' or 'troublesome.' Risk assessments are developed as responses to 'need' through measuring 'risk', and the 'problem' is then dealt with through structured interventions (France and Utting 2005). In youth justice these tend to aim to reduce the potential for future offending and make young people more 'responsible' (France 2006; Newburn 2002) rather than tackling need. For many young people this type of response feels inappropriate and inadequate.

For example, Jake meets with his youth offending team (YOT) worker twice a week but he has negotiated it to once a week because he is working. He has had relationships with other 'social workers' and does not have much time for them. They have never 'made a difference to my life ... it's the streets what's made a difference though, a difference, it's life realised ...'

From his YOT worker's perspective Jake is not a problem, just facing difficulties around balancing his life. Conflict exists over the amount of time he has to spend at work and the lack of space he has for friends. He is, however, not a priority; he does enough to make the YOT worker have a view of him as 'an alright person.'

Jake does what is required to fulfil his requirements with the YOT but does not feel it has much to offer him. The YOT worker talks about Jake mainly through his relationship with crime by drawing upon models provided in the risk assessment form. His explanation and understanding of 'the problem' is framed in the language not only of targets and assessment but also of the measurement of individual attributes. For example, when asked about the offence he committed, the YOT worker explained it as follows:

> I don't think he is impulsive, and I think his cognitive skills, there are not really any deficits there that I can think of, he would think twice and walk away. Whereas a lot of the young people I work with it's compulsive behaviour, egocentric behaviour, I don't think there's any of this with Jake.

Jake is actually into some serious forms of criminal activity, especially around drug-dealing, yet none of this is picked up in the assessment process. Neither are Jake's needs given serious consideration, nor an understanding attempted of the broader context to his offending.

Many other young people showed similar cynicism about professional intervention. Structured programmes were seen as unhelpful and of little use to their future lives. Programmes that aimed to change their lives through cognitive and behavioural change skills techniques seemed to offer little help to their everyday lives in that they tended not to recognise the contexts within which young people have to manage crime and other difficulties. Nathan, for example, was involved in a range of petty offending activities. He was put onto an anger management course and while he said he quite enjoyed it he saw little relevance to his daily life. He believed the course was inappropriate for him, being unrelated to why he was there, and also suggested it would not help him deal with street life in his own neighbourhood.

A strong message that emerges from the ESRC research is that what young people really value is not so much programmes and content but a good supportive relationship with an adult who is not judgemental and is able to offer guidance and advocacy when needed. Trust and respect are important qualities that help young people negotiate their way through difficult decisions and circumstances. Having such assistance was for many of the young people a critical part of helping them move on in their lives. The focus of prevention efforts should be on changing social arrangements to create opportunities and systems that facilitate the formation of such supportive structures.

Conclusion

We have argued in this chapter that pathways and prevention researchers should place a greater emphasis on the social pathways or societal access routes that influence young people's pathways into and out of crime. Pathways research should encompass analysis of the power of structural, political and cultural processes and contexts, and how they can influence criminal behaviour. We have also argued that to gain a greater understanding of these processes we need to listen to the voices and perspectives of young people themselves.

These proposals challenge mainstream criminology, requiring it to recognise the contributions of a broader set of disciplines, theories and empirical evidence not only for a greater understanding of social pathways but also for the design of preventive initiatives. But our proposals also raise questions for other disciplines. For example, sociology, childhood and youth studies, and cultural studies are disciplines that have shown a limited interest in issues of pathways into and out of crime and the challenge of prevention. Yet as we have illustrated, they have the potential to make a significant contribution to our understanding of youth crime. Similar issues are raised in terms of methodology. If we are to include young people's voices more needs to be done to develop methods that encourage the inclusion of those most excluded, but that are also ethical, developmentally appropriate, robust and capable of withstanding both academic and political scrutiny. While childhood and youth studies have come a long way in terms of methodology much still needs to be done.

Fundamental to our position is the contention that prevention researchers should be as concerned with the social arrangements that create or block societal access routes as they currently are with the study of individual developmental pathways. The kinds of 'ecological "conspiracies" that envelop children in high-risk social environments' (Garbarino and Ganzel 2000: 91) and lock them out of the supportive relationships and opportunities that are taken for granted by their more privileged counterparts are the product of interconnected structural, cultural and political forces that must be understood and modified if truly effective prevention policies are to be formulated. Although this is a daunting challenge, we believe that many of the theoretical and research tools required in order to make solid progress are already within our grasp.

Acknowledgements

We should like to thank Paul Mazerolle and three anonymous referees for their perceptive and constructive criticisms. The *Pathways Into and Out of Crime* project was funded by the Economic and Social Research Council UK Grant number LE 330 25 3001.

References

Armstrong, D. (2004) 'A risky business? Research, policy, governmentality and youth offending', *Youth Justice*, 4: 100–17.

Armstrong, D., France, A. and Hine, J. (2006) *Risk and Resilience in Children who are Offending, Excluded from School or Have Behaviour Problems*, Economic and Social Research Council End of Award Report LE330253001.

Bessant, J., Hil, R. and Watts, R. (2003) *'Discovering' Risk*. Oxford: Peter Lang.

Blumstein, A. (2005) 'An overview of the symposium and some next steps', *Annals of the American Academy of Political and Social Science*, 602: 242–58.

Bottoms, A., Shapland, J., Costello, A., Holmes, D. and Muir, G. (2004) 'Towards desistance: Theoretical underpinnings for an empirical study', *Howard Journal*, 4: 368–89.

Bourdieu, P. (1991) *The Logic of Practice*. Cambridge: Polity Press.

Brown, A. (2004) 'Anti-social behaviour, crime control and social control', *Howard Journal of Criminal Justice*, 43: 203–11.

Connell, R.W. (1982) *Making the Difference: Schools, Families and Social Division*. Sydney: George Allen & Unwin.

Connolly, P. and Neill, J. (2001) 'Constructions of locality and gender and their impact on the educational aspirations of working class children', *International Studies in Sociology of Education*, 1: 107–29.

Craine, S. (1997) 'The Black Magic Roundabout: Cyclical Transitions, Social Exclusion and Alternative Careers', in R. MacDonald (ed.) *Youth, the 'Underclass' and Social Exclusion*. London: Routledge, pp. 135–52.

Department for Education and Employment (2000) *Influence or Irrelevance: Can Social Science Improve Government?* London: DfEE.

Department for Education and Skills (2004) *Every Child Matters*. London: DfES.

Developmental Crime Prevention Consortium (1999) *Pathways to Prevention: Developmental and Early Intervention Approaches to Crime in Australia*. Canberra: Australian Government Publishing Service.

Devine, F., Savage, M., Scott, J. and Crompton, R. (2005) *Rethinking Class, Culture, Identities and Lifestyle*. London: Palgrave.

Elder, G.H. Jr, Kirkpatrick Johnson, M. and Crosnoe, R. (2004). 'The Emergence and Development of Life Course Theory', in J.T. Mortimer and M.J. Shanahan (eds), *Handbook of the Life Course*. New York: Springer, pp. 3–22.

Farrington, D. (1996) *Understanding and Preventing Youth Crime*. York: Joseph Rowntree Foundation.

Farrington, D. (2002) 'Developmental Criminology and Risk Focused Prevention', in M. Maguire, R. Morgan and R. Reiner (eds) *The Oxford Handbook of Criminology*, 3rd edn. Oxford: Oxford University Press, pp. 657–701.

Farrington, D. (2003) 'Key Results from the First Forty Years of the Cambridge Study in Delinquent Development', in T.P. Thornberry and M. Krohn (eds) *Taking Stock of Delinquency: An Overview of Findings from Contemporary Longitudinal Studies*. New York: Kluwer, pp. 137–84.

Farrington, D. (2005) 'Conclusions about Developmental and Life-course Theories', in D.P. Farrington (ed.) *Integrated Developmental and Life-course Theories of Offending. Advances in Criminological Theory*, Vol. 14. New Brunswick, NJ: Transaction Publishers, pp. 247–56.

France, A. (2006) *Youth in Late Modernity*. Buckingham: Open University Press.

France, A. and Utting, D. (2005) 'The paradigm of "risk and protection-focused prevention" and its impact on services for children and families', *Children and Society*, 19: 77–90.

France, A., Bendelow, G. and Williams, S. (1999) ' "Risky business": Researching the Health Beliefs of Children and Young People,' in A. Lewis and G. Lindsay (eds.) *Researching Children's Perspectives*. Buckingham: Open University Press, pp. 150–61.

Furstenberg, F. (2004) 'Reflections on the Future of the Life Course', in J.T. Mortimer and M.J. Shanahan (eds), *Handbook of the Life Course*. New York: Springer, pp. 661–70.

Garbarino, J. and Ganzel, B. (2000) 'The Human Ecology of Early Risk', in J.P. Shonkoff and S.J. Meisels (eds) *Handbook of Early Childhood Intervention*, 2nd edn. Cambridge: Cambridge University Press, pp. 76–93.

Gecas, V. (2004) 'Self-agency and the Life Course,' in J.T. Mortimer and M.J. Shanahan (eds), *Handbook of the Life Course*. New York: Springer, pp. 369–88.

Giddens, A. (1991) *Modernity and Self-identity*. Cambridge: Polity Press.

Hall, S. and Jefferson, T. (eds) (1975) *Resistance through Rituals*. London: Routledge & Kegan Paul.

Homel, R. (2005) 'Developmental Crime Prevention', in N. Tilley (ed.) *Handbook of Crime Prevention and Community Safety* Cullompton: Willan Publishing, pp. 71–106.

James, A. and Prout, A. (eds) (1997) *Constructing and Reconstructing Childhood*. London: Falmer Press.

Keating, D.P. and Hertzman, C. (eds) (1999) *Developmental Health and the Wealth of Nations: Social, Biological and Educational Dynamics*. New York: Guilford Press.

Lewis, V., Kellett, M., Robinson, C., Fraser, S. and Ding, S. (2004) *The Reality of Research with Children and Young People*. London: Sage.

Loader, I. (1996) *Youth Policing and Democracy*. London: Macmillan.

MacDonald, R. and Marsh, J. (2005) *Disconnected Youth? Growing up in Poor Britain*. Basingstoke: Palgrave.

McAra, L. and McVie, S. (2005) 'The usual suspects? Street life, young people and the police', *Criminal Justice*, 5: 5–36.

McCahill, M. (2002) *The Surveillance Web*. Cullompton: Willan Publishing.

Malone, K. (1999) 'Growing up in cities: as a model of participative planning and "place making" ', *Youth Studies Australia*, 20: 17–23.

Maughan, B. (2005) 'Developmental trajectory modeling: A view from developmental psychopathology', *Annals of the American Academy of Political and Social Science*, 602: 118–30.

Mortimer, J. and Shanahan, M. (2004) 'Preface', in J.T. Mortimer and M.J. Shanahan (eds) *Handbook of the Life Course*. New York: Springer, pp. xi–xvi.

Muncie, J. (2004) *Youth and Crime.* London: Sage.

Nagin, D. and Tremblay, R. (2005) 'Further reflections on modeling and analysing developmental trajectories: A response to Maughan and Raudenbush', *Annals of the American Academy of Political and Social Science,* 602: 145–54.

Newburn, T. (2002) 'Young People and Youth Justice', in M. Maguire, R. Morgan and R. Reiner (eds) *The Oxford Handbook of Criminology,* 3rd edn. Oxford: Oxford University Press, pp. 531–79.

Norris, C. and Armstrong, G. (1999) *The Maximum Surveillance Society.* Oxford: Berg.

Payne, M., Williams, M. and Chamberland, S. (2004) 'Methodological pluralism in British sociology', *Sociology,* 38: 153–64.

Prout, A. (2000) *The Body, Childhood and Society.* London: Palgrave.

Qvortrup, J. (1997) 'A Voice for Children in Statistical and Social Accounting: A Plea for Children's Right to be Heard', in A. James and A. Prout (eds) *Constructing and Reconstructing Childhood.* London: Falmer Press, pp. 85–106.

Raudenbush, S. (2005) 'How do we study "what happens next"?', *Annals of the American Academy of Political and Social Science,* 602: 131–44.

Sampson, R.J. and Laub, J.H. (1993) *Crime in the Making: Pathways and Turning Points through Life.* Cambridge, MA: Harvard University Press.

Sampson, R.J. and Laub, J.H. (2005) 'When prediction fails: From crime-prone boys to heterogeneity in adulthood', *Annals of the American Academy of Political and Social Science,* 602: 73–9.

Smith, N., Lister, R., Middleton, S. and Cox, L. (2005) 'Young people as real citizens: Towards an inclusionary understanding of citizenship', *Journal of Youth Studies,* 8: 425–44.

Taylor, I., Evans, K. and Fraser, P. (1996) *A Tale of Two Cities.* London: Routledge.

Wikström, P.O. (2004) 'Crime as an Alternative: Towards a Cross-level Situational Action Theory of Crime Causation', in J. McCord (ed.) *Beyond Empiricism: Institutions and Intentions in the study of Crime.* New Brunswick, NJ: Transaction Publishers, pp. 1–38.

Chapter 2

Taking the developmental pathways approach to understanding and preventing antisocial behavour

Jeanette A. Lawrence

Abstract

In this chapter, I focus on the meaning of the pathways imagery from a contemporary developmental perspective and examine the contribution of a developmental pathways approach to understanding how young people become involved in crime. From a developmental perspective a 'pathway' focuses attention on people's experiences. As a heuristic device for interpreting life events, it allows researchers to make sense of how patterns of criminal behaviour start, progress and stop. Such a developmental perspective undergirds crime prevention strategies by supplying a general normative description of the life course and a way of analysing both typical and atypical patterns of experience in relation to normative life periods. It allows criminologists to link prevention strategies to inter-individual and intra-individual variability in patterns of behaviour that have been broadly discussed as 'antisocial'.

Introduction

The long-standing debate about the value of a developmental pathways approach to crime prevention (e.g. Hil 1999; Homel 2000; Wyn and White 1997) makes it timely to consider what are the implications of this favoured imagery of developmental science for understanding how young people become involved in crime. In this chapter, I focus on the meaning of 'a developmental pathway' as formulated in a contemporary life-span developmental perspective. This developmental perspective proposes ways of analysing people's normative life-course experiences and also their exceptional experiences into and out of antisocial activities. I make the case that analyses of the features of developmental pathways give a basis for prevention strategies that pays due attention to the patterns that arise in people's common and exceptional experiences. The chapter is organised in five sections that focus on using a developmental pathways approach as the framework for prevention. That framework comes from the meaning and uses of the pathways concept as it is imbedded in a life-course developmental understanding of patterns of experience over time and social institutions. The framework provides a basis for analysing different patterns of experience in and out of trouble, and links between earlier and later experiences, and it has specific implications in relation to the current debate about pathways models in developmental criminology and their significance for designing prevention strategies.

What is meant by a 'pathway of development'?

Essentially, a pathway of development refers to the *experiences* of a human life – experiences that, considered holistically over time and social situations, have a shape, a coherence: a story to tell about a life being lived out in particular ways. Some patterns of experience are life-long, some emerge in particular life periods or social circumstances, and some cease, either naturally or with intervention. All gain their meaning in relation to the whole of a life stretching temporally over years and spatially over situations. This life is constantly 'developing', that is, changing in lasting and substantial ways as the person is in the process of adapting to and acting upon a changing environment. The dual concepts of a 'whole-of-life experience' and 'change-prompting movements' between interim experiences are readily captured by the pathways imagery. That imagery prompts suggestions for analysing different patterns of experience against which to generate prevention strategies.

The idea of the life pathway as a description of experience is not a radical psychological invention. It is deeply imbedded in classical and popular literature, providing an accessible heuristic for analysing what happens to people as they live – the regular and irregular patterns that social scientists pursue in human experience. We resonate to the Argonaut's wanderings, to the Pilgrim's progress and to Dorothy's adventures along the yellow brick road to Oz. The common storyline is that 'the pathway is trod' as things happen within and around the person: as she/he initiates and responds to events and relationships. The story unfolds, the life is lived. The person may, for example, enter into activities that lead either deeper into trouble (e.g. Pilgrim in the Slough of Despond), or right out of trouble and towards problems resolved (e.g. Jason finds the golden fleece, Dick Whittington 'turns again' to fame and fortune in London).

Each pathway has a beginning (an onset), an end (an outcome) and a series of interim experiences (that link together the beginning and the end in a way that gives the pathway its particular characterisation: usually as problems encountered and solved). Together, these elements make a coherent, interpretable whole, and gain their meaning and significance in relation to that whole. The elements (beginning, ending, and linked-up interim experiences) adhere to each other in different ways in people's lives, so that the 'pathway' becomes a distinctive way of describing the particular patterns in which they combine. There are straight, unerring pathways that compare with twisting, turning pathways, predictable or unexpected pathways, and common or uncommon pathways. The imagery of these forms of interpretable sets of experiences helps us make sense of things that happen over time and space in different configurations. It is by discerning the patterns in the various combinations of experiences that developmental scientists distinguish Pathway X from Pathway Y, with the distinction most coarsely, but not exclusively, used to describe sets of activities and relationships in positive (upward) or negative (downward) terms. Other imageries have a similar holistic quality (e.g. a life story, a narrative, a career), but the pathways concept consistently bears the sense of people 'moving on' through experiences.

Uses of the pathways imagery

The pathway is a useful metaphor for prevention strategists, because it assists social scientists to organise information about individual lives into coherent and interpretable patterns. In reality, people's lives are likely to be less organised and continuous than we suggest in the empirical stories we create to give us a handle on human experience (Steinberg 1995). Consequently, part of the contemporary debate about the value of typologies of pathways to crime revolves around whether the characterisations of the groups reduce too much diversity to uniform descriptions (for a discussion of the issues see Nagin and Tremblay 2005; Sampson and Laub 2005).

Nevertheless, according to Steinberg (1995), the heuristic usefulness of the pathway metaphor lies in its potential for integrating the personal, interpersonal and contextual dimensions of development over time and situations. For prevention strategists, the ability to find both regularities and irregularities in connections across early and later experiences offers a conceptual framework for planning diversions out of antisocial, unproductive patterns, and for facilitating movement into more socially productive patterns. Primarily, the developmental pathway contributes to this kind of strategic planning by allowing us to make sense of how patterns of criminal behaviour start, progress, and stop. It suggests ways of highlighting the interacting features of certain patterns of antisocial activities against the framework of normative development. Imbedding one set of activities in another, larger set should suggest where some patterns are likely to be open to intervention. In effect, the path *is* the story – the story of a way of life, and also within that life, the story of a 'career of crime' (Blumstein *et al.* 1988), whether that career be long or short.

The pathways imagery, then, is used in developmental science in two ways that are particularly relevant to crime prevention. It provides a general, normative description of the life course with its periods, transitions and milestones – the developmental framework. It prompts identification of specific forms of atypical sets of experiences as they are lived out by individuals within social institutions – the specification of the exceptional. For developmental scientists, both these uses point to the identification of different configurations in which beginnings, sequences of interim experiences and ends combine to make sense of discernible sets of experience. Common and uncommon sets of connected events and relationships are observed and analysed using the pathway heuristic in particular domains (e.g. criminal behaviour, pathology, skill development).

The potential for confusing long-term life-course experiences with periodic sets of experiences have led some researchers to reserve 'trajectory' for the larger life-course experience and 'path' for particular interim parts of the life course (e.g. Elder 1998; LeBlanc and Loeber 1998). A 'trajectory', however, carries extra semiotic baggage about impetus, velocity and shape. Following the popular pathways imagery, and focusing on patterns of experience, I prefer to use it for both life-course and specific, interim sets of experience, acknowledging the potential confusion, while avoiding the extra conceptual baggage of implying impetus and force.

Regardless of terminology, however, there is great merit in Rutter and Sroufe's (2000: 272) emphasis on the 'coherence' of a developmental pathway: a criterion that directs attention back to the elements of the pathway and how they combine. Clear analyses of how pathways begin, persist or decline, and ultimately end should dispel some of the ghosts of the strict developmental stage models of the past. These ghosts continue to attract the criticism that a pathways model of development is a deterministic account of preformed dispositions or ideologically normative prescriptions of how life should proceed in relation to chronological age (e.g. te Riele 2004; Wyn and White 1997; and see Lerner 2002 for a contemporary account of how life-course developmental processes are probabilistic and non-deterministic).

A developmental framework for analysing pathways

In its most general application, the life-course developmental pathway encapsulates within-person and across-person variability in people's progressions from infancy to childhood, to adolescence and into and through adulthood. This general idea of people moving through varying sets of experiences in their social environments lies behind any other levels of analysis we may apply to the changing and continuing events in the lives of individuals or groups. Rather than specifying a prescriptive pathway by which all persons *do* or ideally *should* proceed through life, the life-span approach sees development as occurring in a variety of directions (e.g. positive, negative or neutral), over a variety of dimensions of life (e.g. cognitive, affective, behavioural: Baltes 1987). Development is always contextualised and constructed in dynamic, interactive processes (Lerner *et al.* 2006). The person's life is not preformed, but rather, its dimensions emerge, are built up, become refined, and either persist or are superseded as the person engages with social others (persons and institutions). Drawing on concepts of human plasticity and amenability to variation, we should expect to find individual differences in how people and their interactions with their social worlds affect their changing experiences (Lerner 2002).

The same or similar beginnings may have different outcomes as the consequences of changing environmental opportunities and challenges, as these interact with changing personal styles of responding. Connecting chains of earlier to later problems, for instance, may differ for children caught up in similarly unfortunate early parent–child interactions. Sroufe and Jacobvitz (1989) found different forms of unproductive behaviours appearing some time later in boys whose mothers behaved towards them seductively in their second and third years. Years later, some boys exhibited hyperactivity and impulsivity, others anxiety and tension, and yet others inappropriate physical (sexual) contact. Their early experiences became part of subsequent networks of relationships, or at least opened up the boys to further chains of specific problematic interactions.

Different beginnings, likewise, may issue in similar outcomes. Adolescent criminal behaviour, for example, does not have a single, definitive precursor. At the very least, Moffitt's (1997) distinction of 'life-course persistent' and 'adolescent onset' adolescent delinquency indicates that different patterns of activity are likely to lie behind the same overt behaviours of a group of young offenders. For example, the same shoplifting behaviours may be taken up as a way to express adolescent risk-taking, or as another manifestation of a well-entrenched style of acquiring things by taking them. Thornberry and Krohn (2001) show that different interacting configurations of personal, familial and structural variables have distinctive consequences later in time, with the cumulative effects of interacting personal, familial and structural factors adding to the explanation of how adolescents find themselves on different pathways. For example, better financial resources may be able to buffer some of the consequences of negative temperament or poor intellectual skills, while poverty exacerbates the deficits by denying access to appropriate buffering factors such as counselling or coaching.

Regularities and irregularities in developmentally relevant experiences arise as people live out their lives within the social institutions of their culture. Each culture organises the lives of its members through its institutions that pay attention to the common dimensions of human growth and decline. Social institutions lay down the culture's general expectations about where people should be directing their energies at particular phases of their lives, and about the competencies they should be achieving within and across a range of ages and circumstances (e.g. learning to get along with peers in middle childhood, achieving emotional independence in adolescence and young adulthood). Within the parameters of cultural expectations, people are guided into forms of acceptable participation for those of their maturity and station by the discourse, rules and relationships that engage them in the home, school and other formal and informal institutions.

Although personal development is socially organised and constrained, nothing to do with human living is completely predictable.

There always is the possibility of novelty in how people construct their engagements with institutions. People are intentionally active and constrain back on the institutional boundaries that are imposed on their activities (Valsiner and Lawrence 1997). They make choices, complying with or resisting institutionalised behavioural boundaries, taking up or missing opportunities, meeting or avoiding challenges. Once forms of culturally approved experiences are identified, we can analyse the common features of people's developmental experiences, together with the departures from common experiences that may lead people into troubled areas (e.g. the socially 'on time' and 'off time' accomplishment of culturally expected social skills). The working tools of such a life-course analysis of normative and exceptional change revolve around being able to break up the life course into periods that reflect how people typically live out their lives, and being able to describe when and how they move between these periods.

Setting the pathway in time: life periods

While chronological age is commonly used to mark out the course of a life, it is too rough a tool to deal with the complexities of people's life experiences. Experiences may be speeded up or delayed across life periods for a number of reasons, and the reasons may be as adaptive in some circumstances as they are maladaptive in others (e.g. efforts to preserve one's unique identity under pressure to conform). Consequently, it has become useful for developmental scientists to think in broad bands that break up the life course to reflect both large-scale developmental changes and the social arrangements that commonly mark progression through those bands: (1) the early years (usually marked by some large-scale accomplishments at around three or four, Shonkoff and Philips 2000), with significant experiences focused on family processes and the preschool years; (2) pre-primary and primary school years; (3) early adolescence and high school years; (4) late adolescence and early adulthood and the beginnings of working careers and independence – as an elastic period that takes on different connotations with cultural and historical variations; (5) middle adulthood; and (6) late adulthood.

Finer analyses naturally will be focused on experiences belonging to specific periods in order to identify specific developmental problems (e.g. attachments in the first years, readiness for starting school) or towards the socially significant accomplishments that occur with a particular period (e.g. negotiating the transition to high school). The broad periods, however, permit us to concentrate on the expected common experiences of developing persons, while allowing for ranges in so-called 'normal growth' that take the general descriptions beyond specific ages (see Developmental Crime Prevention Consortium 1999; Shonkoff and Philips 2000; Valsiner and Lawrence 1997).

Within each period, culturally defined 'developmental tasks' identify what a person is expected to master in that culture. A developmental task is a skill to be accomplished or a piece of knowledge to be acquired in order to meet the inner and social expectations attached to a life period. Its successful achievement is expected to add to a person's general well-being and to prepare the way for further success with the tasks associated with later periods. According to Havighurst (1952), who first identified the developmental tasks of the life course, failure to accomplish the developmental tasks associated with a particular life period is likely to contribute to personal unhappiness, social disapproval, and future developmental difficulties. Prevention strategies cannot afford to ignore the periodic tasks that are likely to absorb attention and energies of their targeted groups. It would be shortsighted, for instance, to ignore the identity issues that absorb much of the energies of adolescence (Coté and Schwartz 2002). Programmes for prevention, accordingly, should reflect the central tasks that attract people's attention in particular life periods and how their accomplishment is assisted or impeded by contextual factors. This kind of focus changes the perspective from a deficit base for intervention to a more positive perspective on what can be reasonably expected to absorb people's interests. It would be inappropriate, for instance, to ignore the significance of peer acceptance in designing any programmes for adolescents.

Transitions between life periods

Transitions are the social 'way-stations', 'milestones' or social markers that divide up the life experience in terms of people's movements between primary institutions, and the developmental tasks that are mostly associated with distinct social institutions associated with the life periods. Each transition between a phase of life and a related social institution presents its own challenges and opportunities. Movement is temporal, but also can involve an actual physical diversion from one comfortable, known situation into the unknown, as occurs for instance in the move from one form of schooling to another. One learns the rules, the expectations and the possibilities that belong to the new institution. In some Australian school systems, for example, fourth-graders must obtain a 'penmanship licence' before they can progress from writing in pencil to using a pen. When asked why she was so distressed at being slow to manage the new skill, one girl explained, 'Mummy, it's like you graduating from university. It's what allows you to go on.'

Faced with new situations to negotiate and new skills to master, people do not always 'go on' or progress. They instead may fall back on previously acquired and comfortable developmental resources (Keating and Hertzman 1999). The old resources, however, may not be appropriate for the new situation. Handling the first playground conflict with peers or the first experience of the authority of sporting coaches, young people may draw on comfortable, well-used practices developed in dealing with their own family conflicts, trying to stretch old resources to cover fresh demands. The young child who comes to school equipped only with the aggressive strategies that made his wishes known around the home, for example, is at a distinct disadvantage when dealing with peers in the rough and tumble of school play (Shonkoff and Philips 2000). Similarly, the adolescent used to parental sensitivities and indulgences is rudely awakened by the strict codes of the coach or the manager of the fast food outlet. If previously appropriate resources are inadequate, and if the new socially available resources are out of reach (e.g. require greater cognitive or social skills than the person can muster), then the developing person is caught in a person-by-institution 'bad fit' (Eccles *et al.* 1993).

The expected passage through society's institutional entry, exit and interim checkpoints also may become difficult, because young people find the social supports are pulled out from under them. Davis (2003), for example, points to the additional hurdles faced by American young people with serious emotional disturbance who are classified and resourced as 'adults' as soon as they turn 18. As supportive child-oriented services dry up, these young people may fumble the transition, because they are thrown back on their inadequate resources.

Despair and failure can divert energy towards transitions and tasks that are more easily mastered (e.g. into crime instead of work). Deskilled and resource-poor young people who go searching for alternative markers of an emerging adult identity may find themselves caught in vicious cycles of relationships and attempted strategies that keep them on antisocial pathways (Patterson and Yoerger 1993). Adolescents may, for example, try out the antisocial activity, find some interim success and become entrapped in establishing and then maintaining a 'cool' persona that demands further chains of activities unacceptable to mainstream society.

Life-period tasks and encounters, then, form the backdrop of movements into and out of crime. The developmental accomplishments of specific periods and transitions point to individual variability in people's ability to negotiate life experiences, particularly transitional experiences. Being unable to meet the normative cultural expectations for one's time of life for whatever reason (e.g. lack of intelligence, social skills, fear, the absence of supportive others to ease the way) adds to the challenge or threat of new social situations.

Prevention strategists need to be aware of the accomplishments that typically absorb people's attention and resources, and they need to be aware of the enormous consequences for individuals who fail to meet the transitions and their associated social norms. Strategies, accordingly, need to be generated with due sensitivity to the normative tasks and institutional demands that contextualise a given person's or group's patterns of social behaviours. Such sensitivity is a strong counter to the simplistic criticisms that a developmental pathways approach involves 'one pathway fits all' (e.g. te Kiele 2004; Wyn and White 1997). This constitutes a misunderstanding.

Awareness of the likely range of the normatively acceptable alerts the strategist to specific factors that may take people out of that socially acceptable range and bring them into collision with social norms (e.g. teenage pregnancy, dropping out of school). Strategies need to identify patterns of common experiences (e.g. features of a 'well-trod' path) that most people can expect to achieve as they live in their own culture (e.g. those experiences usually channelled through social institutions of family, school, work, etc.). It also should be possible to identify the specific kinds of features that mark out an interim set of experiences (a personal pathway) that is unusual or exceptional (e.g. when a person's life takes off into unusual sequences under conditions of illness, poverty or involvement with criminal associates).

Life periods have provided the framework for several descriptions of sets of experiences in antisocial or criminal involvement (e.g. Moffitt 1997; Nagin and Tremblay 2005; Thornberry 2005). These descriptions of atypical, antisocial patterns of behaviour are set against what is usually accepted as normative ways of dealing with the challenges of particular life periods. When the interpretive and measurement lenses are finely honed and appropriately aligned to the life-course developmental perspective, these analyses are able to pinpoint potential hot spots. They focus attention on why and how antisocial experiences arise, are maintained and end. Possibilities for prevention action, then, are guided by descriptions of both common and uncommon sets of experiences. For example, it is fairly well established that an exceptional expression of disruptive behaviour in early school grades would be a likely precursor of later antisocial behaviour (Tremblay *et al.* 1995). By the same token, the non-exceptional aggressive behaviour of toddlers would not be a useful predictor (Tremblay 2002).

Analysing pathways of development in and out of offending

As people move through the life course, some specific sequences of activities become easier to negotiate and maintain, because there is adequate support for the negotiating activities, and adequate buffering of potentially destructive experiences. Other pathways become less attractive in light of poor social support or personal motivation, or in the face of the personal by institutional 'bad fit' (Eccles *et al.* 1993).

Figure 2.1 describes several different hypothetical paths a person may take into, along and out of trouble, where 'trouble' signifies general social and legal offending and antisocial behaviour. For simplicity, it shows a limited set of the multiple possible paths that a person's life experiences may take across life periods and also within a specific period.

Some people's experiences never get them into trouble (line a). Their lives are lived out within the accepted boundaries of society's institutions. This type of pathway describes the social experience of 'persons of good character' as far as the justice system is concerned. They do not come to notice. They are not recognised as offenders, although they may live close to the edge of legal boundaries, committing petty offences, but avoiding being caught. This pathway can be applied, for instance, to the large numbers of adolescents who engage in shoplifting without being caught, and the large numbers of adults who pilfer without detection. In most characterisations of types of offenders, there is a class of non-offending or minimally offending young people (e.g. Nagin and Tremblay 2005; Thornberry 2005). Their distinguishing characteristic is that their experiences do not bring them into conflict with authorities.

Other people begin and continue in trouble (line b). People whose patterns of experience are described by line b, in contrast, are likely to have difficult in-utero and birth experiences, and to be

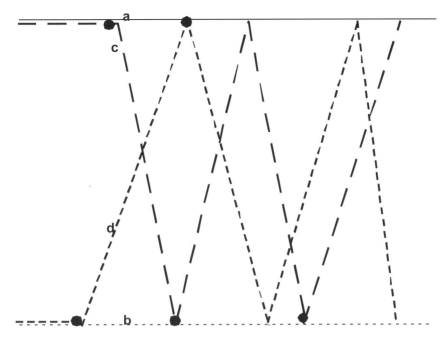

Figure 2.1 Sample pathways of experiences in and out of trouble

fractious babies. They may start off in families already noticed by the law (e.g. for domestic violence or parental offences). They live in unsupportive, risky social environments, and go on to careers of crime, at least through adolescence. These people's patterns of life experiences, by and large, are lived out in zones of trouble. They are likely to appear regularly in court and frequently find themselves paying fines or doing time in prison. They have been called 'career criminals' (Blumstein *et al.* 1988), 'persons with propensities for criminal behaviour' (Gottfredson and Hirschi 1990), or 'life-course persistent offenders' (Moffitt 1997). They form the 5 or 6 per cent of people who are continually known to the criminal justice system.

One of the most contentious issues for developmental approaches to criminology is to account for desistance in these people's criminal careers. Sampson and Laub (2005), for example, propose from their longitudinal data that most will desist, making 'life-long offenders' a misnomer. Their desistance can be seen as a natural, age-related falling off of criminal activities, or as the corollary of patterns of adult work and romantic relationships, particularly marriage. Sampson and Laub's (2005) analyses would suggest that this line b should have a natural upturn away from trouble if it is to be applicable to life-course criminal careers. Its straightness here is to illustrate one hypothetical, persistent pathway rather than to enter the debate of universal desistance from involvement in crime. Even in the case of close to universal desistance, there must remain at least the possibility of continuance, unless all old offenders enter the system or come to notice as old novices.

Initially free of trouble then in trouble people (line c) begin well, but become involved in patterns of activities that move between intermittent involvement and non-involvement in trouble. Their move into offending may vary in its timing, and in relation to social challenges and opportunities that bring them to turning points where the antisocial alternatives are more attractive and available than the prosocial. The pathways of Moffitt's (1997) adolescent-limited delinquents fit here, although line c in Figure 2.1 is describing a more general type of involvement. Its several dips into trouble and out again are not tied to a particular life period. This sample line of varying involvement in trouble, together with the following line d, describes the variability in people's experiences.

The negative pathway opens up, but its effective precursors may have been building up over time. Jimerson *et al.* (2000: 544), for instance, found that the steps towards dropping out of school had many 'mid-course markers of a process rooted in early development'. More immediate precursors of dropping out such as school discipline problems and truancy, failing grades and peer rejection did not add to the predictive power of these young people's poor home experiences before they started school. The initial move into trouble may occur when a critical factor in the dynamic goes missing or is overridden. For instance, Thornberry (2005) points to the absence of parental buffering that previously helped avoid the contribution of a difficult temperament to social interactions. The pathways analysis is not deterministic. Changes in direction are not only possible, but to be expected. It speaks against the 'myth' of single patterns of criminal behaviours with single causes, and against the 'myth' that the critical factors can be found solely in either the person or the environment (Developmental Crime Prevention Consortium 1999: 83).

In and out of trouble people (line d) are of particular interest to designers of preventive and intervention programmes. Their pathway begins in trouble (perhaps again as temperamentally difficult infants in dysfunctional families in poverty). At some point, their patterns of behaviour take a change out of trouble and into socially acceptable patterns of experience. In planning preventive action, we need to be informed about the circumstances that will assist this form of productive change for children in particular combinations of circumstances. Among these line d people, for instance, may be those men in the Glueck sample whose persistence and desistance demonstrated a 'zig-zag' pattern (Laub and Sampson 2003), or the children who were supported onto more productive social paths by preschool interventions (for an overview, see Developmental Crime Prevention Consortium 1999). That is why interventionists act – to promote positive change.

The triggers of change (both negative and positive in lines c and d) and the individualised turning points in activities that take people out of or bring them back into mainstream life are relevant. Do young people simply give up on delinquency, are opportunities less available, or do social forces constrain ways of behaving in early adulthood? Mostly it is thought that the positive change is triggered by marriage or a move away from deviant friends, or a mix of both (Sampson and Laub 2005). A group of prison inmates were able to identify life events over a ten-month period for Horney *et al.* (1995). The prisoners then identified their criminal activities over the same period. The researchers were able to correlate how being criminally active or inactive correlated with the men's experience of being in and out of work and in and out of marriage relationships. More data are needed on the dynamics of such moving in and out.

In summary, this differentiation of some sample pathways illustrates the stable and changing patterns of behaviours across time. Points on the pathways (shown as dots) signify specific events that can trigger changes in direction. For some pathways, changing events are geared to life periods and transitions. Sampson and Laub (2005), for instance, see people as particularly open to common forms of turning point during transition phases. Other events may be highly individualised, eliciting change as personal turning points either into or out of trouble (Rönkä *et al.* 2002). A person comes to a consciousness-raising decision that triggers a change in orientation and direction. Hughes (1998) tells how a young African-American man left the drug scene because he had a gun pointed at him when pushing his baby's pram. It also covers the ways that events at different points along the pathway are linked to each other (especially as earlier lead into later events). Lightfoot (1997) describes how a young member of a drug-defined gang realised he had to leave the gang when he could not meet the critical condition for sustained membership (being willing to drop acid).

My purpose in tracing out the sample pathways in Figure 2.1 is not to propose yet another classification system. Rather, it is to highlight the multiple sets of linked experiences that may be involved in a person's antisocial activities over time. Individual experiences and the links between them can be given meaning as they combine in patterns that developmental scientists can discern (Steinberg 1995). However, this pattern-discerning and interpreting is not a simple business. One interesting *caveat* raised by Sampson and Laub (2005) is that the more time-related data available to developmental scientists, the more different patterns of antisocial experiences are likely to emerge. Categorisations of groups of offenders that fall short of including data on considerable adult experience, for example, are not entitled to describe classes of people as 'life-course persistent offenders'.

There is a general message for preventive action. Efforts either to block a particular line of activity in anticipation or to cut off a started line will have a better chance if those efforts come with understanding of the pathway being lived out (e.g. patterns of actual or likely offending). There is no single pathway. Nor are there only four. Figure 2.1 suggests some major routes related to trouble that could be examined when considering interventions for particular groups.

Critical questions for prevention strategists revolve around the links that allow some sets of experience to reliably form sequences. What weak links in the criminal career pathway are open to modification? The critical analytic tools for tracing out specific pathways need to go beyond descriptions of common sets of experiences to examining the beginning, maintenance and ending of specific forms of behaviour.

Looking within patterns of offending

An insightful account of looking for links across forms of offending comes from the work of LeBlanc and Loeber (1998). They propose two promising focuses for tracing through chains of linked experiences – the *levels* and *phases* of specific patterns of activity.

Levels refer to the links between different activities, working from earlier and less serious to later and more serious forms of offences (Loeber and Hay 1997; LeBlanc and Loeber 1998). These researchers proposed three forms of pathway, depending on whether an offence is overt, covert or authority-avoiding in form. Forms of offending patterns have their own ways of evolving, with levels of overt offending suggesting that the progressive acquisition of violence escalates through a chain, for example (Loeber and Hay 1997: 385):

[bullying and annoying others ^{to}→ physical fighting and gang fighting ^{to}→ rape, attack and strongarm activities]

Thus, levels of progression into more serious offending activities provide a way of interpreting progressions in related antisocial competencies, where the levels have distinctive markers that may not be automatically recognised as flowing on from one to another. Applications to prevention depend on being able to specify the links across circumstances that promote escalating involvement in offending.

Phases of offending refer to the successive steps or stages that identify an activity's start-up, escalation and end (called by them activation, aggravation and desistance). Applying this analytic tool directly to the multiple pathway model, we expect to find that each level of an offence will have its own life cycle. The natural down-turn of an initial activity (e.g. bullying) may be the signal of the up-turn of its more serious successor (physical fighting). The repertoire of antisocial forms is extended and the move into deeper antisocial activities is forged.

These levels and phases of lines of offending provide some leads for planning preventive action at different points in a discernible pathway. They give, for instance, new meaning to 'intervene early'. Intervening early in a new form of offending may involve targeting new, fragile forms of offence like violent behaviour in order to block progression to their later, more serious manifestations. Take, for example, the progression in physical aggression in the Loeber and Hay (1997) model above. If the bullying, fighting, attacking sequence is established, intervening early in the first, bullying phase not only has the potential for blocking its specific development but also involves intervening early or even in advance of the second and third phase activities. In Le Blanc and Loeber's (1998) terms, they can be treated as different expressions of the same, underlying problem of aggression and violent behaviour. The timing of an early intervention would be well informed by knowledge of cyclical and cumulative progressions. From the same perspective, it may not be cost-effective to work on trying to deter bullying, if the offender is already moving on to physical fighting.

Does this kind of fine-tuned targeting of sequenced activities depend on what seems to be an empirically unattainable accuracy? Not necessarily. One intervention strategy may seek to target, for instance, bullying and fighting differently in the same prevention package, once their links are known. It does require, however, studies that can identify the progressions and processes of the pathways of sequenced forms of offending. Programmes more finely tuned to the natural processes involved in specialised skill acquisition would show if a programme is dealing with an initiate like Oliver Twist or a seasoned perpetrator like the Artful Dodger. Some boys as young as 10 or 11, for instance, can be experts in hot-wiring cars. Diagnostic fine-tuning will be sensitive to the level of individual involvement as well as social environmental factors.

Implications of contemporary pathways issues for prevention

It would seem that the developmental approach to understanding criminal behaviours is now well enough established that the issues shift from whether the pathways imagery is useful for prevention, to how it can be best applied. In particular, there is strong evidence of this coming of age in the devotion of an edition of the *Annals of the American Academy of Political and Social Science* (2005) to the merits of different accounts of the trajectories (pathways) of criminal behaviour. The debate now revolves around the ability to empirically characterise different developmental pathways in and out of crime. For preventionists, the issues emerging from this critical examination of different models relate to the elements I have identified: how pathways of crime begin, escalate or are maintained, and how they end.

I have already mentioned two of Sampson and Laub's (2005) contributions. The first is their insistence on having more points of longitudinal data in order to describe life-course patterns, especially for characterising involvement as life-course persistent. Their 'roughly fifty-year window' (2005: 16) on the offending experience of 52 of the original Glueck delinquent sample is impressive, although its generalisability is yet to be established. The long-term longitudinal data may be backed up with retrospective accounts of temporally linked experiences and past turnings points of the kind Clausen (1996) identified.

I do not see the second issue of the natural desistance from crime promoting a serious prevention policy of 'leave them alone and they will come home'. Surely not all old offenders are novices. Non-intervention in the years prior to progressive adult desistance can bring social ruin for young offenders left with criminal records that debar them from various social entries. It also can be costly for society and its institutions. In combination with the age crime curve,

Sampson and Laub's downward trends and their interpretation highlight the importance of focusing resources on forms of antisocial and criminal behaviour that are significant within as well as across age periods.

Sampson and Laub's current attention to the potential for personalised choices to sway the dynamics of what evolves brings developmental criminology closer to the kind of probabilistic account of development belonging to life-span, interactionist developmental models (e.g. Gottlieb 2003; Lerner *et al.* 2006). While this move may make the meaning of 'development' in developmental criminology less 'fuzzy' in Sampson and Laub's (2005: 39) terms, it does not make its applications to prevention strategies any easier. It may support closer focus on micro-level changes in sequences of activities (e.g. in transition periods or in the changes of form in the LeBlanc and Loeber 1998 analyses).

When and how in the life course to target prevention and intervention activities are questions tied to another aspect of the contemporary debate – questions that focus on the comprehensiveness and precision of empirically derived typologies of trajectories (see the debate around Nagin and Tremblay's contribution to the *Annals* 2005). The pertinent issues for prevention here relate to the source of characterisation of different groups (whether based on *a priori* assumptions or empirical findings), the fit of members to groups (whether descriptors involve over-fitting or under-fitting), and the suitability of prospective prediction (whether this is possible within a probabilistic developmental model that sees development as being worked out dynamically in interactions). Of particular interest to framing programmes developmentally is the weight of the odds of forward prediction against the cost of non-intervention.

The more subgroup trajectories (pathways) that can be reliably established, the greater the possibility of tailoring prevention and intervention to specific patterns of behaviour. The heuristic patterns of the developmental scientist (Steinberg 1995) are critical tools for designing strategic interventions. High-level likelihoods add to value, both in the characterisation of groups and in the links drawn between early onset and later involvement. Nagin and Tremblay (2005) present an impressive array of information about likely different patterns of physical aggression, and this fine-grained specification adds to the persuasiveness of their claims (e.g. the greater odds of later physical aggression by boys who are hyperactive and oppositional in kindergarten; 2005: 106). Their epidemiological analogies are well taken. There is ample evidence now of the cost/benefit ratios of opening up better possibilities for some (possibly many) children compared with after-the-fact handling by the justice system (e.g. see Aos *et al.* 2001). Ultimately, the preventionist's confidence in competing models may come down to the relative merits of the density and extensiveness of the data and the relative power of the statistical modelling techniques. Yet we may continue to ask if preventionists can reasonably afford to ignore the indicators of potential trouble (e.g. early parental neglect). The strategies for dealing with beginnings, middles and ends of patterns may be distinctive.

In sum, instead of simply tracing single pathways of development, we could be taking seriously both intra-individual and inter-individual forms of variability that are endemic to the developmental perspective. Instead of simply acknowledging that certain forms of offending may have different histories, we would do well to pinpoint their particular levels of manifestation and the phases of beginning, ending and passing on to new forms of an offence that may be open to intervention. For fine-tuning interventions it would be useful, for instance, to be able to identify the different offending pathways that consistently proceed from early child abuse, following Sroufe and Jacobvitz's (1989) lead.

Measurement issues come to the fore in this analysis of sequences. Being able to make fine-grained analyses of the start-up or aggravation of an offence holds out some promise of teasing apart some strands of the network of exacerbating or inhibiting conditions appearing early and late in an offence. For example, Nagin and Tremblay (1999) point to the inadequacies of several standard measures of aggression. These measures fail to precisely identify physical aggression in childhood well enough to use them as predictors of later behaviours (e.g. items are too few or too coarse). Yet if, as Nagin and Tremblay demonstrate, physical aggression develops in distinctive ways (e.g. in comparison to verbal aggression), any initially inadequate measurement will not be able to identify the distinctive features of the progression of this problem, especially when the problem is repeated over time.

Conclusion

In this chapter I have argued that the developmental pathways imagery suggests forms of analysis to undergird prevention strategies. Taking development pathways as the basis of prevention chiefly means attending to observations and analyses of typical and atypical patterns of experience in people's lives. Analysing these pathways should incorporate their elements (beginnings, linked sequences of events, and ends) and also should deal with the set as a whole.

The starting place is the analysis of normative pathways of development across the life course. By developing realistic, culturally sensitive analyses of common pathways of development through social institutions, we lay the foundation of further analyses of pathways of particular sets of experience, including pathways in and out of trouble and antisocial activities. A contemporary life-course developmental approach not only admits, but expects diversity in people's experiences, challenging strategists to think about ranges of possible pathways at different periods of life. Analyses of sequential steps in particular patterns of offending promotes the fine-tuned diagnosis of hot spots where prevention and intervention may be effective, because it attends to the common experiences of developing people. Some chains of activities are likely to be long term and persistent (especially early conduct disorders and the quality of early family life and nurturance). We may focus on the webs of intertwining personal and social factors that assist some people into antisocial chains of activity, or on the circumstances that open up positive turning points. We should consider the social transitions and developmental tasks that demand developmental resources, making people vulnerable to forms of offending or providing opportunities for change.

The developmental pathways approach has no easy formulas for prevention strategists. It, in fact, makes quick-fix strategies less appropriate, by directing attention to both the common and uncommon experiences of developing people. It invites us to couple prevention strategies to developmental processes, so that they can be planned and paced in light of the complex ways in which people's lives progress in and out of socially acceptable and unacceptable patterns of activity over time and circumstances.

References

Aos, S., Phipps, P., Barnoski, R. and Lieb, R. (2001) *The Comparative Costs and Benefits of Programs to Reduce Crime.* Washington, DC: Washington State Institute for Public Policy.

Baltes, P.B. (1987) 'Theoretical propositions of lifespan developmental psychology: On the dynamics between growth and decline', *Developmental Psychology,* 23(5), 611–26.

Blumstein, A., Cohen, J. and Farrington, D.P. (1988) 'Criminal career research: Its value for criminology', *Criminology*, 26(1), 1–35.

Clausen, J.A. (1996) 'Gender, Contexts, and Turning Points in Adults' Lives', in P. Moen, G.H. Elder, Jr and K. Lüscher (eds) *Examining Lives in Context: Perspectives on the Ecology of Human Development*. Washington, DC: American Psychological Association, pp. 365–89.

Coté, J.E. and Schwartz, S.J. (2002). 'Comparing psychological and sociological approaches to identity: Identity status, identity capital, and the individualization process', *Journal of Adolescence*, 25: 571–86.

Davis, M. (2003) 'Addressing the needs of youth in transition to adulthood', *Administration and Policy and Mental Health*, 30(6): 495–509.

Developmental Crime Prevention Consortium (1999) *Pathways to Prevention: Developmental and Early Intervention Approaches to Crime in Australia.* Canberra: Attorney-General's Department.

Eccles, J.S., Midgley, C., Wigfield, A., Buchanan, C.M., Reuman, D., Flanagan, C. and MacIver, D. (1993) 'Development during adolescence: The impact of stage-environment fit on young adolescents' experiences in school and in families', *American Psychologist*, 48(2): 90–101.

Elder, G.H. Jr (1998) 'The Life Course and Human Development', in W. Damon and R.M. Lerner (eds) *Handbook of Child Psychology: Theoretical Models of Human Development 5th edn*, Vol. 1. New York: John Wiley, pp. 939–91.

Gottfredson, M.R. and Hirschi, T. (1990) *A General Theory of Crime*. Stanford, CA: Stanford University Press

Gottlieb, G. (2003) 'Probabilistic Epigenesis of Development', in J. Valsiner and K. Connolly (eds) *Handbook of Developmental Psychology*. London: Sage, pp. 3–17.

Havighurst, R.J. (1952) *Developmental Tasks and Education.* New York: McKay.

Hil, R. (1999) 'Beating the developmental path: Critical notes on the "Pathways to Prevention Report"', *Youth Studies Australia*, 18(4): 49–50.

Homel, R. (2000) 'Blazing the developmental trail: A reply to Richard Hil', *Youth Studies Australia*, 19(1): 44–50.

Horney, J.D., Osgood, W. and Marshall, I.H. (1995) 'Criminal careers in the short-term: Intra-individual variability in crime and its relation to local life circumstances', *American Sociological Review*, 60: 655–73.

Hughes, M. (1998) 'Turning points in the lives of young inner-city men forgoing destructive criminal behaviors: A qualitative study', *Social Work Research*, 22(3): 143–151.

Jimerson, S., Egeland, B.L., Sroufe, A. and Carlson, B. (2000) 'A prospective longitudinal study of high school dropouts examining multiple predictors across development', *Journal of School Psychology*, 38(6): 525–49.

Keating, D.P. and Hertzman, C. (eds) (1999) *Developmental Health and the Wealth of Nations: Social, Biological and Educational Dynamics.* New York: Guilford Press.

Laub, J.H. and Sampson, R.J. (2003) *Shared Beginnings, Divergent Lives: Delinquent Boys at Age 70.* Cambridge, MA: Harvard University Press.

LeBlanc, M. and Loeber, R. (1998) 'Developmental criminology updated', *Crime and Justice: A Review of Research*, 23: 115–83.

Lerner, R.M. (2002) *Concepts and Theories of Human Development.* Mahwah, NJ: Lawrence Erlbaum Associates.

Lerner, R.M., Lerner, J.V., Almerigi, J. and Theokas, C. (2006) 'Dynamics of Individual Relations in Human Development: A Developmental Systems Perspective', in J.C. Thomas, D. Segal and M. Hersen (eds) *Comprehensive Handbook of Personality and Psychopathology, Vol. 1: Personality and Everyday Functioning.* New York: John Wiley, pp. 23–43.

Lightfoot, C. (1997) *The Culture of Adolescent Risk-taking.* New York: Guilford Press.

Loeber, R. and Hay, D. (1997) 'Key issues in the development of aggression and violence from childhood to early adulthood', *Annual Review of Psychology*, 48: 371–411.

Moffitt, T.E. (1997) 'Adolescence-limited and Life-course-persistent Offending: A Complementary Pair of Developmental Theories', in T.P. Thornberry (ed.) *Developmental Theories of Crime and Delinquency: Advances in Criminological Theory*, Vol. 7. New Brunswick, NJ: Transaction Publishers, pp. 11–54.

Nagin, D. and Tremblay, R.E. (1999) 'Trajectories of boys' physical aggression, opposition, and hyperactivity on the path to physically violent and non-violent juvenile delinquency', *Child Development*, 70(5): 1181–96.

Nagin, D. and Tremblay, R.E. (2005) 'What has been learned from group-based trajectory modelling? Examples from physical aggression and other problem behaviours', *Annals of the American Academy of Political and Social Science*, 602: 82–117.

Patterson, G.R. and Yoerger, K. (1993) 'Developmental Models for Delinquent Behaviour', in S. Hodgins (ed.) *Mental Disorders and Crime.* London: Sage, pp. 140–73.

Rönkä, A., Oravala, S. and Pulkkinen, L. (2002) '"I met this wife of mine and things got onto a better track": Turning points in risk development', *Journal of Adolescence*, 25: 47–63.

Rutter, M. and Sroufe, L.A. (2000) 'Developmental psychopathology: Concepts and challenges', *Development and Psychopathology*, 12: 265–96.

Sampson, R.J. and Laub, J.H. (2005) 'A life-course view of the development of crime', *Annals of the American Academy of Political and Social Science*, 602: 12–45.

Shonkoff, J.P. and Phillips, D.A. (2000) *Neurons to Neighborhoods: The Science of Early Child Development.* Washington, DC: National Academy Press.

Sroufe, L.A. and Jacobvitz, D. (1989) 'Diverging pathways, developmental transformations, multiple etiologies and the problem of continuity in development', *Human Development*, 32(3–4): 196–203.

Steinberg, L. (1995) 'Commentary on: Developmental Pathways and Social Contexts in Adolescence', in L.J. Crockett and A.C. Crouter (eds) *Pathways Through Adolescence: Individual Development in Relation to Social Contexts*. Mahwah, NJ: Lawrence Erlbaum Associates, pp. 245–53.

te Riele, K. (2004) 'Youth transition in Australia: Challenging assumptions of linearity and choice', *Journal of Youth Studies*, 7(3): 243–57.

Thornberry, T.P. (2005) 'Explaining multiple patterns of offending across the life course and across generations', *Annals of the American Academy of Political and Social Science*, 602: 156–95.

Thornberry, T.P. and Krohn, M.D. (2001) 'The Development of Delinquency: An Interactional Perspective', in S.O. White (ed.) *Handbook of Youth and Justice*. New York: Klumwer Academic/Penum Publishers, pp. 289–305.

Tremblay, R.E. (2002) 'The origins of physical aggression', *International Society for the Study of Behavioral Development Newsletter*, 2, Serial No. 42: 4–6.

Tremblay, R.E., Pagani-Kurtz, L., Masse, L.C., Vitaro, F. and Pihl, R.O. (1995) 'A bimodal preventive intervention for disruptive kindergarten boys: Its impact through mid-adolescence', *Journal of Consulting and Clinical Psychology*, 63(4): 560–68.

Valsiner, J. and Lawrence, J.A. (1997) 'Human Development in Culture Across the Life Span', In J.W. Berry, P.R. Dasen and T.S. Saraswathi (eds) *Handbook of Cross-cultural Psychology, Vol. 2: Basic Processes and Developmental Psychology*, 2nd edn. Boston: Allyn and Bacon, pp. 69–106.

Wyn, J. and White, R. (1997) *Rethinking Youth*. Sydney: Allen and Unwin.

Chapter 3

Adding social contexts to developmental analyses of crime prevention

Jacqueline J. Goodnow

Abstract

To link analyses of contexts with analyses of developmental change, this chapter takes as a starting point ways of describing social contexts. Two are given particular attention: one in terms of available routes/ opportunities/options, the other in terms of activities/routines/ practices. Each of these two approaches to contexts may be aligned with some particular descriptions of continuity or change. Each prompts also some particular proposals for forms of intervention or prevention. Considered more briefly are specifications of contexts in terms of ideologies or values, and in terms of a general quality: homogeneity/heterogeneity. The aim throughout is integrative: reducing the array of current positions by bringing together a variety of descriptions of context, in ways that use similar dimensions for the specification of descriptions of development and that suggest particular steps towards bringing about change.

Introduction

Within analyses of acts against the law, two points have long been recognised. One is that social contexts make a difference to what people do. The other is that people change from one age or one life phase to another. Acts against the law, for example, first appear, are sustained or escalate, or come to desist. Still present is the challenge of bringing together the varied descriptions of contexts that have been offered, linking them to descriptions of change, and moving towards actions that might alter the directions of change.

That challenge prompts this chapter. To meet at least part of it, I draw from more than one field. Anthropologists, criminologists and developmental psychologists, for example, share a common interest in social contexts and their links to variations in behaviours over time and place. Across fields, however, there has been little exchange or integration. Attempting to bring them together may even seem to invite making matters worse: increasing still further, for example, the variety of descriptions of contexts. There are, however, common threads and frameworks and each field, I propose, can enrich the other.

Structurally, the chapter begins with a brief statement of why it is important to take a life-span view of development and of contexts. In essence, the argument is that we limit our understanding of both when we place an exclusive or heavy emphasis on 'the early years' of life and the contexts existing at that time. The main body of the chapter then uses ways of describing contexts as a starting point. In all, four kinds of description are noted. These cover descriptions in terms of (1) paths, routes and opportunities; (2) practices, activities and routines; (3) values, ideologies and norms; and (4) qualities such as homogeneity, consensus and 'contest'. The first two are given the larger space, while the latter two are noted more briefly, with an emphasis on some of the particular questions they provoke, used as a way of rounding off the general argument for moving towards approaches that cut across contexts (from families to neighbourhoods), across actions (from crime to schooling or paid work) and across disciplines.

Taking a life-span view

Any attempt at linking contexts to development needs to start from the recognition of two broad kinds of ways to describe development: one emphasising 'the early years' in life, the other – the one I would argue for – taking more of a life-span perspective. Why avoid regarding development as completely shaped by what happens in the early years of life? A first reason is that an 'early years only' perspective leads to a *limited view of development*. It overlooks the occurrence of changes in direction, turning points, recovery routes. Left out also are the internal pushes towards change that occur as people grow older. Puberty, for example, may bring with it an increase in 'impulsivity' (McDonald 1995). Adolescence may bring with it a perception of 'risk-taking' as the expected and appropriate style for one's age (Lightfoot 1997). Left out overall is attention to how behaviours come not only to be established but also to be maintained or to 'desist': issues central to many analyses of crime (cf. Sampson and Laub 1994).

A further reason is that focusing only on the early years leads to a *limited view of contextual influences*. Overlooked is the extent to which maintaining what is established in the early years may depend on social situations continuing to be much the same. Overlooked also is the extent to which social settings change, with shifts occurring in demands, rewards, opportunities, challenges and hazards. Each new setting, to take a description from Wikström and Sampson (2003), may bring particular choices, temptations and provocations. Ways of learning to deal with anger provide an example. Young children can be taught ways of dealing with anger and of resolving conflicts that contribute to a decrease in aggressive behaviour occurring and lasting (e.g. Tremblay *et al.* 1995). The nature of provocations to anger, however, can change over time. We should, in fact, expect them to do so.

As if these difficulties were not enough, a focus on only the first few years promotes a *limited view of action and prevention*. Attention comes to focus on how to stop something getting started. We can then neglect other goals, e.g. the goal of avoiding behaviours becoming entrenched, escalating in seriousness, or increasing in frequency. We may ignore the course of change without intervention, pouring resources into putting an end to activities that people have already begun to phase out themselves. We may interpret 'early intervention' as meaning only that intervention should occur in the early years of life, disregarding the feasibility of taking action at several later points, the importance of recovery routes, and the shifting challenges that people meet. Smoking, substance use, unprotected sex, risky driving: these hazards or temptations are not likely to be covered by putting all our resources or advice into early childhood, ignoring the situations encountered at later points. 'Early in the pathway' or 'close to a point of encounter' are more productive meanings of 'early' (e.g. Developmental Crime Consortium 1999).

This is not to deny the importance of early childhood. Those years can be the start of cumulative disadvantage. Over the first three years of life, there can also occur changes that carry forward in positive fashion. We need, however, to look carefully at what is usefully carried forward to particular future situations. Stattin and his colleagues, for example, in a longitudinal study of adolescents (covering delinquency, school problems and mood), have pointed to the importance of children developing a willingness to disclose to parents what they do away from home (e.g. Kerr and Stattin 2000). That predisposition comes to be of particular importance as adolescents move into contexts where the possibility of parental supervision declines. In effect, the impact of any predisposition – positive or negative – needs always to be considered in the light of the future situations that are likely to be encountered.

Contexts as available paths/routes/opportunities/maps

This first way of describing contexts is essentially spatial or navigational. The emphasis falls, for example, on the ways in which it is possible to move (the available paths, routes, options or opportunities) and on the conditions that facilitate or block various moves. Setting aside for the moment what people see as possible, those contextual conditions may be described in terms such as the prerequisites set, the distances to be covered, the skills and resources required or, an aspect still in need of increased attention, the whims and vested interests of gatekeepers.

Descriptions of contexts in terms of available paths have several advantages. They can be found, for example, in several content areas: within analyses of moves in and out not only of crime but also of school, families, paid work, group memberships and social relationships. They can be found as well in analyses of both physical and social contexts. (Physical contexts are often overlooked by developmental psychologists. Criminologists, in contrast, are more aware of how both the natural and the built environment can pattern the social routes that are available or easy to take.)

A particular advantage is that these descriptions are easy to link with accounts of development. Development may be described, for example, in terms of paths taken or not taken, turning points, or recoveries from an unhappy choice of direction. That conceptual alignment avoids the problem of using different dimensions for the two descriptions, making any cross-mapping difficult. It also opens a search for the specific ways in which the two go together. To take a particular example, the usual progressions into crime may be up two separate ladders: one into increasingly serious crimes against property, the other into crimes against people (Loeber and LeBlanc 1990). The unexpected event may then be a move across ladders, or a jump into the serious end of involvement. An offence against property, for example, turns into a major first crime against people, without any preceding small steps up this ladder. That break in the usual progression may come about from a move into new social contexts and new influences. An adolescent may become involved, for example, with a peer group that is already well up the ladder, making the first act to be copied or used as a base for claiming membership an action at 'the deep end' (Wikström and Loeber 2000).

We have still a great deal to learn about what creates various kinds of match between paths available and paths taken. One way to approach the issue, however, comes from asking: What does this way of looking at contexts offer that is particularly relevant to actions that might be taken? That is not a new question within analyses of crime or antisocial acts. One example of concern is Braithwaite's (1988) argument that, to achieve change in acts against the law, we may need both to open one path and to block another. Expressed in terms related to early aggression against others, children may need to learn a double path. They may need to learn both that being aggressive carries costs and that there are other ways of acting that bring benefits (Tremblay *et al.* 1995). Less familiar are likely to be proposals that come from other fields. Studies of routes through school, for example, contain several that are eminently extendable to 'crime'. They underline the following:

- *Making routes available and keeping them open.* One school-related example is the analysis of options that are 'foreclosed' when pregnant teenagers are cut off from continued schooling (Furstenberg *et al.* 1987). Moffitt (1993) is one of several who make a similar point within analyses of crime, noting the way that convictions 'knife off' later options.

- *Considering the information about routes and prerequisites that people are likely to hold and increasing their 'cultural capital'.* For an example, I reach back to a rich but now neglected study by Jackson and Marsden (1966). The difficulty for many working-class children and parents in this English sample was not a lack of interest in moving through school and into university. Often, however, they had inaccurate maps of progressions and prerequisites, and were reluctant to ask teachers for information. The teachers, in their turn, assumed that of course the parents and children knew what the routes were: they simply made strange choices. In Bourdieu and Passeron's (1977) terms, these families lacked 'cultural capital':

a knowledge of 'how the system works'. That capital, however, could certainly be increased.

- *Doing more than providing information about what is available.* Links to identities are also critical. In Willis' (1981) classic study *Learning to Labour*, for example, 'the lads' often knew the routes they could in theory take. They saw these routes, however, as incompatible with who they were or who they wanted to become. In effect, we need to consider not only the information people may have available but also the way they (and others) construct its relevance to themselves.

An ongoing intervention project provides an example of action. This project started from a concern with the limited number of Hispanic and other minority children in Californian schools who progressed all the way through high school and on to university (Cooper *et al.* 2005). Two steps turned out to be needed to change that pattern. One was to make sure that the students knew the routes that could be taken and the steps involved (e.g. the prerequisites and grade levels that were needed at various points). The other was to work towards having students see those steps and goals as part of their 'possible selves': as both achievable and also in keeping with who they were or might be. To be taken into account was then not only the information each student held but also their sense of worthwhile costs and of the acceptability of progression to their families and the social groups they identified with. We have a great deal yet to learn, I suggest, about that second step: about how the sense of various routes as 'not for me' or 'OK for me' is constructed.

Contexts as activities/routines/cultural practices

Like many criminologists, developmentalists are interested not only in the nature of thinking (e.g. the perception of options, the views held about consequences or about the right and proper thing to do) but also in the nature of action and the links between the two. Several lines of research in fact start from an emphasis on ways of acting as the optimal way of describing both social contexts and developmental shifts. An example with a direct relevance to antisocial or illegal acts is Caldwell and Smith's (this volume) analysis of recreational and leisure activities. They have argued especially for the need to build a stronger theoretical picture for how leisure activities affect involvement in other actions, ranging from crime to prosocial behaviours: effects mediated by opportunities for participation in ways that do more than fill time, offering as well ways to select what one does and to follow through in ways that are rewarding.

Compatible with that kind of analysis is a general approach to contexts in terms of the 'cultural practices' they contain and to development in terms of shifts in participation. The term 'cultural practices' refers to ways of acting that are followed by all or most members of a social group (in this sense, they are 'cultural'), that are carried out in routine, everyday, taken-for-granted fashion, and that attract little reflection or questioning, that come to be felt as 'natural'. Descriptions of contexts in terms of such practices are prominent within anthropology (cf. Bourdieu 1977; Lave and Wenger 1991; Ortner 1984) and are moving into developmental psychology (Goodnow *et al.* 1995, provide several examples; others are to be found in Rogoff 2003, and in a review chapter by Shweder *et al.* 2006).

The attractiveness of practice descriptions lies partly in the emphasis placed on the way cultural practices can limit what is 'thought about' or considered as possible: in Wikström and Sampson's (2003) terms, what is seen as an option. It lies also in the argument that the views people hold arise from their actions (the direction to consider is then from actions to thought rather than the more usual thought to action). The practice of 'doing gender' (West and Zimmerman 1987) provides a case in point. The distinctions we make between 'male' and 'female' are embedded in different ways of acting towards males and females, starting with differences in names, clothing and games and persisting through customary ways of greeting, addressing, inviting, dividing or occupying space, etc. Little or nothing then needs to be said about the importance of distinguishing males from females.

Links to accounts of development

Descriptions of contexts in terms of practices direct attention towards changes in the nature of activities and in the nature of participation. They bring also recognition of the extent to which other people are involved in any activity and of the need to ask always how they are involved. Others may, for example, work directly with us. Even if not physically present, they may structure the tasks we face and the actions we can take: allocating problems, setting standards or norms, judging and evaluating what we do. In some form or other – as team members, competitors, coaches, fans, referees, judges, scorekeepers – others are always part of any action. No action is really 'solo'.

For a specific example of how that kind of description alters views of development, I take the emergence of a second look at the development of 'expertise' or 'skill', drawing especially from analyses by Lave and Wenger (1991) and Rogoff (2003). That second look has involved a turn towards regarding 'expertise' as not only a matter of knowledge but also as competence in action. Increasingly, it has involved as well a turn away from seeing the development of skill as a change occurring only within the individual. In this alternate view, all skills start in interactions with others. Over time, what may change is an understanding both of what we do and also of what others are doing, can do, or are expected to do. Over time, what may change also is the level of instruction, support or control by others (the exchange between 'experts' and 'novices' in some descriptions). Over time, what may change as well is the relationship among the people involved. As 'expertise' increases, for example, people shift from 'peripheral' positions in a group (e.g. tolerated as long as they draw little attention to themselves) to being accepted and recognised members of a 'community of practitioners' (Lave and Wenger 1991). They may, to extend the argument, come to expect that shift, with disaffection and resentment following if that expectation is not met.

Implications for action

Do descriptions of contexts in terms of practices do more than open up new ways of considering development? Offered also are some proposals about change that pick up or add to analyses of acts against the law. A first proposal stems from the emphasis on practices as the basis for ways of viewing the world. *Change may need to focus on practices rather than on information or on ways of thinking.* Altering views about gender provides an example. The points of challenge may be linguistic practices (e.g. the earlier use of 'he' or 'man' to cover both genders). They may also be the conventional division of occupations and spaces into those marked as only for males or only for females. In essence, the changes to aim for are changes in practice. The views held (e.g. views about 'proper' distinctions by gender) may change slowly, or perhaps not at all. The changes in practice, however, create a different climate and in time a different sense of 'normal' ways to act. Similar kinds of change seem likely to be effective in relation to acts against the law or to the everyday activities that make acts against the law more likely.

Some further implications stem from an emphasis on development as changes in the nature of participation and membership. One is the *need always to ask just what others provide*. In developmental analyses of skill, for example, others may provide (a) the strategic tools, (b) a 'scaffolding' of help that is gradually withdrawn as competence increases, or (c) the motivational-affective resources needed to get through a difficult patch. The same kind of breakdown applies also to acts against the law. What others offer, for example, may be expertise in ways to avoid getting caught (Weatherburn and Lind 2001), or a level of information about illegitimate alternatives to paid work that far exceeds the information available about paid work (Hagan 1993). Needed always, however, in any account of the influence of peers or adults, is a specification of what they offer and how that fits with what the individual seeks or brings to an activity.

A further implication is the *need to consider always the nature of membership and of participation*. We need to ask, for example, about the expected and the actual links between changing competence and changing membership. In Moffitt's (1993) terms, there may be for many adolescents a troubling gap (a 'maturity gap') between what they see themselves as capable of (and are capable of) and the adult status that others are willing to grant them. Membership and relationships are also at the core of proposals for the need to consider and to foster social bonds when we seek to change involvement in various activities. Social bonds have long held a significant place in analyses of acts against the law. They are, for example, a prominent part of Gottfredsen and Hirschi's (1990) emphasis on impulse control. That quality they see as established early in life, as persisting over the life course (largely because of weak parental supervision), and as promoting weakness in the social bonds that promote conventional beliefs and activities. That position has prompted several kinds of questions. Raised, for example, have been questions about the relevant conditions in early life, the extent of persistence, and the view taken of social bonds as an outcome rather than as a prompting condition in their own right (cf. Enter Wright *et al.* 1999).

Similar questions have been raised in relation to acts other than those against the law. Social bonds have been pointed to, for example, as a major factor in establishing and maintaining a sense of 'engagement' in activities. 'Engagement' in the academic tasks of school, for example, appears to depend more on the quality of the teacher–student relationship than on the intrinsic appeal of a task (Blumenfeld *et al.* 2005). In effect, both the nature of activities and the nature of participation in them, with participation linked to membership and social bonds, now move to a central position in accounts of how various kinds of activity may come to occur and to change.

Further ways of theorising contexts

I have so far focused on two ways of specifying the nature of social contexts: one in terms of available paths, the other in terms of practices or activities. These are not, however, the only kinds of specification that offer ways of expanding the usual analyses of contexts in relation to acts against the law. Two further ways have to do with (1) contexts as ideologies/values/norms and (2) contexts specified by a general quality (homogeneity/heterogeneity) that applies to all forms of content (routes, practices or ideologies). I take up these further approaches in briefer fashion, with an emphasis on interesting but unfinished possibilities.

Contexts as ideologies, values or/and norms

Analyses of contexts contain a long-standing interest in the nature of distinctions between right and wrong, between what is regarded as 'proper' and what is regarded as not. Analyses of development also contain a long-standing interest in what is usually called 'moral development' and in its bases (most often referred to as 'socialisation'). Within developmental psychology, for example, the nature of 'moral' progression has attracted descriptions in terms of shifts from convention to principle, from situational variations to consistency, commitment and the sense of a viewpoint as being part of one's identity. There seems no need to list the several forms in which interest in these aspects of development has appeared within analyses of acts against the law. I single out instead two lines of questioning that seem to me to present some particular challenges.

One of these has to do with the nature of progression, the other with the bases of change. The question about progression has to do with the ways in which a particular aspect of moral judgement comes about. This is the aspect that Wikström and Sampson (2003) have called 'morality': the perception of an action as 'not an option'. Many of our actions seem to depend on the evaluation of options: evaluating, for example, the costs and the chances of being caught, set against the benefits that might occur if one is successful. Some actions, however, are not seen or considered as options. They are simply 'not on'. Fiske (1991) highlights a similar aspect of moral thinking in his analysis of shared and divergent views among cultures. Cultures may vary, he points out, in what they regard as illegitimate to sell. In some it will be sex, in others drugs or people. In each, however, there is a sense that some actions are 'taboo', some ways of viewing the world 'heretical' or 'unthinkable' (Fiske and Tetlock 1997; Tetlock *et al.* 2004).

How that aspect of development – that deterrent to particular kinds of action – comes about is not as yet well covered in accounts of acts against the law or of moral development in general. Two changes in those accounts, however, begin to fill in part of the gap and to promise links to intervention action. One of these has already been noted. This is the move towards giving a larger space to routines and practices that come to be felt to be 'natural' and to be 'unquestioned'.

The other is a move towards breaking socialisation into more specific processing steps, with different conditions affecting various steps. In one analysis of family socialisation, for example (Grusec and Goodnow 1994), the first step has to do with children's perception of an adult message: a perception that may or may not be accurate. The critical condition seems likely to be the clarity of the parent's message. The second step consists of whether the perceived message is accepted or rejected. For that step, the critical conditions are seen as the quality of the relationship between parent and child, and the presence of contrary messages from others (e.g. from the other parent, from peers or from media models). The third step consists of coming to regard a particular view as one's own, as generated by oneself rather than being a simple compliance. That 'internalisation' step is seen as depending especially on experiencing opportunities to exercise some degree of decision-making or choice. Each step and its associated conditions may then influence the extent to which we come to hold or not hold the views that others present to us. Analysis and intervention, this approach implies, should first pin down the specific steps in processing on the way to agreement or disagreement and the specific conditions associated with them.

Contexts specified by degrees and forms of homogeneity/heterogeneity

This way of describing contexts is regarded as relatively new among anthropologists and developmental psychologists. It is salutary, however, to find it as part of Shaw and McKay's (1942/1969) early analysis of neighbourhoods. Of importance, they argued, was the presence and nature of an 'ethnic mix', with a mix diminishing the likelihood of 'collective control' and the likelihood of parental views becoming the only views held. Important also was the extent to which several groups worked with or against one another. Ethnic groups, for example, might actively devalue one another, business interests invade residential space, legitimate and illegitimate groups combine to resist or to protect 'their' space or 'their' people.

In other fields, a similar kind of emphasis – applied now to a variety of behaviours and values – is to be found under labels such as 'multiplicity and contest'. Multiplicity refers to a view of contexts as never being 'monolithic'. There is always more than one way of acting, one view of how people should act, one approach to areas such as schooling, medicine or work (even of 'crime', one might add). Contest refers to there always being forms of tension and competition among these several ways. Some may be 'dominant' over others, may be 'central' rather than 'marginal'. Between them there are likely to occur putdowns, claims of higher status, attempts at suppression, takeover bids, alliances, resistances, negotiations, and doubts about each other's goodwill: attempts, to use some further terms, by one group to 'colonialise' or 'marginalise' others.

This view of contexts and social life is now widespread in analyses of cultures (e.g. D'Andrade and Strauss 1992; Goodnow and Warton 1992, provide a brief summary of some other accounts). Like the previous descriptions of contexts, this kind of specification also tends to fit well with some particular ways of considering development and possible intervention actions. Development, for example, may be seen as stemming from a series of encounters with diversity: with others' jokes or narratives, others' ways of viewing possible options. Some of these encounters may be positive. Others may be less so. When children from minority groups enter school, for example, they often encounter teachers who devalue their ways of speaking and attempt to replace them with styles the teacher values. They are also likely to encounter others (peers or school staff) who make them aware that they are a 'minority' group with lesser status. What occurs then is the development of both views about self and others and ways of coping with the negative evaluations that may be met.

The main implications for action are of two kinds. The first starts mainly from considering 'multiplicity': from the recognition that alternate views of the world are unlikely to be encountered if the groups one joins hold only values similar to one's own. If a change in views or actions is needed, exposure to alternatives in more heterogeneous groups appears to be the more likely route to success. A specific example comes from a study that mixed antisocial with prosocial peers (Tremblay *et al.* 1995). Teaching young boys to be less aggressive was easier with a group that mixed antisocial and prosocial children than it was with a group made up only of 'offenders'.

The second kind of implication comes more from the concept of 'contest'. Groups do not simply differ from one another in the views that they hold. They also develop 'stances' towards each other. Towards the views and practices of others, for example, the stance most often taken may be one of tolerance, mixed with respect or with amusement. The stance taken may also be more negative: more dismissive, for example, or more concerned with putting these alternatives in their 'proper place', perhaps even 'beyond the pale'. The success of intervention actions may then depend on anticipating the specific kinds of encounter that are likely to be met and on working out specific ways of coping with them or taking advantage of them.

To date, the closest analyses of such preparation appear to come from studies of how African-American parents prepare children for encounters that may devalue them (e.g. Hughes and Chen 1999) or tempt them to move 'off track', to lose interest in academic achievement (e.g. Steinberg *et al.* 1995). The emphasis in those studies on encounters with others' views or values, and on the ways in which these may be resisted or countered, seems potentially very useful for analyses of progressions and interventions in relation to acts against the law or acts that can lead in that direction.

Conclusion

Analyses of culture by anthropologists and sociologists cover far more than the analyses I have noted. The same is true for analyses of settings and neighbourhoods by criminologists (Weatherburn and Lind 2001 provides one overview and a particular kind of analysis; see also Sampson and Laub 1994; Wikström 1998). I have started, however, from a view often stated in analyses of acts against the law: namely, the need to anchor analyses of crime in general theories of behaviour and its settings. Bringing out analyses of contexts that cut across fields is one step towards that broad goal.

More narrowly, I have aimed at bringing out points of overlap and possible expansion that can alert people involved in analyses of crime to material they might not usually encounter, can link to accounts of development, and can use towards the analysis of how action and intervention may proceed. My own views of contexts and development have certainly been enlarged by analyses that focus on acts against the law. My hope is that for people focused to start with on acts against the law, similar benefit comes from considering how others approach the tasks of specifying the features of contexts, the features of development or change, and the interconnections between them.

Acknowledgements

An earlier version of this chapter, a paper presented at the International Symposium on Pathways and Prevention at Brisbane in September 2005, benefited from several papers and discussions at that conference. I happily acknowledge my debt to those who were present: a debt added to some already owed to several members of an earlier Developmental Crime Prevention Consortium, alphabetically Judy Cashmore, Alan Hayes, Ross Homel and Jeanette Lawrence.

References

Blumenfeld, P., Modell, J., Bartko, W.T., Secada, W.G., Fredricks, J.A., Friedel, J. and Parks, A. (2005) 'School Engagement of Inner-city Students During Middle Childhood', in C.R. Cooper, C. García Coll, W.T. Bartko, H. Davis and C. Chatman (eds) *Developmental Pathways Through Middle Childhood: Rethinking Diversity and Contexts as Resources*. Mahwah, NJ: Erlbaum, pp. 145–70.

Bourdieu, P. (1977) *Outline of a Theory of Practice*. New York: Cambridge University Press.

Bourdieu, P. and Passeron, J-C. (1977) *Reproduction in Education, Society and Culture*. Beverly Hills, CA: Sage.

Braithwaite, J. (1988) *Crime, Shame, and Reintegration*. Cambridge: Cambridge University Press.

Cooper, C.R., Dominquez, E. and Rosas, S. (2005) 'Soledad's Dream: How Immigrant Children Bridge their Multiple Worlds and Build Pathways to College', in C.R. Cooper, C. García Coll, W. T. Bartko, H. Davis and C. Chatman (eds) *Developmental Pathways Through Middle Childhood: Rethinking Diversity and Contexts as Resources*. Mahwah, NJ: Erlbaum, pp. 235–60.

D'Andrade, R.G. and Strauss, C. (eds) (1992) *Human Motives and Cultural Models*. Cambridge: Cambridge University Press.

Developmental Crime Prevention Consortium (1999) *Pathways to Prevention: Developmental and Early Intervention Approaches to Crime*. Canberra: Attorney-General's Department.

Enter Wright, B.R., Caspi, A., Moffitt, T.E. and Silva, P. (1999) 'Low self-control, social bonds, and crime: Social causation, social selection, or both?' *Criminology*, 37: 479–509.

Fiske, A.P. (1991) *Structures of Social Life: The Four Elementary Forms of Social Relations*. New York: Free Press.

Fiske, A.P. and Tetlock, P.E. (1997) 'Taboo trade-offs: Reactions to transactions that transgress spheres of justice', *Political Psychology*, 18: 255–97.

Furstenberg, F.F. Jr, Brooks-Gunn, J. and Morgan, S.P. (1987) 'Adolescent mothers and their children in later life', *Family Planning Perspectives*, 19: 142–51.

Goodnow, J.J., Miller, P.J. and Kessel, F. (eds.) (1995) *Cultural Practices as Contexts for Development*. San Francisco: Jossey-Bass.

Goodnow, J.J. and Warton, P. (1992) 'Contexts and Cognition: Taking a Pluralist View', in P. Light and G. Butterworth (eds), *Context and Cognition*. Hertfordshire: Harvester Wheatsheaf, pp. 157–77.

Grusec, J.E. and Goodnow, J.J. (1994) 'The impact of parental discipline methods on the child's internalization of value', *Developmental Psychology*, 30: 4–19.

Gottfredsen, M. and Hirschi, R. (1990) *A General Theory of Crime*. Stanford, CA: Stanford University Press.

Hagan, J. (1993) 'The social embeddedness of crime and unemployment', *Criminology*, 31: 465–92.

Hughes, D. and Chen, L. (1999) 'The Nature of Parents' Race-related Communications to Children', in L. Balter and C.S. Tamis-LeMonda (eds) *Child Psychology: A Handbook of Contemporary Issues*. Philadelphia, PA: Psychology Press, pp. 467–90.

Jackson, B. and Marsden, D. (1966) *Education and the Working Class*. Harmondsworth: Penguin.

Kerr, M. and Stattin, H. (2000) 'What parents know, how they know it, and several forms of adolescent adjustment: Further support for a reinterpretation of monitoring', *Developmental Psychology*, 36: 366–80.

Lave, J. and Wenger, E. (1991) *Situated Learning: Legitimate Peripheral Participation*. New York: Cambridge University Press.

Lightfoot, C. (1997) *The Culture of Adolescent Risk-taking*. New York: Guilford Press.

Loeber, R. and LeBlanc, M. (1990) 'Toward a developmental criminology', *Crime and Justice – An Overview of Research*, 12: 375–473.

McDonald, K.B. (1995) 'Evolution, the five factor model, and levels of personality', *Journal of Personality*, 63: 525–67.

Moffitt, T. E. (1993) 'Life-course persistent and adolescence-limited antisocial behavior: A developmental taxonomy', *Psychological Review*, 100: 674–701.

Ortner, S. (1984) 'Theory in anthropology since the sixties', *Society for Comparative Study of Society and History*, 26: 126–66.

Rogoff, B. (2003) *The Cultural Nature of Human Development*. New York: Oxford University Press.

Sampson, R.J. and Laub, J.H. (1994) 'Urban poverty and the family context of delinquency: A new look at structure and process in a classic study', *Child Development*, 65: 523–40.

Shaw, C.R. and McKay, H.D. (1942, revised edition 1969) *Juvenile Delinquency and Urban Areas*. Chicago: University of Chicago Press.

Shweder, R.A., Goodnow, J.J., Hatano, G., Levine R., Markus, H.R. and Miller, P.J. (2006) The Cultural Psychology of Development: One Mind, Many Mentalities', in W. Damon and R.M. Lerner (eds) *Handbook of Child Psychology*, Vol. 1. New York: John Wiley.

Steinberg, L., Darling, N.E. and Fletcher, A.C. (1995) Authoritative Parenting and Adolescent Adjustment: An Ecological Journey', in P. Moen, G.H. Elder Jr and Lüscher, K. (eds) *Examining Lives in Context*. Washington, DC: American Psychological Association, pp. 423–55.

Tetlock, P.E., McGraw, A.P. and Kristel, O.V. (2004). Proscribed Forms of Social Cognition: Taboo Trade-offs, Blocked Exchanges, Forbidden Base Rates, and Heretical Counterfactuals', in N. Haslam (ed.), *Relational Models Theory: Contemporary Perspectives*. Mahwah, NJ: Erlbaum, pp. 247–62.

Tremblay, R.E., Kurtaz, L., Mâsse, L. C., Vitaro, F. and Phil, R.O. (1995) 'A bimodal preventive intervention for disruptive kindergarten boys: Its impact through adolescence', *Journal of Consulting and Clinical Psychology*, 63: 560–8.

Weatherburn, D. and Lind, B. (2001) *Delinquent-prone Communities*. Cambridge: Cambridge University Press.

West, C. and Zimmerman, D. (1987) 'Doing gender', *Gender and Society*, 1: 125–51.

Wikström, P-O.H. (1998) 'Communities and Crime', in M. Tonry (ed.) *The Handbook of Crime and Punishment*. New York: Oxford University Press, pp. 269–301.

Wikström, P-O.H. and Loeber, R. (2000) 'Do disadvantaged neighborhoods cause well-adjusted children to become delinquent adolescents? A study of male juvenile serious offending, individual risk and protective factors, and neighborhood context', *Criminology*, 38: 1109–42.

Wikström, P-O.H. and Sampson, R.J. (2003) 'Social Mechanisms of Community Influences on Crime and Pathways in Criminality', in B.B. Lahey, T.E. Moffitt and A. Caspi (eds) *Causes of Conduct Disorder and Juvenile Delinquency*. New York: Guilford Press, pp. 118–48.

Willis, P. (1981) *Learning to Labor: Working Class Kids get Working Class Jobs*. New York: Columbia University Press.

Chapter 4

Risk factors and pathways into and out of crime: misleading, misinterpreted or mythic? From generative metaphor to professional myth

Kaye Haw

Abstract

The purpose of this chapter is to explore how the notions of risk-factor research and pathways into and out of crime have attained the status of professional myth. The argument put forward is not about the rights or wrongs of policy or practice based on risk-factor research. Partly this is because the author is not a criminologist but a researcher interested in ethnographic work with young people and their local communities. Neither is the argument primarily about the truthfulness or falsehood of myths, but rather a discussion of how a model has moved from being a generative metaphor to a professional myth. In making this argument this chapter offers a critique of the complex relationship between the values and beliefs of practitioners and their interactions with the discourses, ideologies and structures around them.

In arguing that 'pathways' has moved from a generative metaphor (Schon 1993) to professional myth, I explore how myths function socially within different groups of professions, and the relationship between their social function and individual use. This argument is in part derived from an exploration of the cultural status of any given myth within a profession and the metaphors that underpin them. The discussion of the process of myth-making, and its impact on professionals, is illustrated principally through an analysis of the narratives offered by two different professionals working with young people.

Introduction

This chapter is a view from the outside looking in. It is written from the perspective of a researcher working ethnographically within urban communities interested in issues of identity and how practitioners respond to the discourses around them, rather than a criminologist with an extensive knowledge of the literature generated in this field. The aims are threefold. First, to argue that the notion of the pathway as a means of explaining young people's engagement in criminal and deviant behaviour is increasingly problematic as it has gained mythic status. Second, to argue that the failure to recognise the notion of the pathway as ideologically marked and mythopoeic (Flood 2002) means that it has become part of a disabling rather than enabling discourse. Third, to argue this has repercussions for how young people, like those from Urbanfields who participated in this research, are treated in the criminal justice system.

To achieve these aims the discussion first traces the movement between the risk-factor model and the notion of the 'pathway' as a 'generative' metaphor to its becoming a part of the belief systems of different communities of practice concerned with young people and deviancy. From here I explore how the notion of the pathway has attained the status of professional myth as these groups seek to resolve the dilemmas they are faced with in their everyday practice. This is not an argument fundamentally with the world of risk-factor research or the models that have sprung from it. Nor is it an argument based around myth as speech acts or sense making practices, although mythical language is commonly used as a linguistic device and short cut (Barthes 2000). Instead, the perspective I want to take on myth is similar to that adopted by anthropologists like Douglas (1966), who use the notion of taboo and taboo-breaking and link these to notions of deviance and breaking cultural norms. From this perspective the argument presented concerns the 'sacred' aspect of empirically based knowledge and the way the work becomes taken up and used.

The last sections of this chapter use the data generated by the research to illustrate the argument that the pathway metaphor has achieved the status of ideologically marked conventional wisdom and has attained mythic status. This, it is argued, is to the detriment of the work ethics of some professionals and the young people they work with.

From model to metaphor

In the 1960s Becker wrote about the 'deviant career'. He explored rule-breaking behaviour and used the term 'outsider' to describe a labelled rule-breaker or deviant as an individual that accepts the label attached to them. He then built this into the notion of the deviant career by linking this to the idea of a career in crime and describing the process by which deviant outsiders become involved in secondary deviance. Becker contended that the final stage in the creation of a career delinquent is their involvement in a deviant subculture providing the individual with moral support and a self-justifying rationale (Becker 1963). From this point this model evolved and the dominant metaphor in the area came to be that of the 'criminal career' (Blumstein *et al.* 1986). This perspective was concerned with

> the prevalence of offending, the frequency of offending by offenders, and the onset, persistence, escalation, de-escalation, and desistance of offending. It documented how a small fraction of the population committed large numbers of offences and had long criminal careers. (Farrington 2000: 2)

This work was originally concerned with the serious and violent offender. The internal logic of this work took into account overlapping causalities, and its natural trajectory was to identify frequent offenders in advance and to devise and implement strategies to prevent their delinquent development. This is a particular bounded model in that it specifically looks at a subset of criminal activity and a subset of individuals within that, those with serious and violent criminal careers. However, when this model was combined with the notion of risk factors in the 1990s and applied not just to the abnormal career criminal but to the normal and everyday using the notion of the pathway instead of a career, a new generative metaphor emerged.

A generative metaphor (Schon 1993) is one that in a sense exists already but as it is taken up, combined with other factors and then applied to a new area where it has not previously been used, it generates different insights and understandings. In this instance the combination of the career path with risk factors when applied to young people not only generated new ideas and frameworks within different disciplines, it allowed their understandings to cross between disciplines. This ability to cross between disciplines means that the metaphor of the pathway acts as a 'boundary object'. Boundary objects can be pieces of information, conversations, goals or rules that provide a mechanism for meanings to be shared and constructed across professional boundaries (Engeström *et al.* 1999; Engeström 2001a, 2001b). The metaphor becomes a 'boundary' object as it is worked upon simultaneously by diverse sets of actors and used differently by the corresponding communities, providing a means to think and talk about an idea without the necessity of any one community completely adopting the perspective of the other. Boundary objects provide key moments of meaning creation, renewing learning through collaboration and linking different communities of practice that are

> formed by people who engage in a process of collective learning in a shared domain of human endeavour: a tribe learning to survive, a band of artists seeking new forms of expression, a group of engineers working on similar problems ... In a nutshell Communities of Practice are groups of people who share a concern or passion for something they do and learn how to do it better as they interact regularly. (Wenger 2006: 1)

Where practitioners from diverse professional cultures, such as education, health or youth offending teams, are engaged in shared activities, their professional learning is expanded as they negotiate working practices that cross traditional professional boundaries marking different communities of practice. Currently the practices required to support 'at-risk' young people and families are no longer considered to be the discrete province of any one profession but require planned configurations of complementary expertise drawn from across education, health and social services. Many of the recent key developments in forms of social provision, which aim to enhance the capabilities of children, young people and their families by addressing their complex social needs, have been predicated upon these forms of interagency collaboration (Easen *et al.* 2000). This has included initiatives such as the Social Exclusion Unit, Sure Start, Education Action Zones, Health Action Zones, Connexions, the Children's Fund and Children's Trusts. All these policy initiatives are supported by disciplines that draw on risk-factor research. Connections are made between them by using boundary objects, like the pathways metaphor in the process of brokering (Wenger 1998). The boundary object does not in itself achieve the connection but enables the participative action that brings about the connection through the process of brokering. Brokering occurs when a participant from one community of practice enters another and convinces this latter community to adopt an interpretation of a procedure from the former community. The metaphor of the pathway is a boundary object because it has the potential to create consensual meaning during the brokerage process.

As a generative metaphor, the pathway adds to the setting and framing of the social problem that all individuals are to an extent surrounded by opportunities and threats that may lead them into aspects of criminal or deviant behaviour. The point is not that we ought to think metaphorically about this particular social policy problem but that we already do in terms of this powerful and pervasive generative metaphor. As such, this metaphor has the potential to be both creative and analytical and underpin the ideologies of a range of professions, defined from the non-Marxist political belief system perspective as

sets of ideas by which men [and women] posit, explain and justify ends and means of organised social action, and specifically political action, irrespective of whether such action aims to preserve, amend, uproot or rebuild a given social order. (Seliger 1976: 14)

The ability of the pathway to act as a generative metaphor that links various communities of practice is in part due to how 'risk' has been conceptualised more broadly within society. Fascination with the notion of risk among the media, politicians and the public is recorded in a range of academic disciplines: politics, science, health, economics, employment relations and the environment. Each, while borrowing from the other, has a distinct academic knowledge base and approach but all are increasingly treating risk as central to our discussion of 'being' human in the early twenty-first century.

Various aspects of this broader conceptualisation of risk and risk-taking have fed back into the discourse of youth crime. First, through anthropological approaches investigating variations in understandings of risk between individuals and different communities (see Douglas 1985, 1992). Second, through studies particularly within psychology and social psychology that focus on risk in the everyday such as among extreme sportspeople, environmental and public health and decision-making within group dynamics (see Lupton 1999; Slovic 1987, 1992, 2000). Third, through those that have used Foucault's work concerning the disciplinary effects of discourse (Foucault 1978, 1991) accentuating the role of social institutions in constructing understandings of risk that restrict and regiment human behaviour

(Castel 1991; Dean 1999; O'Malley 2001). Fourth, through the risk society perspective popularised through the work of Beck (1992, 1999) and Giddens (1998, 1999) pointing out the pervasive effects of risk on everyday life (see Bujra 2000; Caplan 2000; Simon 1987). We now have a context where risk theories, such as actuarialism, treat risk as defining the 'everyday'. From this perspective risks are aggregated, statistically calculated, and used as a means of social control, in a sense subsuming values as a means of directing and shaping personal and social life because

> there is no longer so much a concern with justice as with community defence and protection and where causes of crime and deviance are not seen as the vital clue to the solution to the problem of crime. The actuarial stance is calculative of risk, it is wary and probabilistic, it is not concerned with causes but with probabilities, not with justice but with harm minimisation ... The actuarial stance reflects the fact that risk both to individuals and collectivities has increased, crime has become a normalised part of everyday life, the offender is seemingly everywhere in the street and in high office, within the poor parts of town but also in those institutions which were set up to rehabilitate and protect, within the public world of encounters with strangers but within the family itself in relationships with husband and wife and parent and child. (Young 2006: 4–5)

As the notion of risk has been more broadly conceptualised so have risk factors and the metaphor of the pathway to explain the crime and deviancy of young people. The roots of the pathway metaphor lie in the need to structure and identify our environment. It has moved on from traditional interpretations such as 'straying from the straight and narrow' to ideas of multiple pathways, some leading into and some out of crime. In the criminal justice system professionals – social workers or the police – have reified a certain form of knowledge creating its own reference points and sometimes language. This makes it difficult for other groups to understand what part of their knowledge they see as important or significant and engage with them in collaborative activities. The potential of the metaphor as a boundary object is that it allows individuals with different beliefs or ideologies to have conversations across boundaries. This is particularly important in a climate where these groups are increasingly required to implement multi-agency approaches so there is a desire to come to a shared understanding of the various belief systems on which the different approaches and practices within each service are founded. There are two problems here.

The first is as the use of metaphor becomes reified over time there is no equivalent recognition of the differential application of this dominant metaphor in different communities of practice. The second is that while an analysis at the level of ideology and belief systems goes some way to understand relations of power between these groups, it fails to pay sufficient attention to values and emotions. This is important because the professionals working with young people in these circumstances have jobs that are riven with value judgements and emotional contacts that are about communication and relationship-building, in which they are continually called upon to make decisions and resolve a series of dilemmas and tensions. This is where myth is useful to the analysis because it brings in notions of values and emotions, the resolution of contradictions and the space where discourses operate:

> Myth is a value; truth is no guarantee for it ... the meaning is always there to present the form; the form is always there to outdistance the meaning ... there is never any contradiction, conflict or split between the meaning and the form. (Barthes 2000: 123)

From powerful generative metaphor to professional myth

Myths are generally conceived of as narrative elements of broader belief systems that underpin their 'believers' view of reality, or 'truth'. Non-believers of the myth treat these views as 'false' and open to challenge on the basis of empirical findings or other myths. However, the approach adopted here is primarily to treat myths in the same way as they are by many anthropologists and historians of religion, as being defined by their discursive form, content, cultural status and social function rather than their truth (see Segal 1999). Every myth in this sense has its own history, its own geography, and its own set of functions.

One of the key social functions of myth is that it helps us resolve any one of the series of contradictions we are faced with and feel as private individuals and social actors, for example, between what is meant by normal or ordinary and what is deviant or extraordinary. We do not resolve these contradictions purely cognitively. They are also worked out within the social world through narrative, research, policy-making and individual or collective actions, and individually by reference to values and emotions. In the social world these contradictions become 'facts' or real as they shape practices and procedures. As other individuals or groups also try to resolve their own internal contradictions they exhibit similar practices. Over time these take on symbolic meaning and begin to shape how others resolve their 'felt' contradictions, either emotional or values based, leading to further actions that impact on and affect others. Losev terms this the mythic feedback loop (Losev 2003). The loop is a dynamic that flows from an internal 'felt' contradiction which is then synthesised as 'fact' in the social world by action and practice, and which then takes on a symbolic function as it returns to shape the internal sense-making of the individual.

From this perspective, myth possesses a dynamic that breaches the boundary between the internally 'felt' world of the individual and the external world of social action. Myths, once internalised, form a deep structure and act as intermediaries between the unconscious and consciousness (Bennett 1980), the individual and the social. This movement between the internal and external worlds of individuals is the point at which a useful distinction can be made between myth and ideology.

Professional myths in the criminal justice system arise from underlying tensions, such as, for example, the protection of the community versus the rehabilitation of the offender. These tensions accrete through the social cultural context of the professions within this system but also live within the actions of individual professionals in their everyday decisions. In this sense myths need to carry sufficient authority to have paradigmatic value as being simultaneously a 'model of' and a 'model for' reality among those who believe them (Flood 2002). Myths are 'accounts of a more or less common sequence of events involving more or less the same principal actors, subject to more or less the same overall interpretation and implied meaning, that circulate within a social group' (2002: 179).

Once accepted by different communities of practice, myths function to convey an explicit or implicit invitation to assent to a particular ideological standpoint and potentially to act in accordance with it. Myths therefore carry with them the imprint of assumptions values and goals associated with particular belief systems and are ideologically marked accounts (Flood 2002). As the pathway metaphor accretes through use it becomes reified over time, becoming ideologically marked as it comes to have symbolic meaning influencing the belief systems of professionals. In this process it becomes, in this case, both a 'model of' and a 'model for' risk factors and the notion of a pathway into and out of crime. The metaphor of the pathway can therefore be described as mythopoeic (Flood 2002).

Professional myths are both vehicles of ideological beliefs and support for ideological arguments and function to resolve professional contradictions but they also carry with them values and emotions as they move between the internal and external worlds of individuals. This distinguishes them from ideologies. Myths are used by individuals to act as intermediaries between their internal and external worlds and help them temporarily to resolve their 'felt' contradictions. Professional myths have their own specific feedback loops linking 'felt' contradictions of individuals and 'recognised' professional issues.

The 'felt' contradictions expressed by professionals throughout the research tended to be based around value conflicts and their emotional connections with young people. The nature of these professional contradictions reflected how those professionals working with young people in Urbanfields constructed their professional roles. They primarily saw their role as one of working towards the development of the values and morals of the young people they worked with and this necessarily involved emotions as they tried to make connections through the relationships they formed. The 'pathways' myth provided a partial resolution of these felt contradictions but was simultaneously changing the nature of what was felt by these professionals through a series of mythic feedback loops. To understand how these 'loops' operate the relationship between the social functions of myth and their use by individuals needs to be explored. This is because the generic function of 'myth' is to make 'natural' the worlds shaped by individuals over time and make 'reasonable' the notions and intentions of others (Barthes 2000).

Using the Urbanfields research to explore the relationship between individual use of 'pathways' research and to track the social function of the mythic loop from policy to practice

The study adapted an approach developed over several years of research with inner-city communities and drew on two main sources of work. First, that of visual ethnographers and anthropologists who are interested in researching the construction of individual lives and representation within the media (Banks 1995; MacCannell 1994; Margolis 1998). A combination of the analytical frameworks used in visual anthropology, 'the anthropology of visual systems, or more broadly visual cultural forms' (Banks and Morphy 1997), with the methodological frameworks within the field of visual ethnography, anthropology's key research method (Pink 2004), was adopted. This was then combined with a second approach that explores group self-representation, and collective and individual identity using a series of projective tasks to trigger discussion (Melucci 1989, 1996). The resulting representations of everyday life involved young people in the production of videos, video diaries and photographic materials. The individual and group discussions that took place among young people and professionals in the making of these materials were recorded and used as an additional data source. It is the discussions with professionals that are mainly drawn upon here.

The project worked with six groups of young people. The numbers making up these groups fluctuated over the three years it took to complete the research, but it totalled some 70 young people. The project also worked with and carried out multiple interviews with 16 adults representing a range of services. These were the police, social workers, youth offending team workers, probation officers, community drugs workers, youth workers and teachers. Six community researchers from Urbanfields also supported the research. They had no previous research experience but were trained in video production and interviewing techniques. The only criteria for these researchers were that they lived within the community and were members of a minority ethnic group or a significant part of the friendship group or extended family. Their role was to provide an insider's view of the materials being produced by the young people and happenings within Urbanfields. Another of their roles was concerned with the ethical issues of working with video, especially as many of these young people had a criminal record or were involved in criminal activity (Prosser 2002).

The research began with several key questions grouped into two main areas. The first was the relationship between risk factors and the pathways of young people into and out of crime, and how young people identified as being 'at risk' of offending negotiated pathways into and out of crime, including their interaction with professionals. The second was the social processes of protection, resilience and resistance that mediate between risk factors and pathways into and out of crime, again including their interaction with professionals.

There were three distinct but overlapping strands of data collection. The first phase involved interviewing professionals about their personal theories of risk and resilience. These were incorporated into 'trigger' videos aimed at promoting group discussion with young people as they made decisions about the content of their videos. Each of these discussions was recorded and incorporated into subsequent trigger videos (Haw, forthcoming). The second strand of data collection involved more participatory methods, as these young people with their families and friends created visual materials that captured aspects of their lives. These provided an insight into how they managed the everyday risks and opportunities that came their way. The individual and group discussions that occurred while these materials were edited and produced were also recorded to give a further layer of data. The third strand involved multiple group and individual interviews with professionals and young people using materials generated in the previous phases. One topic that came up frequently in the discussions with these professionals was the time-consuming nature of filling in the appropriate documentation on each young person.

In England the ASSET form is used as a means of assessing 'criminal' behaviour or risk-taking and as the basis for selecting intervention strategies to control and rehabilitate young people back into society. It was developed from the work of Farrington (1995, 2000) concerning the predictive power of risk factors. This is a model that is both additive and causal. The key theoretical question is why a study originally based on a statistically small sample that was entirely male and predominantly white became the basis of current risk-factor and preventive work in the UK. The answer partially lies in the claim that a key advantage of the risk-factor paradigm is that it is easy to understand and communicate and that risk factors and interventions are based on empirical research rather than on theories (Farrington 2000). The answer also lies in the dominance of technical-rationalist ideologies that support the procedures of governmentality (Armstrong 2004) embedded within the context of a New Labour government that seeks to initiate policies that promise to offer a rational instrument for managing the risks that confront society.

What is of significance to this discussion is how this work was transformed through various mythic feedback loops, from a piece of explanation as a result of multivariate statistical analysis to become 'fact' as it entered the social world as an assessment tool. When this particular model was taken up, used and refined as a diagnostic and assessment tool in the criminal justice system it became a symbolic expression of a specific model within professions as it supported resolutions of contradictions in practice.

As young people are assessed the form becomes a symbolic expression of how 'at risk' they are. Its symbolic meaning, its mythical function, you could say, is to turn back on them and affect the way in which other individuals make sense of them. The adults administering the form are required to think about young people and themselves in relation to so-called 'risk factors':

> You only have to see it now in terms of some of the high-profile youngsters. Mental health is a key one and that can be identified very early, certainly at 10. Certain sexual offences, violence, aggressive behaviour can be identified very young and with a number of cases you can talk about where it started at 8. There was bereavement in the family, breaking windows. Riding in stolen cars, look-outs for burglars. Now 16-year-olds are wielding knives and committing acts of violence. You just think, why wasn't that person identified at an early age. There are lots of examples like that here. You just think, why have we waited to put all these resources in to the point where the problem has become so acute. (*Youth offending team manager*)

This particular articulation is of a linear causal notion of the pathway, regardless of whether that was or is the intention of the research, on which the form is based. There are two significant points here. The first point relates to how individuals retrospectively account for their professional involvement with young people in terms of a metaphorical pathway that has become subtly ingrained in their own thinking, thus illustrating how the metaphor has become reified, ideologically marked and mythopoeic. The second point regards how young people are symbolically 'bundled', so what is labelled as normal or deviant is dependent on the beliefs related to young people and crime that are in ascendancy and a particular view of the pathway in a given cultural and historical context. The following quote is from a professional who grew up in the 1950s and 1960s, before the notions of a criminal career, the risk-factor paradigm and the pathway into and out of crime were developed.

> I think if the YOT preventative programme was around when I was 10 then I would probably have been on it, mainly through what I was doing at school around violence and things like that. I was excluded from my primary school for a while for fighting and I think, I believe looking back on myself then when I was

around 9, 10, 11, then I was a prime candidate. There was always that potential back then, even when I was at primary school. I remember I certainly pulled a knife. Things are managed in a slightly different way now. The people I was with at the time protected me from possibly a life of crime. (*YOT manager*)

As professionals 'buy into' a notion of a pathway, the metaphor takes on greater and greater symbolic meaning. In this process the metaphor feeds back on itself, becoming a myth as it helps to resolve both 'felt' and 'recognised' professional dilemmas to explain and justify specific treatments. Because the metaphor is predictive its inherent logic drives professionals towards identifying earlier and earlier key factors where interactions are potentially less complex but make potentially more powerful predictions. So if externally set targets, with regard to recidivism for example, are not being met, for some professionals the answer must be that we are not reaching these young people early enough to positively influence them:

> Over the last ten years it's become all about young people, offending and reducing offending. I believe, and I'm passionate about this, that it is not in young people's interest to have antisocial behaviour unchallenged and unchecked without somebody trying to intervene. I know from my life experience, and also from research, that the earlier people start, the more likely they are going to go on to be criminals if something doesn't happen. (*YOT manager*)

These interpretations of early interventions are based on more and more refined and complex models of risk factors, fed back to professionals as part of a belief system of evidence-based practice set within a context of externally imposed targets. The mythic feedback loop now becomes intensified. It is driven forward by new 'felt' tensions. These are the tensions concerning economic pressures to cut costs, and social and political pressures to come up with solutions to address the rising tide of moral panic about young people, while not compromising professional values and the necessity to make emotional contact with young people. At this point it becomes part of a disabling discourse as the metaphor working through myth legitimates and allows for working 'on' the individual, not 'with' the individual. Some professionals are uncomfortable with this:

The casework relationship is absolutely crucial and they think they can solve it by having these abstinence orders, you mustn't do this, you mustn't do that, this anti-social behaviour order here; without a relationship you won't get anything and you won't achieve anything. Good practice used to be enabling people to do things they want to, self-determination. It isn't now, it's being able to complete a case without a breach and to complete it perhaps by early revocation and to enable them to say right, OK, we have completed that case and achieved our target with our particular statistics. We've got a certain percentage of people to complete their orders. That's all they're focused on now. Very, very sad. (*Probation officer*)

Current strategies highlight the tension between supporting young people to be self-aware and the emphasis on 'closing a case'. It is constructing a tension between helping young people mature and develop through their own agency and efforts aimed at removing dangerous contexts and behaviour, such as drug-taking. For some professionals positioned between these two extremes, the repercussions are that there is little opportunity for them to build up substantive relationships with young people who are not yet in the most extreme situations – relationships that they and the young people themselves often identified as being the most helpful to them:

The people that have respect for us and spend time with us and talk to us and everything which we thank them for because not a lot of people put their faith in us or anything so we don't want to disappoint them. (*Young person*)

Others, though, are more comfortable with the power of the model to resolve the contradiction between values-based and evidenced-based practice as they apply the metaphor differently:

I think my practice now is more shaped around, I suppose, what works research. I suppose back then it was more about me as an individual, my own personal skills, my ability to relate and get on alongside youngsters and try and influence them. Now I am more concerned about effectiveness, outcomes and services. (*YOT manager*)

These quotes illustrate how the tensions and contradictions faced by professionals working with young people in the criminal justice system are changing based upon their different interpretations of the metaphor of 'pathways' and the risk factors along it. They also illustrate how individuals from different communities of practice are caught up in a variety of mythic feedback loops that construct the different contradictions they are faced with, and those they feel in their everyday practice. These mythic loops build on the frequently acknowledged cultural and value differences between services and are exacerbated by how new professionals are encultured into their profession. Different communities of practice are now marked by targets, outcomes and the notion of evidence-based approaches, all of which are likely to hamper the espoused desires to move towards greater multi-agency working.

> I think younger people coming in now, they're trained in a degree now into meeting standards and achieving certain things, performance-related stuff, and they are not as politically aware. They like to see things in black and white terms. Grey areas don't exist with them and I don't feel sometimes they are as emotional. They are not allowed to by their training, and although I would be seen as the old school, that's where you were able to become emotional within boundaries. I don't think that new people that come into the probation service have been allowed the opportunity to develop those skills, it's all about programmes and community protection. There are an odd few but they tend to leave the service or remain as probation officers – they don't get promoted. (*Probation officer*)

At this point issues of truth and falseness re-enter the debate. The utility of the metaphor of the pathway as a boundary object that can cross the boundaries between communities of practice is considerable, but within professions it creates either the solidarity of believers or the fragmentation between believers and non-believers. The divisiveness that arises between those who accept the myth as true, compared with those who see it as false, has a number of consequences for professionals working with young people. It also impacts on the broader possibilities of effective multi-agency working in dealing with the often complex and multifaceted problems of young people with consequences for them as they are labelled by the criminal justice system. The failure to recognise the notion of a pathway as ideologically marked contributes to its potential to be part of a disabling rather than enabling discourse. It is disabling at a professional level, as it leads to fragmentation between believers and non-believers, and also because of its impact on professional client relationships as it contributes to a 'working on' not 'working with' culture.

This is because for young people like these, labelled by multiple risk factors, the shift is towards affecting those external factors that are indicative of antisocial behaviour. For example, mentoring becomes a way of changing their interaction with adults, while antisocial behaviour orders prevent them from associating with certain peers in certain places. But these more extreme interventions can impact negatively on a sense of individual choice and agency:

> You can't give us role models. Sometimes I think I would like to be a good role model but it's easier said than done. You could say 'yeah, I'd like to be a good role model', but it's not like there's no manual for this or a manual for that. You just do it and you find out if you have done the right thing in the end. That's how it is. (*Young person*)

Conclusion: critically unpacking the myth

An analysis of the approaches of different groups of professionals working with young people in the criminal justice system based on ideology reveals and concentrates on issues of power and not values and emotions. This is well covered within existing literature but fails to take account of the emotional landscapes that this research revealed and which some academics are calling for (Armstrong 2004). I have used the notion of myth to draw this back into the centre of the discussion.

This chapter has used the mythic process to understand why the metaphor of the pathway based on risk factors has become increasingly problematic. Three potential ramifications or outcomes have been highlighted. First, the analysis has identified the tensions or dilemmas within professions and between professionals and how these 'felt' and 'recognised' contradictions are being differentially constructed within various mythic feedback loops. Second, it has provided an understanding of how these tensions are resolved by different professionals and highlighted how what was seen as an adequate way of working with young people is being changed by the risk-factor and pathways metaphors. Third, an analysis based on values and emotions has provided an insight into how these different constructions are impacting upon practice and the work of these professionals, to the extent that it fundamentally affects what is seen as good practice with repercussions for relationship-building with young people.

The notions of a pathway and risk factor-research have become part of a larger professional myth in that they are accepted uncritically as 'true' by policy-makers and by large elements of the professionals working with young people, and false by others. This is because they provide a temporary and partial resolution for policy-makers and some professionals:

> The risk factor paradigm has brought enormous benefits to criminology in the late 1990s. This approach has greatly fostered linkages between explanation and prevention, fundamental and applied research, and scholars, policy makers and practitioners. Since the choice of interventions is based on empirically established risk factors, the approach is research based but easily understandable and attractive to policy makers and practitioners. (Farrington 2000: 16)

As a dominant myth promoted by policy-makers, this has inadvertently had a divisive effect upon those working with young people in the criminal justice system. It has created its own series of dichotomies between those that place professional values and forging effective relationships with young people at the forefront of their work and those who rely upon notions of evidence and effectiveness. For some the model gives credence to the idea that detailed knowledge and strong relationships with young people are not necessary, beyond that required to make assessments of their risk factors, offending behaviour and current situation, as professionals grow confident in matching symptoms with known cures.

As the risk-factor model becomes increasingly paradigmatic it seeks greater predictive power by accounting for multiple interactions between an increasing number of risk and protective factors. The policy outcomes from this have meant a greater number of young people being drawn into some form of 'light touch' early prevention strategies and the use of more 'extreme' interventions with targeted groups perceived at greatest risk, or those who represent the most significant risk to local communities. Armstrong (2004) refers to this as a 'new industry of early intervention based on an ideology of "risk"' and this, he argues, 'has become a tool of governmentality in the lives of young people, their families and their schools in some of our most deprived communities' (2004: 102).

As the metaphor has become a dominant professional myth for researchers, policy-makers and practitioners alike, it becomes less likely to be generative of new solutions and approaches, as it becomes the solution.

> Improving the risk factor prevention paradigm is not merely an academic exercise designed to advance knowledge about explaining and preventing crime. It is also an intensely practical exercise designed to reduce crime and to improve people's lives. The twin aims of advancing knowledge and increasing the sum of human happiness is what criminology is all about. (Farrington 2000: 19)

My question is, whose knowledge and whose happiness? Currently not the young people living in a deprived community such as Urbanfields, who are overtly labelled by risk factors normalised and made everyday via the mythic feedback loops in which these professionals find themselves.

> People usually think, Urbanfields, 'oh, they're not going to get nowhere in life, they're going to get pregnant at a young age, prison. They are going to be committing crimes.' But they don't think of all the good things they just look at the bad side. I know people from West Fields [Wealthy suburb adjacent to Urbanfields] that have beat people up and got away with it, but as soon as we do anything we get arrested straight away. If you've got your reputation as too big and you're out of control. It's not good and everyone wants to prove they're better than you, harder than you all the time, then you get in fights and it's not good. You won't hardly get a job when you're older and it's going to ruin your career. (*Young person*)

References

Armstrong, D. (2004) 'A risky business? Research, policy, governmentality and youth offending', *Youth Justice*, 4(2): 100–16.

Banks, M. (1995) *Visual Research Methods in Social Research*, update Issue 11, Winter, University of Surrey.

Banks, M. and Morphy, H. (1997) *Rethinking Visual Anthropology*. New Haven, CT: Yale University Press.

Barthes, R. (2000) *Mythologies*. New York: Vintage.

Beck, U. (1992) *Risk Society: Towards a New Modernity*. London: Sage.

Beck, U. (1999) *World Risk Society*. Cambridge: Polity Press.

Becker, H. (1963) *Outsiders: Studies in the Sociology of Deviance*. New York: Free Press.

Bennett, W.L. (1980) 'Myth, ritual and political control', *Journal of Communication*, 30(1): 66–79.

Blumstein, A., Cohen, J., Roth, J.A. and Visher, C.A. (eds) (1986) *Criminal Careers and 'Career Criminals'*. Washington, DC: National Academy Press.

Bujra, J. (2000) 'Risk and Trust: Unsafe Sex, Gender and AIDS in Tanzania', in P. Caplan (ed.) *Risk Revisited*. London: Pluto Press, pp. 59–84.

Caplan, P. (2000) *Risk Revisited*. London: Pluto Press.

Castel, R. (1991) 'From Dangerousness to Risk', in G. Burchell, C. Gordon and P. Miller (eds) *The Foucault Effect: Studies in Governmentality*. London: Harvester Wheatsheaf, pp. 281–98.

Dean, M. (1999) 'Risk Calculable and Incalculable', in D. Lupton (ed.) *New Directions and Perspectives: Risk and Sociocultural Theory*. Cambridge: Cambridge University Press, pp. 131–59.

Douglas, M. (1966) *Purity and Danger: An Analysis of Concepts of Purity and Taboo*. London: Routledge and Kegan Paul.

Douglas, M. (1985) *Risk Acceptability According to the Social Sciences*. New York: Russell Sage Foundation.

Douglas, M. (1992) *Risk and Blame: Essays in Cultural Theory*. London: Routledge.

Easen, P., Atkins, M. and Dyson, A. (2000) 'Inter-professional collaboration and conceptualisations of practice', *Children and Society*, 14(5): 355–67.

Engeström, Y. (2001a) 'Expansive learning at work: Toward an activity theoretical reconceptualization', *Journal of Education and Work*, 14(1): 133–56.

Engeström, Y. (2001b) 'The Horizontal Dimension of Expansive Learning: Weaving a Texture of Cognitive Trails in the Terrain of Health Care in Helsinki', paper presented at the international symposium *New Challenges to Research on Learning*, University of Helsinki, Finland.

Engeström, Y., Engeström , R. and Vahaaho, T. (1999) 'When the Center Does Not Hold: The Importance of Knotworking', in S. Chaiklin, M. Hedegaard and U. Jensen (eds) *Activity Theory and Social Practice*. Aarhus University Press.

Farrington, D.P. (1995) 'The development of offending and antisocial behaviour from childhood: Key findings from the Cambridge study, in delinquent development', *Journal of Child Psychology and Psychiatry*, 36: 929–64.

Farrington, D.P. (2000) 'Explaining and preventing crime: The globalisation of knowledge', *Criminology*, 38(2): 1–24.

Flood, C. (2002) 'Myth and Ideology', in K. Schilbrack (ed.) *Thinking Through Myths: Philosophical Perspectives*. Routledge: London and New York.

Foucault, M. (1978) *The History of Sexuality*. Harmondsworth: Penguin.

Foucault, M. (1991) 'Governmentality', in G. Burchell, C. Gordon and P. Miller (eds) *The Foucault Effect: Studies in Governmentality*. London: Harvester Wheatsheaf, pp. 87–104.

Giddens, A. (1998) 'Risk Society: The Context of British Politics', in J. Franklin (ed.) *The Politics of Risk Society*. Cambridge: Polity Press, pp. 23–34.

Giddens, A. (1999) *The Reith Lectures Risk*, BBC News Online, available at http://news.bbc.co.uk.reith_99

Haw, K.F. (forthcoming) 'Voice and Video: Seen Heard and Listened to?', in P. Thomson (ed.) *Get the Picture: Visual Research with Children and Young People*. London: Routledge.

Losev, A.F. (2003) *The Dialectics of Myth*, trans. V. Marchenkov. London and New York: Routledge Taylor and Francis Group.

Lupton, D. (1999) *Risk*. London and New York: Routledge.

MacCannell, D. (1994) 'Cannibal Tours', in L. Taylor (ed.) *Visualizing Theory. Selected Essays from V.A.R. 1990–1994*. New York and London: Routledge.

Margolis, E. (1998) 'Picturing labour: A visual ethnography of the coal mine labour process', *Visual Sociology*, 13(2): 5–37.

Melucci, A. (1989) *Nomads of the Present*. Philadelphia: Temple University Press.

Melucci, A. (1996) *The Playing Self: Person and Meaning in the Planetary Society*. New York: Cambridge University Press.

O'Malley, P. (2001) 'Policing Crime Risks in the Neo-Liberal Era', in K. Stenson and R. Sullivan (eds) *Crime, Risk and Justice*. Cullompton: Willan Publishing, pp. 89–103.

Pink, S. (2004) 'Making links: on situating a new web site', *Cambridge Journal of Education*, 34(2): 211–22.

Prosser, J. (2002) 'Image-based Research', in H. Simons and R. Usher (eds) *Situated Ethics*. London: Routledge.

Schon, D.A. (1993) 'Generative Metaphor: A Perspective on Problem Setting in Social Policy', in A. Ortony (ed.) *Metaphor and Thought*, 2nd edn. Cambridge: Cambridge University Press.

Segal, R. (1999) *Theorizing About Myth*. Amherst, MA: University of Massachusetts Press.

Seliger, M. (1976) *Ideology and Politics*. London: Allen and Unwin.

Simon, J. (1987) 'The emergence of a risk society: Insurance, law and the state', *Socialist Review*, 95(4): 61–89.

Slovic, P. (1987) 'Perception of Risk', *Science*, 236: 280–5.

Slovic, P. (1992) 'Perception of Risk: Reflections on the Psychometric Paradigm', in S. Krimsky and D. Golding (eds) *Social Theories of Risk*. Westport, CT: Praeger, pp. 117–52.

Slovic, P. (2000) *The Perception of Risk*. London: Earthscan.

Wenger, E. (1998) *Communities of Practice: Learning, Meaning, and Identity*. New York: Cambridge University Press.

Wenger, E. (2006) 'Communities of Practice: A Brief Introduction', available online at www.ewenger.com/theory/communities_of_practice_intro.htm

Young, J. (2006) *Cannibalism and Bulimia: Patterns of Social Control in Late Modernity*. Available online at http://www.malcolmread.co.uk/JockYoung/cannibal.htm

Chapter 5

Young people, pathways and crime: beyond risk factors

Hazel Kemshall, Louise Marsland, Thilo Boeck and Leigh Dunkerton

Abstract

Research and policy approaches to risk are recognised as falling into two cultures, most commonly referred to as *artefact* and *constructionist*. Moreover, within constructionism, a continuum of positions exists, from weak constructionist in which risks may be viewed as cultural mediations of 'real' dangers or hazards, to strong constructionist in which the 'dangers' or 'hazards' are themselves perceived as socially constructed. In this chapter a similar continuum of epistemological positions in relation to pathways is developed; then findings from projects in the ESRC network 'pathways into and out of crime' demonstrate how constructionist perspectives have generated new insights into the way in which traditional risk factors operate for young people. Examples based on three classically identified risk factors are presented. First, the complex and multi-dimensional effects of school exclusion are highlighted. Second, the nature of social networks is explicated and the role of their components as both potential risk and protective factors proposed. Third, the need for drugs to be understood within their cultural and historical contexts is identified, and the potential role of drugs as a mediator between other life stresses and offending portrayed. In conclusion, the value of synthesising rather than disputing paradigms to produce different layers of knowledge is discussed.

Approaches to risk and crime pathways

Research and policy approaches to risk have been described as falling into 'two cultures' (Jasanoff 1993) although they are often 'blurred in practice' (Bradbury 1989: 381). These are most often referred to as 'artefact' and 'constructionist' or 'socially constructed' risk. The relationship between how risk is conceptualised and investigated has been much explored (Hood and Jones 1996), and differing conceptualisations of risk are reflected in the choice and construction of research methods, how risk problems are framed and subsequently resolved (Brown 2000). Thus risk can be investigated through a number of different, and at times competing, research perspectives, as diverse as traditional positivism on the one hand and governmentality analyses on the other. Disputes between research paradigms can be reframed as disputes not about the validity or refinement of the research method, but about the nature of risk and its measurability (Kemshall 2003).

'Pathway' has become a significant term in crime prevention, particularly in relation to youth crime (Farrington 1995; Sampson and Laub 1993). As with risk, pathway has been differentially constructed in research investigations and, we argue, framings of risk are reflected in framings of pathway. The parallel epistemological continuums of risk and pathway are summarised together in Table 5.1. Inevitably, the table is a heuristic device, simplifying the complexities of the nature of knowledge; in particular, the positions do not exist as discrete entities.

Artefact risk and predetermined pathways

In the artefact approach, risk is framed as objectively knowable and amenable to probabilistic calculation (Horlick-Jones 1998), typified by early twentieth-century scientific investigation of risk (Ansell and Wharton 1992). It is embedded in empiricism, scientific canons of proof, and a realist epistemology to the study of risk. In the penal realm this conceptualisation of risk is epitomised by the pursuit of statistically valid and predicatively useful risk factors (e.g. Farrington 1989, 1995; West and Farrington 1977). Corresponding to artefact risk, a realist or positivist position views pathways as linear, predetermined and characterised by risk markers. Quantitative methods and statistical analyses are used to determine those risk factors most likely to predict crime initiation and persistence, and the reduction or manipulation of these factors is seen as key to prevention. The 'preventative paradigm' (Farrington 2000) has contributed much to practice and policy, generating risk assessment tools and identifying 'at risk' youngsters for early intervention (Farrington 1995).

More recently, however, Farrington (2000: 7) has argued that the risk -prevention paradigm should also be concerned with the 'processes or developmental pathways that intervene between risk factors and outcomes, and to bridge the gap between risk factor research and more complex explanatory theories'. This may require the recognition that pathways are social processes that have multiple causes, and that such causes are not merely additive (Farrington 2000), and that subtle differences in initial conditions may over time produce large differences in outcomes (Byrne 1998). This would help to explain why children initially risk marked similarly (e.g. by individual and family risk markers) go on to have different crime pathways, and why a proportion of children 'high risk' for later delinquency do not offend. These concerns have resulted in growing attention to social risk and constructionist approaches to crime, risk and pathway.

Social constructionist risk and the social construction of crime pathways

While the term 'constructionist' is used to describe this paradigm, it actually has a number of positions on a continuum from 'weak' to 'strong' constructionism (Lupton 1999: 35). In crime-risk research, weak constructionism has resulted in attention to the immediate context and environment within which risk decisions are made. This approach reintroduces a limited notion of the 'social' and extends the locus of attention from individuals and 'pathologised' families to their immediate context. This perspective is most often associated with the work of Wikström (e.g. Wikström 2004; Wikström and Sampson 2003), and focuses on the interaction between the 'propensity' of the individual to react to 'temptations' or 'deterrents' located in the various settings she/he enters. The emphasis is on an interactive approach and an examination of the social mechanisms that influence the individual's routines and decision-making processes. Individual agency is seen as important (Clarke and Cornish 1983), and research focus is given to the decision-making of individual offenders usually investigated through self-report studies or in-depth interviews. Similarly, weak constructionism sees pathways as social processes with multiple causes, the focus being on the interaction between

Table 5.1. A continuum of epistemological approaches to risk and crime pathways

	Risk (adapted from Lupton 1999)	Pathways
Artefact	Risk as an objective hazard.	**Pathways** Pathways predetermined, linear and characterised by risk markers. Quantitative methods and statistical analyses used to determine those risk factors most likely to predict crime initiation and persistence.
Weak constructionist	Risk viewed as an objective hazard mediated through social and cultural processes. Risk factors socially, culturally and historically defined and situated. Locus of attention broadened to immediate social context.	**Situational and contextual approaches** Pathways as social processes with multiple causes. Focus on interaction between individual and the immediate setting – social mechanisms that influence decision-making.
Moderate constructionist		**Pathways as a negotiated process** How crime process is negotiated – continuous interaction between agency and structure.

Strong constructionist	Risk as a (total) product of a historically, socially and politically contingent 'way of seeing'. Two key features – individualisation and responsibilisation.	Social context wider than situational context of situational and contextual approaches = social structure (external constraint on agency) and culture/habitus.
		Involves the reproduction of social practices and normative values.
		Negotiation through crime seen as dependent upon individual agency, constraint and opportunity, contingency and context, power, and cultural/structural processes.
		Pathways as governance Pathways highly politicised.

the individual and the immediate setting. Here, protection is seen as a process, and resilience as a personal product of the individual, generated and supported by positive networks such as parenting programmes and school inclusion.

Next along the continuum, an additional position may be identified in relation to pathways: moderate constructionism. Here pathways are viewed as a negotiated process, a continuous interaction between agency and structure, and negotiation through crime is then seen as dependent upon individual agency, constraint and opportunity, contingency and context, power and cultural/structural processes.

At the opposite end of the continuum, strong constructionism, of which social constructionism and cultural theory are the main exponents (Douglas 1992), poses that 'risk is always a social product' (Thompson and Wildavsky 1982: 148). Research focuses on opportunities and power to desist, and the social factors and resources that play a role in such decisions (Farrall 2002; Maruna 2001). The interaction of agency and structure is increasingly posed as a key empirical and theoretical concern of such research (Farrall and Bowling 1999), and social action theories are a key component of such investigations. Individuals are viewed as social actors and the focus is upon how social processes work and impact upon risk decisions, and how risk decisions vary across different contexts.

Cultural theory, the other main exponent of strong constructionism, focuses on how some rationalities gain credibility, acceptance and legitimacy while others do not (Wynne 1996). Within this framing the focus is not individual risk decision-making, but on how some risks are chosen for attention while others are not. Attention is paid to the symbolic and cultural meanings of risk (Douglas 1992), and the political rationalities and strategies that underpin them (Sparks 2001). Here, pathways are viewed as highly politicised, although the key question remains of how discourses and practices operate in the construction of pathways.

Studies of crime pathways undertaken from a constructionist perspective may enhance the artefact approach to risk, generating new insights into how traditional risk factors operate for young people. Examples based on three classically identified risk factors are presented to illustrate the 'added value' that may emerge from a social constructionist perspective: school exclusion, networks and drug use. The research from which these examples are taken was completed as part of an ESRC network: Pathways Into and Out of Crime (www.sheffield.ac.uk/pathways-into-and-out-of-crime/index. htm).

Defining young people as problematic: exploring young people's perspectives on school exclusion

A study undertaken by Sheffield University involved in-depth interviews with young people from three cohorts: young people who had been permanently excluded from school; those who had early contact in their offending history with youth offending teams (YOTs); and children receiving statements of special educational needs specifying 'emotional and behavioural difficulties'. The research gave emphasis to young people's voices exploring their perceptions and experiences of offending and the educational processes that identify them as a 'problem' and as potential offenders. A semi-structured interview schedule was used to encourage young people to tell detailed stories of their lives. In total, 110 young people were interviewed over a two-year period; 75 per cent (83) boys and 25 per cent (27) girls. The research was longitudinal, with 47 young people interviewed on two occasions approximately six–nine months apart, and a further 13 participants constituting a case study sample involving third and fourth interviews. Interviews lasted on average an hour and were conducted either within their home or at school. Interviews were audiotaped and verbatim transcripts produced. The most common type of intervention that occurred in the sample was permanent exclusion from school (68 per cent of participants). While 55 per cent had official contact with the YOT, and 50 per cent had received 'statements of emotional or behavioural difficulty'. Here specific attention is given to young people's perspectives around permanent exclusion, exploring the processes of exclusion and the impact upon their self-identity.

Preliminary findings indicated that critical attention needs to be given to the arbitrary process that exclusion involves; for some young people, being excluded was a result of being in the 'wrong place at the wrong time'. A strong feeling of unfairness was experienced through being labelled as a 'problem' and yet similar behaviour by fellow pupils was ignored; this was perceived as them 'getting away' with it. In some circumstances exclusion was experienced as a process that involved the school gathering evidence through the formal recording of incidents. This kind of recording resulted in the school's interpretation of events, and behaviour being formalised:

> I had been excluded but it was mainly because of me background and me record. Most people have records a centimetre thick and mine would be a foot thick or something like that, it would be huge. (*Mathew*)

The young people described a range of experiences from a one-off permanent exclusion to a number of exclusions, and experience of alternative educational provision, such as special schools and pupil referral units (PRUs). Sometimes negotiation occurred between the school, the young person and his/her parents to withdraw voluntarily, thus avoiding an official record of school exclusion. Alternative forms of recording seemed particularly prominent for girls, who were not always officially excluded but who excluded themselves through non-attendance, supporting previous research by Osler and Vincent (2003).

The range of experiences in relation to exclusion was diverse, but far from emerging as a predictor of offending, only one young person believed that his offending was related to being out of school for a lengthy time. Despite the negativity of the event many young people showed resilience to the exclusion event, putting it behind them and getting on with their life.

> *John*: It might sound weird but I think getting expelled was a very bad thing but also a good thing. Because getting expelled made me realise. Like now, I ain't how I used to be.
>
> *R*: So one thing is, you actually feel you're a better person because of your exclusion.
>
> *John*: Yeah, I've stopped smoking, I dress normal, I speak normal, do you know what I mean, I ain't how I used to be, I'm polite. If someone shows me respect they'll get it back.

For others, exclusion appeared to operate as a protective mechanism in the knowledge that they would have been unable to cope within a mainstream school. In some circumstances this was related to a learning difficulty, but mainstream education was also described as a more risky environment, with more pupils and greater peer pressure that potentially increased the likelihood of them getting into further trouble.

> I find it quite good because I passed my English test and I've done better than what I would have done in school, I know that for a fact. Because it's the crowd I used to hang around with in school and in here there isn't a lot of people to hang around with and I've got on with my work fine. But when I come here people thought, 'I don't know how she got kicked out of school'

because I'm not that kind of person, which I ain't but things happen and things don't, you never know when. (*Tracy*)

Hence, attending an alternative education environment (PRU or special school), precipitated by the exclusion event, may have helped them to cope better. As Munn and Lloyd (2005) suggest, this may be due to support they had previously not received. Research by Hodgson and Webb (2005: 23) also suggests that 'in certain instances school exclusion may actually reduce or indeed prevent offending'.

Research in the field of juvenile delinquency has suggested strong links between truancy, exclusion from school, 'troublesomeness', aggressiveness, bullying and later delinquency (Farrington 1995). The Audit Commission (1996) report *Misspent Youth: Young People and Crime* highlighted the link between truancy and exclusion and offending behaviour, with more than 75 per cent of those permanently excluded from school offending:

Young people who truant or are excluded from school are more likely to offend. Exclusion and truancy are therefore both key indicators of trouble to come if corrective action is not taken. Forty-two per cent of offenders of school age who are sentenced in the youth court have been excluded from school. (Audit Commission 1999: 66)

A number of problems emerge, however, in assuming a causal relationship. First, the direction of causality is unknown. Is offending the result of the exclusion event and the consequences that school exclusion brings, or is exclusion an indicator of a young person's pre-existing 'problems', the school only identifying antisocial or offending behaviour that is already there? Second, the precise mechanisms through which the relationship between school experiences and offending is mediated require explicating. Third, while 'rates of offending' have been problematised, the social construction of school exclusion figures is often ignored (see Vulliamy and Webb 2000). Risk-factor models fail to take into account the arbitrary processes of official and unofficial exclusion, e.g. when parents are encouraged to 'voluntarily' remove their children from school, thus avoiding an official record of school exclusion. One consequence of such arbitrary processes is that only a small proportion of exclusions are included in official statistics. Hence young people may offend and not have an official record of exclusion recorded against them, and equally young people not officially recorded as excluded may not have offended.

Thus any statistical correlations are an artefact. Further to this, a more critical understanding is needed of what exclusion represents. Rather than seeing the problem within the child, questions arise as to how particular children become labelled through professional constructions of 'problem' children.

The complex and multi-dimensional effects of school exclusion were increasingly apparent in this cohort. These findings indicate the complexities that exist around both the process and experience of school exclusion. To assume that school exclusion operates as a risk factor for offending in a direct causal relationship is over-simplistic. From a social constructionist perspective, both the processes of the institution in terms of labelling children as 'problem' and the unofficial and official routes of exclusion are important. The nature of risk's construction must be contextualised within the institutional frameworks that help to create risk, as 'the apparatuses of surveillance and discipline ... routinely produce the risks they assess and manage' (Crook 1999: 171). In addition the meaning and impact of exclusion is not the same for everyone.

Networks, sense of belonging and outlook in life

A multi-modal study undertaken at De Montfort University (DMU) involved 24 in-depth interviews 17 focus groups with 60 young people, and a questionnaire (500) administered individually and in groups. The total sample comprised 589 young people aged 11–19 and was drawn from the Midlands area. It consisted of 131 young people accessed largely through YOTs and Youth Inclusion Projects (YIPs) which include both known offenders and those deemed to be 'at risk' of offending, plus 458 young people accessed through local schools and youth groups; this group included some young people who have offended (since for ethical reasons it was not possible to screen them out) but this part of the sample comprised mostly non-offenders. The data were analysed using NUDIST QSR 6 and SPSS, and key findings were re-examined with a small sample of persistent offenders (n=12) through in-depth interviews (see Boeck *et al.* 2006).

Networks, family and kin have been identified by previous research as central to young people's lives, and act as a considerable resource for them as they navigate key life transitions (MacDonald and Marsh 2001). Such networks are intrinsic to self-identity (Sullivan 2002), and to a 'sense of belonging' (Morrow 2004). Initial findings from the DMU study highlight two groups of young people: those with a tightly bonded network based upon their immediate locale of the street, local park and home; and those with a more diverse network centred on school/college. The tight networks are often small, static in nature and engage in a restricted range of activities, e.g. 'hanging about the street', visiting friends' houses:

Q: So you said that you hang a lot around on the street?
A: Yes, because there aren't many places to go ... just hang around the streets with my friends.
Q: If you think about important places in [the neighbourhood], which would you say were important places for you?
A: Important, my family's houses, I think that's about it really.

The other group of young people have more extended networks, based upon school or college. These networks are more dynamic and young people engage in more after-school activities. In addition, these networks are more diverse and members have greater opportunity to connect with other networks beyond the immediate locale.

A significant correlation exists between the 'locality-based networks' and young people contacted through YOTs/YIPs, and between the 'school/college-based networks' and young people contacted through schools and youth groups. While 60 per cent of young people contacted through the YOTs and YIPs had medium to high locality- based networks, 91 per cent of young people contacted through schools and colleges had medium to high school-based networks. There is an overlap between the two groups that suggests a continuum and certain fluidity between these two network groups. It is important to mention here that a considerable percentage (70 per cent) of the young people contacted through the YOTs and YIPs at the time of the survey were attending schools or colleges.

Previous research has highlighted that young offenders associate with other young offenders (Poulin et al. 1999; Sampson et al. 1997). The current research suggests that school is not facilitating diverse networks for this group, and that opportunities for them 'to act' and 'to be different' are restricted by membership of a tightly bonded locality-based group (Bloor 1995). This restrictive network has implications for young people's (and in this case young offenders') outlook in life and perceptions of self-efficacy.

The young people recruited via the YOTs/YIPs expressed a fatalistic and often hopeless outlook in life. This was evidenced in their passivity about their futures, and their perception that their own actions would have little impact on their life course. Their future aspirations were unrelated to present skills and competences, and in answer to what they would be doing in five years' time responses (75 per cent) varied from being 'a footballer', to 'being a millionaire' to 'being in jail'. Interestingly, those in this group were the least likely to involve anyone else in the resolution of problems in their life or in assisting them with crucial moments in the life course, again underlining their potential isolation. Young people contacted through the YOTs/YIPs were especially fatalistic about their futures. Sometimes this seemed to relate to apathy, or a sense of boredom, and, at other times to hopelessness and frustration. A majority of the young people contacted through schools and colleges (75 per cent) showed that they had a much clearer idea about their future, related to their identified skills and abilities.

Sullivan (2002: 4) has argued that 'perception of possible self, that is, the connection between present self, motivation, behaviour and possible or future self' is essential to personal (and in some contexts community) change. On the basis of these initial findings, it is possible to speculate that young offenders have a limited perception of possible self, and that this is compounded by membership of a tight network of similar persons. Conversely, access to more diverse networks enables an increased self-perception of alternative self (selves), as well as providing important structural opportunities for change (e.g. employment, training: Aguilera 2002).

The young people from YOTs/YIPs who expressed the more hopeless and fatalistic approach to life may be viewed as being in a state of 'risk stagnation', unwilling to take the risk to leave their present situation, immediate network and locale. They are typified by strong bonds to a limited group, a restricted sense of belonging and a fatalistic outlook in life. For these young people, leaving their present high-risk and crime lifestyles is itself a risk, and one they are ill-equipped to take. This resonates with work by MacDonald and Marsh (2001) who found that while 'connections to local networks could help in coping with the problems of "social exclusion" and generate "inclusion", paradoxically they could simultaneously limit the possibilities of escaping the conditions of "social exclusion"' (2001: 384). This contrasts with those young people who are in a situation of 'risk navigation'. These young people are characterised by diverse and wider-ranging networks, a sense of belonging to a wider locale, and a focused and active outlook in life. Edwards and Foley (1998) argue that it is not just about the 'size and density' of the network, it is also about the resources that the network brings.

Networks are an important resource for young people and their decision-making on risk, and the differing types (tightly bonded or diverse) have implications for their power and opportunity to act differently, in essence for their situational agency. Constructionist research adds insight into the role of networks in crime-risk pathways by highlighting that the role of this traditional risk factor is highly complex, with networks functioning potentially as both a risk and a resilience factor, depending not merely upon their type (i.e. criminal or non-criminal) but in terms of key features: restricted or diverse; closed or linking; and in the type of outlook and potential self such networks afford young people.

Substance use and offending: drugs as a mediator

The aim of a study undertaken by Essex and Glasgow Caledonian universities was to examine patterns of substance use among young offenders and identify relationships between substance misuse, offending and personal and social risk-factors, to further illuminate the associations that are traditionally identified by risk factor models. Participants were 293 young offenders recruited from 11 YOTs across England and Wales. Data were collected at two time-points 18 months apart (see Hammersley *et al.* 2003 for details of the first wave). Of the original cohort, 34 per cent (102) were retained to the second wave. Data were collected on a one-to-one basis using an extensive structured questionnaire covering the four areas of basic demographic data, substance use, offending, and risk and protective factors (Table 5.2).

Longitudinal studies of substance use and offending (see Robins and Rutter 1990) have found that substance use and offending develop together in a 'common causal configuration' (Elliott *et al.* 1985) underpinned by the same constellation of risk factors. Thus young offenders are a group who are likely to use substances more than their peers, and the combination of substance use with offending may increase the risk of developing substance dependence and/or of becoming a persistent offender. The risk-factors approach to the development of young people's substance use and offending tends to be actuarial in orientation, however, assuming that different types of risk factor are equivalent and can be summed together to predict consequences. Developmental pathways through substance use and offending are rarely theorised, and when they are have tended to focus on stereotypes. One common model is that the use of 'soft' drugs

Table 5.2 Questionnaire items for study of substance misuse and offending

---

Substance use
- Use of 20 substances:
  prevalence ever
  prevalence during the previous four weeks
  aged first used
  frequency of use over last 12 months
- Assessment of Substance Misuse in Adolescents (ASMA) (Willner 2000)
- Severity of Dependence Scales (Gossop *et al.* 1992)

Offending
- Self-reported measures of offending (Graham and Bowling 1996) with additional items exploring drug-related offences and one to soliciting
- Offences resulting in referral to the YOT
- Number of previous convictions or warnings
- Referral to drug/alcohol project

Risk/protective factors
- Life events (the most common problems/stressors known to have long-term effects on adolescent development)
- Life problems (occurred within previous 2 years, and whose effects are largest within two years of occurrence)
- Coping style (Carver *et al.* 1989)
- Self-esteem (Rosenberg 1965)
- Family structure
- Perceived parenting style
- School affiliation
- Qualifications
- Social networks
- Social support

---

leads to use of 'harder'/addictive type drugs (known as Gateway Theory), hence it would be expected that drug use would increase as youth age. With this generic increase in use comes a proportionate increase in substance use problems and dependence, and the increase in drug use/problems/dependency is a major explanation for youth crime. It is these expectations then that have been regarded as sufficient reasons to intervene against substance use with the aim of reducing offending. Gateway Theory ignores the context of the drugs–crime relationship, neglects alternative causal relationships between drug use and offending, and ignores alternative pathways (for example, of young people who try a new substance one year but have stopped again by the next). One highly salient aspect of the contemporary context is a substantial rise in the prevalence of drug use among adolescents in the UK over the last 25 years. According to Gateway Theory this should have resulted in an epidemic of drug dependence and a crime wave. Actually, it is debatable whether as drug use has increased, offending by young people has decreased over this period. This study proposes that pathways other than the stereotypical image of increased offending are more likely as drug use becomes more prevalent.

Two sets of findings generated from a social constructionist perspective provide additional insights to the relationships between drugs and crime as described by the traditional risk-factor approach. First is the need for risks to be understood within their cultural and historical contexts. The first-wave study data supported other evidence that drug use is becoming normalised among young people in the UK (that is not to say that drug use is typical or average, but rather that there is a cultural incorporation of drugs by young people into their everyday lives) (Parker *et al.* 1998). Whereas in the 1980s and earlier, substance use predicted offending and hard injectable drugs such as heroin and cocaine showed the strongest relationship, in the current study exploratory linear regression analyses showed different results. A stepwise entry design was used, so that only variables that accounted for significant variance were entered. In addition to the offending index, substance use factors and ASMA score, the regression equations included four blocks of variables: block 1, socio-demographics; block 2, risk and coping; block 3, traits and attitudes; block 4, substance use. In this design of analysis, variables in earlier blocks are assumed to be causally prior to variables in later blocks.

This analysis showed that while offending in the past 12 months was predicted by a number of factors (e.g. life problems 8 per cent of variance, expecting to be in trouble again 5 per cent of variance, low positive coping 2 per cent or variance), it was the socially accepted substances – alcohol, tobacco and cannabis – that were more related than the other drugs (Table 5.3). It was surprising that addictive-type drugs did not predict offending, so identical analyses were conducted using some common key offences as the dependent variables. Shoplifting was related to addictive-type drug use, whereas stealing from cars and beating people up were related to stimulant/polydrug use. This implies that heroin or crack use is not a major correlate of offending in this cohort, although a minority of respondents fit the classic pattern of progressing to dependence and increased offending. Moreover, the classic risk factors that previously underpinned both substance use and offending, in this study predicted offending more strongly and drug use less. In other words, the 'delinquent' minority of approximately 20 per cent of youth who offend as teenagers remain delinquent but drugs use has become more widespread than that and can now occur even among young offenders without it being a remarkable or potentially pathological occurrence.

Second, findings from the first and second waves provided new information about the role of drugs in offending. Small cell sizes rendered multivariate analyses inappropriate, so instead t-tests and analyses of variance were used to explore the relationship between a range of variables, substance use and offending. The increased prevalence of substance use among young people, together with the normalisation of drug use, resulted in different pathways from those previously predicted. Although, as could have been expected, there was a persistence or even increase over time in the frequency with which the majority of the youngsters were taking drugs, this increase was *not* associated with an increase in offending. None of the patterns of substance use (socially accepted, addictive type or stimulant/polydrug use) predicted subsequent extent of offending among this cohort; in fact, increased criminal activity was only associated with the number of life events experienced at the second wave ($F[2,80]=5.691$, $p=.005$). In contrast, various aspects of substance use were associated with factors including school affiliation, life problems in the previous two years and expecting to be in trouble again. Rather than drugs existing as a risk factor for offending, then, these findings suggest that it may operate as a mediator between

Table 5.3 Percentages of offending variance predicted by substance use in regression analyses

Predictor	Frequency in last 12 months			
	Total offending	Shoplifting	Stealing from cars	Beating up non-family
Stimulant/polydrug use			2	3
Addictive type drug use		2		
Socially acceptable drug use	9			
TOTAL Adjusted R²	0.22	0.13	0.26	0.26

Note: All effects shown are significant at $p < 0.005$ adjusted for the effects of Blocks 1, 2 and 3 (see text for explanation).

other stressors and offending. Both drug use and offending are likely to lead to official identification as a 'problem' young person, and this official status can involve more inquiries about behaviour, which in turn can reveal problems of offending or drug use where none were recognised before. This alone can make drugs–crime links seem bigger than they are. Using drugs, offending and being a known problem are all stressful, which worsens personal functioning and potentially increases drug use further. While the links between immediate life problems and longer-term life events require further exploration, this study suggests that drug use may exist as a symptom of the difficulties young people encounter *adjusting* to other risk factors, rather than as a risk factor *per se*.

These findings demonstrate how a social constructionist position illuminates the complex relationship between drugs and crime. First, such associations need to be understood within their cultural and historical contexts; they cannot be assumed to be static. Second, rather than existing as a 'causal' risk factor, drugs may be part of the context within which young people interact to negotiate their pathways. The role of drugs may therefore be seen as a mediator between other risk factors which underpin both drug use and crime.

Conclusion

For decades criminological thinking has been dominated by the risk-factor paradigm in which it is assumed that offending is caused by a range of objective, durable and measurable phenomena. More recently, the constructionist perspective has argued that behaviours are criminalised only as part of the process by which the social world is individually and collectively negotiated (Armstrong 2004). In this chapter a continuum of epistemological positions of pathways is developed, and findings from three studies investigating pathways into and out of crime are presented to demonstrate how constructionist perspectives have generated new insights into the way in which traditional risk factors operate for young people. First, preliminary findings from the study of young people's perspectives of school exclusion demonstrated a strong constructionist position, illustrated through the institutional constructions of exclusion rates and the arbitrary process of recording exclusion. Particularly important is the way in which children become routinely managed and defined as a 'problem' within particular institutional settings and professional discourses. While the school context may be a powerful force in shaping opportunities and choices, young people expressed their own agency through resisting and avoiding potential labels, illuminating children's ability to cope, reflect and be resilient. A new school and on some occasions important support mechanisms may have helped to aid children's own reconstruction of themselves, as they are routinely managed and constructed differently.

The second study, of social capital and risk-taking, suggests that social capital is a resource that influences the negotiation of pathways. A moderate constructionist perspective is demonstrated here by evidence of a continuous interaction between agency and structure exemplified by the notions of 'risk stagnation' and 'risk navigation'. Opportunities for young people 'to act' and 'to be different' are restricted or enhanced through different types of social capital. Through this moderate constructionist perspective networks are an important resource for young people and their decision-making on risk, and the differing types (tightly bonded or diverse) have implications for their power and opportunity to act differently, in essence for their situational agency. These findings underline that pathways are social processes that have multiple causes, and that such causes are not merely additive.

The third set of findings from a study of substance use and offending adds new understanding to the relationships previously thought to exist between drugs, crime and classic risk factors. A weak constructionist perspective is demonstrated by evidence of the normalisation of drug use and the changing pathways through substance use and offending that result; associations between classically identified risk factors cannot be assumed to be static but need to be understood within their cultural and historical contexts. Moreover, findings can be interpreted from this constructionist perspective to include the interaction between individual and the immediate setting. In this way, then, rather than a causal risk factor, drugs may be viewed as part of the context within which young people interact to negotiate their pathways.

Epistemological disputes and 'method wars' do not necessarily get us very far, (Layder 1993). Layder (1998: 117, 201), for example, has argued for 'co-operative dialogue' across both disciplinary boundaries and epistemological positions in order to investigate more completely the complexity of social reality. Difference, diversity and context continue to prove challenging to researchers. As Layder puts it, social reality is multi-faceted and variable, and as such it cannot be captured by one analytical approach. Thus he argues that researchers should 'operate with a plural knowledge base in order to maximise understanding and explanatory power' although this may result in difficult debates about the compatibility and validity of differing forms of knowledge (1998: 177). Within criminology this has resulted in the pursuit of integrative theory, capable of answering the 'rates question', that is, the extent to which a behaviour occurs in the population as a whole, and the 'conduct question', that is, why particular individuals do what they do (Leavitt 1999). Such theorising has attempted to integrate behavioural, individual, situational and social factors into a more complete explanatory theory of risk and pathway (Byrne and Trew 2005; Catalano and Hawkins 1996). Byrne and Trew argue: 'These accounts improve on other approaches by incorporating multiple levels of analysis and including dynamic and developmental processes that had often been ignored in the past' (2005: 186).

The pursuit of an integrative theory in criminology is not a new enterprise (Bottoms 2000), and it is accepted that theories in criminology often have partial coverage. Integrative approaches have, however, been critiqued on the grounds that they fail to capture the interactive nature of action and context (Emler and Reicher 1995), and the sheer complexity of social life (Byrne and Trew 2005). The need to operate at the levels of both epidemiology and individual conduct is also problematic (Leavitt 1999). In effect, integrative approaches struggle to function at both the micro and macro levels (Leavitt 1999). The concept of a single integrative theory is therefore perhaps too ambitious. Rather, the goal should be the generation of complementary theories (Layder 1998) producing differing layers of knowledge yet grounded in empirical research. However, Bottoms warns against confusing eclecticism with synthesis, and argues for the 'selective adoption' of key concepts from general social theories, as long as this is done with 'sensitivity and theoretical awareness' (2000: 24). For Bottoms, Layder's 'adaptive grounded theory' approach provides 'principled and defensible procedures for synthesis' (2000: 46).

Perhaps the issue, then, is not about competing epistemological positions, but about what each of them can contribute to differing levels of investigation. The issue therefore becomes one of 'fit' across differing levels of analysis rather than an issue of 'grand explanatory theory' – a question of synthesising not disputing. Academic networks themselves provide one mechanism for attempting this, particularly if they are able to link methods and data sets, and can enable future secondary analysis of combined project data. As Bammer has expressed it, 'The time is ripe for coalescence and co-ordination'

(2003: 1) and for valuing different ways of understanding the world (2003: 11).

References

Aguilera, M. B. (2002) 'The impact of social capital on labour force participation: Evidence from the 2000 Social Capital Benchmark Survey', *Social Science Quarterly*, 83: 853–74.

Ansell, J. and Wharton, F. (1992) *Risk: Analysis, Assessment and Management*. Chichester: John Wiley.

Armstrong, D. (2004) 'A risky business? Research, policy, governmentality and youth offending', *Youth Justice*, 4: 100–17.

Audit Commission (1996) *Misspent Youth: Young People and Crime*. London: Audit Commission.

Bammer, G. (2003) *Integration and Implementation Sciences: Will Developing a New Specialism Improve our Effectiveness in Tackling Complex Issues?* http://www.anu.edu.au/issn/, posted to the Science, Environment and Development Group Website 19 September 2003.

Bloor, M. (1995) *The Sociology of HIV Transmission*. London: Sage.

Boeck, T., Fleming, J. and Kemshall, H. (2006) 'The context of risk decisions: Does social capital make a difference?', in *Qualitative Social Research*, available online at: www.qualitative-research.net/fqs-eng.htm

Bottoms, A. (2000) 'The Relationship Between Theory and Research in Criminology,' in R.D. King and E. Wincup (eds) *Doing Research on Crime and Justice*. Oxford: Oxford University Press, pp. 15–60.

Bradbury, J. (1989) 'The policy implications of differing concepts of risk', *Science, Technology, and Human Values*, 14: 380–99.

Brown, M. (2000) 'Calculations of Risk in Contemporary Penal Practice', in M. Brown and J. Pratt (eds) *Dangerous Offenders: Punishment and Social Order*. London: Routledge, pp. 93–108.

Byrne, C.F. and Trew, K.F. (2005) 'Crime orientations, social relations and involvement in crime: Patterns emerging from offenders' accounts', *Howard Journal of Criminal Justice*, 44: 185–205.

Byrne, D. (1998) *Complexity Theory and the Social Sciences*. London: Routledge.

Carver, C.S., Scheier, M.F. and Weintraub, J.K. (1989) 'Assessing coping strategies: A theoretically-based approach', *Journal of Personality and Social Psychology*, 56: 267–83.

Catalano, R.F. and Hawkins, J.D. (1996) 'The Social Development Model: A Theory of Antisocial Behaviour', in J.D. Hawkins (ed.) *Delinquency and Crime: Current Theories* Cambridge: Cambridge University Press, pp. 149–97.

Clarke, R.V. and Cornish, D. (1983) *Crime Control in Britain: A Review of Policy Research*. Albany, NY: State University of New York Press.

Crook, S. (1999) 'Ordering Risks', in D. Lupton (ed.) *Risk and Sociocultural Theory.* Cambridge: Cambridge University Press, pp. 160–85.

Douglas, M. (1992) *Risk and Blame.* London: Routledge.

Edwards, B. and Foley, M.W. (1998) 'Civil society and social capital beyond Putnam', *American Behavioural Scientist*, 42: 124–39.

Elliott, D.S., Huizinga, D. and Ageton, S.S. (1985) *Explaining Delinquency and Drug Use.* London: Sage.

Emler, N. and Reicher, S. (1995) *Adolescence and Delinquency.* Oxford: Blackwell.

Farrall, S. (2002) *Rethinking What Works with Offenders: Probation, Social Context, and Desistance from Crime*, Cullompton: Willan Publishing.

Farrall, S. and Bowling, B. (1999) 'Structuration, human development and desistance from crime', *British Journal of Criminology*, 39: 252–67.

Farrington, D.P. (1989) *The Origins of Crime: The Cambridge Study of Delinquent Development*, Home Office Research Bulletin 27. London: HMSO.

Farrington, D.P. (1995) 'The development of offending and antisocial behaviour from childhood: Key findings from the Cambridge study in delinquent development', *Journal of Child Psychology and Psychiatry*, 36: 929–64.

Farrington, D.P. (2000) 'Explaining and preventing crime: The globalization of knowledge', American Society of Criminology 1999 Presidential Address, *Criminology*, 38: 1–24.

Gossop, M., Griffiths, P., Powis, B. and Strang, J. (1992) 'Severity of dependence and route of administration of heroin, cocaine and amphetamines', *British Journal of Addiction*, 87: 1527–36.

Graham, J., and Bowling, B. (1996) *Young People and Crime,* Home Office Research Study 145. London: Home Office Research and Statistics Directorate.

Hammersley, R., Marsland, L. and Reid, M. (2003) *Substance Misuse by Young Offenders: The Impact of Normalisation of Drug Use in the Early Years of the 21st Century*, Home Office Research Study 261. London: Home Office.

Hodgson, P. and Webb, D. (2005) 'Young people, crime and school exclusion: A case of some surprises', *Howard Journal of Criminal Justice*, 44: 12–28.

Hood, C. and Jones, D. (1996) (eds) *Accident Design: Contemporary Debates in Risk Management.* London: UCL Press.

Horlick-Jones, T. (1998) 'Meaning and contextualisation in risk assessment', *Reliability Engineering and System Safety*, 5: 79–89.

Jasanoff, S. (1993) 'Bridging the two cultures of risk analysis', *Risk Analysis*, 13: 123–9.

Kemshall, H. (2003) *Understanding Risk in Criminal Justice.* Buckingham: Open University Press.

Layder, D. (1993) *New Strategies in Social Research.* Cambridge: Blackwell Publishers/Polity Press.

Layder, D. (1998) *Sociological Practice: Linking Theory and Social Research.* London: Sage.

Leavitt, G. (1999) 'Criminological theory as an art form: Implications for criminal justice policy', *Crime and Delinquency*, 45: 389–99.

Lupton, D. (1999) *Risk*. London: Routledge.

MacDonald, R. and Marsh, J. (2001) 'Disconnected youth?', *Journal of Youth Studies*, 4: 373–91.

Maruna, S. (2001). *Making Good: How Ex-convicts Reform and Rebuild their Lives*. Washington, DC: American Psychological Association.

Morrow, V. (2004) 'Children's "social capital": Implications for health and well-being', *Health Education*, 104: 211–25.

Munn, P. and Lloyd, G. (2005) 'Exclusion and excluded pupils', *British Educational Research Journal*, 31: 205–21.

Osler, A. and Vincent, K. (2003) *Girls and Exclusion: Rethinking the Agenda*. London: RoutledgeFalmer.

Parker, H., Aldridge, J. and Measham, F. (1998) *Illegal Leisure: The Normalization of Adolescent Recreational Drug Use*. London: Routledge.

Poulin, F., Dishion, T.J. and Haas, E. (1999) 'The peer influence paradox: Friendship quality and deviancy training within male adolescent friendships', *Merrill-Palmer Quarterly*, 1: 42–61.

Robins, L. and Rutter, M. (1990) *Straight and Devious Pathways from Childhood to Adulthood*. Cambridge: Cambridge University Press.

Rosenberg, M. (1965) *Society and the Adolescent Self-image*. Princeton, NJ: Princeton University Press.

Sampson, R.J. and Laub, J.H. (1993) *Crime in the Making: Pathways and Turning Points Through Life*. Cambridge, MA: Harvard University Press.

Sampson, R.J., Raudenbush, S.W. and Earls, F. (1997) 'Neighbourhoods and violent crime: A multilevel study of collective efficacy', *Science*, 277: 918–24.

Sparks, R. (2001) 'Degrees of estrangement: The cultural theory of risk and comparative penology', *Theoretical Criminology*, 5: 159–76.

Sullivan, E. (2002) 'Social Exclusion, Social Identity and Social Capital: Reuniting the Global, the Local and the Personal', discussion paper for the Conference de l'Association Internationale des Ecoles de Travail Social, Montpelier, July.

Thompson, M. and Wildavsky, A. (1982) 'A Proposal to Create a Cultural Theory of Risk', in H.C. Kunreuther and E.V. Ley (eds) *The Risk Analysis Controversy: An Institutional Perspective*. New York: Springer-Verlag, pp. 145–61.

Vulliamy, G. and Webb, R. (2000) 'Stemming the tide of rising school exclusions: Problems and possibilities', *British Journal of Education Studies*, 48: 119–33.

West, D.J. and Farrington, D.P. (1977) *The Delinquent Way of Life*. London: Heinemann.

Wikström, P-O. (2004) 'Crime as Alternative: Towards a Cross-level Situational Action Theory of Crime Causation', in J. McCord (ed.) *Beyond Empiricism: Institutions and Intentions in the Study of Crime*. New Brunswick, NJ: Transaction Publishers, pp. 1–38.

Wikström, P-O. and Sampson, R.J. (2003) 'Social Mechanisms of Community Influences on Crime and Pathways in Criminality', in B. Lahey, T. Moffitt and A. Caspi (eds) *Causes of Conduct Disorder and Juvenile Delinquency.* New York: Guildford Press, pp. 118–52.

Willner, P. (2000). 'Further validation and development of a screening instrument for the assessment of substance misuse in adolescents', *Addiction*, 95: 1691–8.

Wynne, B. (1996) 'May the Sheep Safely Graze? A Reflexive View of the Expert–Lay Knowledge Divide', in S. Lash, B. Szerszynski and B. Wynne (eds) *Risk, Environment and Modernity.* London: Sage, pp. 44–83.

Chapter 6

Social exclusion, youth transitions and criminal careers: five critical reflections on 'risk'

Robert MacDonald

Abstract

This chapter draws upon recent youth research in some of Britain's poorest neighbourhoods (in Teesside, north-east England). It stresses the importance of a qualitative, biographical and long-term perspective in attempting to understand drug-using and criminal careers (and wider youth transitions) and points to some difficulties in applying – straightforwardly – influential models of risk assessment and prediction to individual biographies.

In a context of deep, collective disadvantage, most research participants shared many of the risk factors associated with social exclusion in early adulthood. Yet the majority did *not* pursue full-blown criminal or drug-using careers and the research struggled to identify background factors that seemed to play a causal role in separating out more 'delinquent' transitions from more 'conventional' ones. Youth biographies were marked by flux; they did not roll on deterministically to foregone conclusions. Unpredictable 'critical moments' turned transitions in unpredictable directions; sometimes towards crime, sometimes away. This chapter concludes that there is danger in criminal career research – as in studies of youth transition – in prioritising individual-level explanations at the expense of an assessment of the 'risks' presented by socio-spatial and historical context.

Introduction

This chapter reports recent studies from some of the poorest neighbourhoods in Britain – in Teesside, north-east England – that sought to understand young people's biographies qualitatively, holistically and longitudinally. Their close-up description of the experience of growing up here enabled critical examination of popular, controversial theories that claim to capture these processes of transition (i.e. theories of 'the underclass' and 'social exclusion'). The research was therefore not designed to be, exactly or solely, a study of youth offending or criminal careers and even less so an assessment of important theories of risk prediction and management in respect of these. Nevertheless, it does suggest some useful critical questions about the *application* of risk assessments and predictions to *individual* young people as their lives unfold.

The chapter begins by outlining our theoretical take on debates about youth transition and goes on to describe, in brief, our research methodology. The dominant, social scientific approach to understanding criminal careers and risk is then outlined. This is followed by a sketch of criminal and drug-using careers as uncovered in our research in Teesside. This is used to raise five critical reflections on orthodox, risk-based paradigms.

A note about youth transitions

The value of the concept of transition (and alternative metaphors such as 'pathway') has been hotly contested in youth sociology. Because the movement to adulthood has become more fragmented and unpredictable (Du Bois-Reymond 1998; Cohen and Ainley 2000; EGRIS 2001), critics have distanced themselves from structurally-oriented, class-based analyses of youth transitions in favour of theories about individualisation and the 'risk society' (Giddens 1990, 1991; Beck 1992; Beck *et al.* 1994).

It is true that since the 1970s youth transitions in the UK have become more complicated, extended and apparently less class-bound. This does not, however, invalidate the *concept* of transition (see MacDonald and Marsh 2005 for fuller discussion). As Furlong and Cartmel (1997) and Roberts (2000) show, a young person's opportunities and destination are still strongly influenced by original class location, even though the choices and risks of restructured transitions tend to engender a greater sense of individual autonomy. Thus, summarising much recent youth research in the UK, Jones (2002) stresses the hardening up of 'the youth divide'. Those (typically working-class) young people that make the speediest transitions into the labour market, to parenthood and to independent living face greater risks of the negative outcomes associated with social exclusion.

In drawing upon the sociological concept of 'career' (Becker 1963; Berger and Berger 1972), our studies in Teesside have explored the way that individual decision-making, informed by young people's cultures and subcultures, interacts with socially structured opportunities to create individual, and shared, paths of transition. Coles (1995, 2000) broadens the scope of transition studies to include 'family careers' (the attainment of relative independence from family of origin) and 'housing careers' (the move away from the parental home) alongside the study of 'school-to-work careers' (educational and employment experiences). In some contexts 'criminal careers', 'drug-using careers' and 'leisure careers' can also become important in shaping youth transitions (MacDonald and Marsh 2005 explain these terms). These six 'careers' became the focus of our interviews with young people.

The Teesside studies

This chapter is based on three studies that shared similar aims, research sites and methods.[1] The first of these was published as *Snakes and Ladders* (Johnston *et al.* 2000). It was interested in how 15–25 year olds (n = 98) from the same neighbourhood (Willowdene in the town of Kelby, Teesside), and sharing the same class and ethnic backgrounds, evolved 'alternative' and 'mainstream' transitions to adulthood. The second study, *Disconnected Youth?* (MacDonald and Marsh 2005), examined controversial underclass theories and concepts of social exclusion and their connection with the lived realities of 15–25 year olds (n = 88) who were growing up in the poor neighbourhoods of East Kelby.

In the late 1990s, the seven wards of these studies featured in the top 5 per cent most deprived nationally (DETR 2000) and two of them were in the worst five – of 8,414 – in England. Both projects involved periods of participant observation and interviews with professionals who worked with young people. At their core, though, they relied on lengthy, tape-recorded, biographical interviews (Chamberlayne *et al.* 2002) with a total of 186 young people (82 females and 104 males) from the predominantly white, (ex) manual working-class population resident in 'one of the most de-industrialised locales in the UK' (Byrne 1999: 93).

There is not the room here to review these studies' findings. We note only that whereas at the level of the individual case informants described differentiated family, housing, leisure, criminal and drug-using careers, they were united by a common experience of economic marginality. The majority displayed highly conventional attitudes to employment but their late teenage years school-to-work careers struggled to progress beyond low-paid, low-skill, insecure 'poor work' (Byrne 1999).

Our most recent study, *Poor Transitions* (Webster *et al.* 2004), carried out in 2003, was designed as a follow-up to the two earlier ones. Where did such transitions *lead* individuals in their mid to late twenties? Were people eventually able to carve out more progressive transitions, even in unpromising circumstances? Or were longer-term problems of social exclusion cemented in place by early experiences of economic marginality?

We chose to re-interview 34 individuals (18 females and 16 males), drawn from the two original samples, who were now aged 23 to 29 years. We sampled theoretically so as to understand better the longer-term transitions of: young women who, at last interview, had been committed to full-time parenting (n = 11); those with enduring but unrewarding commitment to education, training and employment (n = 11); and individuals seriously involved in criminal and/or drug-using careers (n = 12).

Our analytic approach combined standard, qualitative analysis of recurrent and divergent themes and responses across the sample(s) and longitudinal analysis of individual, retrospective biographical interviews from all three projects. In doing so, the research presented is relatively unusual in contemporary British social science. Not only are the nearly two hundred participants often described as 'hard to reach' (Merton 1998), they allowed a rare, close-up insight into the ways people at the sharp end live through conditions of social exclusion.

Young adults, risk and crime

At a general, social theoretical level, theories of risk, individualisation and the risk society have had considerable impact on youth studies (e.g. Furlong and Cartmel 1997; France 2000; Mitchell *et al.* 2004). More particularly, 'the risk factor paradigm dominates a range of policy developments and is seen by many agencies as the solution to the 'youth problem' (Crow *et al.* 2004: 73). Coles (2000) provides a useful critical summary of risk approaches to teenage pregnancy, unemployment, mental health and 'NEET' (i.e. young people who are not in education, employment and training).

One of the most influential examples of the risk approach in youth studies is the criminal career perspective. Its key exponent in the UK – and 'globally' according to Muncie (2004: 277) – has been David Farrington. The theoretical promise, and policy influence, of this type of criminology is that offenders and offending can be predicted, known and controlled.[2] Farrington concludes that a small group of chronic offenders is responsible for a large proportion of crime and that 'these chronics might have been identified with reasonable accuracy at age 10' (1994: 566). Longitudinal, quantitative studies (usually of young men) are used to identify, measure and model the early life influences on offenders. Individual psychopathology, from an early age, *predicts* later forms of anti-social behaviour and crime:

> hyperactivity at age 2 may lead to cruelty to animals at 6, shoplifting at 10, burglary at 15, robbery at 20, and eventually spouse assault, child abuse and neglect, alcohol abuse, and employment and accommodation problems later on in life. Typically, a career of childhood anti-social behaviour leads to a criminal career, which often coincides with a career of teenage anti-social behaviour and leads to a career of adult anti-social behaviour. (Farrington 1994: 512)

The major risk factors for juvenile offending (Farrington 1996: 2–3) range through individual personality and intelligence, parental supervision, parental conflict and separation, school, peer and community influences and socio-economic status. This positivist, 'actuarial' approach to crime (see Young 1999) has found favour in youth policy and practice interventions. A good example can be found in the Communities that Care programme for reducing antisocial behaviour (e.g. Beinart *et al.* 2002). Devised in the United States, it has been imported to the UK with major funding from the Joseph Rowntree Foundation. It aims to 'tackle risk factors that are problematic within particular communities' (Farrington 1996: 5). Crow *et al.*'s evaluation (2004) highlights the severe difficulties that have been faced in implementing this model in practice.

The same stress on detecting risk factors among the young and intervening to ward against the predicted, later outcomes is central to the British government's youth crime strategy (see Home Office 2004: 41). It is evident in the OASys system of offender risk assessment and prediction operated by the probation service (Horsefield 2003) and in the programme of Youth Inclusion Projects (YIPs),[3] wherein local, multi-agency teams identify and work with those 50 young residents of high crime areas at greatest *risk* of offending (even if some individuals have, in fact, no record of offending at that point).

A sketch of criminal and drug-using careers on Teesside

Ours were not statistically representative samples of young people in these neighbourhoods but interviewees' biographical accounts did help us sketch out the *nature* and *shape* of criminal careers. While proportions of interviewees with criminal involvement differed a little, the *Snakes and Ladders* and *Disconnected Youth* studies came to very similar theoretical descriptions of criminal careers.[4] Just over half of the 88 young people in the latter project had committed a criminal offence on at least one occasion. For the majority of these, however, their criminal careers were limited, typically to one-off, petty shoplifting in their early to mid-teenage. For most, their transgressions ceased there. Two key movements can be identified in the consolidation of the most serious, longer-term criminal careers (of the sort displayed by 20 interviewees).

The first of these was the hardening up of school disaffection (again, a common experience of the samples overall) into full-blown educational disengagement, usually displayed in frequent, persistent truancy. Simultaneous disengagement from school and engagement with 'street corner society' further established oppositional identities and was the cornerstone for the evolution of most careers of crime that extended beyond early to mid-teenage:

> ... just me and this other lad used to nick off all the time ...Just go and hang about the town ... that was me starting days of crime and that, yeah ... shoplifting and pinching bikes, that's what it was. (*Danny, 21*, Young Offenders Institute inmate)

Dull truant time was enlivened by the camaraderie of shoplifting jaunts, other petty thieving and speeding around the estates in stolen vehicles: crime as leisure for bored, out-of-school teenagers. Although 17-year-old Richy said that he had often 'mooched [stolen from garden] sheds', he did not consider himself 'a bad lad, a real thief'. Acquisitive crime did raise cash but the main motivation was to relieve boredom: 'when you pinch summat, like a barbecue set you can sell on for £10, you can buy yourselves a few bottles of cider, can't you? You can cure your boredom then' (see Stephen and Squires 2003).

For some, this marked the early phases of criminal apprenticeships. They began to learn the routines of acquisitively oriented offending (e.g. how and what to thieve from cars) and were drawn into local criminal markets (e.g. where to fence stolen property, the market rate for 'knock-off gear', etc.). For many, though, these sort of infringements – coupled with underage drinking and recreational drug use – marked the extent, and end point, of criminal careers.

Thus, the large numbers involved in (petty) offending in early teenage lessened as the years passed. The second, most significant moment – that helped to drag out a smaller number of individuals' criminal career into later years and to transmute them into something more destructive – is when heroin enters the scene. Local police and drugs workers reported how cheap, smokeable heroin flooded into Teesside's working-class housing estates in the mid-1990s, prior to which there had been a negligible local heroin-using population. Teesside's young people seem unprepared to resist the temptations of this 'poverty drug' and made speedy transitions from occasional, recreational use of drugs such as cannabis to often daily, dependent use of heroin (and later in the 1990s, crack cocaine).

For this minority of interviewees (n = 11 from 88 in the *Disconnected Youth* study), dependent use of heroin was the driving force behind exclusionary transitions which distanced them from their families, their previous lifestyles, from the labour market and which entangled them in chaotic, damaging careers of drug-driven crime (see Simpson 2003). Heroin use became central to an understanding of their unfolding biographies.

For individuals like Richard, desperate acquisitive criminality was fuelled by the need for daily drug money. By the age of 20, this close combination of drug and crime careers had progressively closed down options for a more 'mainstream' lifestyle. He had failed to complete several training programmes, been employed only once – briefly – and been unemployed recurrently, become estranged from his family, been homeless, had a lengthy, worsening record of offending and had been imprisoned twice. He was living in a bail hostel, struggling to remain committed to a methadone programme and scratching around trying to find ways, beyond heroin, to fill tedious, directionless days.

Questions can be asked about the descriptive purchase provided by the concept, but if anyone is 'socially excluded', Richard is.

Yet our follow up study (Webster *et al*. 2004) produced some surprises. Richard was one of those re-interviewed for *Poor Transitions*, three years later. The intervening period had seen a familiar pattern of heroin use, offending, prison, desistance and relapse to heroin use. He said:

> It's like a vicious circle. It's like one, big, magnetic circle ... when you get out of jail it starts again. You're slowly getting drawn back in all the time ... back on the circle again, moving round and round and back in the same direction all the time. (*Richard*)

At the most recent interview, Richard – like most in this sub-group in the follow-up study – was in a state of 'fragile desistance' from crime and dependent drug use. By this we mean that *we* agreed that he was making a sustained, genuine and – at that point – apparently successful attempt to take the long, arduous, risk-laden struggle back to 'a normal life', as he described it. We stress the fragility of desistance as a *process* (rather than a single, simple event) because the biographies of this sub-sample were replete with failed attempts and because success was contingent on several factors beyond individual motivation.

Just as the perceived purposelessness of school was the context for the drift into offending – and later unemployment meant informants sometimes went down 'the wrong path' into more serious crime – the availability of purposeful activity in which individuals could invest their time, energy and identity aided this 'fragile desistance'. This purposefulness could be found in normal aspects of youth transition; and, confirming other criminological research, the getting of jobs, the forming of new partnerships and becoming a parent motivated and facilitated the process of 'growing out of crime' (Rutherford 1992). The problem, though, is that a corollary of sustained, heroin-driven crime is often largely 'empty' school-to-work careers punctuated by repeated spells of imprisonment. This makes the achievement of these sorts of resolution much harder. People like Richard are unlikely to appear attractive as potential employees, partners and fathers. With purposeful activity to engage energies and through which to redefine personal identity, liberating oneself from addiction was hard enough. Without it, relapse was common. Heroin helped 'fill the void [and] make life bearable' (Foster 2000: 322).

Easy access to therapeutic, non-punitive drug treatment services was also a significant aid to desistance, as was physical and emotional detachment from earlier subcultural lives and alliances. Dependent heroin users were unanimous on this point; their lives since their mid-teens had been lived within social networks that reinforced drug behaviour. Imprisonment sometimes provided a welcome opportunity to 'get clean' (albeit under a harsh, non-therapeutic regime). A few had even purposefully sought a custodial rather than a community-based sentence as a way of escaping the recurrent drug temptations they encountered 'on the street'. Prison release signalled a return to the environment that had generated initial drug dependency and was often viewed with trepidation: 'You're just going back to the same place, the same group of people and it's easy to get back into it' (Stu, 20).

Five critical reflections on theories of risk and criminal career

It is important to reiterate that our research was not designed to evaluate risk-assessment approaches in relation to offending. It could not, for instance, include any proper measure of important risk factors such as parental supervision. It did confirm empirical findings from larger, more statistically representative studies (e.g. gender as an influence on offending and the factors that aid desistance). Our studies do not cast doubt on the importance, influence and rigour of studies on risk and criminal career but do suggest, we believe, some useful theoretical and methodological questions for such approaches and for their application in policy and practice.

First, we should be wary about presuming a tight, causal fit between particular risk indicators and later, or concurrent, behaviour. For instance, the research literature (e.g. Graham and Bowling 1995) and our own studies suggest a strong *association* between persistent school truancy and offending. According to our evidence, however, the first did not *determine* the second (as implied by the Social Exclusion Unit 1997). The majority (n = 16) of those with more sustained, criminal careers (n = 20) in the *Disconnected Youth* sample *had* been frequent school truants. Yet a substantial minority (n = 14) of frequent truants (n = 40) reported no offending whatsoever. Talking of the risk-factor approach, Coles (2000: 194) worries that it:

> employs a remarkably 'deductive', 'positivistic' and 'normative' approach to problem identification and problem solving. It

suggests that social science is supremely confident that it knows the causes of problem behaviours and poor outcomes during youth transitions. This might be a very questionable assumption.

Second, our studies struggled to identify *any* earlier single, individual or family-level factor that would predict confidently those who would follow delinquent transitions. According to our research evidence, those in these studies with the most persistent, extensive later criminality could *not* 'have been identified with reasonable accuracy at age 10' (Farrington 1994: 566). The samples as a whole shared many socio-economic (i.e. low socio-economic class), educational (e.g. poor school performance) and family (e.g. parental separation, bereavement) risk factors. These were not, however, able to explain why a minority of individuals pursued criminal careers and a majority did not. Of course, proponents of risk-factor approaches would stress that theirs are theories that suggest (or are meant to suggest) probabilistic, *general* associations between risks and later outcomes that might, therefore, not be applicable to individual cases.[5]

Webster's analysis of the combined data from the *Snakes and Ladders* and *Disconnected Youth* studies does confirm 'the link between having experienced risk factors and being a frequent offender' (2005: 5). What he means is that the majority of the latter 'possessed' more of the former (i.e. frequent truancy, family conflict, no qualifications, troubled backgrounds) than those who had never offended. As such, on this point, it may be that there is no substantial disagreement between orthodox criminal career research and our findings. Nevertheless, while academic proponents of risk-factor approaches rightly tend to demur from using risk factors to predict *individual* behaviour, this is not always the case with some of the policy and practice outcroppings of risk theory. As noted earlier, the offender risk-assessment system used by the UK probation service and the British government's programme of Youth Inclusion Projects do *exactly* this. Furthermore, the fact that around a third of non-offenders in our studies also shared the same type and number of risk factors as the frequent offenders raises interesting questions, we think, about the level of probable effect of risk factors and their relationship to later outcomes. One such question concerns the uneven distribution of 'protective' factors against risk, which might help explain why some do not follow the 'probable' path to crime. Farrington (1996: 3) notes that 'comparatively little attention' has been paid to these, especially among 'those from high-risk backgrounds' (see Scott and Chaudhary 2003).[6]

This problem of how to explain why some people with a heavy burden of criminogenic risk factors do *not* evolve criminal careers is also identified by Smith and McVie (2003: 170): 'the substantial limitation' of childhood risk predictions is 'that there are many "false positives" … [for example] among children who are difficult to control there are many who turn out not to have criminal careers as adolescents or adults'.

Contrary to some theorisations of crime in poor neighbourhoods (e.g. Dennis 1993; *Guardian*, 5 April 2001), for instance, the *Disconnected Youth* study found no association at all between family type and later criminality. Only four of those 20 who reported frequent, longer-term offending were brought up in lone-parent families. Interviewing siblings who followed quite different paths confirmed our wariness about the 'actuarial positivism' present in some contemporary criminology (Young 1999).[7] Many were called, but few were chosen. Long-term educational disengagement and engagement with street-based peer groups *was* a necessary condition for the evolution of serious criminal careers but it was not a *sufficient* condition.[8]

Third, which of the multitudinous risks experienced by our samples might be most significant? Which risks propel some young people towards crime (and which do not)? Sorting out 'which risk factors have causal effects' is a 'difficult question', but Farrington and Painter (2004: 57) go on to suggest that 'if all modifiable risk factors are targeted' by intervention programmes they 'will be effective because at least some of the risk factors will be causes'. The current UK ESRC research network on *Pathways In and Out of Crime* also highlights the theoretical 'difficulty in attributing causality to single and universal "risk" factors. For example, life-histories show that the same "factor" can have different consequences for different people at different times' (ESRC 2004: 3). The Teesside studies go further: the same risk factor can have quite different consequences *for the same individual*, at different points in the life course. For instance, *Poor Transitions* (Webster *et al.* 2004) shows how in the biography of one young man, the deaths of close family members became, at different points, the major psychological triggers for the *turn to* and *turn away* from heroin.

This leads us to our fourth critical reflection on risk orthodoxies. Methodologically, large-scale, quantitative studies of criminal careers help show co-relations between a range of variables and outcomes across larger, representative samples. They are less able than qualitative studies to get close up to social actors' own subjective, complicated accounts and life stories.[9] Although class, ethnicity and place united these interviewees, their subjective *experiences* of transition were different. The combined influence of school-to-work, family, housing, leisure, criminal and drug-using careers meant that individual transitions were complex, fluid and unpredictable. Biographical interviews highlighted the significance of contingent, unpredictable events and experiences in the creation of *youth* transitions of different sorts. Youth is emphasised here because, like Smith and McVie (2003), we are interested in post-childhood influences on criminal careers (such as the role of leisure lifestyles and social networks: see also Wikström n.d.; Armstrong 2003). Criminal – and non-criminal – destinies are not set in stone in childhood. Teenage and young adulthood presented unpredictable 'critical moments', with unpredictable consequences for some transitions (Johnston *et al.* 2000; Thomson *et al.* 2002).[10] Events and encounters in one sphere could have dramatic repercussions in another. 'Stuff happens' and more 'stuff happens' as the years pass, remarks Webster (2005: 1). Physical and mental ill health was widespread among interviewees and their families, unsurprisingly so given what we know about the socio-spatial concentration of health inequalities (Mitchell *et al.* 2000). Experiences of loss – particularly of bereavement and parental separation – proved to be especially important in shaping the course of individuals' lives thereafter.

Again, though, *how* such events impact on transitions would be unknowable without the benefit of interviewees' *retrospective* biographical accounts. Seemingly following uneventful, 'normal' transitions until that point, a few interviewees highlighted family traumas as the moment when they started 'going off the rails'. Learning at the age of 11 that her 'father' was not actually her father was identified by Sarah as the 'turning point' (Hodkinson and Sparkes 1997) that set in train a series of turbulent relationships with family members and, later, boyfriends, which in turn motivated a very chaotic, nomadic housing career. Conversely, Martin is a good example of a person who, despite multiple personal hardships ('risk factors'), such as the suicides of his best friend and father when Martin was in his late teens and, later, the perinatal death of his first child, remained steadfastly committed to a 'conventional' working-class lifestyle.

Fifth, and finally, there is a tendency in much criminal career research to overplay individual-level risks at the expense of those that are presented by the historical and spatial contexts in which youth transitions are made (Smith and McVie 2003). According to our research, it would be impossible to understand the contemporary criminal careers of disadvantaged youth in Teesside without reference to two, crucial historical–spatial processes (Webster *et al.* 2006). The first is the rapid and widespread deindustrialisation of this locale (Byrne 1999) and the concomitant rise of economic marginality and poverty for working-class youth. Talking of our research, Webster (2005: 1) puts it like this:

> ... our cohorts were born on the cusp or in the depths of accelerated social transformation (i.e. between 1974 and the mid-80s), which de-industrialised and destabilised their neighbourhoods, polarising their experiences and class positions. These crises were shifted onto the life histories of individuals.

The second is the historically unprecedented influx of cheap heroin in the mid-1990s. The testimonies of drugs workers, police officers, adult residents and young people all pointed to the devastating, localised and recent effects of 'poverty drugs' in enmeshing some young people in the most damaging forms of criminal career. Prior to the mid-1990s, it would have been difficult to locate any individuals who had the sort of transition described by Richard (earlier). In other words, new, imported risks bear down on young people's lives here; risks which were unknown just a few years earlier and which are 'scarcely recognised in risk and prediction studies' (Webster *et al.* 2006).

Of course, it would be foolish to argue that persistent youth crime is and has always been rooted in drug dependency. Craine (1997) shows how economically marginal transitions can readily generate minority 'alternative careers' of crime, regardless of any contact with 'poverty drugs'. Nevertheless, the form of drug-crime career sketched in this chapter explains much of, and the most pernicious examples of, current youth offending in this locale. The implication of this argument is that in emphasising childhood experiences and ingrained personality factors, criminal career research can underestimate the influence of *changing* community conditions (specific to particular places and times) and how these are encountered in *youth* transitions in generating the most serious forms of criminal career.[11]

Summary and conclusion

In making their transitions, our interviewees collided with the numerous hardships of socially excluded, poor neighbourhoods.

Direct, cumulative experience of, *inter alia*, poverty, personal and family ill-health, criminal victimisation, unemployment, poor schooling, offending, problematic drug use and homelessness undeniably affected the sort of lives they led. These were the sort of risks allotted to young people born in these neighbourhoods during the latter part of the twentieth century. Exactly what sort of effects such experiences had, at the level of individual transitions, was much less certain. 'Stuff happens' (Webster 2005: 1) – sometimes for the better, sometimes for the worse and sometimes with unclear, equivocal outcomes. A key conclusion of these studies is, then, about the contingency of life biographies: transitions of whatever sort – whether they be 'conventional', 'delinquent' or somewhere in-between – do not roll on deterministically to foregone conclusions.

It is not easy – and perhaps not helpful – therefore to apply orthodox risk assessments and predictions to lives like these. Experience of school disengagement, parental separation, low educational attainment, early offending and so on was widespread, but the most serious forms of social exclusion – experienced as long-term criminal and drug-using careers – were limited to a minority. Conversely, economic marginality in late teenage and early adulthood – signified by recurrent episodes of 'poor work' and unemployment – was the preserve of all, despite differential levels of school engagement and educational qualification.

In conclusion, we stress the value of ethnography in understanding how young people experience risks as they grow up in poor neighbourhoods. At the same time, we should be wary of studies (of youth transitions in general, of the criminal career in particular) that cease there. The Teesside studies emphasise how individual youth transitions must be understood in relation to changing, place-specific and unequal 'structures of opportunity'. They suggest an approach that situates the current academic and policy fascination with the twists and turns of individual careers and transitions within that panorama of social structural processes that *create* 'risk' and 'exclusion' – in some places, during some times, for some young people.

Acknowledgements

While this chapter is individually authored it is based on the research and analysis of a wider team. Particular thanks go to the key fieldwork researchers – Paul Mason, Jane Marsh and Donald Simpson – and to Tracy Shildrick and Colin Webster for their insightful thinking on our shared questions, to the Economic and Social Research Council and Joseph Rowntree Foundation for funding and to the research participants.

Notes

1   For discussion of the methodological design and details of these studies: see Webster *et al.* (2004), MacDonald and Marsh (2005) and MacDonald *et al.* (2005). Names of neighbourhoods and interviewees are pseudonyms.

2   Other studies that operate with a less deterministic theory of criminal career and/or give a more *sociological* account of such careers include Sampson and Laub (1993), Laub and Sampson (2003) and Craine (1997).

3   See www.crimereduction.gov.uk/gpyc05.htm (accessed 21 October 2004).

4   Other publications provide a more detailed account. There is not the space here, for instance, to discuss the role of gender in shaping the forms, prevalence and content of criminal careers among our samples.

5   As did a very helpful, anonymous, critical reviewer of this chapter.

6   And this question is one that we are attempting to interrogate more closely in future analysis and writing.

7   Farrington and Painter's (2004) study of the siblings of the offenders in the Cambridge Study in Delinquent Development also raises queries. (Only) 44 per cent of brothers and 12 per cent of sisters had a conviction despite the fact – presumably – that these siblings shared many of the same risk factors as their offending brothers.

8   We are unable to say much about early childhood behaviours, personality types or the sort of parenting that interviewees had received. These risk factors *might* explain involvement in criminal careers among our sample. It is possible but unlikely, however, that the rate and form of youth offending in Teesside in the 1990s can be explained by a sudden change in local parenting styles or preponderance of antisocial personality types (Smith and McVie 2003).

9   For instance, when *non-offenders* were pushed about why they, as individuals, were *not* criminally inclined they reached for shorthand versions of underclass theory: 'bad' parents produced 'bad' children. This was sometimes despite the facts of their own family history (e.g. of siblings who had become embroiled in crime) and of their own, occasional offending. Stronger evidence against the 'bad parenting/bad parents' thesis is the fact those interviewees who *had* been involved in serious offending *also* described, remorsefully, their own parents' conventional morality and heroic, failed attempts to keep them on 'the straight and narrow'.

10 For instance, traumatic critical moments sometimes spurred desistance and caused people to reorient their lives. Lisa used to be 'in with a

crowd getting into trouble and doing drugs' until she was raped by one of them. Zack explained how 'the turning point' in his life was when 'my best mate hung 'imself'. He had since 'calmed down now' and given up 'all sorts of mad stuff'.

11 Webster (2005: 2) asks:

> Has political expediency and scientific attrition narrowed down risk factors to the family, parenting, truancy and peer groups because these individualised factors are amenable to early micro interventions, thus ignoring the more intractable influences of social exclusion and neighbourhood destabilisation resulting from social and economic change?

References

Armstrong, D. (2003) 'Pathways Into and Out of Crime: Risk, Resilience and Diversity', ESRC Research Priority Network conference, University of Sheffield.

Beck, U. (1992) *Risk Society*. London: Sage.

Beck, U., Giddens, A. and Lash, S. (eds) (1994) *Reflexive Modernization*. Cambridge: Polity Press.

Becker, H. (1963) *Outsiders*. Glencoe: Free Press.

Beinart, S., Anderson, B., Lee, S. and Utting, D. (2002) *Youth at Risk?* London: Communities that Care.

Berger, P. and Berger, B. (1972) *Sociology: A Biographical Approach*. New York: Basic Books.

Byrne, D. (1999) *Social Exclusion*. Milton Keynes: Open University Press.

Chamberlayne, P., Rustin, M. and Wengraf, T. (eds) (2002) *Biography and Social Exclusion in Europe*. Bristol: Policy Press.

Cohen, P. and Ainley, P. (2000) 'In the country of the blind? Youth studies and cultural studies in Britain', *Journal of Youth Studies*, 3: 79–95.

Coles, B. (1995) *Youth and Social Policy*. London: UCL Press.

Coles, B. (2000) *Joined Up Youth Research, Policy and Practice*. Leicester: Youth Work Press.

Craine, S. (1997) 'The Black Magic Roundabout', in R. MacDonald (ed.) *Youth, the 'Underclass' and Social Exclusion*. London: Routledge, pp. 130–52.

Crow, I., France, A., Hacking, S. and Hart, M. (2004) *Does Communities that Care Work?* York: Joseph Rowntree Foundation.

Dennis, N. (1993) *Rising Crime and the Dismembered Family*. London: Institute of Economic Affairs.

DETR (2000) *Index of Multiple Deprivation*. London: Department of the Environment, Transport and the Regions.

Du Bois-Reymond, M. (1998) '"I don't want to commit myself yet": Young people's life concepts', *Journal of Youth Studies*, 1: 63–80.

EGRIS (European Group for Integrated Social Research) (2001) 'Misleading trajectories', *Journal of Youth Studies*, 4: 101–18.

ESRC (2004) *Pathways Into and Out of Crime*. Sheffield: University of Sheffield.

Farrington, D. (1994) 'Human Development and Criminal Careers', in M. Maguire, R. Morgan and R. Reiner (eds) *Oxford Handbook of Criminology*. Oxford: Oxford University Press, pp. 511–584.

Farrington, D. (1996) *Understanding and Preventing Youth Crime*, Joseph Rowntree Foundation Social Policy Findings 93. York: Joseph Rowntree Foundation.

Farrington, D. and Painter, K. (2004) *Gender Differences in Offending*. Home Office Online Report 09/04. London: Home Office.

Foster, J. (2000) 'Social exclusion, crime and drugs', *Drugs: Education, Prevention and Policy*, 7(4): 317–30.

France, A. (2000) 'Towards a sociological understanding of youth and the risk-taking', *Journal of Youth Studies*, 3: 317–31.

Furlong, A. and Cartmel, F. (1997) *Young People and Social Change*. London: Open University Press.

Giddens, A. (1990) *The Consequences of Modernity*. Cambridge: Polity Press.

Giddens, A. (1991) *Modernity and Self-identity*. Cambridge: Polity Press.

Graham, J. and Bowling, B. (1995) *Young People and Crime*, Home Office Research Study 145. London: HMSO.

Hodkinson, P. and Sparkes, A. (1997) 'Careership: A sociological theory of career decision making', *British Journal of Sociology of Education*, 18: 29–44.

Home Office (2004) *Confident Communities in a Secure Britain*, CM 6287. London: Home Office.

Horsefield, A. (2003) 'Risk assessment: Who needs it?', *Probation Journal*, 50: 374–79.

Johnston, L., MacDonald, R., Mason, P., Ridley, L. and Webster, C. (2000) *Snakes & Ladders*. Bristol: Policy Press

Jones, G. (2002) *The Youth Divide*. York: Joseph Rowntree Foundation.

Laub J. and Sampson, R. (2003) *Shared Beginnings, Divergent Lives*. Cambridge, MA: Harvard University Press.

MacDonald, R. and Marsh, J. (2005) *Disconnected Youth? Growing Up in Britain's Poor Neighbourhoods*. Basingstoke: Palgrave.

MacDonald, R., Shildrick, T., Webster, C. and Simpson, D. (2005) 'Growing up in poor neighbourhoods: The significance of class and place in the extended transitions of "socially excluded" young adults', *Sociology*, 39(5): 873–91.

Merton, B. (1998) *Finding the Missing*. Leicester: Youth Work Press.

Mitchell R., Shaw, M. and Dorling, D. (2000) *Inequalities in Life and Death: What if Britain Were More Equal?* Bristol: Policy Press.

Mitchell, W., Bunton, R. and Green, E. (2004) *Young People, Risk and Leisure*. Basingstoke: Palgrave.

Muncie, J. (2004) *Youth and Crime*, 2nd edn. London: Sage.

Roberts, K. (2000) 'The Sociology of Youth: Problems, Priorities and Methods', British Sociological Association Youth Study Group Conference, University of Surrey, July.

Rutherford, A. (1992) *Growing Out of Crime: The New Era*. London: Waterside Press.

Sampson, R. and Laub, R. (1993) *Crime in the Making*. London: Harvard University Press.

Scott, J. and Chaudhary, C. (2003) *Beating the Odds*. Leicester: National Youth Agency.

Simpson, M. (2003) 'The relationship between drug use and crime', *International Journal of Drug Policy*, 14: 307–19.

Smith, D. and McVie, S. (2003) 'Theory and method in the Edinburgh Study of Youth Transitions and Crime', *British Journal of Criminology*, 43: 169–95.

Social Exclusion Unit (1997) *Tackling Truancy*. London: Social Exclusion Unit.

Stephen D. and Squires, P. (2003) 'Adults don't realize how sheltered they are', *Journal of Youth Studies*, 6: 145–64.

Thomson, R., Bell, R., Holland, J., Henderson, S., McGrellis, S. and Sharpe, S. (2002b) 'Critical moments: Choice, chance and opportunity in young people's narratives of transition', *Sociology*, 36: 335–54.

Webster, C. (2005) 'Predicting Criminal Careers Through Risk Assessment', British Society for Criminology Annual Conference, University of Leeds.

Webster, C., MacDonald, R. and Simpson, M. (2006) 'Predicting criminality? Risk factors, neighbourhood influence and desistance', *Youth Justice*, 6(1): 7–22.

Webster, C., Simpson, D., MacDonald, R., Abbas, A., Cieslik, M., Shildrick, T. and Simpson, M. (2004) *Poor Transitions*. Bristol: Policy Press.

Wikström, P-O. (n.d.) 'Individual Risk, Life-style Risk and Adolescent Offending', available online at www.scopic.ac.uk (retrieved 11 March 2004).

Young, J. (1999) *The Exclusive Society*. London: Sage.

Chapter 7

What mediates the macro-level effects of economic and social stress on crime?

Don Weatherburn and Bronwyn Lind

Abstract

Social disorganisation theorists maintain that structural variables, such as poverty, ethnic heterogeneity and geographic mobility, exert their effects on crime by reducing the level of informal social control or collective efficacy in a neighbourhood. There is a large body of individual level evidence, however, that suggests that structural variables exert their effects on offending by disrupting the parenting process (e.g. by reducing the level of parental supervision). The purpose of this chapter is to report the results of an aggregate-level study designed to investigate whether the aggregate-level effects of poverty, ethnic heterogeneity and geographic mobility on rates of juvenile participation in crime are produced by raising the level of child neglect in a neighbourhood. The results support this hypothesis. Possible limitations of the study are discussed and suggestions for more definitive research are put forward.

Introduction

Over the last 20 years there has been a resurgence of interest in social disorganisation theory, led in the main by Rob Sampson and his colleagues (e.g. Sampson and Groves 1989; Sampson and Lauritsen 1990; Sampson and Laub 1993; Sampson *et al.* 1997; Morenoff *et al.* 2001; Sampson 2002). Like Shaw and McKay (1969), these scholars argue that structural (or 'background') factors like poverty, geographic mobility, family dissolution and/or their ethnic heterogeneity, weaken a community's 'informal social controls', by which they mean:

> the capacity of a group to regulate its members according to desired principles – to realise collective, as opposed to forced, goals ... Examples of informal social control include the monitoring of spontaneous play groups among children, a willingness to intervene to prevent acts such as truancy and street-corner 'hanging' by teenage peer groups, and the confrontation of persons who are exploiting or disturbing public space. (Sampson *et al.* 1997: 918)

In recent times the hypothesised effects of these structural factors have been extended to include a reduction in what social disorganisation theorists refer to as 'collective efficacy'. By this term they mean:

> the differential ability of communities to extract resources and respond to cuts in public services (such as police patrols, fire stations, garbage collection, and housing code enforcement) looms large when we consider the known link between public signs of disorder (such as vacant housing, burned-out buildings, vandalism and litter) and more serious crime. (Sampson *et al.* 1997: 918)

The notion that the collective social acts of individual citizens play a key role in setting crime levels is quite beguiling but it is important to note that the re-emergence of social disorganisation theory has not come about as a result of its triumphs over any other competing theory of crime. In fact, most putative tests of social disorganisation theory make no attempt to compare its predictions with those of a rival theory in some domain where those predictions conflict. The dominant research strategy has simply been to see whether crime-prone communities are characterised by weak informal social controls (or low collective efficacy) and whether and to what extent measures of these controls 'mediate' (in a statistical sense) the effects of structural variables on crime. This is a weak test of social disorganisation theory because it leaves open the possibility that some other theory or set of theories can explain the same phenomena in different terms.

The aim of this chapter is threefold. First, we seek to argue that the apparent effect of structural variables like poverty, ethnic heterogeneity and geographic mobility on crime can be explained without recourse to concepts like informal social control or collective efficacy. In particular, we argue that there is a large body of evidence (including some gathered by Sampson and his colleagues) supporting the assumption that parenting factors mediate most if not all of the relationship between structural variables and juvenile participation in crime. Second, we seek to show that a model based on this assumption passes at least some of the same sorts of general tests that social disorganisation theory has been subjected to. Finally, we contrast the prevention policy implications of this model with those of social disorganisation theory.

The transmission mechanism(s) linking structural factors to crime

Twenty years ago Loeber and Stouthamer-Loeber (1986) published a review that revealed just how critical family factors are in the genesis of juvenile delinquency. They gave particular attention to variables associated with child neglect (e.g. parental rejection, poor parental supervision), which they said showed the strongest correlation with delinquency. Two years later, Laub and Sampson (1988) reanalysed data originally collected by Sheldon and Eleanor Glueck and found evidence that parenting variables mediated some 80 per cent of the effect of factors like family dissolution, unemployment, geographic mobility and household crowding on juvenile participation in crime. They concluded on the basis of this study that family factors mediate nearly all of the influence of background factors on juvenile delinquency.

For reasons we will come to shortly, Sampson subsequently abandoned this view. It is worth noting, however, that following the publication of Laub and Sampson's (1988) study, a large body of evidence began to accumulate supporting their conclusion. A large number of studies, for example, found a strong positive correlation between various measures of household poverty and the risk of child maltreatment (particularly child neglect), both at the aggregate and at the individual level (Young and Gately 1988; Garbarino and Kostelny 1992; Coulton and Pandey 1992; Coulton et al. 1995; Chaffin et al. 1996; Lempers et al. 1989; Silbereisen et al. 1990; McLoyd and Wilson 1990; Conger et al. 1992; Larzelere and Patterson 1990; Sampson and Laub 1994; Harris and Marmer 1996). Rates of neglect and abuse were found to be higher in areas with higher levels of geographical mobility and among disadvantaged minority groups, such as African and Mexican-Americans (Spearly and Lauderdale 1983; Garbarino and Kostelny 1992; Coulton and Pandey 1992; Krishnan and Morrison 1995; Coulton et al. 1995; Chaffin et al. 1996). Family dissolution and social isolation were also shown to be strong independent predictors of child maltreatment (Coohey 1996; Cotterell 1986; Young and Gately 1988; Creighton and Noyes 1989; Garbarino and Kostelny 1992; Coulton and Pandey 1992; Nelson et al. 1993; Pett et al. 1994; Kotch et al. 1995; Chaffin et al. 1996; Coulton et al. 1995; Zuravin and DiBlasio 1996).

Quite apart from this indirect evidence, a number of studies also actually managed to replicate the original findings by Laub and Sampson (1988). These included Lempers et al. (1989), Silbereisen et al. (1990), Larzelere and Patterson (1990) and, in Australia, Smart et al. (2003). The most compelling recent evidence that family factors mediate the effects of structural factors on juvenile involvement in crime has come from a study by Fergusson et al. (2004). Using data from 1,265 children in the Christchurch Health and Development Study, they examined the interrelationship between socio-economic status, parenting, peers and delinquency (measured through both self-reports and official records). Their analysis revealed that low socio-economic status was associated with higher rates of physical punishment and child abuse; reduced levels of maternal care; low attachment to parents; childhood adjustment problems; poor school performance and truancy; and association with delinquent peers. Importantly, the more of these factors Fergusson et al. controlled for in their analysis, the weaker the observed relationship between socio-economic status and involvement in crime. When all intervening variables were included in the analysis the relationship between socio-economic status and involvement in crime completely disappeared.

Sampson does not appear to have been persuaded by this evidence to adhere to the position he articulated in Laub and Sampson (1988) that family factors mediate all or most of the effect of structural variables on offending. Instead, he shifted to the view that background factors influence crime by reducing the level of 'informal social control' and 'collective efficacy' in a neighbourhood (Sampson et al. 1997). While these terms might be thought of as encompassing the effects of parental variables on delinquency, as can be seen from the quotations above, they encompass a great deal that cannot be characterised as parenting at all. They include acts on the part of individual citizens that have no effects on child development but instead limit the opportunities for offending or increase the risks (of detection and intervention) associated with it.

It is hard to understand why Sampson felt compelled to invoke 'informal social control' or 'collective efficacy' to explain the relationship between structural factors and crime. One might readily concede that neighbourhoods vary in the willingness of their residents to monitor and respond to nascent threats to law and order. There is, however, very little direct observational evidence that community or neighbourhood-level surveillance and intervention play a critical role in limiting the amount of crime that actually occurs. The only evidence we have which suggests that informal social control/collective efficacy are important comes from studies like Sampson *et al.* (1997), which find that the regression coefficients on structural variables predicting area crime rates are rendered weak or insignificant in the presence of controls for informal social control/collective efficacy. This is credible evidence only as long as one assumes that Sampson's measures of informal social control/collective efficacy are not acting as a proxy for some other unmeasured factor. What, though, if these analyses have omitted some important factor that is strongly correlated with collective efficacy/informal social control? In this case the variables measuring collective efficacy and/or informal social control will simply end up acting as proxy for the omitted factor (or factors).

This is an important point. There is, as we have seen, abundant evidence indicating that parenting variables mediate a large part of the association between structural factors and crime. It would not be surprising if these same variables also influence the extent to which residents in a neighbourhood bond with one another or act in concert to achieve shared goals (see, for example, Browning *et al.* 2005). Yet none of the studies purporting to show the importance of collective efficacy/informal social control include any direct measure of the quality of parenting in the neighbourhoods they examined. It is entirely possible, then, that what appears to be an effect of weak informal social control or collective efficacy, is actually a product of poor parenting (and therefore poor socialisation).

There is little point conducting yet another individual-level study showing that parenting variables mediate most if not all of the effects of structural variables on individual offending. That must surely by now be regarded as a settled issue. It could be argued, however, that the transmission mechanisms linking structural variables to aggregate rates of offending differ from those that link structural variables to individual offending behaviour. It is conceivable, for example, that factors like poverty weaken both parental and collective efficacy but that it is the latter which plays the dominant role in shaping rates of juvenile participation crime across a neighbourhood.

In the next section we explore this possibility by seeing whether the findings of individual-level studies examining the interrelationship between structural factors, parenting processes and juvenile involvement in crime can be replicated at the aggregate level. Our specific aim is to see whether most or all of the effects of poverty, ethnic heterogeneity and geographic mobility on rates of juvenile participation in crime disappear after we control for the level of child neglect in a neighbourhood. We focus on child neglect because Loeber and Stouthamer-Loeber (1986) found variables associated with neglect to be the strongest family-level correlates of juvenile involvement in crime. Our general strategy is to construct a series of regression models and compare the amount of variation in crime explained by a model including only a measure of child neglect, with the amount of variation in crime explained by a model that includes both child neglect and the structural variables, which, we maintain, influence rates of involvement in crime via their effect on rates of child neglect. Our expectation is that the structural variables in question will add little or no explanatory power to a model of juvenile involvement in crime once we have controlled for the parenting defects which mediate the effects of structural variables on crime.

Method

Since our focus is on the aggregate-level relationship between structural factors and juvenile participation in crime we need aggregate-level measures of all of our key variables. The spatial units of analysis for this study were the urban postcodes in New South Wales (NSW). Aggregate level measures of poverty, ethnic heterogeneity and geographic mobility for these units can be obtained from the 1991 Census. The key challenge is to find aggregate-level measures of child neglect and juvenile participation in crime.

We measure the prevalence of child neglect in a postcode via the percentage of children resident in the postcode who have been the subject of a report of neglect to the NSW Department of Community Services. It is sometimes suggested that the correlation between poverty and officially recorded rates of neglect reflects nothing more than a tendency on the part of authorities to subject those who live in poor areas to much greater surveillance than those who live in wealthy areas. There are two reasons for rejecting this 'surveillance' hypothesis. First, a large number of studies that rely on direct observation rather than official records to measure poor parenting have found a strong relationship between various measures of poor parenting (e.g. child rejection, child neglect, poor parental supervision) and family income (Elder *et al.* 1985; Lempers *et al.* 1989; Silbereisen *et al.* 1990; McLoyd and Wilson 1990; Larzelere and Patterson 1990). Second, if the 'surveillance' hypothesis were true, one would expect to find little or no correlation between the level of poverty and child neglect in areas that are all comparatively poor and which therefore presumably have to endure uniformly high (and constant) surveillance. As it turns out, there is a strong relationship between income and child neglect even within the lowest decile of the income distribution (Weatherburn and Lind 2001: 84).

We measure the prevalence of juvenile participation in crime via the percentage of juveniles who have appeared in court for a property or violent crime (data on which was obtained from the NSW Department of Juvenile Justice). As with neglect, questions are sometimes raised about the reliability of officially recorded delinquency as a measure of juvenile involvement in crime. Such concerns may have some validity where minor crime is concerned (Hindelang *et al.* 1979) but there is a strong correlation between self-reported and officially recorded offending where the offence in question is serious (Blumstein *et al.* 1986: 46). Nevertheless, as an added precaution we exclude court appearances for offences such as illicit drug use and public order, on the grounds that they may be influenced by policing policy and the way in which police in different postcodes choose to exercise their discretion. We also ignore multiple appearances by the same juvenile because we wish to explore the factors that influence juvenile participation in crime, not juvenile recidivism.

The variables included in the analysis, therefore, were as follows:

- *Neglect*: the number of children with at least one notification during the five-year period 1 July 1986 to 30 June 1991 for either neglect or emotional abuse (but not for physical or sexual abuse), divided by the number of 0–15 year olds resident in the postcode at the 1991 census.

- *Delinquency*: the number of juveniles with at least one court appearance during the five-year period 1 July 1990 to 30 June 1995 where the most serious offence was a property or violent offence, divided by the number of 10–17 year olds resident in the postcode at the 1991 census.

- *Poverty*: households with an annual income of less than A$16,000, as a proportion of all households at the 1991 census.

- *Geographic mobility*: families who had a different address five years earlier, as a proportion of all families at the 1991 census.

- *Ethnic heterogeneity*: persons who arrived in Australia less than five years previously, and who do not speak English well, as a proportion of all persons at the 1991 census.

It should be noted that the measures of neglect and delinquency were each based on a five-year period. Given the nature of the hypothesis being tested (i.e. that delinquency is caused by child neglect) the data for child neglect were deliberately drawn from an earlier time period than the data for delinquency.

To test the hypotheses we used multiple linear regression and path analysis. In the regression models parameters were estimated using weighted least squares because the response variable, delinquency, was in effect a proportion (and the variance of a proportion is dependent on the sample size on which it is based). Because the distribution of delinquency was skewed, with a long upper tail, it was normalised in the regression models by applying a logistic transformation, in which y was replaced by its logit function $\ln[y/(1-y)]$. Predictor variables were left untransformed in all regression models. Because we were analysing spatial data, we wanted to control for possible spatial autocorrelation because near-neighbour postcodes may be similar and therefore not independent of each other. Commonly used measures of spatial autocorrelation use the distance between spatial units. There is no readily available data on the distances between postcodes in New South Wales nor is there any readily available source of information indicating which pairs of postcodes share a border. We therefore constructed a measure of delinquency in the surrounding neighbourhood where 'neighbourhood' was defined to be all other postcodes falling within the same local government area(s) as the postcode of interest, that is, the neighbourhood consisted of bordering or near-neighbour postcodes. This measure of neighbourhood delinquency was used to control for spatial correlation in the regression models. In effect it is a measure of the causal influence of delinquent peers in nearby postcodes.

The adequacy of each fitted model was assessed in a number of ways. Variance inflation factors were calculated to check for multicollinearity. The normality of the residuals from each fitted model was checked by examining probability plots of the residuals. Finally, studentised residuals were examined to check for outliers. Generally, there were, at most, one or two outliers for any fitted regression model. No outliers were removed because the focus was on hypothesis testing rather than prediction and, for this purpose, the influence of one or two outliers was deemed to be negligible.

We used path analysis techniques to assess the causal influence of the structural variables. Path coefficients were estimated using the best linear predictor method, applied to untransformed standardised variables, as described by Kang and Seneta (1980). Using this method, no assumptions need be made about the variables in a path analysis other than that they are random (i.e. not controlled as in an experiment) and that the sample size is relatively large (so that large sample theory can be applied to use the sample correlation matrix as an estimate of the population correlation matrix). Because untransformed standardised variables are used in the regression models, the estimated path coefficients do not vary when there are changes in the units of measurement of the variables, and hence can be interpreted as absolute measures of direct causal influence.

Results

Correlations

We begin with a brief description of the data, then examine the pairwise correlations between variables and show the scatter plots of poverty, ethnic heterogeneity and geographic mobility, before moving on to the tests of hypotheses.

The rates of delinquency in the 262 NSW urban postcodes ranged from 6 per 1,000 juveniles to 232 per 1,000 juveniles, with an average of 45 per 1,000 juveniles. Ninety per cent of postcodes had rates below 80 per 1,000 juveniles. Poverty – the proportion of households with low income – ranged from 2 per cent of households to 56 per cent of households, with an average of 18 per cent. Geographic mobility – the proportion of families with a different address five years earlier – ranged from 19 per cent of families to 62 per cent of families, with an average of 35 per cent. Ethnic heterogeneity – the proportion of persons who are recent arrivals with poor English – ranged from 0 to 12 per cent of persons, with an average of 1 per cent.

Table 7.1 shows Pearson correlation coefficients for each pair of variables in our analysis. As the table shows delinquency is significantly correlated with poverty, geographic mobility and ethnic heterogeneity. Each of these structural variables is also significantly correlated with neglect.

Table 7.1 Pearson correlation coefficients for 262 urban postcodes, NSW

	Delinquency	Poverty	Geographic mobility	Ethnic heterogeneity	Neglect
Delinquency	1.00				
Poverty	0.64	1.00			
Geographic mobility	0.24	NS	1.00		
Ethnic heterogeneity	0.23	0.15	NS	1.00	
Neglect	0.80	0.60	0.17	0.14	1.00

Note: 'NS' indicates the correlation is not statistically significant ($p>0.05$)

Figures 7.1, 7.2 and 7.3 illustrate the correlations of delinquency with each of the structural variables. They show scatter plots of delinquency with each of poverty, geographic mobility and ethnic heterogeneity, respectively. In each of the figures the straight line is the software-generated line of best fit.

Regression models

Table 7.2 presents the results of fitting three separate models each with delinquency (actually the logistic transformation of delinquency) as the response variable. Each of the models includes the measure of neighbourhood delinquency as a predictor. Model 1 has neglect as

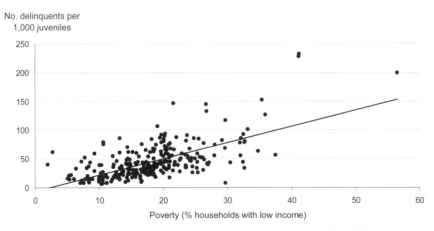

Figure 7.1 Delinquency and poverty in 262 urban postcodes, NSW

No. delinquents per
1,000 juveniles

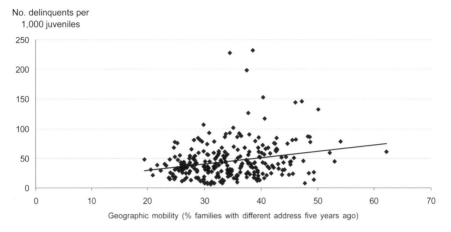

Figure 7.2 Delinquency and geographic mobility in 262 urban postcodes, NSW

No. delinquents per
1,000 juveniles

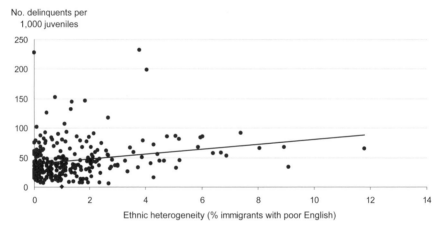

Figure 7.3 Delinquency and ethnic heterogeneity in 262 urban postcodes, NSW

the only other predictor. Model 2 has poverty, geographic mobility and ethnic heterogeneity as predictors. Model 3 includes the whole set of predictor variables.

Comparing the first two models in Table 7.2, it can be seen that in the presence of neighbourhood delinquency, the variation explained by neglect is substantially greater than the variation explained by poverty, geographic mobility and ethnic heterogeneity. When poverty, geographic mobility and ethnic heterogeneity are added to

Table 7.2 Regression models for delinquency

Term in model	Model 1 Parameter estimate	p	Model 2 Parameter estimate	p	Model 3 Parameter estimate	p
Intercept	−4.016	<0.0001	−4.550	<0.0001	−4.421	<0.0001
Neglect	0.014	<0.0001	−	−	0.013	<0.0001
Poverty	−	−	0.035	<0.0001	0.015	<0.0001
Geographic mobility	−	−	0.010	0.0323	0.007	0.0354
Ethnic heterogeneity	−	−	0.028	0.0188	0.037	<0.0001
Neighbourhood delinquency	11.024	<0.0001	11.907	<0.0001	8.326	<0.0001
R^2		0.65		0.43		0.71

the regression model, with neglect and neighbourhood delinquency, each of them is a significant predictor and the increase in explained variation is statistically significant ($F_{3,256}$ = 16.5, p<0.0001). However, the full model explains only an additional 6 percentage points more than the percentage of variation explained by the model containing neglect and neighbourhood delinquency alone. It is clear, then, that a substantial amount of the variation explained by poverty, geographic mobility and ethnic heterogeneity is accounted for by neglect.

Perhaps the best way to illustrate this point is to use path analysis techniques to assess the relative importance of the causal influences. Figure 7.4 shows the path diagram for posited causes of neglect and delinquency. The double-headed arrows between pairs of structural variables indicate their pairwise correlations (where statistically significant). The single-headed arrows show the causal relationships. The structural variables are assumed to be causes of both neglect and delinquency; neglect and neighbourhood delinquency are assumed to be additional causes of delinquency.

It can be seen that poverty is the strongest of the causal pathways for neglect with a path coefficient of 0.60. However, poverty has a much smaller causal influence on delinquency with a path coefficient of 0.22. Neglect has the strongest causal influence on delinquency with a path coefficient of 0.57, more than double that of any of the path coefficients for the structural variables. In short, the path analysis supports the hypothesis that most of the effects of poverty,

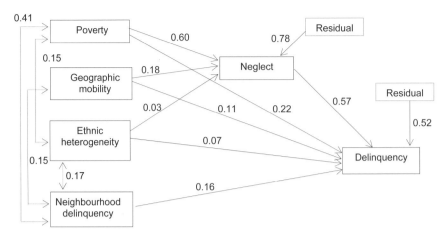

Figure 7.4 Path diagram for posited causes of neglect and delinquency

geographic mobility and ethnic heterogeneity on crime are mediated by parenting processes.

Discussion

Standard tests of social disorganisation theory find that the coefficients on structural variables predicting area crime rates are rendered weak or insignificant in the presence of controls for collective efficacy/ informal social control. This finding has been interpreted as evidence that the latter mediates the effects of the structural variables. The results obtained in the present study show that when a measure of child neglect (rather than informal social control or collective efficacy) is included in a regression equation linking poverty, ethnic heterogeneity and geographic mobility to crime, we see precisely the same effect: the coefficients of most of the structural variables diminish in magnitude and the variable measuring the level of child neglect ends up explaining much of the variation in juvenile participation in crime. Further, the path analysis shows that the measure of child neglect has the strongest causal influence on juvenile participation in crime. Our results mirror those obtained in earlier individual-level studies. This is the first time to our knowledge, however, that an aggregate level variable measuring parenting quality has been shown to mediate the effects of structural variables on crime.

These findings suggest that past research purporting to show the importance of informal social control and collective efficacy (e.g.

Sampson *et al.* 1997) is open to question. The apparent effect of informal social control/collective efficacy may in fact be attributable to defects in the quality of parenting children receive. Of course, as one of our anonymous reviewers pointed out, it would be open to defenders of social disorganisation theory to reverse this argument and contend that our measure of neglect plays a mediating role only because it is acting as a proxy for lack of informal social control or collective efficacy (which we have not measured). We acknowledge this possibility but it only serves to underscore our point that the theoretical implications of past research into the processes that mediate the relationship between structural variables and crime are open to debate. Theory testing is always more instructive when two theories are pitted against one another. If we really want to test the hypothesis that collective efficacy mediates the effect of structural variables on crime we ought to compare this hypothesis to one that implicates other mechanisms (e.g. parental efficacy).

This may be easier said than done. It is possible that poverty, geographic mobility, ethnic heterogeneity and poor parenting combine to produce both low levels of collective efficacy and, independently, high levels of crime. If this is true, parental and collective efficacy are always going to be strongly correlated even if the latter plays no significant role in generating crime. A more stringent test of the relative importance of collective as opposed to parental efficacy in preventing crime would seem to require direct evidence of their crime prevention effects. In this regard parental efficacy seems at present to be on a stronger footing. As we have seen, there is prospective, longitudinal evidence that increases in economic stress reduce the quality of parenting children receive. There is experimental evidence that improvements in the quality of parenting children receive can substantially reduce the risk of delinquency. On the other hand, while exponents of social disorganisation theory frequently cite illustrative examples of informal social control (e.g. supervising youth leisure activities, intervention in street corner congregation and challenging youths who seem to be 'up to no good'), there is no direct evidence that these kinds of behaviours occur at the right times, in the right locations or with enough frequency to influence the rate of participation in crime. Nor is there any experimental evidence that crime rates can be reduced through programmes that are designed to strengthen communities or enhance their capacity for informal social control (Welsh and Hoshi 2001).

It is worth noting, in conclusion, that the issues we have been discussing are relevant to policy as well as to criminological theory.

For while there are some similarities in the prevention policy implications of social disorganisation and (our expanded version of) developmental theory, there are also some interesting contrasts. Both theories imply that we can reduce rates of involvement in crime (over the longer term) by reducing the level of poverty among families with dependent children. Both theories also imply that efforts to strengthen community and neighbourhood social bonds should reduce crime, although developmental theory would suggest that the key imperative is to provide poor parents (or those grappling with problems like domestic violence, substance abuse, depression or social isolation) with additional sources of social support, while social disorganisation theory would suggest that the key imperative is to strengthen the capacity of communities to challenge nascent threats to law and order.

Critical differences between the theories in their prevention policy implications emerge at the micro-social level. According to social disorganisation theory, factors like poverty, family dissolution, ethnic heterogeneity and geographic mobility influence crime essentially because they create opportunities and incentives for offending that are not found in better resourced and more socially cohesive communities. The theory therefore provides intellectual support for policies and programmes that are directed at strengthening community ties (e.g. programmes designed to promote greater civic involvement in voluntary organisations and clubs), increasing the capacity of neighbourhoods to supervise the behaviour of young people at risk of involvement in crime (e.g. programmes designed to promote greater youth involvement in organised recreational activity) and/or empowering local communities to monitor and challenge nascent threats to law and order (e.g. neighbourhood watch).

There is nothing in developmental theory that provides a general justification (in terms of crime prevention) for programmes designed to strengthen the capacity of local communities to challenge nascent threats to law and order. If the expanded account of developmental theory we have given here is accepted, the micro-social focus should be upon measures that nullify or attenuate the corrosive effects of poverty, family dissolution, geographic mobility or ethnic heterogeneity on parenting. Such measures would include programmes and policies designed to reduce social isolation; strengthen the parent–child bond; provide practical and emotional support to parents (particularly in cases of family dissolution); and assist parents in the process of child-rearing. They would also include programmes designed to assist adolescents and teenagers overcome the social, educational or intellectual handicaps that economic and social disadvantage might have conferred.

Acknowledgements

We wish to thank our anonymous referees for their helpful comments on an earlier draft of this chapter.

References

Blumstein, A., Cohen, J., Roth, J.A. and Visher, C.A. (eds) (1986) *Criminal Careers and Career Criminals, Vol. 1.* Washington, DC: National Academy Press.

Browning, C.R., Leventhal, T. and Brooks-Gunn, J. (2005) 'Sexual initiation in early adolescence: The nexus of parental and community control', *American Sociological Review*, 70: 758–78.

Chaffin, M., Kelleher, K. and Hollenberg, J. (1996) 'Onset of physical abuse and neglect: Psychiatric, substance abuse, and social risk factors from prospective community data', *Child Abuse and Neglect*, 20: 191–203.

Conger, R.D., Conger, K.J., Elder, G.H., Lorenz, F.O., Simons, R.L. and Whitbeck, L.B. (1992) 'A family process model of economic hardship and adjustment of early adolescent boys', *Child Development*, 63: 526–41.

Coohey, C. (1996) 'Child maltreatment: Testing the social isolation hypothesis', *Child Abuse and Neglect*, 20: 241–54.

Cotterell, J.L. (1986) 'Work and community influences on the quality of child rearing', *Child Development*, 57: 362–74.

Coulton, C.J. and Pandey, S. (1992) 'Geographic concentration of poverty and risk to children in urban neighbourhoods', *American Behavioural Scientist*, 35: 238–57.

Coulton, C.J., Korbin, J. E., Su, M. and Chow, J. (1995) 'Community level factors and child maltreatment rates', *Child Development*, 66: 1262–76.

Creighton, S. and Noyes, P. (1989) *Child Abuse Trends in England and Wales 1983–1987.* London: NSPCC.

Elder, G.H. Jr, Van Nguyen, T. and Caspi, A. (1985) 'Linking family hardship to children's lives', *Child Development*, 56: 361–75.

Fergusson, D., Swain-Campbell, N. and Horwood, J. (2004) 'How does childhood economic disadvantage lead to crime?', *Journal of Child Psychology and Psychiatry*, 45: 956–66.

Garbarino, J. and Kostelny, K. (1992) 'Child maltreatment as a community problem', *Child Abuse and Neglect*, 16; 455–64.

Harris, K.M. and Marmer, J.K. (1996) 'Poverty, paternal involvement, and adolescent well-being', *Journal of Family Issues*, 17: 614–40.

Hindelang, M.J., Hirschi, T. and Weis, J.G. (1979) 'Correlates of delinquency: The illusion of discrepancy between self-report and official measures', *American Sociological Review*, 44: 995–1014.

Kang, K.M. and Seneta, E. (1980) 'Path Analysis: An Exposition', in P.R. Krishnaiah (ed.) *Developments in Statistics, Vol. 3*. New York: Academic Press, pp. 217–46.

Kotch, J.B., Browne, D.C., Ringwalt, C.L., Stewart, P.W., Ruina, E., Holt, K., Lowman, B. and Jung, J. (1995) 'Risk of child abuse or neglect in a cohort of low-income children', *Child Abuse and Neglect*, 19: 1115–30.

Krishnan, V. and Morrison, K.B. (1995) 'An ecological model of child maltreatment in a Canadian province', *Child Abuse and Neglect*, 19, 101–13.

Larzelere, R.E. and Patterson, G.R. (1990) 'Parental management: Mediator of the effect of socioeconomic status on early delinquency', *Criminology*, 28: 301–23.

Laub, J.H. and Sampson, R.J. (1988) 'Unravelling families and delinquency: A reanalysis of the Gluecks' Data', *Criminology*, 26, 355–80.

Lempers, J., Clark-Lempers, D. and Simons, R. (1989) 'Economic hardship, parenting and distress in adolescence', *Child Development*, 60: 25–49.

Loeber, R. and Stouthamer-Loeber, M. (1986) 'Family Factors as Correlates and Predictors of Juvenile Conduct Problems and Delinquency', in M. Tonry and N. Morris (eds) *Crime and Justice: An Annual Review of Research, Vol. 7*. Chicago: University of Chicago Press, pp. 29–149.

McLoyd, V.C. and Wilson, L. (1990) 'Maternal Behaviour, Social Support, and Economic Conditions as Predictors of Distress in Children', in V.C. McLoyd and C.A. Flanagan (eds) *Economic Stress: Effects on Family Life and Child Development*, New Directions for Child Development, Vol. 46. San Francisco: Jossey-Bass, pp. 49–70.

Morenoff, J.D., Sampson, R.J. and Raudenbush, S.W. (2001) 'Neighbourhood inequality, collective efficacy, and the spatial dynamics of urban violence', *Criminology*, 39: 517–60.

Nelson, K.E., Saunders, E.J. and Landsman, M.J. (1993) 'Chronic child neglect in perspective', *Social Work*, 38: 661–71.

Pett, M.A., Vaughan-Cole, B. and Wampold, B.E. (1994) 'Maternal employment and perceived stress: Their impact on children's adjustment and mother–child interaction in young divorced and married families', *Family Relations*, 43: 151–58.

Pratt, T.C. and Cullen, F.T. (2005) 'Assessing Macro-level Predictors and Theories of Crime: A Meta Analysis', in M. Tonry (ed.) *Crime and Justice, A Review of Research, Vol. 32*. Chicago: University of Chicago Press, pp. 373–441.

Sampson, R.J. (1985) 'Neighborhood and crime: The structural determinants of personal victimization', *Journal of Research in Crime and Delinquency*, 22: 7–40.

Sampson, R.J. (2002) 'Transcending tradition: New directions in community research, Chicago style – The American Society of Criminology 2001 Sutherland Address', *Criminology*, 40: 213–30.

Sampson, R.J. and Groves, W.B. (1989) 'Community structure and crime: Testing social-disorganization theory', *American Journal of Sociology*, 94: 774–802.

Sampson, R.J. and Lauritsen, J.L. (1990) 'Deviant lifestyles, proximity to crime, and the offender-victim link in personal violence', *Journal of Research in Crime and Delinquency*, 27: 110–39.

Sampson, R.J. and Laub, J.H. (1993) *Crime in the Making: Pathways and Turning Points Through Life*. Cambridge, MA: Harvard University Press.

Sampson, R.J. and Laub, J.H. (1994) 'Urban poverty and the family context of delinquency: A new look at structure and process in a classic study', *Child Development*, 65: 523–40.

Sampson, R.J., Raudenbush, S.W. and Earls, F. (1997) 'Neighbourhoods and violent crime: A multi-level study of collective efficacy', *Science*, 277: 15 August.

Shaw, C.R. and McKay, H.D. (1969) *Juvenile Delinquency and Urban Areas*. Chicago: University of Chicago Press.

Silbereisen, R.K., Walper, S. and Albrecht, H. (1990) 'Family Income Loss and Economic Hardship: Antecedents of Adolescents' Problem Behaviour', in V.C. McLoyd and C.A. Flanagan (eds) *Economic Stress: Effects on Family Life and Child Development*. New Directions for Child Development, Vol. 46. San Francisco: Jossey-Bass, pp. 27–47.

Smart, D., Vassallo, S., Sanson, A., Richardson, N., Dussuyer, I., McKendry, B., Toumbourou, J., Prior, M. and Oberklaid, F. (2003) *Patterns and Precursors of Adolescent Antisocial Behaviour*. Melbourne: Crime Prevention Victoria.

Spearly, J.L. and Lauderdale, M. (1983) 'Community characteristics and ethnicity in the prediction of child maltreatment rates', *Child Abuse and Neglect*, 7: 91–105.

Weatherburn, D. and Lind, B.L. (2001) *Delinquent-Prone Communities*. Cambridge University Press, London.

Welsh, B.C. and Hoshi, A. (2001) 'Communities and Crime Prevention', in L.W. Sherman, D.P. Farrington, B.C. Welsh and D.L. MacKenzie (eds) *Evidence-Based Crime Prevention*. London: Routledge, pp. 165–97.

Young, G. and Gately, T. (1988) 'Neighbourhood impoverishment and child maltreatment', *Journal of Family Issues*, 9: 240–54.

Zuravin, S.J. and DiBlasio, F.A. (1996) 'The correlates of child physical abuse and neglect by adolescent mothers', *Journal of Family Violence*, 11: 149–66.

Chapter 8

Repeat sexual victimisation among an offender sample: implications for pathways and prevention*

Paul Mazerolle, Margot Legosz, Elena Miceski and Jennifer Sanderson

Abstract

Among its many negative consequences, sexual victimisation has been shown to have links to juvenile offending behaviour, post-traumatic stress disorder, substance abuse, and negative mental health outcomes. While there is reason to expect a high degree of continuity in sexual victimisation across the life course, little is known about these experiences among an offender population. This chapter explores these issues using data from a larger study examining violence across the life course for adults serving community corrections orders (i.e. non-custodial) in Queensland, Australia. We find high levels of sexual victimisation in this group compared with community samples, especially among women, and a high degree of continuity from childhood to adulthood, especially for penetrative sexual victimisation. Logistic regression analyses controlling for a range of individual and lifestyle factors showed that child sexual abuse directly affected the risk of adult sexual victimisation; the relationship was not mediated through alcohol problems and relationships, although these and related factors, including drug abuse, remained salient predictors of sexual victimisation in their own right. The major implications for prevention are to reduce the incidence of childhood sexual victimisation and to address the mental health and lifestyle factors that increase the risks of re-victimisation as an adult.

The opinions expressed in this chapter are those of the authors and do not represent the official position of the Queensland Crime and Misconduct Commission.

Introduction

Research results consistently reveal a range of deleterious consequences associated with sexual victimisation. For example, individuals experiencing child sexual abuse have an increased chance of becoming delinquent (Siegel and Williams 2003), developing substance abuse problems (Grice *et al.* 1995), taking more sexual risks (Fergusson *et al.* 1997; Krahe *et al.* 1999), experiencing post-traumatic stress disorder (Arata 2002) and developing poor mental health outcomes (Janssen *et al.* 2004; Jumper 1995). These findings are consistent across samples and study contexts.

Among the most concerning aspects of sexual victimisation is the issue of repeat victimisation. Past research has indicated that previous victims of sexual abuse are at an increased risk of being re-victimised, and this observation appears to hold across college students, clinical and community-based samples, and in both retrospective and prospective studies (Gidycz *et al.* 1993; Fergusson *et al.* 1997; Messman and Long 1996). For example, the American National Violence Against Women Survey revealed that women who reported being raped as a child were twice as likely to report an adulthood rape as those who had not been raped during childhood (Tjaden and Thoennes 2000; see also Desai *et al.* 2002). Additionally, the Australian component of the International Violence Against Women Survey revealed that the risk of sexual violence in adulthood doubled for women who were abused as children (54 per cent versus 26 per cent) (Mouzos and Makkai 2004). In general, a range of studies uncover a strong relationship between childhood sexual victimisation and adult sexual victimisation, with an increased risk of between two and three times compared to non-prior victims (Gidycz *et al.* 1993; Fleming *et al.* 1999). Messman and Long's (1996) systematic review reveals that between 16 and 72 per cent of women who have experienced child sexual abuse are expected to be re-victimised in the future.

The observation about substantial continuity in sexual victimisation is consistent with research about other forms of criminal victimisation (Lauritsen and Quinet 1995; Wittebrood and Nieuwbeerta 2000). For example, research by Menard and Huizinga (2001) indicated that while the majority of individuals do not experience serious assault, those who do tend to be repeat, rather than one-time, victims. They reported, for example, that approximately 10 per cent of participants in the Denver Youth Survey accounted for over half of all violent victimisation events. These criminological research results, which reveal that previous victimisation is a robust predictor of future victimisation (Pease and Laycock 1996), can sometimes be explained by the presence of consistent or persistent risks, which can include either personal (e.g. low self-control) or lifestyle characteristics (Wittebrood and Nieuwbeerta 2000). Some of these characteristics may be amenable to early intervention and prevention efforts which may go some way towards reducing rates of repeat victimisation.

Despite observations that various forms of victimisation exhibit substantial continuity, there are unique concerns associated with repeat sexual victimisation. Repeat victims of sexual abuse are especially likely to experience heightened levels of anxiety, depression and hostility (Messman and Long 1996) due to the highly personal nature of their sexual victimisation experiences. To a large extent, the theoretical mechanisms required for understanding repeat sexual victimisation appear to be somewhat different from other forms of repeat victimisation. For example, several of the proposed mechanisms, largely drawn from learning theory (Bandura 1973: low self-esteem, learned helplessness, sexualised behaviours, poor relationship choices, etc.) do not easily apply to less personal forms of re-victimisation (Messman and Long 1996). An additional reason for suggesting that sexual re-victimisation is unique, compared to other forms of re-victimisation, involves the risk of intergenerational transmission of victimisation (McClosky and Bailey 2000). Although the findings are somewhat controversial, victims of sexual abuse may be at risk of perpetrating sexual offences in the future (White and Hall Smith 2004), thus increasing the risks for their own children and the chance that a 'cycle of victimisation' will persist across generations. Additionally, there is reason to expect that risks for sexual victimisation in certain environments may persist in some families over time, due to certain conditions, such as continuity in 'at-risk' lifestyle patterns involving drug abuse (McCloskey and Bailey 2000) or other persistent relationship dimensions (e.g. exposure to perpetrators in the extended family). Thus, for a range of theoretical as well as practical reasons, the issue of repeat sexual victimisation requires further empirical examination.

While past research into repeat sexual victimisation has been illuminating and has demonstrated a strong link between past and future victimisation, few studies have examined this issue in a sample of non-institutionalised offenders. This chapter examines the level of exposure to sexual victimisation across different points of the life course (e.g. adolescence and adulthood) for non-custodial offenders. Additionally, the level of repeat sexual victimisation and the characteristics associated with re-victimisation are examined.

The research literature

Research has consistently demonstrated that exposure to various forms of sexual victimisation is common in the general population. For example, James (1996) reviewed community studies in New Zealand, America and Canada and reported that between 10 and 38 per cent of women and 9 and 16 per cent of men have been victims of childhood sexual abuse. In Australia, Fleming's (1997: 66) random survey of 3,958 women found that 35 per cent reported some sexual abuse or sexual experience that was unwanted or distressing during childhood. Based on an Australia-wide randomised retrospective study, Dunne and colleagues (2002) report that 33.6 per cent of women and 15.9 per cent of men had experienced an unwanted childhood non-penetrative sexual act and that 12.2 per cent of women and 4.1 per cent of men had experienced an unwanted penetrative experience. Findings from the Australian Component of the International Violence Against Women Survey published by the Australian Institute of Criminology revealed that 16 per cent of women had reported sexual abuse by a non-parent and 2 per cent had been abused by a parent (Mouzos and Makkai 2004). The consistency of these findings across studies and locations supports the view that sexual victimisation is a common form of victimisation, especially for females.

Similarly, research into sexual re-victimisation finds relatively high levels of prevalence across studies. In a study of children and adolescents, Boney-McCoy and Finkelhor (1995) found that children who had previously experienced child sexual abuse were almost 12 times more likely to be re-victimised than children who had not been formerly victimised. Furthermore, a comprehensive study of 520 females by Fergusson *et al.* (1997) revealed that adolescents with a prior experience of child sexual abuse were three times more likely to have been sexually assaulted and five times more likely to experience rape or attempted rape between ages 16 and 18 than non-child sexual abuse victims. In studies of adults who have been sexually abused, the rates of sexual re-victimisation often exceed 60 per cent of cases (Desai *et al.* 2002; Randall and Haskell 1995; Russell, 1986; Sorenson *et al.* 1987). Overall, research reveals that rates of re-victimsation range between 16 and 72 per cent for women who have previously experienced child sexual abuse (cf. Messman and Long 1996; Sandberg *et al.* 1994).

Various factors associated with repeat sexual victimisation in adulthood have been identified. For example, child sexual abuse (Briere *et al.* 1997; Fergusson *et al.* 1997; Fleming *et al.* 1999) and adolescent sexual victimisation (Humphrey and White 2000) are strong risk factors for sexual victimisation in adulthood. The recency (Himelein 1995), frequency, length of exposure (Classen *et al.* 2005) and extent of invasiveness or severity of previous sexual abuse (Fergusson *et al.* 1997; Merrill *et al.* 1999) are also predictive of sexual re-victimisation.

Both direct and indirect linkages between child sexual abuse and adult re-victimisation have been identified. For example, Tyler *et al.* (2000) found direct links between victimisation and psychological and emotional problems among their sample of 361 homeless and runaway female adolescents, as well as indirect linkages consistent with a risk amplification model. The risk amplification process includes experiences such as running away from home, being exposed to deviant peers while homeless and engaging in survival sexual activity. Essentially, this interpretation lends support to the view that prior child sexual abuse fosters risky lifestyle circumstances that further increase or amplify the risks for sexual re-victimisation.

A number of studies on sexual re-victimisation reveal strong linkages to sexual health and sexualised behaviour, such as prostitution. A study by West and colleagues (2000), for example, found that re-victimised women reported higher involvement in intimate partner violence and prostitution than women who had been victims of child sexual abuse only. Furthermore, their study revealed that repeat victims reported diminished levels of sexual health, in that they experienced more sexually transmitted infections (STIs) and other infections. Sexual re-victimisation has also been found to be associated with other forms of sexual behaviours such as having more sexual partners (Krahe *et al.* 1999), having a higher likelihood of receiving treatment for STIs (Kalichman *et al.* 2001) and trading sex for financial resources (Kalichman *et al.* 2001).

The current study extends prior research on sexual re-victimisation by exploring the prevalence of victimisation and re-victimisation among a sample of offenders serving non-custodial supervision orders in Queensland, Australia. As a group, offenders are expected to have higher levels of exposure to sexual victimisation, re-victimisation and other forms of social dysfunction than community samples, although scant information is available on this issue for offender samples in Australia. The chapter also examines characteristics associated with repeat sexual victimisation and explores which characteristics mediate the relationship between past and future sexual victimisation.

Method

The data presented in this study are drawn from a larger project which examined the life experiences of people serving community corrections orders in Queensland, Australia. The Crime and Misconduct Commission undertook the project in co-operation with the Department of Corrective Services in Queensland. Offenders participated in a detailed face-to-face structured interview which focused on a range of experiences across the life course, including early life experiences such as education and family relationships, and later life experiences such as juvenile and adult offending, peer support, employment, substance abuse, physical and mental health problems and treatment and programme involvement. Information about sexual experiences, exposure to violence, victimisation, mental health, offending behaviour, and a range of demographic information was also collected by face-to-face interviews. Criminal history information was obtained from the Department of Corrective Services' records.

Participants

Participants were offenders serving intensive correction or probation orders through the Queensland Department of Corrective Services' (DCS) area offices between September 2003 and February 2004. Queensland covers an area roughly one fifth of the land size of the United States of America and seven times the size of the United Kingdom. It was therefore necessary to select a representative sample of 25 area offices covering urban and rural areas. Area offices were chosen that were geographically accessible, included a large number of offenders serving intensive correction and probation orders, or included a population with an over-representation of Indigenous offenders. Indigenous offenders were over-sampled to ensure that there were sufficient numbers to permit comparisons based on ethnicity.

Over the course of a one to two-week period, interviewers approached offenders attending area offices for a scheduled meeting with their community corrections supervisor and asked them to participate in the study.[1] As the larger study aimed to examine gender differences, towards the end of the data collection period it was necessary to over-sample female offenders to ensure that there would be a sufficient number to permit meaningful analysis. DCS community corrections supervisors were requested to schedule interview times with female offenders, subject to their agreement to be interviewed. Indigenous participants were also recruited in this way. All respondents were remunerated (A$20) for participating in the interview. The mean interview duration was 74 minutes and interviews generally took place in a private area associated with the community corrections offices.

A total of 562 offenders were approached to participate in the study. Of those approached, 82 offenders (14.6 per cent) refused to participate. No significant differences were found between participants and refusers on a range of demographic variables. In all, 480 offenders completed the interviews. The sample comprised 292 (60.8 per cent) males and 188 (39.2 per cent) females. Ninety-eight (20.4 per cent) participants identified themselves as Indigenous Australians. Participants ranged from 18 to 68 years of age (M=29.35, SD=9.48). Levels of education were low, with 276 (58.0 per cent) participants having left school at the end of Grade 10 or earlier. Levels of unemployment were high with 313 (65.2 per cent) participants unemployed or receiving benefits. Regarding previous offending, 213 participants (44.4 per cent) had no prior convictions in Queensland, 91 (19.0 per cent) had one prior conviction, 72 (15.0 per cent) had two prior convictions and 104 (21.6 per cent) had three or more prior convictions. Offending behaviour was widespread across the sample with approximately three-quarters of male and female respondents self-reporting prior involvement in violent and property crime in adulthood. Approximately half of all respondents reported involvement in drug related crime.

Measures

In the current analysis, various measures of sexual victimisation, mental health problems, drug and alcohol abuse, and relationship characteristics were used to examine key relationships.

Sexual abuse in childhood was measured with a scale used by Fleming (1997), first reported by Wyatt (1985). The scale asks respondents to respond to 12 questions that gauge their exposure to various types of unwanted sexual experiences during childhood (prior to age 16). The questions describe fairly graphic unwanted sexual experiences ranging from non-physical episodes ('someone exposed themselves to me'), to physical events ('someone rubbed their genitals against me'), and more extreme experiences of penetrative sexual victimisation ('someone had intercourse with me'). This measure has been used in several previous studies of childhood sexual abuse (Fleming *et al.* 1997).

Sexual victimisation in adulthood (since 16 years) was gauged by an 11-item measure developed by Koss and Gidycz (1985). As with the measure for childhood sexual abuse, the Koss and Gidycz scale seeks information about exposure to diverse forms of sexual victimisation experiences from non-physical to penetrative since the age of 16 years. In general, the experiences are directly comparable across childhood and adulthood.

Past research has found that sexual abuse victims may develop alcohol-related problems. In this study, patterns of alcohol use and problematic use were assessed by the Alcohol Use Disorders Identification Test (AUDIT) which was developed by the World Health Organisation (Babor *et al.* 1992; Conigrave *et al.* 1995). The AUDIT is a ten-item scale that establishes the prevalence of low, hazardous or harmful patterns of alcohol consumption. Responses to the ten items are added to obtain a total AUDIT score. In this analysis, higher scores reflect more harmful use. The AUDIT also uses different scoring for patterns of alcohol use for males and females. The established risk categories for female AUDIT scores are: low (1–6); hazardous (7–12); and harmful (13+). For males these are: low (1–7); hazardous (8–14); and harmful (15+).

Our study also included several questions about patterns of drug use and problematic drug use. Many of these questions were drawn from questions developed and used by the Australian Institute of Criminology as part of the Drug Use Monitoring in Australia (DUMA) data collection. An additional measure of drug use dependence, the Severity of Dependence Scale, was included. This five-item scale was first developed by Gossop and colleagues (1995) and includes questions that gauge respondents' perceptions about their drug use including their ability to stop use and whether they believed it was out of control ('Did you think your use of [named drug] was out of control?'; 'Did you worry about your use of [named drug]?'; 'Did you wish you could stop?'; 'How difficult did you find it to stop, or go without [named drug]?'; 'Did the prospect of missing a fix [or dose] make you anxious or worried?'). In the current study, the five-item scale had a Cronbach alpha reliability of .74.

For this study, we used measures of depression developed by Beck *et al.* (2000). The Beck Depression Inventory-Fast Screen (BDI-FS) is a brief inventory designed to evaluate current levels of depression. The BDI-FS is a seven-item scale measure that gauges feelings of sadness, discouragement, self-dislike, self-criticism, loss of pleasure, failure, suicide thoughts and wishes. Higher scores on the scale indicate higher levels of depression. Previous studies have found the BDI-FS to be a valid and reliable indictor of depression among high-risk samples, including samples of hospital patients (Beck *et al.* 2001; Benedict *et al.* 2003). In this sample, the Cronbach alpha reliability for the scale was .84.

A series of measures was included to gauge intimate partner relationship quality and satisfaction, as well as exposure to a series of 'at-risk' behaviours and lifestyle circumstances within the context of intimate partner relationships.

Sexual abuse may affect intimate partner relationships, including marital relationship satisfaction. Although speculative, prior victims may encounter more problems in developing meaningful intimate partner relationships, which may exacerbate risks for repeat sexual victimisation. In this study, relationship satisfaction was gauged by the Quality Marriage Index developed by Norton (1983). This six-item scale, which seeks to evaluate the marital relationship holistically, has been used extensively in prior research, and is highly reliable (Feeney 1996). The scale was recoded so that higher scores reflect higher levels of relationship quality and satisfaction. The Cronbach alpha reliability coefficient for the scale was 0.92.

A series of dichotomous measures was included to gauge a range of at-risk partnering behaviours. Prior exposure to child sexual abuse may influence intimate partnering experiences, in part through selective relationship choices. The domains measured in this study included whether a partner had been arrested or in prison; the number of previous serious relationships in which a partner had an alcohol problem; the number of previous serious relationships in which a partner had a drug problem; whether a partner's alcohol use caused problems in the home; whether a partner's alcohol use caused problems outside the home; whether a partner was violent while on alcohol; whether a partner was violent while on drugs; whether a partner's drug use caused problems inside the home; whether a partner's drug use caused problems outside the home; the number of previous physically abusive intimate partner relationships; and the number of previous emotionally abusive intimate partner relationships.

The present analysis also incorporates measures of control variables for age, gender and ethnicity (Indigenous status). Sex and ethnicity were coded as dichotomous variables. Males were coded as 0 and females as 1. Ethnicity was coded as non-Indigenous (0) or Indigenous Australian (1). Age was calculated in years.

Analysis

Information about the prevalence of exposure to child sexual abuse and adult sexual victimisation is presented and comparisons are made by gender where possible. The analysis also includes an examination of the levels of continuity of child and adult sexual victimisation. Finally, a series of logistic regression models is estimated to assess systemically the characteristics associated with adult sexual victimisation. In these models, the relationship between child sexual abuse and adult sexual victimisation are assessed to gauge stability in these relationships. In sum, the models examine whether, in a multivariate sense, prior child sexual victimisation increases the likelihood of adult sexual victimisation, and whether certain factors mediate this relationship. Thus, the analysis explores both direct and indirect relationships (e.g. via depression or relationship satisfaction) between prior and subsequent sexual victimisation.

Results

Levels of exposure to sexual abuse in childhood and adulthood

The level and type of exposure to sexual abuse during childhood by gender is described in Table 8.1. The overall prevalence of exposure to any form of unwanted sexual behaviour among the sample was 47 per cent. This exposure was generally significantly higher for females than males by a factor of 2 to 2.5. Further, the prevalence of exposure to child sexual abuse for this sample of offenders was consistently higher than that observed in other studies that have used the same instrument in community samples (Dunne *et al.* 2002).

The unwanted sexual behaviours referred to in the instrument are collated into three categories (non-physical, physical and penetrative behaviours) in Figure 8.1. Across all three categories, female respondents in the sample experienced higher levels of exposure than males, and the highest category of exposure was physical sexual victimisation, which was experienced by 52 per cent of the female respondents and 28 per cent of the males.

Information about the level and type of exposure to adult (since age 16) sexual victimisation for male and female respondents is shown in Table 8.2. The overall prevalence of exposure to any form of adult sexual victimisation for this sample was 54 per cent. The results shown in Table 8.2 demonstrate that exposure to sexual victimisation in adulthood, much like childhood, ranges across diverse types of

Table 8.1 Unwanted sexual experiences before the age of 16 by gender (n=480)

| | Per cent of sample | |
	Male	Female
Behaviour		
Someone:		
Exposed themselves to me	22	47***
Masturbated in front of me	13	22 *
Tried to sexually arouse me	22	38***
Touched/fondled my body	21	44***
Made me arouse them	16	30***
Rubbed their genitals against me	15	34***
Touched my genitals with their mouth	12	14
Made me touch their genitals with my mouth	9	19***
Tried to have intercourse with me	16	34***
Had intercourse with me	11	27***
Tried to have anal intercourse with me	9	6
Had anal intercourse with me	7	3

Note: *p < .05; ***p < .001
Source: Fleming (1997)

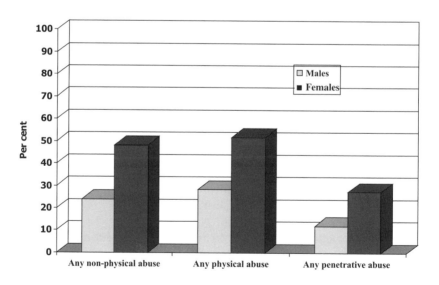

Figure 8.1 Non-physical, physical and penetrative child sexual abuse: comparisons by gender

experiences, such as having someone expose themselves (e.g. non-physical) to more extreme sexual assault behaviours. Females, as a group, experienced significantly more sexual victimisation across all types of victimisation experiences with the gender differences ranging from approximately 2 to 1 for the less invasive behaviours to 6 to 1 for penetrative abuse (i.e. had intercourse because of physical force). In sum, the findings reveal exposure to varied types of unwanted sexual behaviours as an adult as well as higher overall exposure, predominantly by females.

We now turn to the issue of continuity of exposure to sexual victimisation from childhood to adulthood.

Continuity in sexual victimisation

Past research has indicated that individuals who have experienced sexual victimisation are at risk of re-victimisation, yet many of these relationships have not been fully explored within an offender sample. That information is reported in Table 8.3 and Figure 8.2.

Table 8.2 Unwanted sexual experiences since the age of 16 by gender (n=480)

	Per cent of sample	
	Male	Female
Behaviour		
Someone exposed themselves to me	22	39***
Given into sex play when overwhelmed by arguments	15	36***
Given into sex play because of position/authority	6	11
Given into sex play because of force	5	24***
Given into sex play due to drugs/alcohol	18	36***
Experienced attempted intercourse with force	5	28***
Attempted intercourse when someone gave them drugs/alcohol	13	36***
Had sexual intercourse due to power/authority	5	11**
Had sexual intercourse because of drugs/alcohol	12	33***
Agreed to sex but felt used afterwards	21	49***
Had intercourse because of physical force	4	24***

Note: $*p < .05$; $**p < .01$; $*** p < .001$
Source: Koss and Gidycz (1985)

Table 8.3 reveals remarkable continuity in sexual victimisation experiences across childhood and adulthood for this sample. The information is presented across four categories of child sexual abuse experience: no child sexual abuse; non-physical sexual abuse only; physical sexual abuse only; and penetrative abuse. All comparisons in Table 8.3 are statistically significant, which means that prior experiences of child sexual abuse are statistically associated with adult sexual victimisation. The relationships are particularly strong for physical and penetrative child sexual abuse. Individuals experiencing more extreme forms of child sexual abuse reported much higher prevalence rates of adult sexual victimisation than non-child sexual abuse victims and those who had only experienced unwanted non-physical sexual behaviours as a child. These results strongly suggest that there is continuity between child sexual abuse and adult sexual victimisation.

Table 8.3 Relationships between child sexual victimisation and adult (since age 16) sexual victimisation

Behaviour	Severity of childhood sexual victimisation (% of all respondents)			
	No CSA	Non-physical	Physical	Penetrative
Someone exposed themselves to me	14	44	46	55
Given into sex play when overwhelmed by arguments	10	30	41	42
Given into sex play because of position/ authority	2	4	11	24
Given into sex play because of force	5	7	17	33
Given into sex play due to drugs/alcohol	11	22	45	49
Experienced attempted intercourse with force	5	11	27	31
Attempted intercourse when someone gave them drugs/alcohol	9	22	41	42
Had sexual intercourse due to power/authority	2	4	8	23
Had sexual intercourse because of drugs/ alcohol	8	19	37	41
Agreed to sex but felt used afterwards	15	37	52	67
Had intercourse because of physical force	4	11	17	31

Note: All comparisons, $p < .001$
Source: Koss and Gidycz (1985); Fleming (1997)

This observation is reinforced by the information provided in Figure 8.2, which shows that experiencing penetrative child sexual abuse is strongly associated with experiencing penetrative adult sexual victimisation. The information in Figure 8.2 is also consistent with the view that no exposure to child sexual abuse is strongly associated with not experiencing sexual victimisation in adulthood. In short, the results are consistent with continuity in extreme forms of sexual victimisation (i.e. penetrative) between childhood and adulthood, as well as continuity in not being exposed to sexual victimisation over time.

Levels of continuity in sexual victimisation in the sample are generally very high for both males and females. Among prior victims of child sexual abuse in this sample (n=210), 81 per cent reported some form of sexual victimisation in adulthood, which generally exceeds levels observed in other samples by previous research (Gidycz

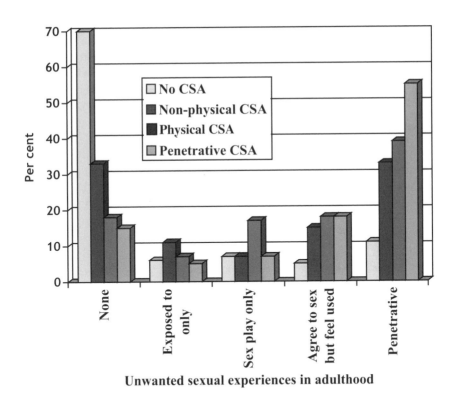

Figure 8.2 Continuity in sexual victimisation by type of abuse

et al. 1993). A high level of persistence in sexual revictimisation is observed for both males and females, but the rate is approximately 10 per cent higher for female respondents (85 per cent vs. 76 per cent). While females experience higher levels of revictimisation, it is important to note that the majority of male victims of child sexual abuse also reported experiencing some form of sexual victimisation in adulthood.[2]

We next present the results from a series of logistic regression models which examine whether the relationships between child sexual abuse and adult sexual victimisation are direct or mediated through other events or conditions.

Predictors of adult sexual victimisation: examining direct and indirect relationships

A series of logistic regression models predicting the prevalence of adult sexual victimisation are presented in Table 8.4. In all 10 models are presented which assess whether experiencing child sexual abuse has a direct influence on the likelihood of experiencing adult sexual victimisation, or whether the effects of child sexual abuse operate through other mediating influences such as depression or alcohol abuse. The models also assess whether other predictors of adult sexual victimisation (e.g. alcohol abuse) are salient, independent of the influences of child sexual abuse.

Regarding mediating influences, one would expect the effects of child sexual abuse on adult sexual victimisation to diminish if the influences were mediated through other processes such as depression, substance abuse problems, or relationships problems. Failure to observe such mediating effects would suggest that child sexual abuse can have a direct influence on adult sexual victimisation. Such an observation would lend support to the view that there is persistent heterogeneity, or stable and persistent risks for repeat victimisation, across individuals in the sample which do not vary over time. Such persistent influences can operate at the individual level (e.g. low self-control, drug addiction), but may also reflect persistent and unchanging risks in the environment (e.g. persistent poverty, a sexually abusive relative).

The results of the baseline model reported in Table 8.4 indicate that females have an increased likelihood of experiencing adult sexual victimisation over males. This finding is consistent with previous research. In model 2, the effects of child sexual abuse are considered, and the results reveal that experiencing child sexual abuse is highly predictive of experiencing adult sexual victimisation (Wald = 86.17). The results of models 3, 4, and 5 lead to a consistent conclusion: depression, alcohol dependence and relationship satisfaction are all salient predictors of adult sexual victimisation, net of the effects of child sexual abuse and demographic controls. In other words, being depressed and being alcohol dependent increases the likelihood of adult sex victimisation, as does having poor intimate partner relationship satisfaction. At the same time, child sexual abuse remains a salient predictor of adult sexual victimisation and is not reduced in any material sense by the other factors. In other words, there is little support for the view that the effects of child sexual abuse on adult sexual victimisation are mediated though depression, alcohol dependence or relationship quality/satisfaction.

Models 6 to 10 allow us to consider whether a series of specific relationship dynamics impact upon adult sexual abuse. The relationship dimensions considered are being exposed to partner violence in previous relationships and being exposed to partners with drug and/or alcohol problems.

The results of model 6, which considers the impact of having intimate partners who experience alcohol-related problems outside of home, over and above other predictors, reveal that child sexual abuse and relationship satisfaction remain salient predictors of adult sexual victimisation. Note that the influences of depression and alcohol dependence are no longer statistically significant which suggests some overlapping influences with this measure. It is interesting to note that while the effects of child sexual abuse are somewhat reduced (Wald = 50.79), it remains a very strong predictor of adult sexual victimisation.

The results of models 7 to 9 lead to some general observations. They reveal that: (a) partnering dimensions are salient and strong predictors of adult sexual victimisation; (b) the effects of depression, alcohol dependence and relationship satisfaction vary but remain salient; and (c) child sexual abuse continues to exert the strongest effects on predicting the likelihood of adult sexual victimisation. There is no evidence in these models of any mediating or indirect effects of child sexual abuse on adult sexual victimisation. Nor is there any influence of age or ethnicity. In sum, therefore, intimate relationship and partner dynamics appear to be independent influences increasing the likelihood of adult sexual victimisation. This suggests, to some extent, that various lifestyle characteristics enhance the risks of sexual victimisation in adulthood.

Table 8.4 Logistic regressions models predicting the likelihood of adult sexual victimisation

Variables	Model 1 B	Wald	Model 2 B	Wald	Model 3 B	Wald	Model 4 B	Wald	Model 5 B	Wald
Ethnicity	.07	.09	.12	.17	.15	.30	-.01	.01	-.04	.01
Age	.01	1.67	.01	.33	.01	.56	.01	.12	.01	.12
Gender	1.28*	38.21	.95*	16.28	.98*	16.45	1.07*	18.45	1.01*	15.48
Child sexual abuse			2.14*	86.17	2.04*	75.37	2.03*	71.11	2.07*	67.92
Depression					.88*	9.73	.72*	5.87	.71*	5.17
Alcohol dependent							.61*	5.18	.54*	3.76
Relationship satisfaction									-.31*	5.05
Constant	-2.20*	23.19	-1.36*	13.12	-1.59*	16.84	-1.611*	16.1	-.62	1.05
model χ^2(df)	43.62*(3)		142.42*(4)		148.38*(5)		149.05*(6)		149.55*(7)	
N=	456		452		445		431		414	

*Note: *p < .05 (two tailed)*

Table 8.4 *continued*

Variables	Model 6 B	Model 6 Wald	Model 7 B	Model 7 Wald	Model 8 B	Model 8 Wald	Model 9 B	Model 9 Wald	Model 10 B	Model 10 Wald
Ethnicity	.03	.01	-.19	.39	-.02	.01	-.11	.14	.29	.38
Age	.02	2.23	-.01	.01	.01	.03	.01	.05	.06*	5.42
Gender	.96*	8.89	.90*	11.94	.91*	12.27	.79*	8.74	.90*	4.65
Child sexual abuse	2.15*	50.79	2.14*	68.67	2.06*	64.24	2.08*	64.94	1.94*	24.87
Depression	.43	1.30	.60	3.52	.60*	3.60	.61*	3.60	.17	.14
Alcohol dependent	.41	1.63	.49	3.03	.57*	4.90	.55*	3.70	.48	1.38
Relationship satisfaction	-.39*	5.10	-.29*	4.25	-.30*	4.55	-.26	3.20	-.45*	3.99
Partner alcohol problems outside	.60	2.23	—	—	—	—	—	—		
#Relationships with alcohol problems			.91*	6.40	—	—	—	—	.68	1.76
#Relationships with drug problems					.94*	9.12	—	—		
DV in previous relationships							.88*	12.37		
Drug dependence									-.74	2.43
Constant	-.88	.74	-.55	.82	-.72	1.34	-1.10	3.05	-1.34	1.87
Model χ²(df)	125.75*(8)		151.37*(8)		154.92*(8)		161.25*(8)		77.07*(9)	
N=	313		406		406		411		196	

Note: *p < .05 (two tailed)

The final model, reported in model 10, tests whether becoming dependent on illicit drugs increases sexual victimisation in adulthood net of other influences and/or mediates the effects of child sexual abuse. The measure for drug dependence is based on the severity of dependence score (SDS), and a dichotomous measure was created with the drug-dependent respondents being coded as 1. Note that because of missing data the sample was reduced by over 50 per cent when this variable was included. This means that some caution should be exercised in interpreting the results.

Model 10 suggests that becoming drug dependent mediates to a reasonably large extent the effects of child sexual abuse on adult sexual victimisation. Although child sexual abuse still remains a significant predictor in the model, its predictive power is greatly reduced. While being drug dependent is not predictive of adult sexual victimisation, it appears to mediate or incorporate the effects of other variables including depression, alcohol dependence and some relationship dimensions, although relationship satisfaction still remains a salient predictor. Note also that age is statistically significant in model 10, suggesting that older respondents are more likely to experience adult sexual victimisation than younger respondents. This finding is unexpected based on the previous nine models and suggests that age and being drug dependent are linked empirically in the model.

In general, the results for model 10 suggest that becoming drug dependent is a salient outcome of child sexual abuse (although the bivariate correlation is modest) which reduces its impact on adult sexual victimisation. A similar process was expected for some other variables in the model (e.g. depression). Overall, however, child sexual abuse and intimate relationship satisfaction remained the salient predicators of adult sexual victimisation. While the effects of child sexual abuse are somewhat mediated, it still remains a robust and direct influence on adult sexual victimisation.

Discussion

This study explored, on several levels, the issue of repeat sexual victimisation among a sample of offenders serving community correction orders in Queensland, Australia. Several interesting findings were observed. First, exposure to sexual victimisation was examined. High levels of exposure compared to community samples were demonstrated and females were shown to have a higher prevalence of exposure to varied forms of sexual victimisation than males. The study also explored continuity in experiences between child and adult sexual victimisation. A high degree of continuity was demonstrated, in particular for penetrative sexual victimisation. The results reveal that for both male and female offenders who are victims of child sexual abuse, the majority will experience revictimisation in adulthood.

The study also estimated a series of logistic regression models to identify the predictors of adult sexual victimisation, and to assess whether child sexual abuse had a direct or indirect relationship with adult sexual victimisation via various factors (e.g. depression). The results suggested that females have an increased likelihood of being adult victims of sexual abuse, and that child sexual abuse experiences have, by far, the strongest impact on the likelihood of adult sexual abuse. Additionally, the results revealed that depression, alcohol problems and poor relationship satisfaction all increased the likelihood of adult sexual victimisation, but did not act as mediating influences. In short, child sexual abuse appeared to affect directly the risk of adult sexual victimisation, and did not operate through its effects on depression, alcohol problems and relationship dissatisfaction.

Further models revealed that relationship and partnering dimensions, including partnering with individuals with drug and alcohol problems and experiencing previous partner violence, are salient predictors of adult sexual victimisation. At the same time, these influences, while salient situational predictors of sexual victimisation in adulthood, do not mediate the effects of child sexual abuse. However, in a final model in which a measure of drug dependence was included, the impact of child sexual abuse was reduced substantially, although it remained the most salient predictor.[3] In this final model, the effects of depression and alcohol problems were also reduced, which suggests that some of the consequences of child sexual abuse may be manifesting themselves in drug problems, at least in this sample.

These results have implications for criminological research and theory development with respect to pathways towards victimisation as well as preventive opportunities across the life course. Regarding theory, the results suggest that the model of cascading influences of victimisation, which are expected to be consequential in heightening the risks for further victimisation, is not correct. In short, state-dependent or experiential effects were not shown to be important in furthering victimisation in this population. In contrast, the results are generally consistent with the persistent heterogeneity view that stable characteristics across individuals (or environments) consistently influence victimisation risks. Persistent risks across individuals may relate to individual characteristics such as low self-control, but also to persistent risks in the environment (e.g. drug-using behaviour, intra-familial risks).

Regarding preventative opportunities, the results indicated a mixed set of options. Clearly, they suggest that continuity in sexual victimisation is very high, at least for this high-risk population of offenders. Thus, in practical terms, there is some urgency associated with the need to minimise exposure to any form of sexual abuse in this population. As a consequence, interventions should be especially directed towards at-risk families where exposure to sexual abuse is prevalent. This approach should foster the provision of proactive educational assistance as well as other forms of preventative support to minimise the harms associated with sexual victimisation, reduce the risks of revictimisation, and the risks for the children of parents who have previously been exposed to sexual abuse. An array of comparisons (not shown) consistently identified that persistent victims experienced the most problems and risks. Thus, there are useful preventative investments to be made in targeting interventions at specific risks and needs. However, the problems among this group of enduring victims can be formidable and overlapping (e.g. drug and alcohol abuse, depression). Addressing this co-morbidity remains a challenge for practitioners.

Research on offending pathways is useful for understanding criminal offending and for illuminating the need for age-appropriate interventions to reduce criminal behaviour (Piquero and Mazerolle 2001). Embracing a pathways model is also useful for understanding the nature of sexual revictimisation. Such an approach allows researchers to consider direct and indirect relationships between past and future sexual victimisation and provides a framework for examining how past victimisation experiences amplify and shape future victimisation risks.

The current study is one of the few to examine repeat sexual victimisation amongst an offender sample. The findings indicate that both direct and indirect, proximate paths to adult sexual victimisation operate. On the one hand, child sexual abuse directly increases the risk of sexual revictimisation in adulthood. These persistent risks stem from the enduring characteristics of individual victims as well as enduring risks in the environment, such as persistent poverty, or persistent exposure to extra-familial risks. On the other hand, many of the more indirect or proximate mechanisms relate to intimate partner characteristics such as the effects of domestic violence, relationship turnover and drug and alcohol abuse. While prior child sexual victimisation may influence pathways towards poor or risky intimate partner choices, the situational dynamics of risky intimate partner characteristics appear to accentuate the risks for sexual victimisation in adulthood. In the current study, the consequences of poor relationship experiences were especially magnified for females.

While it is acknowledged that there are limitations to this study[4] and that the results need to be qualified, the fact that the study was conducted on an at-risk sample of offenders and still revealed consistent and theoretically expected findings suggests that observations are valid. Studies of repeat victimisation are under-represented among offender-based populations and this study seeks to extend knowledge in this area. At the same time, the study raises important opportunities for future research into pathways of victimisation, not the least of which involves examining how persistent victims engage with the criminal justice system and how their experiences shape future victimisation risks and criminal activities. Further research is also required into understanding the intimate partner relationship dynamics of persistent victims of sexual abuse, as well as how extra-familial and neighbourhood risks influence the intergenerational transmission of risks for sexual victimisation. Thus, future research in this area is sure to reveal information of theoretical as well as practical relevance in relation to understanding sexual victimisation across the life course and minimising the associated negative consequences.

Notes

1 Although each area office serviced a reasonably large catchment area, the actual number of offenders physically attending area offices was lower than originally expected due to unexpected cancellations and some instances of telephone reporting.
2 Recall that the measure for sexual victimisation being used in this analysis is a global measure that includes non-physical, physical and penetrative experiences. Different degrees of stability and gender comparisons could be observed when considering sub-types of sexual victimisation (e.g. penetrative).
3 Note that there was a substantial amount of missing data in this final model which could have affected the reliability of the estimates.
4 For example, the cross-sectional sampling design will have an effect on the temporal ordering of key variables, some measures are reliant on recall, and so on.

References

Arata, C.M. (2002). 'Child sexual abuse and sexual revictimization', *Clinical Psychology: Science and Practice*, 9: 135–64.

Babor, T.F., De La Fuente, J.R., Saunders, J. and Grant, M. (1992) *AUDIT – The Alcohol Use Disorders Identification Test: Guidelines for Use in Primary Health Care*. Geneva: World Health Organisation.

Bandura, A. (1973) *Aggression: A Social Learning Analysis*. Englewood Cliffs, NJ: Prentice-Hall.

Beck, A.T., Brown, G.K., Steer, R.A., Kuyken, W. and Grisham, J. (2001) 'Psychometric properties of the Beck Self-Esteem Scales', *Behaviour Research and Therapy*, 29: 115–24.

Beck, A.T., Steer, R.A. and Brown, G.K. (2000) *BDI-Fast Screen for Medical Patients Manual*. San Antonio: Psychological Corporation.

Benedict, R.H.B., Fishman, I., McClellan, M.M., Bakshi, R., and Weinstock-Guttman, B. (2003) 'Validity of the Beck Depression Inventory-Fast Screen in multiple sclerosis', *Multiple Sclerosis*, 9: 393–6.

Boney-McCoy, S. and Finkelhor, D. (1995) 'Prior victimization: A risk factor for child sexual abuse and for PTSD-related symptomatology among sexually abused youth', *Child Abuse and Neglect* 19: 1401–421.

Briere, J., Woo, R., McRae, B., Foltz, J. and Sitzman, R. (1997) 'Lifetime victimization history, demographics and clinical status in female psychiatric emergency room patients', *Journal of Nervous and Mental Disease*, 185: 95–101.

Classen, C.C., Palesh, O.G. and Aggarwal, R. (2005) 'Sexual revictimization: A review of the empirical literature,' *Trauma, Violence and Abuse*, 6(2): 103–29.

Conigrave, K.M., Hall, W.D. and Saunders, J.B. (1995) 'The AUDIT questionnaire: Choosing a cut-off score', *Addiction*, 90: 1349–56.

Desai, S., Arias, I., Thompson, M.P., and Basile, K.C. (2002). 'Childhood victimization and subsequent adult revictimization assessed in a nationally representative sample of women and men', *Violence and Victims*, 17(6): 639–53.

Dunne, M.P., Purdie, D.M., Cook, M.D., Boyle, F.M. and Najman, J.M. (2002) 'Is child sexual abuse declining? Evidence from a population based survey of men and women in Australia', *Child Abuse and Neglect*, 27(2): 141–52.

Feeney, J. (1996) 'Attachment, care giving, and marital satisfaction', *Personal Relationships*, 3: 401–16.

Fergusson, D.M., Horwood, L.J. and Lynskey, M.T. (1997) 'Childhood sexual abuse, adolescent sexual behaviours, and sexual revictimization', *Child Abuse and Neglect*, 21(8): 789–803.

Fleming, J. (1997) 'Prevalence of childhood sexual abuse in a community sample', *The Medical Journal of Australia*, 166: 65–8.

Fleming, J., Mullen, P. and Bammer, G. (1997) 'A study of potential risk factors for sexual abuse in childhood', *Child Abuse and Neglect*, 21: 49–58.

Fleming, J., Mullen, P., Sibthorpe, B. and Bammer, G. (1999) 'The long-term impact of childhood sexual abuse in Australian women', *Child Abuse and Neglect*, 23: 145–59.

Gidycz, C.A., Coble, C.N., Latham, L. and Layman, M.J. (1993) 'Sexual assault experience in adulthood and prior victimization experiences: A prospective analysis', *Psychology of Women Quarterly*, 17: 151–68.

Gossop, M., Darke, S., Griffiths, P., Hando, J., Powis, B., Hall, W. and Strang, J. (1995) 'The severity of dependence scale (SDS): Psychometric properties of the SDS in English and Australian samples of heroin, cocaine and amphetamine users', *Addiction*, 90: 607–14.

Grice, D.E., Brady, K.T., Dustan, L.R., Malcolm, M. and Kilpatrick, D.G. (1995) 'Sexual and physical assault history and posttraumatic stress disorder in substance dependent individuals', *American Journal on Addictions*, 4: 297–305.

Himelein, M.J. (1995) 'Risk factors for sexual victimization in dating: A longitudinal study of college women', *Psychology of Women Quarterly*, 19: 31–48.

Humphrey, J.A. and White, J.W. (2000) 'Women's vulnerability to sexual assault from adolescence to young adulthood', *Journal of Adolescent Health*, 27: 419–24.

James, M. (1996) *Paedophilia, Trends and Issues in Crime and Criminal Justice*, Vol. 57. Canberra: Australian Institute of Criminology.

Janssen, I., Krabbendam, L., Bak, M., Hanseen, M., Vollebergh, W., de Graaf, R. and Van Os, J. (2004) 'Childhood abuse as a risk factor for psychotic experiences', *Acta Physiologica Scandinavia*, 109(1): 38–45.

Jumper, S.A. (1995) 'A meta-analysis of the relationship of child sexual abuse to adult psychological adjustment', *Child Abuse and Neglect*, 19(6): 715–28.

Kalichman, S.C., Benotsch, E., Rompa, D., Gore-Felton, C. Austin, J., Luke, W., DiFronzo, K., Buckles, J., Kyomugisha, F. and Simpson, D. (2001) 'Unwanted sexual experiences and sexual risks in gay and bisexual men: Associations among re-victimization, substance use, and psychiatric symptoms', *Journal of Sex Research*, 38: 1–9.

Koss, M.P. and Gidycz, C.A. (1985) 'Sexual experiences survey: Reliability and validity', *Journal of Consulting and Clinical Psychology*, 53(3): 422–3.

Krahe, B., Scheinberger-Olwig, R., Waizenhofer, E. and Kolpin, S. (1999) 'Childhood sexual abuse and re-victimization in adolescence', *Child Abuse and Neglect*, 23(4): 383–94.

Lauritsen, J.L. and Quinet, K.F.D. (1995) 'Repeat victimization among adolescents and young adults', *Journal of Quantitative Criminology*, 11(2): 143–65.

McCloskey, L.A. and Bailey, J.A. (2000) 'The intergenerational transmission of risk for child sexual abuse', *Journal of Interpersonal Violence*, 15(10): 1019–35.

Menard, S. and Huizinga, D. (2001) 'Repeat victimization in a high-risk sample of adolescents', *Youth and Society*, 32(4): 447–72.

Merrill, L.L., Newell, C.E., Thomsen, C.J., Gold, S.R., Milner, J.S., Koss, M.P. and Rosswork, S.G. (1999) 'Childhood abuse and sexual revictimization in a female navy recruit sample', *Journal of Traumatic Stress*, 12: 211–25.

Messman, T.L. and Long, P. J. (1996) 'Child sexual abuse and its relationship to re-victimization in adult women: A review', *Clinical Psychology Review*, 16(5): 397–420.

Mouzos, J. and Makkai, T. (2004) *Women's Experiences of Male Violence: Findings from the Australian Component of the International Violence Against Women Survey (IVAWS)*, Research and Public Policy Series No 56. Canberra: Australian Institute of Criminology.

Norton, R. (1983) 'Measuring marriage quality: A critical look at the dependent variable', *Journal of Marriage and the Family*, 45: 141–51.

Pease, K. and Laycock, G. (1996) *Revictimization: Reducing the Heat on Hot Victims*, NIJ Research in Action Series. Washington, DC: National Institute of Justice.

Piquero, A. and Mazerolle, P. (2001) *Crime Over the Lifecourse: Contemporary Readings*. Belmont, CA: Wadsworth.

Randall, M. and Haskell, L. (1995) 'Sexual violence in women's lives: Findings from the Women's Safety Project, a community-based survey', *Violence Against Women*, 1: 6–31.

Russell, D. (1986) *The Secret Trauma: Incest in the Lives of Girls and Women*. New York: Basic Books.

Sandberg, D., Lynn, S.J. and Green, J.P. (1994) 'Sexual Abuse and Re-victimization: Mastery, Dysfunctional Learning and Dissociation', in S.J. Lynn and J.W. Rhue (eds) *Dissociation: Clinical and Theoretical Perspectives* New York: Guilford Press, pp. 243–67.

Siegel, J.A. and Williams, L.M. (2003) 'The relationship between child sexual abuse and female delinquency and crime: A prospective study', *Journal of Research in Crime and Delinquency*, 40(1): 71–94.

Sorenson, S.B., Stein, J.A., Siegel, J.M., Golding, J.M. and Burnam, M.A. (1987) 'The prevalence of adult sexual assault: The Los Angeles Epidemiologic Catchment Area Project', *American Journal of Epidemiology*, 126: 1154–64.

Tjaden, P. and Thoennes, N. (2000) *Full Report of the Prevalence, Incidence, and Consequences of Violence against Women: Findings from the National Violence against Women Survey.* Washington, DC: US Department of Justice.

Tyler, K., Hoyt, D. and Whitbeck, L. (2000) 'The effects of early sexual abuse on later sexual victimization among female homeless and runaway adolescents', *Journal of Interpersonal Violence*, 15(3): 235–50.

West, C., Williams, L. and Seigel, J.A. (2000) 'Adult sexual re-victimization among black women sexually abused in childhood: A prospective examination of serious consequences of abuse', *Child Maltreatment*, 5(1): 49–57.

White, J. and Hall Smith, P. (2004) 'Sexual assault perpetration and re-perpetration: From adolescence to young adulthood', *Criminal Justice and Behavior*, 31(2): 182–202.

Wittebrood, K. and Nieuwbeerta, P. (2000) 'Criminal victimisation during one's life-course: The effects of previous victimisation and patterns of routine activities', *Journal of Research in Crime and Delinquency*, 37(1): 91–122.

Wyatt, G.E. (1985) 'The sexual abuse of Afro-American and White American women in childhood', *Child Abuse and Neglect*, 9: 507–19.

Chapter 9

A life-course perspective on bullying

Jacqueline Homel

Abstract

Much remains to be learned about the long-term trajectories of bullying behaviour and the consequences of school bullying experiences in later life. This chapter shows how a life course developmental perspective provides a useful framework for exploring continuity and discontinuity in bullying from childhood to young adulthood, and across different social and institutional contexts. It is argued that bullying is the result of complex interactions between individual, social and contextual resources. These interactions become particularly important at times of developmental transition, when young people are required to negotiate challenges presented by new social and institutional contexts. The way in which individual, social and contextual resources help or hinder these negotiations play a significant role in determining whether people continue to form relationships characterised by bullying and victimisation, or are able to break away from negative patterns of interaction. The chapter concludes with a discussion of the implications of a life-course perspective for prevention of bullying.

Introduction

A considerable amount of research has documented the nature of bullying in primary and high schools, the characteristics of children involved, and the short-term health and behavioural outcomes of being a bully or being a victim. This research accompanies an increasing concern in schools, the media and among parents regarding the damaging effect of bullying and the best ways of handling the problem. Less is known, however, about whether school bullying has long-term effects in late adolescence and young adulthood, and whether it continues once people leave school. For example, are bullied children more likely to develop mental health problems later in life? Do bullies continue to exhibit antisocial behaviour after they leave school? This paper argues that placing bullying and victimisation within a life-course developmental framework is a meaningful way to approach these issues. This is because the life-course developmental perspective provides conceptual tools for linking individual behaviours, characteristics, experiences and social contexts to investigate continuity and discontinuity in bullying and victimisation across the life-span. The argument is illustrated with excerpts from a series of focus groups with young adults about bullying and victimisation that were conducted as part of a larger longitudinal study of bullying.[1]

This chapter falls into five sections. First, I set the stage with a description of the nature of bullying in different contexts. Second, I raise the issue of continuity and discontinuity in bullying and consider how a life-course perspective on bullying might address some of the major questions facing the bullying research field. The remainder of the chapter is devoted to discussion of how to make links between contextual factors and individual factors to understand continuity of bullying behaviour across people, time and settings. The third section suggests some ways in which contextual factors contribute to continuity of bullying behaviour and experience, while the fourth section discusses how developmental transitions facilitate continuity. The concluding section contains a discussion of the implications of this analysis for prevention of bullying.

Settings: school, workplace and home

Bullying and peer victimisation in schools has been the focus of systematic investigation for over 30 years. Beginning in the 1970s with Dan Olweus' (1993) seminal Scandinavian research, the field has expanded to thousands of studies conducted in several countries, including the United Kingdom, Italy, Spain, Japan, the United States and Australia (Ahmed and Braithwaite 2004; Kochenderfer-Ladd 2004; Owens *et al.* 2005; Rigby 1996; Schäfer *et al.* 2005; Slee 1995;

Smith 2004; Smith *et al.* 2004). Most bullying research has been cross-sectional in nature (Hawker and Boulton 2000), investigating the individual characteristics of children who bully and children who are victims, and the contemporaneous effects of victimisation. Rigby (2002, 2003) reviews longitudinal work.

As the focus group findings reported in this chapter were conducted in Australia, this chapter draws on research conducted in Western Europe, Australia and North America. Although research has historically been concentrated in these regions, recent years have seen an increase in studies conducted in non-western countries, including Taiwan, South Korea and Bangladesh (Ahmed and Braithwaite 2006). In Japan, an independent tradition of research developed in the 1980s surrounding the nature and prevalence of *ijime*, a behaviour that corresponds closely to western definitions of school bullying (Smith and Brain 2000). While cross-cultural research is still in its early stages, findings suggest that school bullying occurs in similar forms in most countries studied. For example, a survey of 1,344 South Korean primary school children reported similar patterns of bullying and related psychological distress as western studies (Yang *et al.* 2006). Current work (Taki *et al.* 2006) which directly compares patterns of behaviour in different cultural settings promises to shed further light on what may be a universal developmental experience.

Bullying at school is generally defined as intentional aggressive behaviour against a victim who cannot defend himself or herself, and that is repeated over time (Smith 2004). A broad distinction is made between behaviours that involve direct or overt aggression, such as physical fighting (eg. hitting, pushing) and face-to-face verbal victimisation (eg. name-calling, insults, threats), and indirect or covert aggression. Indirect aggression refers to a wide range of hostile behaviours that are aimed at damaging social relationships (Crick and Grotpeter 1996), such as spreading rumours or gossiping about a third person, or excluding others from social groups and activities (Espelage and Swearer 2003; Owens *et al.* 2000). The nature of bullying, however, changes as children grow older. For example, most studies confirm that bullying among primary school aged children is characterised by higher levels of direct aggression, while an increase in the use of indirect aggression is observed as children progress through high school.

Overall, studies have demonstrated that bullying occurs relatively frequently among children and adolescents in the school environment, causes distress to victims, and is associated with adverse outcomes for those involved. Children who are victims, for example, tend to report low self-esteem, avoid school, and be rejected by their peers (Boulton and Smith 1994; Smith *et al.* 2004), while it is widely agreed that bullies are more aggressive generally, and tend to be impulsive or hyperactive (Baldry and Farrington 1998; Espelage and Swearer 2003). Children who are both bullies and victims appear to be particularly troubled, reporting higher levels of aggression and hyperactivity, depression and anxiety, as well as conflict and difficulties in the home environment (Ahmed and Braithwaite 2004; Austin and Joseph 1996; Swearer *et al.* 2001).

Almost the entire population of the developed world will spend a decade or longer in formal schooling. As such, it is not surprising that the vast majority of bullying research has focused on the school. The school forces together potential offenders and potential victims in an environment that provides ample opportunities for bullying to occur. Beyond school, at least in theory, people are free to exercise greater control in their choice of the people with whom and environments in which they spend their time. In the adult world, we most often hear about bullying in the workplace, prisons and the military, but it can occur in any setting – for example, churches, sports teams, nursing homes, hospitals, and youth groups. Bullying can occur in any environment where people interact for periods of time, particularly social institutions characterised by hierarchical structures with opportunities for individuals to abuse power.

Recognition of workplace bullying as a significant problem, and corresponding research in the area have both increased greatly in the last ten years. Recent studies investigating the nature and prevalence of workplace bullying have been conducted largely in Europe, particularly the UK (Jennifer *et al.* 2003; Rayner 1997) and Scandinavia (Einarsen *et al.* 1994; Einarsen and Skogstad 1996; Leymann 1996). Due to wide variation in measurement and methodology, there is some disagreement in the literature as to how the behaviour should be defined, but many researchers accept the general definition of bullying as a systematic, deliberate abuse of power that is repeated over time (Rigby 2002). Depending on the structure of the workplace (e.g. size, physical environment, proportion of male to female employees) and nature of the work, this abuse of power could take many forms. In a review of research, Rayner and Höel (1997) grouped workplace bullying into five types: *threat to professional status* (e.g. belittling opinion), *threat to personal standing* (e.g. insults, intimidation), *isolation* (e.g. withholding of information, preventing access to opportunities), *overwork* (e.g. impossible deadlines) and *destabilisation* (e.g. meaningless tasks, setting up to fail).

The way in which those in positions of power in the workplace can use these techniques to isolate and destabilise others is illustrated with a quotation from one of the focus groups conducted during the present study. A young female apprentice baker, who was part of the adult Scouting focus group, told the following story:

> At my work, if I don't work supervised by a qualified tradesperson, I'm supposed to get paid tradesperson's rates. I work two-thirds of my time unsupervised and I get paid the same amount as what I always do. But if I told them [managers] that I didn't – I have done it before, and it was the most miserable month I've ever had at my work. They will just make your life hell, and if you try and get out of the store, even if you try and transfer, they will make your life hell. And they will tell every other person who works in your area about you in other stores and you will never be able to work anywhere else as well. (*Female pastry cook, aged 19*)

As a distinct behaviour, bullying in the home has received less attention. This may be because most bullying behaviours in the home setting are not researched as bullying. Although there are an increasing number of studies investigating sibling bullying (Duncan 1999b), aggressive and coercive behaviour involving parents and children is usually analysed as child abuse, and aggressive behaviour between adult partners as domestic violence. If bullying involves a repeated, systematic abuse of power, however, some aspects of these behaviours are consistent with that definition. Rigby (2002) argues that conceptions of domestic violence and abuse that include behaviours intended to emotionally wound, such as withholding affection and belittling, would be more usefully defined as bullying. Take, for example, a female student's description of victimisation between boyfriends and girlfriends:

> There's people who attract each other, but then you always get the dominant and the weaker one. And I think lots of girls get into situations, and I think lots of boys do too, but you hear it more with girls, they say, 'Oh, my boyfriend hates me – but I really love him so I'll just take him doing this.' Like, calling her dumb, or sleeping with other people, and all that stuff. So what if he calls me dumb and stupid and useless, he would never hit me, so that's OK! (*Female high school student, aged 18*)

Similarly, depending on the definition used, child abuse includes physical violence, neglect, sexual assault, exposure to family violence, and psychological or emotional maltreatment. Psychological and emotional maltreatment involves behaviour such as yelling, calling names, criticising and ridicule or humiliation (Duncan 1999a; Finkelhor *et al.* 2005), and similar behaviours are involved in techniques of coercive parenting (Perry *et al.* 2001). Furthermore, there is no doubt that the parent holds a position of power over the child.

Bullying in life-course perspective

Much has been learned about bullying in the past 20 years. Beyond the well-established correlates and short-term effects, however, there are important gaps in our understanding of this complex behaviour. First, there have been few systematic investigations of the post high-school outcomes associated with bullying. Does being bullied produce significant difficulties for young adults, and if so, what are they? For example, does bullying lead directly to emotional problems, or does it affect people's lives by reducing academic achievement, or impairing the ability to form intimate relationships? Second, the consequences of being bullied as an adult (at work, for example) are not well understood. Third, the relationship between bullying and other forms of victimisation is in need of closer scrutiny. Few studies have examined the connections between, for example, bullying and racial and sexual harassment, sibling bullying, child abuse, criminal victimisation and violence in adolescent dating relationships. Similarly, the links between bullying and aggressive and antisocial behaviour, delinquency and offending, and drug and alcohol abuse have not been fully investigated. Finally, although interventions to reduce bullying in the school environment are based on extensive research and have been shown to be effective, questions remain regarding timing of programmes for optimal effect. Is it best to target bullies, victims or everyone, and how much should the family and community be involved (Smith, Pepler and Rigby 2004)?

Researchers have recently begun to recommend that the scope of bullying research be widened to incorporate the growing recognition of ways in which the myriad social and institutional contexts of people's lives interact to foster and inhibit bullying behaviour (Espelage and Swearer 2003). The questions posed in the previous paragraph, however, concern continuity and discontinuity of behaviour and experience across time and contexts. Although stability in bullying has been explored, from primary school to high school (Schäfer *et al.* 2005) there has been little attempt to approach the problem from a contemporary life-course perspective. The life-course perspective provides a useful framework for investigating the mechanisms of continuity in bullying across time because it views individual behaviour, emotions and cognitions as emerging from dynamic interactions between these elements (Elder *et al.* 2003). In order to understand the effects of bullying on later trajectories of development, it is necessary to 'think outside the school box' by making links between context, experience and individual behaviour across time.

Continuity in bullying describes the development over time of both bullying and its consequences. Schulenberg *et al.* (2003) make a distinction between *descriptive* and *ontogenic* continuity. Descriptive continuity or discontinuity refers to the persistence, or not, of the same behaviour or characteristic over time, such as continuation of bully or victim status from high school to the workplace. Ontogenic continuity or discontinuity refers to the presence of a causal link, or not, between earlier experiences and later outcomes, such as observation of a causal relationship between victimisation in high school and depression in young adulthood. The extent to which both descriptive and ontogenic continuity are observed are often largely dependent on the influence of other, more recent experiences. For example, the relationship between being bullied in high school and depression in young adulthood might be mediated by both the response of the young person's school to the situation and their individual coping style. The mechanisms of continuity and discontinuity therefore operate in dynamic interplay between developing individuals and changing contexts.

The following section examines contextual norms in bullying research. This includes an exploration of the influence of norms on bullying in different settings, and the importance of recognising the way in which wider social context affects both more immediate contexts and individual behaviour.

The contribution of contextual factors to continuity and discontinuity

The links between contexts and their influence on individual pathways of development is central to the developmental sciences (Goodnow, this volume; Schulenberg *et al.* 2003). Contextual factors are significant to the study of bullying in the life course because as people move in and out of different settings, it is necessary to use what we know about these links to answer questions about continuity of bullying across different contexts. For example, for whom and under what conditions might parental bullying lead to more serious child abuse, or coercive behaviour in adolescent dating relationships to domestic violence? In addition to examining continuity in behaviour across contexts, it is important to establish the extent to which people experience continuity of context. For example, is the high school bully really likely to become the workplace bully, or does this only occur if that bully is employed in a workplace with a social and institutional structure that allows bullying to occur? One way that the links between contexts and bullying could be more firmly established is through the investigation of contextual norms on both the way people behave, and how they interpret behaviour.

Contextual norms

The varying ways that bullying is defined in the workplace and in the home show that similar behaviours may be perceived differently, or have different meanings in different contexts. Norms are one feature of social and institutional settings that may influence these variations. Norms may be defined as perceived regulatory mechanisms that guide people's behaviour in given situations. They contribute to what people perceive as legitimate behaviour in different settings, as well as legitimate ways to handle behaviour. The norms that operate in a given context will therefore influence people's view about whether it is 'OK' to bully others, and others' responses to this. In the school environment, for example, the effectiveness of interventions to reduce bullying depend in part on teachers' perceptions of both the extent to which bullying is a problem and their ability to improve the situation (Olweus 2004). Studies of workplace bullying have frequently highlighted the way in which different aspects of workplace 'culture' are related to employees' experience of bullying. Overall, organisations with a hierarchical, authoritarian structure, or where there is a high degree of uncertainty and ambiguity surrounding work roles, may produce environments in which employees are bullied (Jennifer *et al.* 2003). Einarsen (2000) argues that this occurs because humiliating and punitive behaviours become accepted practice over time, with management and colleagues favouring those who are tough enough to survive them. The norms of different workplaces will therefore affect what people regard as acceptable behaviour in that particular environment. Young male construction apprentices, for example, considered it perfectly legitimate to give other employees a hard time if they had trouble keeping up with physically demanding labour:

> A: They're just people who can't do their job. Like, you're expected to carry that, and it you're not strong enough to carry it then you're not much good. If you can't do something you can't do something, but if you can't do something for the job you may as well be at home. May as well not even be at work.
>
> *Interviewer*:   So what would people say to them, then?
>
> A: Oh, just give it to them because they're weak.
> (*Male construction apprentice, aged 20*)

The same apprentices described how different bosses would insult junior workers or deliberately assign them menial and boring tasks. This behaviour, however, was accepted as a normal experience of the construction industry:

> Everyone has to have a crap period – just because they [the bosses] might have got picked on and got all the crap jobs and they can just palm it down because they had to do it, so why shouldn't *we* have to do it, so they just more or less keep it going. The apprentices get the shit stuff and as we go up it'll eventually get better. (*Male construction apprentice, aged 18*)

Contextual norms also affect people's perceptions of legitimate and available reactions to bullying and harassment. For example, a well-established workplace procedure for resolution of grievances might prompt employees to take steps about bullying in the confidence that complaints will be taken seriously. The same procedures are not available, however, to an adult being bullied by a partner or family member. Such behaviour is often considered justified, by both perpetrator and victim (Rigby 2002). In some settings, attempts to violate norms against taking action lead to further difficulties:

> At my work, if you try and say no 'cos they're asking you to do something that isn't really in the job description, that you don't really have to do, but you go, 'No, I don't want to', it sort of stands out. And they'll point it out to everyone who *does* do it normally, and so they'll all turn around and go, 'We

all do it, what the hell's wrong with you?' So they make them think badly about you – something about you that the other person might not actually have thought about, and might not have cared about. 'Hey! Hate them!' And the other person goes, 'Yeah, OK.' (*Female public servant, aged 20*)

Finally, if aggressive behaviour is sanctioned in a particular context, others may be reluctant to intervene on behalf of a victimised person. An extensive literature surrounds the various roles played by 'non-participants' in school bullying situations (Pepler *et al.* 1999). This research highlights the role of the whole peer group in reinforcing bullying, often by failure to intervene. The following example of sexual harassment at Rover among a group of young adult peers highlights this process:

We had a problem in our crew about two years ago between two males of significant power, and one female who was very stubborn in her own right, and some of the things that they would say to her, unbelievably derogative, sexual, horrible comments, in front of everybody and nobody would do anything about it. Victimised to the point where she would just sit there crying, and none of us would do anything about it. (*Female public servant, aged 22*)

Wider social context

Thus far, discussion of context has been limited to the immediate settings of workplace, family and school environment. The influence of change in broader contexts (e.g. neighbourhood, national economy, political climate) on these smaller settings and on individual behaviour must also be considered (France and Homel, Chapter 1 this volume). Australia's new industrial relations laws, for example, have granted employers in small businesses widened latitude to dismiss staff without specific reason. This sort of political change could affect victims' willingness to 'make a fuss' about problems in the workplace. At a broader societal level, major changes in the institutional pathways from childhood to adolescence and young adulthood have taken place in the last 20 years (Wyn 2004). Young adults are delaying transitions to full-time work, studying longer, staying at home longer, and marrying and starting families later. This has accompanied a dramatic increase in casual work, particularly among young people. Most Australian adolescents work in casual jobs after school, at the weekends, and in their holidays. This opens up the opportunity for new experiences and behaviours, including victimisation. Young, casual workers are at particular risk for exploitation:

> And I worked in a job before that at Subway. I was under the impression that you could take coupons. So I went to take a few one day, told I wasn't allowed, so I put them back. Then the manager proceeded to write me SMSs telling me I was a thief and a liar and all this sort of stuff. I said, 'When am I next working?' and he said, 'Oh, if you tell me what you stole.' And he was actually telling my friend, who was at the same level as me, to fire me, because he didn't want to. It was just cheap, dodgy. (*Female high school student, aged 18*)

Wider socio-economic context may also wield its influence in subtle ways. For example, the famous study of the effects on children of the Iowa farm crisis (Conger and Elder 1994) showed that economic hardship affected children in negative ways through its influence on parental depression and negative parent–child interaction processes. The following example suggests that an environment characterised by stresses such as economic deprivation can act to increase victimisation and further disadvantage the already marginalised:

> And when you're down in the dumps, don't have much money and there's other people around don't have much money as well, and then you're all, like, you're dealing with each other as well as copping stuff from the rich people – it makes the feuds between the not so fortunate a lot more violent. (*Male youth centre attendee, aged 18*)

In summary, the nature and meaning of bullying vary greatly across different contexts. In order to research continuity and discontinuity in bullying across the life-span, the link between context and behaviour must be central. Establishing these links, however, raises several methodological problems. One issue is the need to sharpen definitions and measurements of behaviour. For example, finer-grained definitions of bullying at school and measures of child and partner abuse in the home have the potential to clarify aspects of both problems. At present, measures of child and partner abuse sometimes include non-violent actions that are behaviourally similar to bullying as defined in the school context, while measures of school incorporate violent behaviours such as hitting and kicking that in other contexts might be defined as assault. More specific categorisation might help researchers establish the different contextual factors that are related to the occurrence of bullying and violence in the home and at school.

Another problem is measurement of context itself. For example, context may be conceptualised using structural features (e.g. number of children in a family) or functional features (e.g. quality of parent–child relationship); or be defined as institutional (e.g. school, workplace) or social (e.g. family, peer group) or both (McLeod and Almazan 2003). The most useful way to measure contextual factors such that links can be made between settings and behaviour is an issue that concerns the developmental sciences generally.

Despite the centrality of context, the study of settings alone will tell only part of the bullying story. Different individuals move into social and institutional settings with varying past experiences, personal capacities and levels of access to social and material resources. The next section discusses how the relationships between individuals and contexts operate at times of developmental transition, and how these transitions can act as a mechanism for continuity or discontinuity of bullying. The links between bullying, offending and victimisation around the transition of puberty are used as an example.

The contribution of developmental transitions to continuity and discontinuity

Developmental transitions go hand in hand with shifts in social and institutional settings, opportunities and relationships. Puberty is a transition that brings the initiation of romantic relationships, increased freedom to roam in public space and reduced parental supervision. At the same time, young people move into new institutional settings, like high school and the workplace, which impose their own demands and new responsibilities (Steinberg and Morris 2001). For some young people, these new settings afford opportunities for continuation of aggressive behaviour. For instance, bullying others at school is a risk factor for antisocial and delinquent behaviour in adolescence (Farrington 1993). Andershed et al. (2001) found that Swedish 14 year olds who bullied others at school were more likely than non-bullies to behave violently or carry weapons on the street. The explanation was that these adolescents were also more likely to loiter in the street and spend nights away from home, thus increasing their exposure to situations holding a potential for antisocial behaviour. Similar patterns of aggression can be observed in other settings. Connolly *et al.* (2000) found that adolescents who reported bullying at school were more likely than non-bullies to report physical and social aggression with their boyfriends and girlfriends. It was argued that the bullying adolescents had learned to use interactional patterns with peers that rewarded the use of aggression to assert power, and that these coercive techniques met with similar 'success' in romantic relationships.

However, the story is not as straightforward as the simple transfer of learned patterns of behaviour from one setting to another. As the life-span perspective emphasises a constant interplay between changing people and changing contexts, it is expected that there will be wide variation in developmental trajectories (Schulenberg *et al.* 2003). That is, the same initial antecedent (such as being a bully in early adolescence) will lead to different patterns of outcomes for different people. In addition, similar outcomes might be observed even when initial antecedents differ. Among the Swedish adolescents, for example, being a bully increased risks for becoming a victim of criminal assault as well as engaging in delinquent behaviour (Andershed *et al.* 2001). Those at highest risk of being violently victimised, however, were those who were both bullies and victims at school. It was suggested that this was a reflection of the personal characteristics of bully-victims, such as hyperactivity, combined with their own violent behaviour. In other words, puberty may bring about situations in which the same factors that contribute to bully-victims' risk of being bullied in school place them at risk of victimisation on the streets. In the context of adolescent dating relationships, both girls and boys who were bullies were aggressive with their romantic partners (Connolly *et al.* 2000). Later in life, however, it is women who are most likely to be victims of partner violence. The authors suggested that girls who become trapped in aggressive interactional patterns in early relationships might find themselves at increased risk for violence in later relationships as their aggression is met with increasingly harsher aggression from increasingly powerful male partners. The antecedents and consequences of bullying therefore vary according to their timing in a person's life (Elder *et al.* 2003).

What are the mechanisms by which developmental transitions lead to varied outcomes? First, individual resources and capacities are important. Transitions require people to engage with challenging new settings and tasks. The extent to which people arrive at transitions equipped with competencies to negotiate associated challenges can serve to magnify existing strengths and weaknesses (Schulenberg *et al.* 2003). For instance, children who are persistently bullied in primary school might lack the skills to negotiate new relationships in high school and continue to be victimised:

> In primary school I basically had no friends, and people would purposely build you up to let you down again, and so I went into high school basically not trusting anyone. I think I sort of hung out with the people that had also been victimised, but because of that they had also become quite bitter and took it out on me. (*Female high school student, aged 18*)

For bullies, some individual competencies appear to be particularly important to this process. A general inability to regulate one's own behaviour and emotions, including impulsivity, have been related to bullying and aggression (Eisenberg *et al.* 2004). At times of transition, the lack of these skills may serve to magnify the aggressive patterns that characterise bullies' relations with their peers:

> I can evaluate my own actions in a seemingly objective manner, and these people just can't do that. They don't look at themselves, they don't see themselves, they do things, but they don't think about what they've done or what they're doing. In primary school I used to bully people, I was always the big bully. But I made a conscious choice, because I was self-aware, that I probably shouldn't do this and that I was not going to. (*Male high school student, aged 18*)

Transitions may contribute to developmental discontinuity. Although most delinquents report having bullied others at school, not all bullies become delinquents (Farrington 1993), and many children experience a change in bullying status (e.g. from victim to non-victim) between primary school and high school (Smith, Talamelli *et al.* 2004). Transitions can therefore serve as turning points that allow people to 'escape' problematic behaviours like bullying. If transitions allow people to move into contexts with opportunities for activities and relationships that afford a better match with their interests and skills, earlier problematic experiences may not continue. For example, children who are bullied for being 'nerds' who do well at school sometimes find that the transition to environments more accepting of academic achievement results in a decrease in victimisation. The focus group high school students provide an example. In Canberra, the final two years of high school are completed in 'colleges' where students enjoy tertiary-like flexibility in timetabling of classes, and have the opportunity to undertake extra tertiary-level or vocational courses. The students described the college environment as much more accepting of academic achievement.

> G: I found in high school things were very different.
>
> *Interviewer*: How have things changed since you've come to college?
>
> T: I think a lot of people have grown a brain and realised there's more to life. (*Female high school students, aged 18*)

In summary, transitions have different effects for different people. For some, transitions contribute to continuity, in the shape of continued aggression and/or continued victimisation. Continuity may also be observed in the shape of outcomes like depression or social anxiety that are linked to earlier bullying experiences. For others, transitions contribute to discontinuity, such that individuals are able to escape from past bullying or victimisation. Likewise, transitions may provide positive experiences that buffer adverse effects of earlier difficulties with bullying and victimisation. This diversity of potential outcomes depends on complex interactions between individuals' past experiences, current relationships, contexts and available social, material and personal resources. An important implication is that transitions may serve to either close off opportunities or open them up. For example, the high school students described significant institutional change in response to bullying between high school and college:

> They don't make it here – they are expelled before they get here. And that is a huge point about why college is so good for people who've come out of a violent high school because so many students have been expelled. You're *arrested* if you stab somebody here, whereas you're *counselled* if you stab somebody in high school. All the people I had conflict with have been through corrective services, and are probably there now. And they really should have been dealt with much harsher much quicker, instead of trying to baby them through to Year 10. (*Male high school student, aged 18*)

For the former bullies, opportunities (e.g. academic) had been curtailed, which may well have affected their ability to negotiate future transitions (e.g. to the workplace). Their absence at college, however, had helped others make a successful transition to a much more pleasant environment where opportunities for academic achievement were readily available. This, in turn, provided them with skills to make further transitions to tertiary study and employment. In other words, strengths were magnified for those doing well prior to the transition, and weakened for those who were already struggling. Being bullied or bullying others has effects that can persist throughout the life course.

Prevention

Prevention of bullying in school has received much research attention, and the Olweus Bullying Prevention Programme has been implemented successfully in a number of different countries (Smith, Pepler and Rigby 2004). However, placing bullying in a life-course perspective suggests that preventive efforts will be improved by taking wider social, family and community factors into account. In general, many of the principles that apply to general developmental prevention, usually aimed at crime reduction, are relevant to reduction of bullying (Farrington 1993).

First, bullying should not be viewed as an isolated behaviour, but as an aspect of aggression and antisocial behaviour in general. As Connolly *et al.* (2000) note, schools often view bullying as transitory and not requiring intervention. This discussion has shown, however, that it has multiple effects across settings and relationships. For high-risk youth in particular, involvement in bullying may facilitate development of other problems like delinquency and school exclusion that contribute to a spiral of cumulative disadvantage. Findings from longitudinal studies of the antisocial behaviours and criminal careers should therefore inform prevention efforts (Farrington 1993).

Second, victimisation should not be viewed as an isolated experience. Like bullying, it will result in different outcomes for different people. For some, victimisation may be part of, or lead to, a larger syndrome of internalising problems, and for others, to aggression and further victimisation. Restorative justice approaches have been employed in schools to address bullying problems (Cameron and Thorsborne 2001; Morrison 2002), and offer a way to reintegrate bullies into the school community while supporting victims. Although more research and evaluation is needed, such programmes have the potential to decrease the negative effects of both bullying and victimisation at school and in other institutional settings such as the workplace.

he nature of interventions should reflect the developmental
the target population. This discussion shows that
:cedents and consequences of victimisation depend on
.nental timing. The fact that bullying peers in adolescence
is rei₎₎₎d to aggressive behaviour with boyfriends and girlfriends
suggests that interventions at high school age should be directed at
prevention of dating violence, as well as aggression in the peer group
(Connolly *et al.* 2000). In addition, interventions should be timed
to take maximum advantage of the potential of transitions to be
turning points. Intensive bullying awareness and conflict resolution
programmes at the beginning of the school year or with first-year
high school students, for example, might prevent the establishment
of power relationships and social norms that lead to bullying.

Fourth, an exclusive focus on bullies and victims will not suffice.
Interventions should also address the norms that operate in specific
contexts. As institutions with a responsibility for people's safety,
interventions to reduce bullying in schools and workplaces could
benefit from the situational crime prevention literature. For example,
situational crime prevention measures have been found to reduce
bullying and victimisation in prison (Wortley 2002). At a wider level,
individuals' social relationships beyond the institution should be a
target of intervention. It is critical to engage families and communities.
Although this discussion has not covered the influence of family
factors such as parenting style on bullying in any depth, family
resources and capacities have important causal and mediating effects
on both bullying and victimisation. In general, school interventions
do not engage families beyond providing information about bullying
and efforts to prevent it. Given the links between bullying, social
relationships and broader social context, bullying prevention efforts
might need to be part of a multiple-component community-based
programme incorporating parenting training and, for disadvantaged
families, services such as financial planning and practical support
(Freiberg *et al.,* this volume).

Fifth, further research is needed on the value of promoting
general social competence alongside the specific prevention of
bullying. Children who bully are often more aggressive, poor at
resolving conflicts with peers, and less able to regulate their actions
and emotions than others (Eisenberg *et al.* 2004). Andershed *et al.*
(2001) recommend that interventions aim to change individuals'
ways of thinking. The Montreal Longitudinal Study (Tremblay *et al.*
1992) showed that social skills training and parent training reduced
aggression and bullying among disruptive boys. As bullying is part

of a spectrum of aggressive and antisocial behaviour, these findings suggest that prevention efforts include cognitive-behavioural social skills training to reduce aggression and promote positive peer relationships. Given the importance of family factors, however, this may be most effective when combined with parent training, as in the Montreal study (Farrington 2005).

Finally, although interventions designed to prevent bullying could learn from developmental crime prevention, successful bullying interventions have much to offer other fields of research. Bullying prevention in schools and workplaces, for instance, potentially involve an equal focus on the victim, the offender, and contextual factors. They are therefore uniquely positioned to draw on findings from situational crime prevention, developmental crime prevention, and restorative justice to change both situations and future trajectories of bullies and victims.

I have argued that the life-course perspective provides a useful framework for addressing questions of continuity and discontinuity in bullying across people, time and settings. The consequences of bullying and victimisation for adult behaviour and functioning are dependent on complex links between people, experiences, relationships and social and institutional setting. Some of the ways in which these links might operate were illustrated by the ways in which contextual factors and developmental transitions influence continuity and discontinuity in bullying. Prevention of bullying and associated problems could improve outcomes in many areas including child and adult relationships, academic achievement, workplace climate, adult well-being, delinquent behaviour and family functioning. Prevention programmes must be based, however, on research that specifically addresses the complexity of bullying. The challenge for these researchers is to widen the scope of investigation far beyond the trio of bully, victim and school to incorporate multiple individual, social and contextual factors.

Notes

1 The 'Life at School' (Ahmed 2001) project is a longitudinal study of bullying and victimisation involving parents and children in Canberra, Australia. Self-report surveys were completed in 1996 by 978 primary school children aged 8–12 years old and one of their parents. In 1999, 368 of these children and parents completed the survey a second time. The surveys included measures of children's bullying and victimisation

experience, well-being, school adjustment, social competence, parenting style and family hassles. The present study involved the collection of a third wave of questionnaire data from these children (now aged 18–22) and their mother or father. The overall aim of the project was to examine the continuity and changes in behaviour and experience of bullying across time (from early adolescence to young adulthood) and context (school to university, the workplace or other settings).

Preliminary focus groups were conducted with a range of late adolescents and young adults to inform the development of a valid quantitative measure of bullying and victimisation for young adults in non-school settings. Participants (n = 34) were: two groups of 19–20-year-old male apprentices in the construction industry; two groups of 19–20-year-old male and female attendees at a drop-in centre for homeless and disadvantaged youth; one group of male and female 18–24-year-old members of an adult Scouting group, which included a mix of university students and workers in industry, education and the public service; and three groups of 18-year-old male and female students in their final year of high school. The aim of the focus groups was to obtain qualitative accounts of victimisation from young people in their own words. I began each session with the question, 'What is victimisation?' As the discussion proceeded, participants were encouraged to tell their stories of victimisation and bullying experiences at home, in the workplace and with friends, and to describe why these behaviours might occur. Each discussion lasted about one hour and was taped and transcribed.

References

Ahmed, E. (2001) 'Shame Management: Regulating Bullying', in E. Ahmed, N. Harris, J. Braithwaite and V. Braithwaite (eds) *Shame Management Through Reintegration*. Cambridge: Cambridge University Press, pp. 211–311.

Ahmed, E. and Braithwaite, V. (2004) 'Bullying and victimization: Cause for concern for both families and schools', *Social Psychology of Education*, 7: 35–54.

Ahmed, E. and Braithwaite, V. (2006) 'Forgiveness, reconciliation and shame: Three key variables in reducing school bullying', *Journal of Social Issues*, 62: 347–70.

Andershed, H., Kerr, M. and Stattin, H. (2001) 'Bullying in school and violence on the streets: Are the same people involved?' *Journal of Scandinavian Studies in Criminology and Crime Prevention*, 2: 31–49.

Austin, S. and Joseph, S. (1996) 'Assessment of bully/victim problems in 8 to 11 year olds', *British Journal of Educational Psychology*, 66: 447–56.

Baldry, A.C. and Farrington, D.P. (1998) 'Parenting influences on bullying and victimization', *Legal and Criminological Psychology*, 3: 237–54.

Boulton, M. and Smith, P.K. (1994) 'Bully/victim problems in middle school children: Stability, perceived competence, peer perception and peer acceptance', *British Journal of Developmental Psychology*, 12: 315–29.

Cameron, L. and Thorsborne, M. (2001) 'Restorative Justice and School Discipline: Mutually Exclusive?', in J. Brathwaite and H. Strang (eds) *Restorative Justice and Civil Society*. Cambridge: Cambridge University Press, pp. 180–94.

Conger, R. and Elder, G. (1994). *Families in Troubled Times: Adapting to Change in Rural America*. Hawthorne, NY: Aldine de Grutyer.

Connolly, J., Pepler, D., Craig, W. M. and Taradash, A. (2000) 'Dating experiences of bullies in early adolescence', *Child Maltreatment*, 5: 299–310.

Crick, N. and Grotpeter, J. (1996) 'Children's treatment by peers: Victims of relational and overt aggression', *Development and Psychopathology*, 8: 36–80.

Duncan, R.D. (1999a) 'Maltreatment by parents and peers: The relationship between child abuse, bully victimization and psychological distress', *Child Maltreatment*, 4: 45–55.

Duncan, R.D. (1999b) 'Peer and sibling aggression: An investigation of intra- and extra-familial bullying', *Journal of Interpersonal Violence*, 14: 871–86.

Einarsen, S. (2000) 'Harassment and violence at work: A review of the Scandinavian approach', *Aggression & Violent Behavior*, 5: 379–401.

Einarsen, S. and Skogstad, A. (1996) 'Bullying at work: Epidemiological findings in public and private oranizations', *European Journal of Work and Organizational Psychology*, 5: 185–201.

Einarsen, S., Raknes, B. and Matthiesen, S.B. (1994) 'Bullying and harassment at work and their relationships to work environment quality: An exploratory study', *European Journal of Work and Organizational Psychology*, 4: 381–401.

Eisenberg, N., Spinrad, T. L., Fabes, R. A., Reiser, M., Cumberland, A., Shepard, S. A. *et al.* (2004) 'The relations of effortful control and impulsivity to children's resiliency and adjustment', *Child Development*, 75: 25–46.

Elder, G., Johnson, M. and Crosnoe, R. (2003) 'The Emergence and Development of Life Course Theory', in J. Mortimer and M. Shanahan (eds) *Handbook of the Life Course*. New York: Kluwer Academic/Plenum Publishers, pp. 3–19.

Espelage, D. and Swearer, S. (2003) 'Research on school bullying and victimization: What have we learned and where do we go from here?', *School Psychology Review*, 32: 365–83.

Farrington, D.P. (1993) 'Understanding and Preventing Bullying', in M. Tonry (ed.) *Crime and Justice: A Review of Research*, Vol. 17. Chicago: University of Chicago Press, pp. 381–458.

Farrington, D.P. (2005) 'Childhood origins of antisocial behavior', *Clinical Psychology & Psychotherapy*, 12: 177–90.

Finkelhor, D., Ormrod, R., Turner, H. and Hamby, S. (2005) 'The victimization of children and youth: A comprehensive, national survey', *Child Maltreatment*, 10: 5–25.

Hawker, D. and Boulton, M. (2000) 'Twenty years' research on peer victimization and pyschosocial maladjustment: A meta-analytic review of cross-sectional studies', *Journal of Child Psychology and Psychiarty*, 41: 441–55.

Jennifer, D., Cowie, H. and Ananiadou, K. (2003) 'Perceptions and experience of workplace bullying in five different working populations', *Aggressive Behavior*, 29: 489–96.

Kochenderfer-Ladd, B. (2004) 'Peer victimization: The role of emotions in adaptive and maladaptive coping', *Social Development*, 13: 329–49.

Leymann, H. (1996) 'The content and development of mobbing at work', *European Journal of Work and Organizational Psychology*, 5: 165–84.

McLeod, J. and Almazan, E. (2003) 'Connections between Childhood and Adulthood', in J. Mortimer and M. Shanahan (eds) *Handbook of the Life Course*. New York: Kluwer Academic/Plenum Publishers, pp. 391–411.

Morrison, B. (2002) *'Bullying and Victimisation in Schools: A Restorative Justice Approach'* (No. 219). Canberra: Australia Institute of Criminology.

Olweus, D. (1993) *Bullying at School: What We Know and What We Can Do.* Oxford: Blackwell Publishers.

Olweus, D. (2004) 'The Olweus Bullying Prevention Programme: Design and Implementation Issues and a New National Initiative in Norway', in P.K. Smith, D. Pepler and K. Rigby (eds) *Bullying in Schools: How Successful Can Interventions Be?* Cambridge: Cambridge University Press, pp. 13–36.

Owens, L., Daly, A. and Slee, P. (2005) 'Sex and age differences in victimisation and conflict resolution among adolescents in a South Australian school', *Aggressive Behavior*, 31: 1–12.

Owens, L., Shute, R. and Slee, P. (2000) 'I'm in and you're out ... Explanations for teenage girls' indirect aggression', *Psychology, Evolution and Gender*, 2: 19–46.

Pepler, D., Craig, W.M. and O'Connell, P. (1999) 'Understanding Bullying from a Dynamic Systems Perspective', in A. Slater and D. Muir (eds) *The Blackwell Reader in Developmental Psychology*. Malden, MA: Blackwell, pp. 440–51.

Perry, D.G., Hodges, E.V.E. and Egan, S.D. (2001) 'Determinants of Chronic Victimization by Peers: A Review and New Model of Family Influence', in J. Juvonen and S. Graham (eds) *Peer Harassment in School: The Plight of the Vulnerable and Victimzed*. New York: Guilford Press, pp. 73–104.

Rayner, C. (1997) 'The incidence of workplace bullying', *Journal of Community and Applied Social Psychology*, 7: 1199–1208.

Rayner, C. and Höel, H. (1997) 'A summary review of literature relating to workplace bullying', *Journal of Community and Applied Social Psychology*, 7: 181–91.

Rigby, K. (1996). *Bullying in Schools: And What To Do About It*. Melbourne: Australian Council for Educational Research.

Rigby, K. (2002) *New Perspectives on Bullying*. London: Jessica Kingsley.

Rigby, K. (2003) 'Consequences of bullying in schools', *Canadian Journal of Psychiatry*, 48: 583–90.

Schäfer, M., Korn, S., Brodbeck, F., Wolke, D. and Schulz, H. (2005) 'Bullying roles in changing contexts: The stability of victim and bully roles from primary school to secondary school', *International Journal of Behavioral Development*, 29: 323–35.

Schulenberg, J., Maggs, J. and O'Malley, P. (2003) How and Why the Understanding of Developmental Continuity and Discontinuity is Important: The Sample Case of Long-term Consequences of Adolescent Substance Use', in J. Mortimer and M. Shanahan (eds) *Handbook of the Life Course*. New York: Kluwer Academic/Plenum Publishers, pp. 391–411.

Slee, P. (1995) 'Peer victimization and its relationship to depression among Australian primary school students', *Personality and Individual Differences*, 18: 57–62.

Smith, P.K. (2004) 'Bullying: Recent developments', *Child and Adolescent Mental Health*, 9: 98–103.

Smith, P.K. and Brain, P. (2000) 'Bullying in schools: Lessons from two decades of research', *Aggressive Behavior*, 26: 1–9.

Smith, P.K., Pepler, D. and Rigby, K. (eds) (2004) *Bullying in Schools: How Successful Can Interventions Be?* Cambridge: Cambridge University Press.

Smith, P.K., Talamelli, L., Cowie, H., Naylor, P. and Chauhan, P. (2004) 'Profiles of non-victims, escaped victims, continuing victims and new victims of school bullying', *British Journal of Educational Psychology*, 47: 565–81.

Steinberg, L. and Morris, A. (2001) 'Adolescent development', *Annual Review of Psychology*, 52: 82–110.

Swearer, S., Song, S., Cary, P., Eagle, J. and Mickelson, W. (2001) 'Psychosocial correlates in bullying and victimization: The relationship between depression, anxiety, and bully/victim status', *Journal of Emotional Abuse*, 2: 95–121.

Taki, M., Sim, H-O., Pepler, D., Hymel, S., Slee, P. and Swearer, S. (2006) 'Bullying Research Involving 5 Pacific Rim Countries', paper presented at the 19th Biennial Meeting of the International Society for the Study of Behavioural Development, Melbourne, Australia, 2–6 July.

Tremblay, R., Vitaro, F., Bertrand, L., LeBlanc, M., Beauchense, H., Bioleau, H. *et al.* (1992) 'Parent and Child Training to Prevent Early Onset of Delinquency: The Montreal Longitudinal-Experimental Study', in J. McCord and R. Tremblay (eds) *Preventing Antisocial Behavior* New York: Guilford Press, pp. 117–38.

Wortley, R. (2002) *Situational Prison Control*. Cambridge: Cambridge University Press.

Wyn, J. (2004) 'Youth Transitions to Work and Further Education in Australia', paper presented at the American Educational Research Association, San Diego, CA (April).

Yang, S-J., Kim, J-M., Kim, S-W., Shin, I-S. and Yoon, J-S. (2006) 'Bullying and victimization behaviors in boys and girls at South Korean primary schools', *Journal of the American Academy of Child and Adolescent Psychiatry*, 45: 69–77.

Part 2

Prevention theory, policy and practice

Introduction

Ross Homel and Alan France

The theoretical debates about the nature of developmental criminology recorded in the November 2005 *Annals of the American Academy of Political and Social Sciences* go to the heart of the criminological enterprise because they are concerned with fundamental issues of causation, the nature of the life course, and the methods we use to think about and to do our research. The North American debate and the arguments proposed in a number of the chapters in this book are also fundamentally important to those interested in the prevention of crime and related social problems, not least because if the critics are correct, accurate prediction from individual traits, from risk factors, and from prior experiences seems largely beyond reach (see Homel 2005 for a discussion of some of the theoretical issues).

Despite these challenges, the authors of the chapters in Part 1 were able to make a range of observations about the implications for prevention planning of their work on pathways. We discussed some of these implications in our introduction to Part 1. In this second part of the book we focus directly on prevention, exploring empirical evidence from evaluations of preventive interventions and in particular the intersections between research, policy and practice. It is this last theme that most dominates the seven chapters in this section.

The first three chapters are directly or indirectly about the *Pathways to Prevention* report and the project in Brisbane that arose from the report. The project is a prevention initiative that was developed in 1999 by one of the editors (Homel) in partnership with the national community agency Mission Australia. It is a universal, 'early intervention', developmental prevention project in a socially disadvantaged area that, in its first phase, combined child-focused programs delivered through state preschools with services for families, within a community development framework.[1] The project had its beginnings in the federal government report, *Pathways to Prevention: Developmental and Early Intervention Approaches to Crime in Australia* (1999), written by a group of scholars from several disciplines who came together as the Developmental Crime Prevention Consortium.

The success of the Developmental Crime Prevention Consortium's report in getting the concept of 'early intervention' onto the policy map in Australia is the starting point for Alan Hayes' chapter. Alan expresses concerns that the policy agenda has been hijacked by an overemphasis on the early years at the expense of 'early in the pathway', the latter being the major focus of the 1999 report. He clarifies the meanings of 'prevention' and 'early intervention', arguing that early intervention is a special case of prevention, and goes on to demonstrate that the empirical evidence on developmental pathways does not support a case for an exclusive focus on the early years. What is needed, at any age, is a central focus on the 'sustaining social systems' both as the loci for prevention and as the engines for the formation and maintenance of positive pathways (p. 203).

In Chapter 11 Kate Freiberg, Ross Homel and Cherie Lamb analyse data from the Pathways Project to explore the relationship between levels of family adversity or strengths and children's developmental competencies, a relationship, they argue, that is largely mediated by parent efficacy, or the sense of confidence and control that parents feel in parenting tasks. This reinforces the importance of family empowerment programmes as a way of promoting positive outcomes for children and moderating the effects of poverty-created stressors, but also highlights the need for society-wide policies to reduce these stressors. Their study therefore illustrates some of the central themes of Alan Hayes' chapter.

The conclusions of Freiberg and her colleagues are also very much in line with the outcomes of the research that helped shape the current 'blizzard of new initiatives and programmes' in the UK that Gillian Pugh describes in Chapter 16 (p. 344). Of course, in scale the Pathways Project, located in only one disadvantaged region of one Australian city, is dwarfed by the massive expenditure in the UK on Sure Start and other government-funded child-oriented programmes, but it does have the advantage of being largely independent of government and founded in a research–practice partnership established for 'the long haul'. Under such conditions innovation and rigorous research and development are possible, producing new knowledge that can inform larger-scale initiatives such as Communities for Children in Australia or Sure Start in the UK.

How to capture the 'learnings' from projects like Pathways to Prevention is the central theme of Chapter 12 by Marie Leech, Caryn Anderson and Catherine Mahoney. As these authors put it, 'How can we tap the intellectual capital generated in projects such as Pathways and therefore improve outcomes across programmes and geographical areas for service users?' (p. 248). To address this question they propose several conceptual lenses that draw on theories of knowledge management and other fields of enquiry that are not generally the bedtime reading of either pathways or prevention researchers – but probably should be. Utilising limited interview data with key people, they assess the extent to which the rather intuitive processes developed in the Pathways Project fitted the description of a learning organisation and created the conditions for successful practice–research engagement.

Chapters 13 to 15 address specific prevention challenges. Linda Caldwell and Edward Smith engage with the criminological literature on youth crime, and propose a much richer framework for theorising the role of leisure in human development and the prevention of risky behaviour than is usually found in that literature. The nub of their theoretical contribution is to enrich our understanding of leisure as simultaneously a social institution most closely associated with the world of adolescence and a context of risk and protection that provides a natural setting for prevention (p. 274). They report the results of an *ad hoc* analysis of the data from a prevention experiment that was designed with other outcomes in mind but which yielded promising results in terms of the effects on rates of property damage of teaching youth to make healthy decisions in their leisure.

Rebecca Denning and Ross Homel use the Youth Justice Service in Queensland as a case study of the challenges involved in embedding developmental prevention principles into the routine practices of a large government department. Their finding that the new policies and programmes did not reduce recidivism, although there were frequent references in the official documents to key research findings and prevention principles, is not itself cause for great surprise. The value of the chapter lies in its analysis of the causes of failure simultaneously in the lack of clarity and goal ambiguities in the policy, and in operational failures that included poor workforce capacity to deal effectively with youth offenders, a lack of commitment to rehabilitative goals, and communication failures and conflicts among caseworkers. Because Queensland is not likely to be the only jurisdiction in which such problems manifest, the results of the case study analysis are likely to have wide application.

Karin Ishimine and David Evans do not address prevention directly in their chapter on the quality of childcare. Their focus rather is on the quality of these settings, the variations in quality between centres in disadvantaged areas compared with 'partially disadvantaged' areas, and the relationship between the quality of long day care centres and the social skills development of the young children who attend them. In a sense, therefore, they are reporting the results of a 'quasi-experiment' in which social processes create the experimental condition of 'disadvantage' and the outcomes are the quality of the setting and the social skills of children. They find clear links between quality and disadvantage but the effects on social skills development are less clear, pointing to the need for larger-scale research into issues that have become urgent given the huge growth in the numbers of young children in childcare.

We conclude this book with Gillian Pugh's chapter on UK policies to promote the well-being of children and young people. Gillian's chapter, to which we alluded earlier, is significant for its lucid summary and insightful analysis of the effects of the huge investment in programmes for children that has been made in the UK in the past decade. Few other countries can match such an investment, and none has made such a serious effort to learn from research and to base practice on evidence of what works. The UK experience is, therefore, a vast experiment that has captured the imagination and interest of many observers around the world. It is an unfinished experiment, and there are political trends identified by Gillian that suggest that some components may be aborted before they have time to develop as intended. The lessons so far are nevertheless instructive, and what she refers to as 'the ambitious change agenda' (p. 337) should serve as a policy template for Australia and other developed countries.

Note

1 Because the Pathways Project is located in a disadvantaged area, it is properly referred to as a 'selective intervention', not 'universal'. However, it was universal in the sense that all children and families in the area were eligible to participate; there was no selection of children on the basis that they were 'high risk', although there is evidence that many families with high-level needs self-selected into the programme.

References

Developmental Crime Prevention Consortium (1999). *Pathways to Prevention: Developmental and Early Intervention Approaches to Crime in Australia*. Canberra: Australian Government Publishing Service.

Homel, R. (2005) 'Developmental Crime Prevention', in N. Tilley (ed.) *Handbook of Crime Prevention and Community Safety*. Cullompton: Willan Publishing, pp. 71–106.

Chapter 10

Why early in life is not enough: timing and sustainability in prevention and early intervention*

Alan Hayes

Abstract

This chapter critically considers some key assumptions underpinning prevention and early intervention. It focuses particularly on the distinction between preventive interventions early in life as opposed to early in the pathway. Key definitional issues are considered, with emphasis placed on the value of a framework that includes universal, selected and indicated prevention. It is argued that early intervention is a class of indicated prevention. To illustrate the distinction between indicated prevention and selective prevention, two landmark studies are considered. The first, the Iowa Orphanage Study of Skeels, illustrates indicated prevention. The second, the High/Scope Perry Preschool Project, illustrates selective prevention. The discussion then turns to consideration of two key questions. The first concerns timing: Which problems require action when, over what timeframe, where and with whom? The second is the sustainability question: How are gains maintained? In exploring the timing question the focus is on the developmental ordering of problems and the precursors of problems that are evident in measures of temperament and personality, across infancy, early childhood, childhood and adolescence. Recent evidence from the field of adolescent development is introduced focusing particularly on the relationship between neurological

The views expressed in this chapter are those of the author and may not reflect the views of the Australian Institute of Family Studies or the Australian government.

change and the emergence of risk-taking behaviours. To address the sustainability question, life-span developmental concepts and longitudinal approaches underpin the argument. Families, childcare provisions, preschools, schools, peer groups, vocational, further and higher education, community organisations, and the world of work, are seen as key sustaining social systems vital both as the loci for prevention and intervention as well as for maintaining their benefits. The chapter concludes that a life-course, comprehensive approach focused on these key sustaining systems, and supported by integrated policy and practice, is needed to address the key issues of timing and sustainability, as well as the reasons why early in life is not enough.

Introduction

The report *Pathways to Prevention* (Developmental Crime Prevention Consortium 1999) has had a major impact on thinking about prevention and early intervention, not only in Australia but also more widely. Focused on crime prevention, it addressed developmental intervention in two senses: early in life and early in the pathway to a problem. In terms of the first sense, it has perhaps been too successful. It has resonated with the recent interest in early childhood that has been stimulated by some new, and not-so-new evidence of the effects of early experience on brain development, especially in the first three years of life (Cynader and Frost 1999; Keating and Hertzman 1999; McCain and Mustard 1999; Nelson and Bloom 1997). In considering the new brain research, of most significance are the links between abuse and neglect and brain development outcomes that may have effects across life. Despite the most compelling evidence relating to abuse and neglect, findings are often extended to all children (Schorr 1997). Less well understood, however, is the extent of neural plasticity, the constraints on this (Fox *et al.* 1994), and the scope for neurological change, across life, including in adolescence and throughout adulthood (Blakemore and Choudhury 2006; Spear 2000, 2004). The limitations of the evidence base also need more explicit acknowledgement (Corrie 2000).

In recent years, developmental science has taken centre stage, though one stage of life, early childhood, has become central to advocacy and policy development initiatives (Shonkoff and Phillips 2000; Dahl 2004). To be clear, the early years are important. The fundamental significance and the longer-term benefits of a good start in life are well recognised (Keating and Hertzman 1999; Shonkoff and Meisels 2000). The current emphasis on this one life stage, however, stands in contrast to the life-course perspectives in mainstream developmental research that have gained prominence across much of the last half century (Goodnow, this volume).

The contemporary focus on early childhood repeats an error that has been widely recognised for at least three decades (Clarke and Clarke 1976). The error is in giving primacy to early life and assuming that all pathways start in the first three, five or eight years, depending on whose perspective one takes. These years are held to set the scene for adult life, across all the domains of development from the cognitive, social and emotional, to the communicational and physical. In the extreme form of this perspective, what happens in between seems largely irrelevant.

Accompanying and promoting this view of the primacy of early experience is a powerful advocacy agenda. At the heart of this agenda is the assumption that problems spanning the spectrum, from school failure to aggressive and antisocial behaviour, and on to juvenile and adult criminality, could be eliminated once we find the right solutions in early childhood.

To reiterate, my concern is not with the focus on early childhood, *per se*, but with those who make at best exaggerated and at worst unsubstantiated claims concerning the benefits of prevention and intervention initiatives in the early years. It is this magical thinking (Brooks-Gunn 2003), and the capacity it has to result in simplistic approaches to prevention and early intervention (Zigler 2003), that is at the heart of my concern.

Since the publication of *Pathways to Prevention* I have reflected on the relative lack of interest from researchers, policy-makers and practitioners in prevention and early intervention in the second sense of addressing pathways that start later in life. I say relative, because of course there are many who have remained focused on developmental epochs other than the early years (Dahl 2004: Blakemore and Choudhury 2006). But they have struggled to have their voices heard in recent years, and some developmental epochs, such as middle childhood, continue to be overlooked. While adolescence is of growing interest (Spear 2004), adulthood is still too often relegated to being merely an end point, rather than a time of developmental change in its own right (Smith 2006).

In this chapter, I address some assumptions underpinning prevention and early intervention, critically considering the early-in-life perspective. I ask two key questions to present a case for why early-in-the-pathway is a better way to approach prevention and early intervention. The first concerns timing, and the second, sustainability of the effects of prevention and early intervention initiatives. Let me begin, however, by defining some key terms.

Prevention and early intervention defined

Prevention is increasingly associated with early intervention and the two are now typically used in combination in the policy and practice literature. Prevention involves planned and organised efforts to reduce the likelihood of potential problems (Little 1999). Intervention starts with evidence of risk, either in terms of the individual's characteristics and/or circumstances or, more typically, as a result of membership of a group that is held to be at risk. Prevention aims to reduce the overall incidence and prevalence of risk. From a pathways perspective, prevention seeks to reduce the overall likelihood of negative pathways and increase the incidence of positive, while early intervention seeks to alter an emergent pathway.

Early intervention is a subset of prevention. In 1957 the US Commission on Chronic Illness classified prevention in terms of primary, and secondary prevention (Gordon 1983). From a medical perspective, primary prevention occurred prior to the recognition of a disease, while secondary prevention took place once a disease had been identified. A third concept, tertiary prevention, was added to encompass the effort to reduce the likelihood of further deterioration in those suffering the disease. Gordon highlighted a number of limitations particularly related to the biological bias of the scheme and its failure to encompass other aetiologies (such as the psychosocial and behavioural). In its place, he offered a classification comprising universal prevention efforts potentially available to the whole population, selective prevention for population subgroups identified as at risk, and indicated prevention, for those with an identified problem or at high risk of its future development. In this scheme, early intervention is a class of indicated prevention (Johnson 2002).

Within the category of indicated prevention, early intervention is a generic term for planned and organised attempts to alter the behaviour or development of individuals who show the early signs of an identified problem and/or who are considered at high risk of developing that problem. An area that has a long history and a recent rediscovery, early intervention initially focused on children with disabilities (Hayes 1991). Since the Second World War, early intervention programmes have been a feature of special education and arguably one of the significant contributions of that field. Early intervention, however, has not solely focused on disability. Amelioration of the effects of disadvantage has been the second major focus. Each focus reflects different contents and approaches but both share the aim of altering the outcomes for individuals at risk of developmental problems (Hayes 1991).

Prevention and early intervention efforts can also be focused on enhancing strengths, amplifying protective factors and enriching the available pathways (France and Utting 2005; Masten 2004). Typically this will be through provision of access to experiences that compensate for disadvantage, vulnerability and adverse life circumstances. Often, the focus will be both on reduction of negative and enrichment of positive factors. Parenting programmes, for example, may focus on both by reducing negative behaviours that are related to harsh, coercive or inconsistent parenting and enriching the parent's sense of competence by the development of positive parenting skills (Sanders *et al.* 2003). As Masten (2004) argues, there is much to be learned from the study of both negative and positive pathways.

By the implementation of well-designed initiatives, prevention and early intervention offer the potential to address and overcome a wide range of problems in development, health, learning, behaviour and well-being. As such, both have a capacity to influence, simultaneously, a range of factors that may have negative short- and longer-term impacts, while amplifying strengths and enriching positive attributes. They can have multiple impacts on multifaceted problems. Problems do, after all, tend to cluster, or as Loeber puts it, 'cascade' (Loeber and Stouthamer-Loeber 1998). Prevention and early intervention are compelling notions that are easily grasped by lay people and professionals alike and are particularly persuasive when evidence of cost effectiveness is provided.

To illustrate some of the origins of the focus on prevention and early intervention, I now turn to two particularly salient examples of interventions in early life. Both have landmark status in the field and each has contributed to the pervasiveness of the focus on early life. The first is the work of Skeels, which illustrates indicated prevention. The other, the High/Scope Perry Preschool Programme, illustrates selective prevention.

Skeels and the Iowa Orphanage Study

One of the developmental studies underpinning early intervention is the work of Skeels (1966). It began serendipitously when Skeels, a young psychologist, visited an orphanage in Iowa in the 1930s. He was informed of the presence of two baby girls who had been abandoned and placed in the institution. Their condition was pitiful and it was clear that they were unlikely to survive, such was the extent of their failure to thrive. Malnutrition, neglect and the lack of loving care had already begun to take their toll. Skeels arranged for the babies to be transferred to an institution for the 'mentally defective' and placed in the care of an adolescent girl, who was a resident of the institution. To his surprise, on returning some weeks later Skeels found that the waifs had flourished with the attention and care provided by the young woman.

On the basis of this experience, he went on to conduct a larger study involving the transfer from orphanages of 13 children aged under three years and placed in the care of women with an intellectual disability, in another institution. A comparison group included 12 children, again under three years of age, who remained in the orphanage. The Second World War intervened and Skeels went on to a distinguished career in psychology.

Some years later, it was suggested that he find the children who had been placed in the care of the young women in the institution for the intellectually disabled, and those who had formed the comparison group. The differences in life experience for the two groups were stark. Of the children reared by the women with an intellectual disability, all were self-supporting and had a median education level greater than the twelfth grade (Skeels 1966). In stark contrast, in the comparison group one child had died in an institution as an adolescent; four were wards of the state, living in institutions; only half were working; and the group had completed less than the fourth grade of school. This was compelling evidence indeed of the importance of early experience and the value of indicated prevention, or early intervention.

The High/Scope Perry Preschool Programme

A second and even more widely cited example of prevention and early intervention is the High/Scope Perry Preschool Programme. This targeted disadvantaged children and used an enriched preschool programme to provide a better start in life. The High/Scope Perry

Preschool Programme was offered to a group of young children, 58 in all, aged three and four years. The children were selected because they were at high risk of the developmental problems that flow from disadvantage. They lived in neighbourhoods that were marked by high rates of parental unemployment (40 per cent of families had no adult in employment) and single-parent families (50 per cent of families) and low rates of completion of school (11 per cent of the fathers and 21 per cent of the mothers).

The focus of the intervention was on the provision of two years of high-quality early childhood education, emphasising active learning, prior to school. In addition to the half-day sessions, involving individual and group work, the teachers provided home visiting, each week, to encourage parent involvement in their child's learning and development.

The influence of the High/Scope Perry Preschool Programme is grounded in its matched group design (with 65 children selected from similarly disadvantaged children who did not receive the intervention), and the availability of longitudinal evaluation data (Schweinhart *et al.* 1993). Over the years since the preschool intervention programme was established in 1962, both groups of children have been followed and assessed, annually from three years to 11 years of age, and then at 15 19, 27 and 40 years. Differences emerged during the primary school years and have widened through life. The children who had received the early childhood programme had higher levels of school achievement and appropriate behaviour at primary school. They were more likely to have completed secondary schooling and entered further education. They had better health outcomes. At 15, they showed lower levels of involvement in criminal activities. At 19, 27 and 40 years of age, they had fewer arrests and shorter incarcerations. Finally, they had higher levels of income and home ownership along with more stable family relationships. Cost-benefit analyses initially showed a US$7 return for every dollar invested; however, the most recent analysis reveals even greater benefits (US$17.07 per dollar invested), with the bulk of the benefit from reduction in the cost of crime for those who took part in the High/Scope Perry Preschool Programme (Schweinhart 2004).

Both examples provide powerful evidence of the value of prevention and intervention, early in life, when the risk factors are clearly evident, in Skeels' case in the form of social, emotional and cognitive deprivation, and in Weikart and Schweinhart's example, in the form of the multiple risks attending social and economic disadvantage. They share a focus on prevention, though through two different approaches. To reiterate, the Iowa study is an example of indicated prevention, while the High/Scope Perry Preschool Programme illustrates selective prevention. The High/Scope Perry Preschool Programme has exerted great influence on contemporary policy. It is widely cited, and its longitudinal follow-up data and evidence of cost-effectiveness have made it a powerful, if small-scale, tool in lobbying for the focus on prevention and early intervention.

As signalled in the introduction, two key questions are the focus of this chapter. The first is the timing question: Which problems require action when, over what time-frame, where and with whom? The second is the sustainability question: How are gains maintained? The discussion now turns to the first of these.

The timing question

To address the first, I draw on Loeber's work (Loeber and Stouthamer-Loeber 1998; Loeber and Farrington 1998; Loeber *et al.* 2003) along with some data from the Australian Temperament Project (ATP) (Prior *et al.* 2000).

The developmental ordering of problems

Loeber highlighted the developmental ordering of problems across the span from early childhood to adolescence. Problems such as difficult temperament, hyperactivity and overt conduct problems and aggressiveness tend to appear in early childhood, whereas withdrawal, poor peer relationships and academic problems are more likely to manifest themselves in the primary school years. Covert or concealing conduct problems, and association with deviant peers appear later and, later still, delinquency and recidivist involvement with juvenile crime.

He makes the point, however, that stability over time tends to be low, except for those showing antisocial behaviour early in life, especially outside the home. Even in this case, there is considerable variability, over time. The low stability of problems makes the timing of intervention a difficult issue. Loeber postulates that there are multiple pathways to criminality, and Loeber and Stouthamer-Loeber label these *overt*, *covert* and *authority conflict*. In their view, the overt pathway is associated with aggression, the covert with property crime, and the authority conflict with defiance and disobedience. The developmental stacking of behaviours suggests multiple points for intervention and, ultimately, the outcomes of early vulnerabilities are a function of the number of risks and problems and the presence of factors that catalyse their emergence. Hyperactivity (attention deficit hyperactivity disorder, ADHD) and substance use, for example, have been shown to be particular catalysts for later criminality.

Temperament and the timing of problems

The ATP provides some very valuable insights, via the lens of early temperament and its relationships to a range of outcomes (Hayes *et al.* 2004; Prior *et al.* 2000; Smart and Vassallo 2005). The study commenced in 1983, when the 2,443 participants were aged between four and eight months. The infants and their parents were broadly representative of the population of the Australian State of Victoria. Of the initial sample, two-thirds remain in the study. The measured variables included 'temperament style, behavioural and emotional adjustment, school attachment, health, social skills, antisocial behaviour, substance use, civic engagement, road safety, peer and family relationships, as well as family functioning, parenting practices, family structure and family socio-economic background' (Smart and Vassallo 2005: p. xiii). Self-, parent- and teacher-report data form the bases of the analyses.

The most recent analyses of the data span the period from infancy to the age of 19 to 20 years and focus, among other things, on alcohol use (Hayes *et al.* 2004) and driving behaviour (Smart and Vassallo 2005). Of particular relevance to the present discussion is the evidence that the ATP provides of the variation in the time when pathways became noticeable, in terms of the temperamental correlates of later problem behaviour.

The first, involving the pathway to multiple substance use at the age of 15 to 16 years, was discernible in infancy. Those who went on to report substance abuse in adolescence were, on parental report, less rhythmic as infants; less persistent and less co-operative as toddlers; less shy from three to four years on; more aggressive from five to six years on; and from primary school on showed greater inflexibility, poorer peer relations, more depressiveness but lower anxiety and fearfulness.

In contrast, the pathway to persistent antisocial behaviour in adolescence only became noticeable in the primary school years. Those who showed problems of antisocial behaviour had noticeably higher levels of acting out, aggression, hyperactivity, attention problems and volatility that became apparent in the primary school years. In turn, they had lower levels of co-operation, self-control and relationship with parents. At least in terms of temperament, however, there were no significant associations with parental reports of their characteristics in infancy.

The final example from the ATP relates to a pathway that was evident early in life for boys and in middle childhood for girls. It focuses on the problem of anxiety in adolescence. Boys who went on to show anxiety in adolescence by the age of three were noticeably more anxious and more likely to be considered to be shy. For girls, their higher anxiety, parent relationship factors and externalising problems only became noticeable at 11 to 12 years of age.

These are interesting data and dovetail, conceptually, with the work of Loeber and Stouthamer-Loeber. They also add further weight to the view that the timing of interventions will differ across problems, given that intervention can only occur when the indicators of a potential problem become discernible. The third example from the ATP highlights the considerable variation within and between children, including between boy and girls. So pathways may be differentiated by key sub-group characteristics such as, in this case, gender, as the work of Edwards (2006) also shows in relation to the greater impact of disadvantage on the early development of boys. Finally, prediction of outcomes is likely to be difficult (Hayes 1990), given the wider representation in the population of the indicators of any problem. Again, this reinforces the need for longitudinal studies designed to trace the various pathways people follow through life (France and Utting 2005).

Windows of opportunity and ports of entry

Timing suggests different 'ports of entry', to use Sameroff's (2004) term. Sameroff and Fiese (2000) apply a transactional model, in which change in one person leads to change in the other, in a cyclical set of transactions. In applying a transactional model to mother–infant prevention and intervention initiatives, Sameroff differentiates three types: *remediation*, which seeks to change the child's behaviour in order to change parental behaviour; *redefinition*, which aims to change the parent's interpretation of the child's behaviour; and *re-education*, which involves changing the parent's behaviour in order to change child behaviour. The ports of entry are likely to differ depending on the target and the timing of intervention. Similarly, Sameroff's typology highlights the need for prevention and early intervention to focus on both beliefs and behaviours, so both thought and action have to be considered (Goodnow, this volume). Recent research in the area of adolescent development illustrates this. Developmental changes in adolescence highlight both alterations in the ways adolescents interpret and construe their worlds and the ways they behave and act, especially in social situations (Blakemore and Choudhury 2006).

Adolescent development and the emergence of risky behaviour

In reading the recent early childhood literature one might conclude that this is the only time in life when key brain developments occur (Blakemore and Choudhury 2006), since this was a view that held considerable sway until quite recently. The technological and scientific breakthroughs that have focused attention on early brain development are now providing a window on development in adolescence that affords powerful insights into some of the hormonal and neurophysiological underpinnings of cognition and behaviour in this life phase.

Adolescence is a paradoxical period in human development (Dahl 2004). On the one hand, adolescents make a quantum leap in physical strength, intellectual processing speed and capacity, and overall resilience. On the other, this is a time of heightened risk, with morbidity and mortality rates doubling over the years of adolescence (Dahl 2004). Changes occur to multiple neurological and endocrinological systems and their interactions (Kelley *et al.* 2004), with brain developmental changes preceding and driving the hormonal changes associated with puberty (Dahl 2004). Changes to myelination and neuronal pruning, especially in the prefrontal cortex, characterise the entry to adolescence (Spear 2000, 2004). The net effects of these changes are profound and in part explain the propensity of adolescents to seek novelty and engage in risky behaviour (Blakemore and Choudhury 2006; Kelley *et al.* 2004; Spear 2000, 2004). Importantly, the neurological changes that occur in adolescence signal changes that continue through life (Blakemore and Choudhury 2006). Prevention and early intervention initiatives need to take account of these key changes that occur beyond early childhood, early in the pathways to later emerging problems.

The sustainability question

If the timing of the interventions to alter different pathways is problematic, then the sustainability of effects is of another order of magnitude entirely. This begs the question, how are gains to be maintained? As Brooks-Gunn (2003) argues, the issue is steeped in magical thinking and there is still much to be learned about the processes that operate to sustain effects. On the one hand, she highlights the fact that the effect sizes of early intervention are impressive (especially early in life, but presumably also early in the pathway), when compared and contrasted with interventions later in life when pathways are more deeply entrenched. On the other, she provides a compelling critique of what might be called the *early childhood error* – the belief that all is evident and active, albeit in some instances in latent form, in early life and therefore remediable then, if only we had the knowledge. What is not clear is what is sustained, as opposed to lost, from early experience. I am reminded of the book by Rutter *et al.* (1979) *Fifteen Thousand Hours*, and the limited residue of all that time spent in school. Not everything experienced is retained!

The evidence for what sustains the effects of early interventions is interesting. As Sameroff (2004) observes, 'developmental achievements are rarely sole consequences of immediate causes and more rarely sole consequences of earlier events' (2004: 9). Outcomes are also influenced by the interpretations of events, and these in turn change over life (Sameroff 2004). There is a need to move beyond simple main effects models of the outcomes of development, including of our efforts to alter developmental pathways through prevention and early intervention, and consider 'more complex pathways, [including] indirect, interactive or transactional effects' (Sanson *et al.* 2004: 160).

The sustainability issue also fits the evaluation data, which shows short- and medium-term effects for many interventions, but questionable long-term outcomes (Wise *et al.* 2005). Wise *et al.* conclude that 'the measured effects of early childhood interventions were mostly limited to the immediate and short term. Reductions in acts of delinquency and crime (which are easily measured) were the most enduring intervention effects reported' (2005: 66).

The importance of longitudinal approaches

As Emde (2003) observes in his commentary on the Brooks-Gunn (2003) paper, prospective longitudinal evaluations are essential if we are to tease out the factors that sustain outcomes. Such studies will provide valuable insights into issues of change and continuity of pathways, and the factors and processes that sustain or change pathways (Masten 2004). Appropriately designed longitudinal evaluations will also provide evidence of the extent of gains across groups. In addition, prospective longitudinal evaluations can shed light on the 'dose' question, or whether higher levels of participation lead to larger effects that are of greater durability (Hill *et al.* 2003; Reynolds *et al.* 2001; Shonkoff and Phillips 2000).

At present, views of the scale of gains are diametrically opposed, with some such as Zigler (2003) arguing that the gains from targeted early intervention with the disadvantaged are less than those for more advantaged groups in the community. In reflecting on the recent evaluation of Sure Start, in the UK, Rutter (2006) concludes that 'there is modest evidence that well planned interventions for young children in disadvantaged families can make a wortwhile difference' (2006: 135). In contrast, on the basis of longitudinal follow-up data from the Chicago Child–Parent Centers Programme for young children from disadvantaged predominantly African-American neighbourhoods, Reynolds and Ou (2003) conclude that the effects are greater for those in greater disadvantage.

There is clearly a need to research the factors and processes that sustain the effects of the experiences involved in early intervention and prevention. These sustaining factors and processes are important mediators and moderators of the impacts of experience. The work of Sampson and Laub (2005; Laub and Sampson 2003) underscores the scope for change and the influence of what I would call *sustaining systems* that, in the case of adult criminality, alter negative pathways and maintain positive ones. They cite the evidence for the world of work, with its regularities and routines, and close personal relationships as two such systems. They further highlight the mediating effect on delinquency in adolescence of informal social control, over and above structural background factors, such as family poverty. Sampson and Laub make a persuasive case for the changing nature of these mediating and moderating factors and processes, illustrating their argument with data on the transition from adolescence to adulthood.

Sustaining systems

So what are some examples of such sustaining systems? The Head Start follow-up studies and the work of Reynolds (Reynolds and Ou 2003; Reynolds *et al.* 2001, 2004; Smokowski *et al.* 2003) and Currie and Thomas (2000a, 2000b), among others, show the importance of high-quality schooling in sustaining the effects of interventions, early in life. Using structural equation modelling of the Child–Parent Centre

Programme data from the Chicago Longitudinal Study, Reynolds and Ou demonstrate that while the cognitive advantage hypothesis best fit the data, the combination of school quality and parent participation were powerful mediators and moderators of longer-term outcomes, with the protective effects of participation in the intervention evident into early adulthood. Quality of schooling especially differentiates the longer-term outcomes for African-American 'graduates' of Head Start when compared with their Anglo counterparts (Currie and Thomas 200b). A recent meta-analysis of school mobility shows that stability of schooling is another dimension that influences later developmental outcomes when taken in combination with the effects of socio-economic disadvantage (Mehana and Reynolds 2004). The results discussed above broadly mirror those of the High/Scope Perry Preschool Programme, although with data from a much larger sample (998 in the intervention group and 550 in the comparison sample, as opposed to 58 and 65 respectively for the High/Scope Perry Preschool Programme).

If one is to avoid magical thinking, the mechanisms that sustain the effects should be given at least as much attention as the prevention initiatives or interventions that result in these effects. The available evidence suggests that social systems such as schools and families will play a considerable role in sustaining the effects of initiatives in early life. As Reynolds *et al.* (2004) conclude in considering the findings of the analyses of the Chicago Child–Parent Centers:

> The widely held belief that enhanced cognitive skills are the sole or primary source of effects was not supported. Although the mechanisms are complex, factors influencing the long-term effects of intervention can be modified by educators, parents, and policy-makers. (2004: 1322)

The data examined by Sampson and Laub (2005), from the Gluecks follow-up study of 500 male delinquents, and 500 matched male non-delinquents, aged 10 to 17 years, provide a rich longitudinal lens through which to view the transition from adolescence to adulthood and the pathways that those studied took across this period of the life course. Data were available at 14, 25 and 32 years. Sampson and Laub's analyses highlight the scope for divergence in the pathways of delinquents, despite their 'shared beginnings'. They challenge the typologies of delinquents: 'Not only is prediction clearly poor at the individual level, our data reveal the tenuous basis for the sorts of distinct groupings that dominate theoretical discussions' (2005: 10).

They show that 'there is stability and change in behaviour over the life course and these changes are systematically linked to the institutions of work and family relations in adulthood' (2005: 8). The presence or absence of connections to the important social systems, in this case work and relationships, explain the patterns of desistance or persistence they observed in the life courses of the juvenile offenders.

In reflecting on the Kauai Longitudinal Study, arguably *the* ground-breaking study of resilience, Werner (2005) extends the list:

> Among the most potent forces for positive changes for high-risk youth who had a record of delinquency and/or mental health problems in adolescence, and for teenage mothers, were continuing education at community colleges; educational and vocational skills acquired during voluntary service in the Armed Forces; marriage to a stable partner; conversion to a religion that required active participation in a 'community of faith'; recovery from a life threatening illness or accident that required a lengthy hospitalisation; and occasionally psychotherapy. (2005: 7)

Homel (2005) reaches a similar conclusion. It is the social institutions that underpin a child-friendly society that will be crucial in ensuring that investments are sustained, be they early in life or early in the pathway. For early in life, availability of quality preschool education, quality schooling, and the social systems that work to ameliorate the effects of poverty are significant sustaining systems. In reflecting on the Chicago Longitudinal Study data on academic, social and mental health outcomes in adolescence, Smokowski *et al.* (2003) conclude that 'early childhood intervention in preschool had the widest ranging protective effects on all three adolescent outcomes' (2003: 63).

The importance of preschool intervention, as highlighted in the Pathways to Prevention project (Freiberg *et al.* 2005), especially on the boys participating in the project, underscores the value of 'broad-spectrum' universal services, such as preschool, in addressing a range of potential developmental problems, in this case early in life. Similarly, writing in the context of Canadian prevention and early intervention initiatives, Hoddinott *et al.* (2002) point to the large cumulative effects of bundles of household characteristics which often occur together (2002: i) which again suggests the need for broadly based prevention and intervention approaches.

Preschool education increasingly is seen as a foundational support for young children that has established short-, medium- and long-term benefits (Research and Policy Committee of the Committee for Economic Development 2002) and offers a base for intervention across a number of developmental domains. The durability of these effects has been demonstrated, impressively, by the most recent analyses of the data from the national Child Development Study in the UK (Goodman and Sianesi 2005). Pre-compulsory education, either through preschool or via early entry to school, has been shown to effect cognitive improvements that are evident at age seven and remain at 16 years of age. In contrast, nursery and playgroups produced only short-term effects. The effects are indeed long term, with the benefits of pre-compulsory education evident in higher qualifications and employment levels at age 33 years (Goodman and Sianesi 2005). In addressing the question, how big are these effects?, they state:

> the gains to early cognition (age 7) are of a comparable size to those associated with growing up in a family where the father is of high social class, and almost completely counteract the negative effects on test scores of growing up in a difficult family environment. However, whilst these latter family background effects either stay the same or grow bigger throughout childhood and adulthood, the effects of early education diminish, and so are small relative to the impact of these family background factors by the time the individual enters adulthood. The addition of wages due to extra schooling before the age of 5 (around 3%) are small compared to the estimated gains from an extra year of schooling later on in a person's school career, which have been estimated at around 6%. On the other hand, for some groups of the population such as those who are not first-born children, the estimated effect on wages is somewhat higher (5 per cent for second or later born children, at age 33 and 42). (Goodman and Sianesi 2005: 23)

In addition to the material reviewed above, Goodman and Sianesi's work highlights the need for closer consideration of the limited duration of early life impacts, unless they connect systems that sustain their impacts, such as schooling, employment and close personal relationships.

Windows of opportunity and ports of entry clearly extend beyond the early years, and family and school-based interventions increasingly are the focus for addressing problems that manifest in later periods of childhood and adolescence. Given the importance of family characteristics on the outcomes of preventive interventions in early life (NICHD 2003; Sammons *et al.* 2002, 2003), it is hardly surprising that programmes later in life focus on the family as a context for intervention and the basis for sustainability beyond the life of the intervention initiative. Increasingly, substance abuse and antisocial behaviour are addressed through family-based approaches (Farrington and Welsh 1999; Hogue and Liddle 1999; Hogue *et al.* 2002; Liddle *et al.* 2004).

Schools are important as a context in which to address a wide range of problems from alcohol abuse (Brown *et al.* 2005) and other substance abuse (Waldron and Kern-Jones 2004) to emotional and behavioural disorders (Conroy *et al.* 2004), including adolescent depression (Kowalenko *et al.* 2005) and conduct disorders (Prinz and Dumas 2004), as well as antisocial, violent behaviour (Hawkins *et al.* 2003; Sprague and Walker 2000). The sustaining social systems – families, childcare provisions, preschools, schools, peer groups, vocational, further and higher education, community organisations, and the world of work – are vital as the loci for prevention and intervention, as well as for maintaining their benefits.

Conclusion

The material reviewed in this chapter highlights the need for thinking systemically about early intervention and prevention and the factors that sustain their benefits. It requires a comprehensive, integrated policy focus, if sustainability is to be achieved. As Appleyard *et al.* (2005) recently observed with regard to child behavioural outcomes: 'given the significant impact of multiple risks from varying family domains, interventions should be designed as comprehensive programs that enhance as many aspects of family life as possible' (2005: 243). I would extend their logic beyond the behavioural focus, and beyond the family.

The timing of the onset of problem behaviours is also related to differences in pathways and their developmental prognoses. Patterson and Yoerger (2002), for example, postulate two pathways to juvenile offending. One, the early onset pathway, has its origins in early childhood and predicts adult career criminality. In the other, the late onset pathway, juvenile offenders are more likely to desist as adults. Others identify five pathways that they label 'non-offenders, late onsetters, desistors, escalators and chronic offenders' (Hawkins *et al.* 2003: 301). Pathways differentiated by the timing of onset have been similarly identified for alcohol abuse, with those who start drinking earlier having a higher probability of adult problem drinking (Spear 2000).

Timing and sustainability are key issues. As Clarke and Clarke (1976) observe, 'what one does for a child at any age, provided it is maintained, plays a part in shaping his development within the limits imposed by genetic and constitutional factors' (1976: 273). Reflecting on the long history of early intervention for children, I am reminded of Farran's (2000) conclusion:

> Somehow, our nation has to move beyond thinking of the problems of young children as being something someone else fixes at an earlier age or in a different place so that other systems do not have to change. A developmental focus that covers the first 12 to 15 years of life would be a good start. (2000: 542)

There is a need to move beyond a focus on individuals to the individual in social context. In reviewing the research from the Montreal Longitudinal and Experimental Study, Tremblay and his colleagues have concluded that a focus on offenders needs to be replaced by 'a lifespan, intergenerational approach to the problem' (Tremblay *et al.* 2003: 244). This resonates with the findings of Hawkins and his colleagues in the Seattle Social Development Project (Hawkins *et al.* 1999), who concluded that 'a package of interventions with teachers, parents, and children provided throughout the elementary grades can have enduring effects in reducing violent behavior, heavy drinking and sexual intercourse by age 18 years among multiethnic urban children' (1999: 226). Such a life-course, comprehensive approach, focused on the key sustaining systems, and supported by integrated policy and practice, both for prevention and early intervention, would be a good start in addressing the issues of timing and sustainability, discussed in this chapter.

Early in life? Or early in the pathway? When it comes to both indicated and selective prevention, early in life is only a matter of early in the pathways that emerge in the early years. Many other pathways emerge later in childhood, adolescence and even adulthood. From a life-span developmental perspective, early in life is never enough!

Acknowledgements

I wish to acknowledge the assistance of my colleagues, Ruth Weston, Matthew Gray, Diana Smart, Suzanne Vassallo, Judy Adams, Gillian Lord, Carole Jean, Anita Emmanouilidis and Nancy Virgona, in the preparation of this chapter. Their assistance, along with the helpful editorial suggestions of Professor Ross Homel and an anonymous reviewer, are greatly appreciated.

References

Appleyard, K., Egeland, B., van Dulmen, M.H.M. and Sroufe, L.A. (2005) 'When more is not better: The role of cumulative risk in child behavior outcomes', *Journal of Child Psychology and Psychiatry*, 46(3): 235–45.

Blakemore, S-J. and Choudhury, S. (2006) 'Development of the adolescent brain: Implications for executive function and social cognition', *Journal of Child Psychology and Psychiatry*, 47 (3/4): 296–312.

Brooks-Gunn, J. (2003) 'Do you believe in magic? What can we expect from early childhood intervention programs', *Social Policy Report*, XVII(1): 3–15.

Brown, S.A., Anderson, K.G., Schulte, M.T., Sintov, N.D. and Frissell, K.C. (2005) 'Facilitating youth self change through school-based intervention', *Addictive Behaviors*, 30(9): 1797–810.

Clarke, A.M. and Clarke, A.D.B. (1976) *Early Experience: Myth and Evidence*. London: Open Books.

Conroy, M., Hendrickson, J.M., and Hester, P.P. (2004) Early Identification and Prevention of Emotional and Behavioural Disorders', in R.E. Rutherford, M.M. Quinn and S.R. Mathur (eds) *Handbook of Research in Emotional and Behavioural Disorders* New York: Guilford Press, pp. 199–215.

Corrie, L. (2000) 'Neuroscience and early childhood? A dangerous liaison', *Australian Journal of Early Childhood*, 26(2): 34–40.

Currie, J. and Thomas, D. (2000a) 'Does Head Start make a difference?', *American Economic Review*, 85(3): 341–64.

Currie, J. and Thomas, D. (2000b) 'School quality and the longer-term effects of Head Start', *Journal of Human Resources*, XXXV(4): 755–74.

Cynader, M.S. and Frost, B. (1999) 'Mechanisms of Brain Development: Neuronal Sculpting by the Physical and Social Environment', in D.P. Keating and C. Hertzman (eds) *Developmental Health and the Wealth of Nations: Social, Biological and Educational Dynamics*. New York: Guilford Press, pp. 153–84.

Dahl, R.E. (2004) 'Adolescent Brain Development: A Period of Vulnerabilities and Opportunities', in R. E. Dahl and L.P. Spear (eds) *Adolescent Brain Development: Vulnerabilities and Opportunities*, *Annals of the New York*

Academy of Science, 1021. New York: New York Academy of Science, pp. 1–22.

Developmental Crime Prevention Consortium (1999) *Pathways to Prevention: Developmental and Early Intervention Approaches to Crime in Australia.* Canberra: Australian Government Publishing Service.

Edwards, B. (2006) 'Does it take a village? An investigation of neighbourhood effects on Australian children's development', *Family Matters*, 72: 36–43.

Emde, R.T. (2003) 'Charting intervention effects over time', *Social Policy Report*, XVII(1): 8.

Farran, D.C. (2000) 'Another Decade of Early Intervention for Children who are Low Income or Disabled: What Do We Know Now?', in J.P. Shonkoff and S.J. Meisels (eds) *Handbook of Early Intervention*, 2nd edn. Cambridge: Cambridge University Press, pp. 510–48.

Farrington, D.P. and Welsh, B.C. (1999) 'Delinquency-based prevention using family-based interventions', *Children and Society*, 13: 287–303.

Fox, N.A., Calkins, S.D. and Bell, M. (1994) 'Neural plasticity and development in the first two years of life: Evidence from cognitive and socioemotional domains of research', *Development and Psychopathology*, 6: 667–96.

France, A., and Utting, D. (2005) 'The paradigm of "risk and protection-focused prevention" and its impact on services for children and families', *Children and Society*, 19: 77–90.

Freiberg, K., Homel, R., Batchelor, S., Carr, A., Lamb, I., Elias, G. and Teague, R. (2005) 'Pathways to participation: A community-based developmental prevention project in Australia', *Children and Society*, 19(2): 144–57.

Goodman, A. and Sianesi, B. (2005) *Early Education and Children's Outcomes: How Long do the Impacts Last?* London: Institute for Fiscal Studies.

Gordon, R.S. Jr (1983) 'An operational classification of disease prevention', *Public Health Reports*, 98(2): 107–09.

Hawkins, J.D., Catalano, R.F., Kosterman, R., Abbott, R. and Hill, K.G. (1999) 'Preventing adolescent health-risk behaviours by strengthening protection during childhood', *Archives of Pediatric and Adolescent Medicine*, 153: 226–34.

Hawkins, J.D., Smith, B.H., Hill, K.G., Kosterman, R. Catalano, R.F. and Abbott, R.D. (2003) 'Understanding and Preventing Crime and Violence: Findings from the Seattle Social Development Project', in T.P. Thornberry and M. Krohn (eds) *Taking Stock of Delinquency: An Overview of Findings from Contemporary Longitudinal Studies* New York: Kluwer, pp. 255–312.

Hayes, A. (1990) 'Developmental psychology, education and the need to move beyond typological thinking', *Australian Journal of Education*, 34(3): 235–41.

Hayes, A. (1991) 'The Changing Face of Early Intervention in Australia: Following Fads and Fashions?', in K. Marfo (ed.) *Early Intervention in Transition: Current Perspectives on Programs for Handicapped Children.* New York: Praeger, pp. 271–98.

Hayes, L., Smart, D., Toumbourou, J. and Sanson, A.V. (2004) *Parenting Influences on Adolescent Alcohol Use*. Melbourne: Australian Institute of Family Studies.

Hill, J.L., Brooks-Gunn, J. and Waldfogel, J. (2003) 'Sustained effects of high participation in an early intervention for low-birth-weight premature infants', *Developmental Psychology*, 39(4): 730–44.

Hoddinott, J., Lethbridge, L. and Phipps, S. (2002) *Is History Destiny? Resources, Transitions and Child Education Attainments in Canada. Final Report*. Hull, Quebec: Human Resources Development Canada.

Hogue, A. and Liddle, H.A. (1999) 'Family-based preventive intervention: An approach to preventing substance use and antisocial behavior', *American Journal of Orthopsychiatry*, 69(3): 278–93.

Hogue, A., Liddle, H.A., Becker, D. and Johnson-Leckrone, J. (2002) 'Family-based counselling for high-risk young adolescents: Immediate outcomes', *Journal of Community Psychology*, 30(1): 1–22.

Homel, R. (2005) 'Developmental Crime Prevention', in N. Tilley (ed.) *Handbook of Crime Prevention and Community Safety*. Cullompton: Willan Publishing.

Johnson, R.L. (2002) 'Pathways to adolescent health: Early intervention', *Journal of Adolescent Health*, 31, 240–50.

Keating, D.P. and Hertzman, C. (1999) 'Modernity's Paradox', in D.P. Keating and C. Hertzman (eds) *Developmental Health and the Wealth of Nations: Social, Biological and Educational Dynamics*. New York: Guilford Press, pp. 1–18.

Kelley, A.E., Schochet, T. and Landry, C.F. (2004) 'Risk-taking and Novelty Seeking in Adolescence', in R.E. Dahl. and L.P. Spear (eds) *Adolescent Brain Development: Vulnerabilities and Opportunities*, Annals of the New York Academy of Science, 1021. New York: New York Academy of Science, pp. 27–32.

Kowalenko, N., Rapee, R., Simmons, J. Wignall, A., Hoge, R., Whitefield, K., Starling, J., Stonehouse, R. and Baillie, A.J. (2005) 'Short-term effectiveness of a school-based early intervention program for adolescent depression', *Clinical Child Psychology and Psychiatry*, 10(4): 493–507.

Laub, J.H. and Sampson, R.J. (2003) *Shared Beginnings, Divergent Lives: Delinquent Boys to Age 70*. Cambridge, MA: Harvard University Press.

Liddle, H.A., Rowe, C.L., Dakof, G.A., Ungaro, R.A. and Henderson, C.E. (2004) 'Early intervention for adolescent substance abuse: Pretreatment to posttreatment outcomes of a randomised clinical trial comparing multidimensional family therapy and peer group treatment', *Journal of Psychoactive Drugs*, 36(1): 49–63.

Little, M. (1999) 'Prevention and early intervention with children in need: Definitions, principles and examples of good practice', *Children and Society*, 13, 304–16.

Loeber, R. and Farrington, D. (1998) 'Never too early, never too late. Risk factors and successful interventions for serious and violent juvenile offenders', *Studies on Crime and Crime Prevention*, 7(1): 7–30.

Loeber, R. and Stouthamer-Loeber, M. (1998) 'Development of juvenile aggression and violence: Some common misconceptions and controversies', *American Psychologist*, 53(2): 242–49.

Loeber, R., Farrington, D.P., Stouthamer-Loeber, M., Moffitt, T.E., Caspi, A., White, H.R., Wei, E.H. and Beyers, J.M. (2003) 'The Development of Male Offending: Key Findings from Fourteen Years of the Pittsburgh Youth Study', in T.P. Thornberry and M. Krohn (eds) *Taking Stock of Delinquency: An Overview of Findings from Contemporary Longitudinal Studies*. New York: Kluwer, pp. 93–136.

Masten, A.S. (2004) 'Regulatory Processes, Risk and Resilience in Adolescent Development', in R.E. Dahl and L.P. Spear (eds) *Adolescent Brain Development: Vulnerabilities and Opportunities, Annals of the New York Academy of Science, 1021*. New York: New York Academy of Science, pp. 310–19.

McCain, M.N. and Mustard, J.F. (1999), *Reversing the Real Brain Drain: Early Years Study Final Report*. Government of Ontario/Founders' Network.

Mehana, M. and Reynolds, A.J. (2004) 'School mobility and achievement: A meta-analysis', *Children and Youth Services Review*, 26: 93–119.

Nelson, C.A. and Bloom, F.E. (1997) 'Child development and neuroscience', *Child Development, 68*: 970–87.

NICHD Early Child Care Research Network (2003) 'Families matter – even for kids in child care', *Journal of Developmental ane Behavioral Pediatrics*, 24: 58–62.

Patterson, G.R. and Yoerger, K. (2002) 'A Developmental Model for Early- and Late-Onset Delinquency', in J.B. Reid, G.R. Patterson and J. Snyder (eds) *Antisocial Behaviour in Children and Adolescents: A Developmental Model for Intervention*. Washington, DC: American Psychological Association, pp. 147–72.

Prior, M., Sanson, A., Smart, D. and Oberklaid, F. (2000) *Pathways from Infancy to Adolescence: Australian Temperament Project 1983–2000*. Melbourne: Australian Institute of Family Studies.

Prinz, R.P. and Dumas, J.E. (2004) 'Prevention of Oppositional Defiant Disorder and Conduct Disorder in Children and Adolescents', in P.M. Barrett and T.H. Ollendick (eds) *Handbook of Interventions that Work with Children and Adolescents: Prevention and Treatment*. Chichester: John Wiley, pp. 475–88.

Research and Policy Committee of the Committee for Economic Development (2002) *Preschool for All: Investing in a Productive and Just Society*. New York: Committee for Economic Development.

Reynolds, A.J. and Ou, S-R. (2003) 'Promoting Resilience Through Early Childhood Intervention', in S.S. Luthar (ed.) *Resilience and Vulnerability: Adaptation in the Context of Childhood Adversities*. Cambridge: Cambridge University Press.

Reynolds, A.J., Ou, S-R. and Topitzes, J.W. (2004) 'Paths of effects of early childhood interventions on educational attainment and delinquency:

A confirmatory analysis of the Chicago Child-Parent Centers', *Child Development*, 75(5): 1299–328.

Reynolds, A.J., Temple, J.A., Robertson, D.L. and Mann, E.A. (2001) 'Long-term effects of an early childhood intervention on educational achievement and juvenile arrest: A 15-year follow-up of low-income children in public schools', *Journal of the American Medical Association*, 285(18): 2339–46.

Rutter, M. (2006) 'Is Sure Start and effective preventive intervention?', *Child and Adolescent Mental Health*, 11(3): 135–41.

Rutter, M., Maugham, B., Mortimer, P. and Ouston, J. (1979). *Fifteen Thousand Hours.* London: Open Books.

Sameroff, A.J. (2004) 'Ports of Entry and the Dynamics of Mother–Infant Interventions', in A.J. Sameroff, S.C. McDonough and K.L. Rosenblum (eds) *Treating Parent–Infant Relationship Problems: Strategies for Intervention* New York: Guilford Press, pp. 3–28.

Sameroff, A. and Fiese, B. (2000), 'Transactional Regulation: The Developmental Ecology of Early Intervention', in J.P. Shonkoff and S.J. Meisels (eds) *Handbook of Early Intervention*, 2nd edn. Cambridge: Cambridge University Press, pp. 135–59.

Sammons, P., Sylva, K., Melhuish, E., Siraj-Blatchford, I., Taggart, B. and Elliott, K. (2002). *Measuring the Impact of Pre-school in Children's Cognitive Progress over the Preschool Period*, Technical Paper 8a. London: Institute of Education, University of London.

Sammons, P., Sylva, K., Melhuish, E., Siraj-Blatchford, I., Taggart, B. and Elliott, K. (2003) *Measuring the Impact of Pre-school in Children's Social Behavioural Development over the Preschool Period*, Technical Paper 8b. London: Institute of Education, University of London.

Sampson, R.J. and Laub, J.H. (2005) 'A General Age Graded Theory of Crime: Lessons Learned and the Future of Life-course Criminology', in D.P. Farrington (ed.) *Integrated Developmental and Life-course Theories of Offending: Advances in Criminological Theory*, Vol. 14. New Brunswick, NJ: Transaction Publishers, pp. 165–81.

Sanders, M., Markie-Dadds, C. and Turner, K. (2003) 'Theoretical, scientific and clinical foundations of the Triple P – Positive Parenting Program: A population approach to the promotion of parenting competence', *Parenting Research and Practice Monograph No. 1:* 1–24.

Sanson, A., Hemphill, S.A. and Smart, D. (2004) 'Connections between temperament and social development: A review', *Social Development*, 13(1): 142–170.

Schorr, L.B. (1997) *Common Purpose: Strengthening Families and Neighbourhoods to Rebuild America.* New York: Anchor Books.

Schweinhart, L.J. (2004) *The High/Scope Perry Preschool Study Through Age 40.* Ypsilanti, MI: High Scope Press.

Schweinhart, L.J., Barnes, H. and Weikhart, D. (1993) *Significant Benefits: The High/Scope Perry Preschool Study Through Age 27.* Ypsilanti, MI: High Scope Press.

Shonkoff, J.P. and Meisels, S.J. (eds) (2000) *Handbook of Early Childhood Intervention*, 2nd edn. Cambridge: Cambridge University Press.

Shonkoff, J.P. and Phillips, D.A. (eds.) (2000) *From Neurons to Neighbourhoods: The Science of Early Childhood Development.* Washington, DC: National Academy Press.

Skeels, H.M. (1966) 'Adult status of children with contrasting early life experiences', *Monographs of the Society for Research in Child Development,* Serial No. 105, 31 (3).

Smart, D. and Vassallo, S. (2005) *In the Driver's Seat: Understanding Young Adults' Driving Behaviour.* Melbourne: Australian Institute of Family Studies.

Smith, J. (2006) 'Psychological Vitality in Old Age: A New Look at an Old Concept'. Keynote Address to the 19th meeting of the International Society for the Study of Behavioral Development, Melbourne, Australia, 2–6 July.

Smokowski, P.R., Mann, E.A., Reynolds, A.R. and Fraser, M.W. (2003) 'Childhood risk and protective factors and late adolescent adjustment in inner city minority youth', *Children and Youth Services Review*, 26: 63–91.

Spear, L.P. (2000) 'The adolescent brain and age-related behavioural manifestations', *Neuroscience and Biobehavioral Reviews*, 24: 417–63.

Spear, L.P. (2004) 'Adolescent Brain Development and Animal Models', in R.E. Dahl and L.P. Spear (eds) *Adolescent Brain Development: Vulnerabilities and opportunities*, *Annals of the New York Academy of Science*, 1021. New York: New York Academy of Science, pp. 23–6.

Sprague, J. and Walker, H. (2000), 'Early identification and intervention for youth with antisocial and violent behavior', *Exceptional Children*, 66(3): 367–79.

Tremblay, R.E., Vitaro, F. and Nagin, D., Pagani, L. and Séguin, J.R. (2003) in 'The Montreal Longitudinal and Experimental Study', T.P. Thornberry and M. Krohn (eds) *Taking Stock of Delinquency: An Overview of Findings from Contemporary Longitudinal Studies.* New York: Kluwer, pp. 205–54.

Waldron, H.B. and Kern-Jones, S. (2004) 'Treatment of Substance Abuse Disorders in Children and Adolescents', in P.M. Barrett and T.H. Ollendick (eds) *Handbook of Interventions that Work with Children and Adolescents: Prevention and Treatment.* Chichester: John Wiley, pp. 329–42.

Werner, E.E. (2005) 'Resilience Research: Past, Present and Future', in R. DeV. Peters, B. Leadbeater and R.J. McMahon (eds) *Resilience in Children, Families and Communities: Linking Context to Practice and Policy.* New York: Kluwer Academic/Plenum, pp. 3–11.

Wise, S., da Silva, L., Webster, E. and Sanson, A. (2005) *The Efficacy of Early Interventions*, Research Report No. 14. Melbourne: Australian Institute of Family Studies.

Zigler, E. (2003) 'Forty years of believing in magic is enough', *Social Policy Report*, XVII(1): 10.

Chapter 11

The pervasive impact of poverty on children: tackling family adversity and promoting child development through the Pathways to Prevention project

Kate Freiberg, Ross Homel and Cherie Lamb

Abstract

The Pathways to Prevention project involves a university–community organisation–schools partnership designed to bring together a range of programmes to reduce the strength of the association between social disadvantage and poor developmental outcomes for children growing up in one of the most disadvantaged urban areas in Queensland. Beginning from an understanding that development is tied to the social contexts in which it occurs, one strategy that became an immediate driving force for programme activity was to provide an accessible and sensitive family support service to strengthen family function and promote positive child-rearing conditions. The Family Independence Programme (FIP) is focused on the goal of family empowerment and supporting families through adversity. Correlation analysis confirmed that level of family adversity was related to children's developmental competence (language, behaviour and prosocial skills) and that this relationship was most likely mediated by parent efficacy. Preliminary analyses of the effect of FIP involvement indicate its positive impact on parents' sense of efficacy and sense of being supported in the parenting role. It is concluded that supporting families in dealing with adversity is a key to promoting positive outcomes for children. Furthermore, it is argued that a comprehensive approach is required wherein family-oriented programmes such as Pathways to Prevention form part of a wider societal movement to reduce the social and economic stressors that impact on family function.

Introduction

Longitudinal research that traces pathways of individual development from birth or childhood to adulthood consistently highlights the way certain disruptive conditions and experiences (so-called 'risk factors' like poverty and abuse) increase the likelihood of poor developmental outcomes. For example, in his summation of evidence from the Cambridge Study of the development of delinquent behaviour that followed a large group of boys over a 35-year period from the ages of approximately 11 to 46, Farrington concluded that:

> The main policy implication of the Cambridge Study is that, in order to reduce offending and antisocial behaviour, early prevention experiments are needed targeting four important predictors that may be both causal and modifiable: low achievement, poor parental child-rearing behaviour, impulsivity, and poverty. (Farrington 2003: 175)

Farrington's (2003) statement encapsulates the 'simple' reality of a complex issue. To begin, it presents a balanced perspective on development that upholds the concept of resilience alongside the recognition of risk (e.g. acknowledging that the effects of exposure to some risks are modifiable through intervention). More important, perhaps, it focuses attention squarely on the reason why single-focus interventions and piecemeal prevention approaches are destined to fail: complex social problems (like crime and antisocial behaviour) are influenced by many interrelated factors and so must be addressed by co-ordinating and linking action across multiple spheres. This means more than running (say) child- and parent-focused programmes in parallel, or even making sure they reinforce each other. It also means understanding the nature of the connections between developmental settings such as home, school and neighbourhood, the impact of forces such as poverty or culture on these connections, and addressing where necessary the gaps, disruptions or conflicts that do so much to undermine healthy development.

Consistent with Farrington's conclusion, the Pathways to Prevention project has been guided from its inception by theory and empirical research about the pathways through which antisocial behaviour develops (Freiberg *et al.* 2005). These pathways encompass individual, family, school, community and societal factors, as well as their interactions. The intervention model used within the Pathways to Prevention project mirrors these processes and pathways and works across those same individual, family, school and community contexts. However, fundamental to our approach is our belief that the ultimate success of programmes like Pathways depends on their being part of a wider social movement that works directly to reduce poverty, or at least to ameliorate its impacts in disadvantaged communities.

In this chapter we discuss the rationale for and the development of the Pathways project, with a particular emphasis on the role of poverty and the ways in which we attempted to understand and address its effects on families and children. We then report the outcomes of an analysis of the links between family functioning (specifically, the extent of family adversity, parental efficacy, and parent involvement with their children) and children's development (specifically, language and social skills). We conclude by reporting preliminary analyses of the way family involvement in the project may promote resilience and contribute to positive developmental outcomes.

Project rationale: the context for intervention

The community as a context for intervention

The impact of poverty is of substantial concern, even for children growing up in an affluent and privileged country like Australia, where it has been reported that 14.7 per cent of children currently live in poverty (UNICEF 2005). The links between poverty and children's development are well documented (e.g. Bradley and Corwyn 2002; Brooks-Gunn and Duncan 1997; McLoyd 1998). One reason why the impact of poverty is so pernicious relates to the changing nature of its distribution. It has been noted that there is a growing trend towards the geographic concentration of poverty and within Australia, as in other countries, there are marked regional variations in socio-economic status (Glover *et al.* 1999). The social environment that develops within these localised pockets of poverty is one where a number of mechanisms that can disrupt development are activated simultaneously. Poverty thus represents not so much a single risk factor as a complex web of interacting processes that create a social context within which the barriers to social participation and the achievement of even simple daily tasks can pile up and become overwhelming, especially for parents with young children.

Children living in poverty are more likely to experience a range of stressors, such as incarceration of family members, substance abuse and mental health problems within the family, poor health, substandard housing, high mobility and disrupted schooling, family conflict, separation from or loss of family members, underemployment and reduced accessibility to jobs, financial hardship and food insecurity (Gorman-Smith *et al.* 2005). For children living in neighbourhoods where poverty is endemic, these within-family stresses are exacerbated by lowered safety and morale at the community level. These environments are frequently characterised by high levels of unrest, violence, drug use, disengagement, alienation, and poor access to informal social supports and quality facilities. Living in poverty, and more specifically in poor neighbourhoods, therefore reduces access not only to financial capital, but to social and human capital as well (Coleman 1988).

It seems likely that the paradoxical rise in social problems observed by Keating and Hertzman (1999) and Stanley *et al.* (2005) will not be reversed unless society is willing to address seriously the issues of poverty and its sequelae (such as growing regional disparities) that create stress within its members – particularly among those charged with the responsibility of raising children. This requires economic and social policy reforms at the national level, addressing issues such as housing support, job security, the way in which welfare-dependent groups are transferred to the 'real' economy, and the availability of affordable quality childcare.

A complementary approach is to focus directly on disadvantaged communities by increasing access to material and social resources with a view to empowering families and communities to participate more effectively in mainstream institutions such as schools and to achieve better outcomes for their children. To some extent this is the approach embodied within the new federal government programme Communities for Children (FaCSIA *Stronger Families and Communities Strategy* 2005), which itself has been strongly influenced by our work in the Pathways to Prevention project. The Pathways project, which has been described in some detail in Freiberg *et al.* (2005) and Homel *et al.* (2006), is implemented as a partnership between the national community organisation Mission Australia and Griffith University. The project operates in a region of Brisbane that has been identified as the poorest urban area in Queensland (Queensland Council of Social Service 1999). Census data show that the income of four in ten families living in the area falls below the poverty line and that the local median weekly household income is little more than 50 per cent of that recorded across the greater Brisbane region (ABS 2001). These data indicate that many children in the Pathways community are living in relative poverty (see Katz *et al.* 2005 for a discussion

229

of relative poverty). This chapter provides further information on the links in our data between family adversity, parental efficacy, and child outcomes.

The family as a context for intervention

The impact of poverty on family function and parenting can occur at a number of levels:

1 *Quality of parenting.* Clear differences in parenting styles have been noted across the SES divide (Bolger *et al.* 1995; Yeung *et al.* 2002). Quality of parenting is impaired in families that are persistently dogged by adversity (even ongoing exposure to minor hassles, let alone to serious burdens). Children in stressed, depressed and preoccupied families receive lower levels of sensitive care, nurturing and stimulation in their home environment and are more likely to experience aversive and coercive patterns of interaction with their parents (Patterson 1986; Webster-Stratton 1990). This can compromise attachment and impede children's cognitive, social and emotional development. It can also contribute to the development of behaviour problems.

2 *Powerlessness.* Chronic stress and adversity can also contribute to a sense of powerlessness and loss of control over one's life and hence to a reduced sense of personal efficacy (Baum *et al.* 1999; Bradley and Corwyn 2002; McLoyd 1998). This sense of helplessness reduces the likelihood that parents will have either the confidence or the motivation to take active and effective steps to solve problems and overcome difficulties because they are less likely to feel capable of influencing outcomes and changing things for the better (Bandura 1977). Poverty, therefore, can contribute to a tendency to become trapped within a cycle of responding reactively on the basis of external demands (Taylor and Sleeman 1999) rather than on the basis of self-generated goals and the adoption of a proactive problem-solving orientation.

3 *Connectedness.* Parents who are very isolated or 'insular' with regard to their social contacts tend to feel unsupported and have been found to be less positive in their parenting practices than non-insular parents (Wahler and Dumas 1985). In contrast, when parents feel supported by strong social and emotional networks they interact with their children in more sensitive, warm and responsive ways (Jennings *et al.* 1991), and are less likely to abuse

their children, better able to handle stressful situations, and more effective and confident in their parenting (Cochran and Niego 1995).

It is apparent that growing up in an insulated or otherwise socially unsupported family struggling to cope with chronic adversity is likely to have a negative impact on children's development because of the effects these conditions have on family energy and capacity to parent effectively. This type of evidence suggests that family function and parental efficacy are key mechanisms via which poverty wields its effect on development. Consequently, one of the major intervention strategies adopted within Pathways to Prevention was the implementation of a family-oriented programme: the Family Independence Programme (FIP).[1] Significantly, evidence of the way poverty and disadvantage influence developmental outcomes via their influence on family function also provides insight and guidelines about *how* to intervene with disadvantaged families and influenced the shape of the Family Independence Programme.

The Family Independence Programme

Programme intervention model

The approach to family support taken in Pathways to Prevention is guided by Bronfenbrenner's (1979) developmental-ecological theory and the understanding that the quality of parenting and family function is influenced by external forces and characteristics of the social, economic and cultural environments within which the family lives. Within this model, therefore, efforts to enhance parenting must include more than simply providing parenting skills training. Rather, emphasis is on increasing access to supportive networks and empowering carers to take control of their lives and manage developmental and environmental challenges more confidently and effectively (i.e. to move away from the predisposition to operate primarily in reaction to the demands of immediate external pressures towards the adoption of a more purposeful strategy of setting and working to achieve one's own goals).

As a family support programme, the Pathways project's main concern is not to influence financial capital directly (although in some small part the programme does assist families to gain access to basic material resources such as food, shelter and welfare benefits).

Rather, the spotlight of the family programme has moved away from a traditional focus on material welfare provision and focuses instead on efforts to enhance social capital by increasing access to non-material resources (e.g. social support, opportunity and education). The overall goal of the FIP was to provide sensitive parent support in order to enhance family resilience and capacity to deal effectively with adversity, to reduce social isolation and to promote positive parenting. The FIP model has a strong focus on family empowerment and aims to strengthen families from within by working alongside parents and carers to develop resources that promote:

- mastery over systems being dealt with (e.g. schools, social security, service agencies);
- better understanding of the needs of children;
- personal efficacy with respect to the parenting role.

To achieve this the FIP operates as a system that offers families free choice to participate as they see fit and to select services to suit individual needs. As such, the format of the FIP in itself provides a model of family empowerment.

Programme delivery method and focus of content

The method of intervention adopted within the Family Independence Programme is that of a practitioner–family partnership. This approach had a number of implications for programme development and delivery. The first implication was that great emphasis was placed on the development of trust. Unless a family support programme can win the trust of the community and reduce barriers to access by the most vulnerable and hard-to-reach families, it will fail to achieve its goal of serving the community. Therefore, FIP efforts and activities were designed to:

1 *Build community-level acceptance of and confidence in the service.* Examples of activity at this level included:
   (a) organising and participating in community celebrations, special events and family fun days;
   (b) working collaboratively with other agencies to establish the service as a key member of the broadly recognised network of care that existed within the community in a way that would facilitate interagency referral to ensure increased access to essential services and a greater continuity or integration of support for families;

(c) membership of cross-agency partnerships to garner funds for joint community projects.

2 *Establish reliable, enduring and caring relationships between family support personnel and family participants.* Family support staff were committed to developing respectful relationships with their clients. These relationships were grounded in a strengths-based philosophy that recognised and sought to bolster existing family capacity and respected the influence of each family's cultural background on parenting and family practices. Examples of practices at this level include:

(a) establishment of a team of skilled family support professionals whose linguistic and cultural backgrounds reflect the community cultural profile;

(b) an 'organic' process of programme development in response to client needs and issues that had a practical problem-solving orientation and worked to achieve immediate and positive changes in participants' lives;

(c) commitment to creating opportunities for ongoing, long-term involvement in the programme that allowed relationships to develop over time;

(d) combining individual support (that facilitated relationships between the family and their support professional) with group support methods (that facilitated the development of relationships and friendship networks between clients).

The second implication of adopting a practitioner–family partnership model was the recognition that different families have different needs and respond differently to different modes of programme delivery. In response to developing this understanding, family support staff tried to tailor programme activities to the particular circumstances of the families with whom they were working. The FIP featured a flexible range of options for participation. This enabled a balance to be struck between the use of structured, curriculum-bound interventions and the construction of an adaptive service (Collins *et al.* 2004). The opportunity to build what was essentially an individualised programme within the FIP also guaranteed more meaningful participation to meet a variety of needs. Examples of individual client needs ranged from requirements to undertake parenting skills training by order of the Department of Child Safety to satisfying a need for social companionship; from crisis relief to dealing with the enduring trauma of a carer's own abuse as a child; from help dealing with addiction or children's health problems to parent literacy skills development or even to development of an interest or hobby activity such as art, craft or cooking.

Options for participation included:

1 *Individual support programmes.* This included activities such as counselling, therapy, home-visiting, to provide personal support with household and family management, advocacy on behalf of the family with a range of family and community services, and providing advice or a friendly/non-judgemental ear to listen to a client's story via a drop-in or phone-in service.

2 *Group support or training programmes* (for carers and/or children). Activities within this set of programmes included parenting skills courses, playgroups, and life-skills education groups that provided training in areas as diverse as computing, budgeting, family nutrition, learning English as a second language, and grief management.

3 *Family relief.* This included elements such as holiday and recreational activities for children, material assistance, childcare and transport for families who attended individual and group support programmes.

This varied menu of activities and opportunities to participate was linked by a common set of objectives:

1 *To inform and educate.* This purpose was clear in programmes that delivered a standardised curriculum (e.g. Triple P: Sanders 1999; Sanders *et al.* 2000). However, even in the more informal parent support groups there was a strong undercurrent that emphasised information (e.g. about child development, health and safety) through the provision of materials, discussions, practical activities or presentations by guest speakers from relevant professions (e.g. paediatricians, teachers, nutritionists).

2 *To empower families.* This involved developing specific skills and personal resources (e.g. for behaviour management, household management, interpersonal relationships, dealing with systems, setting personal goals, problem-solving and creating safe, nurturing and stimulating environments for child development).

3 *To support relationships.* The focus was on strengthening relationships both inside the family (e.g. by promoting positive parent–child interaction) and outside the family (e.g. by developing social networks).

The FIP incorporates a preventive emphasis by working to promote nurturing family contexts. However, it does this by adopting a more traditional treatment-oriented paradigm which concentrates much of its effort on working with families who are already experiencing adversity. This approach constitutes an attempt to overcome exigencies within the family that can jeopardise children's development and well-being. Information about the types of factors that placed strain on family function was collected as families participated in the FIP. Programme activity within the FIP was subsequently guided by this information as staff worked alongside families to promote individual capacity to overcome the specific stressors with which the family was dealing.

Programme implementation and participation

At its outset, the FIP was offered as a free service to the families of all four to six year olds enrolled in preschools within the local community. At the same time, children attending these preschools participated in the Pathways Preschool Intervention Programme (PIP), – which is the second major stream of programme activity incorporated within the overall Pathways to Prevention project. Families' participation in the FIP was a matter of choice on the part of each individual family. Children's participation in the PIP was determined on the basis of whether the preschool each child attended had been chosen to participate as an intervention or a comparison school.

Data collection

As children were entering their preschool year (i.e. prior to the implementation of programme activities within either the FIP or the PIP), baseline data were collected on a range of variables from preschool children and their families.

1 *Child variables*. Measures of children's developmental status were linked to the core competencies that the PIP curriculum was designed to promote: language skills, behaviour and prosocial skills. The measures used to assess these skills included: the Preschool Language Assessment Instrument (PLAI: Blank *et al.* 1978); the Rowe Behaviour Rating Inventory (RBRI: Rowe and Rowe 1995); and the Strengths and Difficulties Questionnaire (SDQ: Goodman 1997). The SDQ yielded a score for level of difficult

or antisocial behaviour as well as a score for level of prosocial behaviour. These data were collected for a total of 594 preschool children. In addition to the data on children's language and social skills, information was also collected about children's attachment to school. This variable was measured by parent report.

2 *Family/parent variables.* Measures of the family factors understood to be indicative of prevailing child-rearing conditions and practices were also collected. These variables included family adversity, parent efficacy, and parent–child relationships (as indicated by level of parent involvement and behaviour management style). The family adversity measure represents the total number of stressful life events to which family members were exposed (or at least those issues known to family-support staff as they were revealed during the course of families' FIP participation). Scores indicating level of family adversity were available only for the 120 preschool children whose families had elected to access FIP services.

Measures of parent efficacy and parent involvement were collected as self-report data via parent surveys that families of all preschool children were invited to participate in during the school year. Respondents were contacted by telephone by trained researchers who conducted interviews in home languages wherever possible. The 26 items used to measure parent efficacy yielded three sub-scores that related to (a) general parenting practices (sense of confidence in undertaking parenting tasks in relation to fostering children's positive development), (b) behaviour management (sense of control tapping disciplinary style and the use of positive and coercive strategies), and (c) school and learning (parents' sense of confidence that they can help their child do well at school and advocate on their child's behalf). The five items used to measure level of parent involvement yielded sub-scores for home-based involvement (activities like playing learning games, reading and talking with child) and school-based involvement (frequency of family contact with school and teacher). During the survey parents also reported on their child's level of attachment to, and enjoyment of, preschool.

Analysis of parent variables in this chapter are based on responses provided by the parents of 147 preschool children who participated in a baseline survey conducted early in the school year (n=45 or 30.6 per cent of this sample subsequently participated in FIP; n=65 or 44.2 per cent of this sample spoke a first language other than English).

The operations and context of the Family Independence Programme

Relationship between child and family variables

Examination of the baseline measures allows us to consider the way family contextual factors are linked to children's development at the time when they are entering preschool and beginning their transition into the education system. It is critical for ongoing development of the programme to identify the mechanisms that underpin children's success. We therefore conducted a correlation analysis to explore the pattern of interrelationships between child and family variables as evidence of the way family processes might have contributed to measured indicators of child competence.

Significant correlations between these variables are summarised in Figure 11.1. For simplicity, Figure 11.1 does not show all correlations

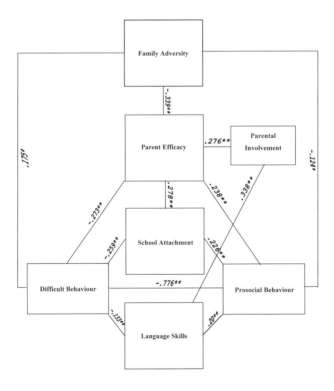

Figure 11.1 Pattern of relationships between child and family measures
*Note: *p<.05 **p<.01*

between every sub-scale within each overall variable. Rather, correlation coefficients indicate the highest level of correlation achieved between any subscale within each variable.

As a guide to interpreting the overall picture, it is useful to begin by considering the way certain groups of variables link together:

1 The level of family adversity (indicated by the number of adverse life events families experience) was related to measures of children's behaviour. The greater the adversity the more disruptive and less prosocial was the child's behaviour.

2 Level of family adversity was associated with lowered levels of general parenting efficacy or confidence in nurturing their child's development.

3 Parenting efficacy is related to child behaviour. In general, the more confident parents are in their role the more positive their child's behaviour is at preschool and the more their child is reported to enjoy preschool.

4 Parent efficacy is positively related to the degree to which parents report being involved in their children's learning.

5 In its turn, parent involvement is positively related to children's language proficiency.

6 Each of the measures of child competence (language, behaviour and prosocial skills) is related to the other (in the expected direction). This corroborates what previous research has found – that behaviour, communication and social skills are linked (e.g. Beitchman *et al.* 1996).

7 There were significant correlations between parents' reports of their child's attachment to preschool and measures of children's social behaviours at preschool. Children who enjoyed preschool were engaged in more prosocial and less difficult behaviour.

8 The relationship between level of adversity and level of parent involvement was not significant. It had been expected that high levels of stress might reduce parents' time, energy and motivation to be involved in their children's learning. However, current findings suggest that it may not be adversity *per se* that has a direct influence on parent involvement, but rather how effectively parents deal with adversity. As noted earlier, parents' reported level of involvement was related to measures of efficacy. This confirms the fundamental role that parent efficacy plays in parenting practices.

It is evident that contextual factors like family adversity affect both parents and children. We found that not only was family adversity related to children's developing social competence but this was likely mediated through the association between adversity and parent efficacy. This pattern of findings validates the purpose of the FIP to support family capacity to respond effectively to stressful life events as a means of reducing the impact of adversity on children's development.

Examining the pre-existing patterns of relationship between child and family variables provides a useful insight into the way subsequent programme input might be transformed into outcomes. It is clear that the FIP has the potential to influence outcomes for children by working to enhance family mechanisms like parenting practice, parent–child relationships, shared engagement in experiences that stimulate children's developing competence, and resilience in the face of adversity. Moreover, while parent efficacy appears to indicate adversity, it is equally clear that sense of efficacy may also serve to moderate the impact of adversity on both child and parent variables. This highlights the way efficacy underpins family function and the critical importance of work within the FIP to foster efficacy: that is, to empower parents by promoting the skills, resources, confidence and support they need to actively seek solutions to problems and reduce the tendency for reactive responses to the vagaries of external pressures.

The correlation analysis helps construct a clearer picture of the way the FIP might drive the change process by influencing the intervening variables (e.g. parent efficacy) that are linked to child outcome variables (e.g. children's skills). These family mechanisms are themselves measurable outcomes sought as goals of the FIP.

The effects of FIP on family mechanisms

If, as intended, the FIP acts to enhance family processes such as parent efficacy, then it is reasonable to expect this would translate to a range of positive effects for children (language, behaviour, attachment to school, etc.). The impact of FIP on outcomes for children will be reported elsewhere. The first step in establishing the efficacy of FIP input, however, is to demonstrate its more proximal effects on outcomes for parents.

To examine the relationship between FIP participation and family factors, data were collected from a group of FIP participants (n=68) to answer questions relating to the most fundamental objectives of FIP efforts: Does the FIP support families and promote their capacity to deal effectively with challenge? To measure these two key constructs, we used a questionnaire that was based on an instrument called the Family Empowerment Scale (Koren *et al.* 1992). Adaptations to the original scale were made after an extended period of consultation with family-support staff who provided insight into the appropriateness of questions for FIP clients. The main changes involved reducing the number of questions to 25 items, including new items focused on connectedness, and rewording some of the items. The two constructs tapped in the adapted Family Scale were:

1 *Parent efficacy*: Confidence in handling the tasks of parenthood. Does the parent have a sense that the challenges associated with parenting are manageable? (11 items)

2 *Parent support*: Sense of connection to a supportive network. Does the parent feel supported and that help is available and accessible if needed? (14 items)

Monitoring outcomes for families is considered an essential component of programme accountability as well as critical to continued programme development. As such, it is our goal to be able to demonstrate the impact of FIP participation by comparing pre-intervention baseline scores on the Family Scale to scores on a follow-up measure taken after families have made use of the service. Despite our commitment to evaluation we encountered some initial difficulties in collecting systematic data from FIP participants (some of whom were experiencing extreme hardship). These difficulties placed some limits on the approach we were able to take in the analysis of outcomes at the time of writing this report. The most notable complication has been that, in spite of every effort to administer the baseline measure of the Family Scale at the point of each client's first contact with the service, a considerable period of time often elapsed before the scales were actually collected from some families. Given these conditions, a decision was made to conduct a preliminary analysis of FIP effects by comparing scores on the Family Scale across three distinct groups of FIP clients:

1 A group who completed the scale within two months of their first contact with the service (n=31).
2 A group who completed the scale after having had between two and five months of contact (n=17).

3 A group who did not complete the scale until having been in contact with the service for at least six months (n=20).

Analyses of variance were used to investigate whether there were any significant differences in the levels of parent efficacy and parent sense of support between these three groups. It was predicted that if the FIP were effective, both feelings of efficacy and sense of support would increase as length of contact increased.

Results indicate that parent efficacy was significantly influenced by the length of time clients had been in contact with the FIP service ($p<.01$). The mean score on the measure of parent efficacy was 51.1 for the group who had been with the service for less than two months, compared to 57.4 for two to five months and 58.7 for over six months of service. That is, parent efficacy was higher within the two groups who had longer association with the service. This is an effect size of about .82, and is depicted graphically in Figure 11.2.[2]

Although the overall effect of length of contact with the FIP service on parent sense of support was not statistically significant, pairwise comparisons between groups shows that there was a significant difference between sense of support in the groups with less than two months' and greater than six months' contact (effect size = .59, $p<.05$: Figure 11.2). This highlights the value of providing a programme that offers opportunities for sustained contact when working with families who experience considerable disadvantage, and validates the FIP model.

While these results do not provide conclusive evidence of the effectiveness of the FIP (due to our current inability to demonstrate change over time within individual families) they provide early indications of the positive impact that the FIP has on parent efficacy and sense of support. This supports the theoretical assumptions upon which the approach was based, although we acknowledge the need to continue our evaluation of the way the FIP influences the multiple factors and processes that contribute to family function.

Discussion

The correlation analysis helps paint a clear picture of the way children's developing competence is linked not only to the experience of family adversity but to family strengths (e.g. efficacy) that can moderate the impact of those external influences (as long as these factors are themselves not weakened by adversity). The preliminary

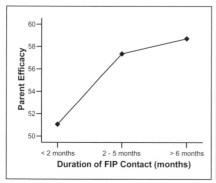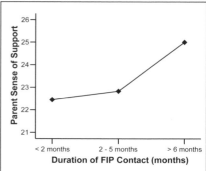

Figure 11.2 Relationship between duration of FIP contact and scores on measures of parent efficacy and parent sense of support

data showing that involvement in the FIP led to increased levels of parent efficacy and sense of connectedness are a promising sign that the approach to family support taken within the Pathways family programme is an effective way of lessening the potential effects of adversity on family function and children's development.

Our experience within the FIP is very much in line with Halpern's (2000) observation that, to be effective, interventions must start where families are developmentally so they are immediately relevant and responsive to vulnerable participants' own experiences and preoccupations. The implications of this approach are the prioritisation of unique family needs and individualisation of services within programme delivery. The difficulties that this approach creates for evaluation are well rehearsed in the literature (e.g. inability to control for selection effects through random allocation when services are tailored specifically to family need). These types of difficulties have prompted authorities such as Halpern (2000) and Schorr (1998) to level criticism on the over-reliance on positivist purity at the expense of methods that, while providing persuasive (if not conclusive) evidence of programme effects, also take into account the contextualised and multifaceted nature of the interventions. It is for this reason that we have not attempted to evaluate individual programme components within the family programme, opting rather to treat FIP as a single activity, albeit with different levels of duration and intensity for different participants.

What nevertheless remains an essential task is to work within a valid research design to continue to collect data that may reveal in a more persuasive way how the FIP acts as a catalyst that initiates and sustains changes in parenting behaviour and in family functioning that, in turn, influence outcomes for children. Ongoing evaluation and the strengthening of methodological rigour with respect to the systematic collection of family mechanism variables from FIP participants will ultimately determine how effectively the programme promotes family resilience in the face of poverty and adversity.

In the absence of broader social policy initiatives designed to reduce inequalities in the distribution of resources, it is not possible for individual preventive programmes such as Pathways to Prevention (or Communities for Children) to eliminate the effects of poverty on a large scale for young Australian children. However, the present results show that it is possible for family-oriented programmes such as the FIP to strengthen the features of family context that facilitate positive child development but which are often the casualties of poverty. It is by promoting these family mechanisms that programmes like Pathways to Prevention have the potential to ameliorate some of the effects of poverty and social deprivation. However, it is abundantly clear that these mechanisms must be simultaneously strengthened on a much wider scale through reform of social and economic environments within which family life is embedded. Efforts to bring such approaches to scale for the large numbers (14.7 per cent) of Australian children who live in poverty will, in the end, depend on a fundamental reassessment of national priorities and values.

Notes

1 Another major programme strategy within the Pathways to Prevention project was a child-focused Preschool Intervention Programme (PIP) designed to promote developmental competencies that are foundational to social and academic achievement. This preschool-based intervention component of the project is described in Freiberg *et al.* (2005).
2 An effect size of 0.3 to 0.4 is considered fairly average for successful child and parent interventions (Farrington and Welsh 2003), while anything over 0.5 is generally considered a moderate to large effect (Cohen 1988). In other words, in this field the obtained effect size in analyses of programme effects indicates a substantial programme impact.

References

Australian Bureau of Statistics (2001) *Census of Population and Housing*.

Bandura, A. (1977) 'Self-efficacy: Toward a unifying theory of behavioural change', *Psychological Review*, 84: 191–215.

Baum, A., Garofalo, J. and Yali, A. (1999) 'SES and Chronic Stress: Does Stress Account for SES Effects on Health?', in N. Adler, M. Marmot, B. McEwen and J. Stewart (eds) (1999) *Socio-economic Status and Health in Industrialised Nations*. New York: NY Academy of Science.

Beitchman, J., Wilson, B., Brownlie, E., Walters, H., Inglis, A. and Lancee, W. (1996) 'Long-term consistency in speech/language profiles: II. Behavioural, emotional, and social outcomes', *Journal of the American Academy of Child and Adolescent Psychiatry*, 35: 815–25.

Blank, M., Rose, S.A. and Berlin, L.J. (1978) *Preschool Language Assessment Instrument: The Language of Learning in Practice*. Austin, TX: PRO-ED, Inc.

Bolger, K., Patterson, C., Thompson, W. and Kupersmidt, J. (1995) 'Psychological adjustment among children experiencing persistent and intermittent family economic hardship', *Child Development*, 66: 1107–29.

Bradley, R. and Corwyn, R. (2002) 'Socioeconomic status and child development', *Annual Review of Psychology*, 53: 371–99.

Bronfenbrenner, U. (1979) *The Ecology of Human Development: Experiments by Nature and Design*. Cambridge, MA: Harvard University Press.

Brooks-Gunn, J. and Duncan, G. (1997) 'The effects of poverty on children', *Future Child*, 7: 55–71.

Cochran, M. and Niego, S. (1995) 'Parenting and Social Networks', in M.H. Bornstein (ed.) *Handbook of Parenting, Vol. 3: Status and Social Conditions of Parenting*. Mahwah, NJ: Erlbaum, pp. 393–418.

Cohen, J. (1988) *Statistical Power Analysis for the Behavioural Sciences,* 2nd edn. Hillsdale, NJ: Lawrence Erlbaum Associates.

Coleman, J. (1988) 'Social capital in the creation of human capital', *American Journal of Sociology*, 94 (Suppl.): 95–120.

Collins, L., Murphy, S. and Bierman, K. (2004) 'A conceptual framework for adaptive preventive interventions', *Prevention Science*, 5(3): 185–96.

FaCSIA (2005) *Stronger Families and Communities Strategy*. (2005) Available online at: http://www.facs.gov.au/internet/facsinternet.nsf/aboutfacs/programs/sfsc-communities_for_children.htm

Farrington, D. (2003) 'Key Results from the First Forty Years of the Cambridge Study in Delinquent Development', in T.P. Thornberry and M. Krohn (eds) *Taking Stock of Delinquency: An Overview of Findings from Contemporary Longitudinal Studies*. New York: Kluwer, pp. 137–84.

Farrington, D.P. and Welsh, B.C. (2003) 'Family-based prevention of offending: A meta-analysis', *Australian and New Zealand Journal of Criminology*, 36(2): 127–51.

Freiberg, K., Homel, R., Batchelor, S., Carr, A., Hay, I., Elias, G., Teague, R. and Lamb, C. (2005) 'Creating pathways to participation: A community-based developmental prevention project in Australia', *Children and Society*, 19: 144–57.

Glover, J., Harris, K. and Tennant, S. (1999) *A Social Health Atlas of Australia, Vol. 1: Australia*, 2nd edn. Adelaide: Openbook Publishers.

Goodman, R. (1997) 'The Strengths and Difficulties Questionnaire: A research note', *Journal of Child Psychology and Psychiatry*, 38(5): 581–6.

Gorman-Smith, D., Tolan, P. and Henry, D. (2005) 'Promoting Resilience in the Inner City: Families as a Venue for Protection, Support, and Opportunity', in R. deV. Peters, B. Leadbeater and R.J. McMahon (eds) *Resilience in Children, Families, and Communities: Linking Context to Practice and Policy* New York: Kluwer Academic/Plenum, pp. 137–55.

Halpern, R. (2000) 'Early Intervention for Low-income Children and Families', in J.P. Shonkoff and S.J. Meisels (eds) *Handbook of Early Childhood Intervention*, 2nd edn. Cambridge: Cambridge University Press, pp. 361–86.

Homel, R., Freiberg, K., Lamb, C., Leech, M., Carr, A., Hay, I., Elias, G., Manning, M., Teague, R. and Batchelor, S. (2006) *The Pathways to Prevention Project: The First Five Years, 1999–2004*. Brisbane: Mission Australia and Griffith University.

Jennings, K., Stagg, V. and Connors, R. (1991) 'Social networks and mothers' interactions with their preschool children', *Child Development*, 62: 572–82.

Katz, I., Corlyon, J., La Placa, V. and Hunter, S. (2005) *The Relationship Between Parenting and Poverty*, Report to the Joseph Rountree Foundation. York: Joseph Rowntree Foundation.

Keating, D.P. and C. Hertzman (eds) (1999) *Developmental Health and the Wealth of Nations: Social, Biological, and Educational Dynamics*. New York: Guilford Press.

Koren, P., DeChillo, N. and Friesen, B. (1992) 'Measuring empowerment in families whose children have emotional disabilities: A brief questionnaire', *Rehabilitation Psychology*, 37: 305–21.

McLoyd, V. (1998) 'Socioeconomic disadvantage and child development', *American Psychologist*, 53: 185–204.

Patterson, G. (1986) 'Performance models for antisocial boys', *American Psychologist*, 41: 432–444.

Queensland Council of Social Service (1999) *People & Places – A Profile of Growing Disadvantage in Queensland*. Kelvin Grove: Queensland Council of Social Service Inc. and Social Action Office.

Rowe, K. and Rowe, K. (1995) *RBRI Profile User's Guide*. Melbourne: Centre for Applied Educational Research and Department of Paediatrics, University of Melbourne.

Sanders, M. (1999) 'Triple Positive Parenting Program: Towards an empirically validated multilevel parenting and family support strategy for the prevention of behavior and emotional problems in children', *Clinical Child and Family Psychology Review*, 2: 71–90.

Sanders, M.R. (2000) 'The Triple-P Positive Parenting Program: A comparison of enhanced, standard and self-directed behavioral family intervention for parents of children with early onset conduct problems', *Journal of Consulting and Clinical Psychology*, 68(4): 624–40.

Schorr, L. (1998). *Common Purpose: Strengthening Families and Neighbourhoods to Rebuild America.* New York: Anchor Books.

Stanley, F., Richardson, S. and Prior, M. (2005) *Children of the Lucky Country? How Australian Society has Turned its Back on Children and Why Children Matter.* Sydney: Pan Macmillan.

Taylor, S. and Sleeman, T. (1999) 'Psychosocial Resources and the SES–Health Relationship', in N. Adler, M. Marmot, B. McEwen and J. Stewart, (eds) (1999) *Socio-economic Status and Health in Industrialised Nations.* New York: NY Academy of Science.

UNICEF (2005) *Child Poverty in Rich Countries,* Innocenti Report Card No. 6. Florence: UNICEF Innocenti Research Centre.

Wahler, R. and Dumas, J. (1985) 'Stimulus Class Determinants of Mother–Child Coercive Interchanges in Multidistressed Families: Assessment and Interventions', in J. Burchard and S. Burchard (eds) *Prevention of Delinquent Behavior.* New York: Sage.

Webster-Stratton, C. (1990) 'Stress: A potential disrupter of parent perceptions and family interactions', *Journal of Clinical Child Psychology*, 19: 302–12.

Yeung, J., Linver, M. and Brooks-Gunn, J. (2002) 'How money matters for young children's development: Parental investment and family processes', *Child Development*, 73: 1861–79.

Chapter 12

Research–practice–policy intersections in the Pathways to Prevention project: reflections on theory and experience

Marie Leech, Caryn Anderson and Catherine Mahoney

Abstract

Pathways to Prevention is a multidimensional, early intervention crime prevention project integrating family support programmes with preschools and school-based programmes in a highly disadvantaged suburb of Brisbane. It is a partnership between Mission Australia, a practice-based direct service provider, and Griffith University, a research institution. As well as providing sound practice and policy relevant research, the project constituted a unique resource for generating much needed new knowledge about organisational learning, integration and implementation in multidisciplinary environments, and knowledge management specific to the areas of intersectoral, interorganisational collaboration and research–practice–policy partnerships. This paper examines the Pathways to Prevention Project through five different theoretical lenses to stimulate awareness of theories that others may find useful and to identify opportunities for studying the structures and processes involved in complex, public good partnerships. The lenses used to explore the project are organisational learning, knowledge management, integration and implementation sciences, public policy transformation, and practice–research engagement. For each lens we present key intellectual foundations, discuss relevant learning experiences from the Pathways project, and suggest future lines of study and experimentation to develop new knowledge pathways in each area.

Introduction

The multilayered knowledge generated in projects such as Pathways to Prevention, about both programmes and processes, is often complex, hard to encapsulate, and hard to separate from the people who created it. How do we preserve learning? How do we plug gaps in the process? How can we tap the intellectual capital generated in projects such as Pathways and therefore improve outcomes across programmes and geographical areas for service users? We begin to address these questions by examining current theories of organisational learning, knowledge management and research–practice collaboration. The aim is to develop a more predictable and sustainable process for linking research and practice, embedding both in the volatile and capricious policy process. This chapter analyses the Pathways to Prevention project using these theories as lenses to explore how the research–practice–policy trio can work to create a 'new knowledge' developmental pathway.

The Pathways Project was designed as a partnership between Mission Australia, a practice-based direct service provider, and Griffith University, a research institution, to provide a sound research foundation for programme activities and to provide fertile ground for basic research in the areas of crime prevention and early intervention. As the project progressed, the diversity of stakeholder needs, contributions and patterns played themselves out – in conjunction with programmatic and process innovations, challenges and successes – in a variety of unexpected ways. Over time, as difficulties turned into learning opportunities, and apprehension turned into trust, it became clear that the structural characteristics of the project, the innovative and creative spirit of the operational environment, and the collaborative and adaptive behaviour of the stakeholders together created unique examples of a learning organisation; of the processes of linking research, practice and policy; of learning and collaborating across sectoral and professional boundaries; and of integrating and implementing multidimensional interventions across complex, interdisciplinary environments.

This chapter examines the Pathways to Prevention Project through five different theoretical lenses. For each lens we present some key intellectual foundations and discuss the relevant learning experiences of the Pathways Project. Our aim is not to be comprehensive in terms of concepts or their intellectual foundations, nor to present a highly sophisticated analysis of the Pathways learning experiences. Rather we seek to stimulate awareness of theories that others may find useful and to give a flavour of their applicability through the Pathways experience. We hope that researchers will find this preliminary scoping of conceptual frameworks to be an open invitation to propose more structured investigations of the Pathways Project along these lines. Such investigation would generate much needed new knowledge in the areas of intersectoral, interorganisational collaboration and research–practice–policy partnerships. This chapter will also serve as a launching point for further guided self-reflection and analysis to improve the Pathways Project itself. We expect that many of the project stakeholders will find it useful to have a range of larger theoretical frameworks within which to position the outstanding practical outcomes they have achieved, and by which to guide future strategies.

We begin by considering the work of Argyris and Senge on a systems approach to organisational learning and specifically analyse the learning dynamics of the Pathways Project in the context of their theories. We follow on with a discussion of knowledge management, including a preliminary measure of the project's success in knowledge mediation and a framework for further analysis.

We then turn to the matter of integrated interventions and consider Bammer's work developing the specialisation of Integration and Implementation Sciences, identifying where the principles have already been demonstrated in the project. Pathways is a public good project first and foremost, and we move next to considering the public policy transformation process and the ways in which Pathways has already had a direct effect on Australian federal government policy. The final area we consider is collaboration and partnerships. We outline the Practice Research Engagement framework developed by Brown and colleagues and use this to explore the nuances of the researcher–practitioner dynamic of the Mission Australia and Griffith University partnership. This leads us to recommend actions for influencing the direction of the developmental pathway to new knowledge for research–practice–policy engagement and intersectoral, collaborative learning partnerships.

The Pathways Project was established using a number of intuitive processes, which have turned out to be characteristic of learning organisations. It has also charted successes in Practice Research Engagement across institutions and sectors. The theoretical lenses used here help explain its success, but also point to further areas of improvement and provide models and guidance for other similar projects.

About pathways

This early intervention crime prevention project, based in a highly disadvantaged area of Brisbane (Inala), is multilayered and, in its first phase in the years 2001–2004, integrated family support programmes with preschool and school-based programmes in seven local schools. In its current form, which has evolved on the basis of the learnings from the first phase, the emphasis has moved from the development and implementation of 'bolted on' programmes and services to building stronger connections between families, schools and community agencies, and creating sustainable preventive practices through a transformation of the routine activities of schools and other developmentally relevant institutions (including the Pathways service itself). The overall goal of the Pathways Project remains to support families, schools and communities in their efforts to create positive pathways for children's development and for success at school through the promotion of nurturing contexts for development. Such a goal necessarily implies diverse stakeholders including schools, local community organisations and government departments. Funding for the project is derived from a variety of sponsors and includes private foundations, research councils, state and federal government departments and the partner organisations (Homel *et al.* 2006).

This brief overview of the Pathways Project provides an insight into the volume and density of the intersections, accountabilities and relationships involved. The overall project management structure that supports the project is detailed in Figure 12.1.

The structures of the Pathways Project, by and large, are consistent with systems thinking. Peter Senge, who has been highly influential in the field of learning organisations, regards systems thinking (i.e. a 'whole system' perspective) as the cornerstone of the learning organisation, and argues that very few people in management approach their operations as the complex systems that they are (1990). We argue that each player on the Pathways management team demonstrated a strong capacity to focus on the whole, comprehending the interrelationship between the parts and understanding the project as a dynamic process. Thus from the beginning, Pathways had embedded in its structures one of the cornerstones of the learning organisation.

Project Management Structure:
Roles, Responsibilities and Reporting

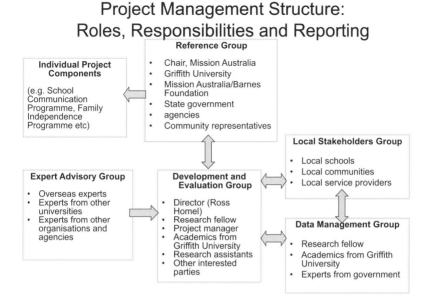

Reference Group
- Chair, Mission Australia
- Griffith University
- Mission Australia/Barnes Foundation
- State government
- agencies
- Community representatives

Individual Project Components

(e.g. School Communication Programme, Family Independence Programme etc)

Local Stakeholders Group
- Local schools
- Local communities
- Local service providers

Expert Advisory Group
- Overseas experts
- Experts from other universities
- Experts from other organisations and agencies

Development and Evaluation Group
- Director (Ross Homel)
- Research fellow
- Project manager
- Academics from Griffith University
- Research assistants
- Other interested parties

Data Management Group
- Research fellow
- Academics from Griffith University
- Experts from government

Figure 12.1   Pathways project management structure

Lens 1: Organisational learning

Organisational learning is a branch of knowledge within organisational theory that examines the way an organisation learns and adapts and is informed by complexity theory, systems thinking more broadly, and knowledge management. Some of the major models of organisational learning include those of Argyris (1977), March and Olson (1975), Senge (1990) and Kim (1993). The treatment provided in this chapter will be limited to a brief overview of two major theorists, Argyris and Senge. Argyris, an organisational psychologist, defined organisational learning as the process of 'detection and correction of error' (1977: 121). His work with Schön (Argyris and Schön 1978), informed by the earlier work of Gregory Bateson (1972), detailed three levels of learning:

- *Single loop learning* involves improving the *status quo* by adaptive learning. The focus is on current problem solving and gradual improvement. Single loop learning informed what Argyris called

Model 1, which is characterised by organisational conformity, 'learning disabilities' and mediocre performance, in short, coping or 'getting by'.

- *Double loop learning*, also known as generative learning, questions and challenges assumptions as well as the *status quo*. Double loop learning informed what Argyris called Model 2, which is characterised by personal mastery, collaboration, critiquing of assumptions and continuous experimentation.

- *Deutero learning* involves transformational change, with double loop learning or Model 2 as a prerequisite for this to occur. Deutero learning is characterised by the examination and improvement of the learning process.

For Argyris, the type of learning is determined by the 'ecology' of the organisation or the organisational learning system. For example, if the organisational ecology or culture values the reinforcement of existing assumptions and norms, it is unlikely to result in double loop learning and less likely to promote transformational change. Peter Senge's book *The Fifth Discipline* (1990) popularised and built on many of Argyris' theories. Senge advocates five 'disciplines' for a successful learning organisation:

1 *Personal mastery*: the discipline of continually clarifying and deepening personal vision, of focusing energies, of developing patience, and of seeing reality objectively.

2 *Mental models*: working with mental models which allow individuals to unearth the assumptions and generalisations that influence their understanding of the world and shape action.

3 *Building shared vision*: unearthing 'shared pictures of the future' that foster genuine commitment and enrolment (rather than compliance), encouraging people to excel and learn.

4 *Team learning*: builds the capacity of team members to suspend assumptions and enter into a genuine thinking together. Dialogue (the free and creative exploration of complex issues) and discussion (the presentation and defence of different perspectives) are important features.

5 *Systems thinking*: studies systems using holistic rather than reductionist methods, and is concerned with complexity and interdependency. Systems thinking understands the organisation

as an open system that is dependent on its internal and external environmental context; it is a relational model.

According to Senge, these disciplines promote generative learning, which is vital to work environments that need to continually respond to change, complexity and uncertainty. Systems thinking, especially complexity theory, is key to much current organisational learning theory and although the terms are often used interchangeably, complexity theory is actually one aspect of systems thinking. Broadly speaking, complexity studies consider patterns of order and disorder in systems and these studies indicate that the powerful innovative phase in natural systems often occurs at the point between order and chaos. Much of the literature on organisational learning emphasises the importance of 'creative tension' in promoting change and innovation. For a number of theorists, complexity theory enables us to understand how cognition occurs in social systems and this is a critical question for organisational learning.

Theorist Edgar H. Schein highlights the difficulties of fostering an organisational learning culture. While Schein maintains that organisational change is possible, 'it is also unbelievably painful and slow' (Coutu 2002: 107). While emphasising the difficulties of transformational learning, Schein does also acknowledge that 'learning anxiety' can be reduced by the creation of an organisational environment where it is safe to both learn and unlearn. He draws parallels between ex-prisoners of war and organisational behaviour to highlight how passivity becomes a survival tool preferred by the majority. It is perhaps the prevalence of this type of conservative internal culture that results in most organisations conforming to Model 1 (Argyris and Schön 1978) and only engaging in single loop learning. For organisational learning to flourish and maximise human resources in the current environment of rapid change and increasing competition, an internal culture is required that promotes an environment of 'challenge and be challenged', characterised by openness, learning from mistakes, risk-taking and experimentation.

Where Pathways ranks, when viewed through the lenses of the indicators of organisational learning above (i.e. Senge's five disciplines and Argyris and Schön's levels of learning), has been canvassed with the key players. Structured phone interviews were conducted with ten stakeholders from the academic and service delivery aspects of this Pathways partnership in August/September 2005 by one of the authors (Mahoney). Interviewees were selected based on their close involvement with Pathways and were asked questions specifically about the learning dynamics of the project. Key players noted that the Pathways Project *as an organisation* clearly adopted a set of characteristics quite different from its two parent bodies (Mission Australia and Griffith University), as well as from its range of funding bodies. The root of these distinctions remains to be explored.

Responses relating to the work of Argyris and Senge highlighted some key differences in perspective between researchers and practitioners, as well as ongoing challenges for the project.

From an academic perspective:

- Service delivery staff are often too busy to engage in the 'learning' process. They may also lack a knowledge and understanding of aspects of the theoretical framework of the project.

- There is a level of resentment from service delivery staff in terms of systematic measurement of performance, leading to a 'culture gap' between service delivery staff and researchers.

- Academics are regularly engaged in active reflection about the project. They tend to have both formal and informal processes for this activity and it often culminates in the writing stage.

- Service delivery staff have a great deal of practitioner knowledge that has not as yet been effectively accessed. More needs to be known about how they problem-solve and the process of their interventions at the practical level.

From a service delivery perspective:

- A lack of integration between those entering the data (service delivery staff) and those undertaking the evaluation (researchers) can be a problem for the project. Service delivery staff do not receive sufficient feedback on the results of their input. This can lead to lack of motivation/interest.

- Time lags between data collection, analysis and findings are too long for a service that needs to be flexible and responsive. By the time findings are available, changes have already been made to service implementation.

- Service delivery staff tend to take more of an action research approach to gauge the effectiveness of their programmes and rely on daily feedback from clients about what works and what doesn't. Improvements are implemented as the need dictates.

- Service delivery staff have difficulty in finding the time and space for reflecting on their work and the project as a whole. Regular scheduled time 'off line' with an external facilitator would be of real assistance.

- Within the current funding environment service delivery staff are constantly searching for sources of funding and writing submissions, as well as addressing a multitude of unmet needs in a very disadvantaged community. This is the priority and it leaves little time for considering the 'big picture', although service delivery staff want to be part of the learning and new knowledge that leads to better lives for clients.

However, in terms of the project *as an organisation* stakeholders noted:

- A high and significant level of deutero learning during the all too infrequent points of meeting between researchers and practitioners; and also between the more senior staff in the two camps.
- A very high score for Pathways on the 'shared vision' and 'team learning' aspects of Senge's five disciplines.
- Creative tension and constructive non-conformity were greeted with complete recognition and regarded as part of everyday interactions within the project.
- Learning anxiety was considerably reduced through the life of the project.

Stakeholders agreed that deutero or double loop learning was less likely in the very busy and demanding human services working environment of the service delivery staff. The problem-solving that is likely to occur is about meeting immediate and medium-term needs and issues (single loop learning). Stakeholders also identified a number of strategies that would move Pathways further along the new knowledge development pathway, for example:

- Increase opportunities for service delivery staff and academic staff to meet together to reflect, share information, and to interpret and build joint knowledge.

- Develop a more integrated approach to the data needs of the researchers and the service providers so that the process is conducive to learning across professional boundaries.

- Work towards a common language, a common understanding of and purpose for the learning.

Thus, though frustrations exist within subsystems of the project, there appears to be evidence that overall Pathways has incorporated a number of the cornerstones of learning organisations without conscious incorporation of the theory and practice of organisational learning. Key facilitators of this intuitive development are likely to have been: autonomy generated by non-prescriptive funding; autonomy of individual programmes within large multiservice non-governmental organisations; the nature of the unique multilevel and fully engaged partnership between Mission Australia and Griffith University; and the shared vision of key players at multiple levels in the parent organisations.

Lens 2: Theories of knowledge management

Knowledge management is one of the engines of organisational learning. There are many definitions, theories and perspectives of knowledge management, but most specialists would agree that the primary aim of knowledge management is to ensure the best possible use of available knowledge to encourage innovation and the reuse of best practices in order to add value to the enterprise.

In 2005, Kimiz Dalkir synthesised the work of dozens of knowledge management theorists and practitioners in *Knowledge Management in Theory and Practice*. She concluded that 'the sources of innovation and knowledge reuse consist of either internal or external discoveries, or they may stem from business practices or from knowledge workers' competencies. More often, improvements will result from some combination of these types of sources' (2005: 248). The implied diversity of these possible 'combinations' hints at the diversity of knowledge management approaches, which also reflect multifarious internal and external enterprise environments.

In short, effective knowledge management can only be conducted in a customised way. Every organisation that consciously wishes to manage their knowledge more effectively is advised to audit their environments carefully and review the theoretical approaches and available tools thoroughly to craft a strategy that is best for their circumstances. Nevertheless, it is possible to synthesise key components of knowledge management approaches into four integrated and interdependent dimensions:

- *Types of knowledge*: tacit and explicit.
- *Phases of the knowledge management cycle*: capture and/or creation, sharing and dissemination, acquisition and application.
- *Components of approach*: theories, content, tools, people, processes.
- *Levels of actors*: individual, group or community, organisation as a whole.

The three basic phases of the cycle (creation/capture, sharing and dissemination, acquisition and application) represent Dalkir's synthesis of the work of other authors, especially Wiig, Zack, McElroy, and Bukowitz and Williams, in which she also simplifies the concepts. These phases also correspond closely with what have been considered successive 'generations' in the evolution of knowledge management. Initially, knowledge is either captured (from internal or external sources) or created. The first generation of knowledge management initiatives were primarily concerned with identifying, cataloguing and storing best practices and lessons learned in explicit forms. These early days can be characterised by efforts to design specific information technology tools to respond to the sentiment 'If only we knew what we know.' Today, this phase includes the identification of knowledge experts (individuals or teams) with tacit knowledge as well as the capture and creation of explicit content.

After capturing or creating knowledge, content is then assessed and codified to support the second phase, which focuses on sharing and disseminating the content among people. This corresponds to the second generation of knowledge management initiatives, which began to recognise the importance and complexity of people and the social networks and political environments they operate in. These new crops of projects focused on being nimble enough to adequately respond to the dynamic and rapidly changing enterprise environments. Managers began to say, 'If only we knew who knows about what.' The focus turned towards communities of practice (groups of individuals focused on specific topical areas), and these communities are now recognised as being tacit knowledge experts/resources in addition to being consumers or producers of explicit knowledge.

In the third phase of the knowledge management cycle, 'knowledge is then contextualised in order to be understood ("acquisition") and used ("application"). This stage then feeds back into the first one in order to update the knowledge content' (Dalkir 2005: 43). Knowledge managers have come to recognise that effective knowledge management can 'only be possible if people know what there is to be known, can find it when they need to, can understand it, and

257

are convinced that this knowledge should be put to work' (2005: 18). This involves providing more context for both explicit content and tacit knowledge experts/resources, and also for the knowledge management initiative as a whole.

A successful knowledge management approach is not just a tool or technology designed to hold explicit content or list topic experts. It is essential that a context of 'networks, practices, and incentives are instituted to facilitate person-to-person knowledge transfer as well as person-knowledge content connections' (2005: 26). Each component (theories, content, tools/technologies, people, processes) must be considered carefully. As Davenport and Prusak (1998) said, 'knowledge is as much an act or process as an artifact or thing' (1998: 53).

Acts and processes are engaged in, and governed by, actors. Davenport and Prusak (1998) go on to describe these acts, processes and actors as a knowledge market:

> Like markets for goods and services, the knowledge market has buyers and sellers who negotiate to reach a mutually satisfactory price for the goods exchanged. It has brokers who bring buyers and sellers together and even entrepreneurs who use their market knowledge to create internal power bases. (1998: 25)

This market perspective highlights the need for knowledge management initiatives to understand and respond to the different roles played by individuals, groups/communities, and the organisation itself, in different circumstances and at different times. There are many factors that affect the relationships between buyers, sellers, brokers and entrepreneurs, including reciprocity, reputation, altruism, and, perhaps most important trust.

As an intersectoral partnership, the Pathways Project involvement of researchers and practitioners in many contexts created an extremely diverse and challenging knowledge environment. While no structured knowledge management system was consciously instituted at the outset of the Pathways Project, knowledge creation, exchange and application patterns did emerge over time. Even without benchmark measures, it is still possible to begin to evaluate the success of the knowledge exchange environment using Ford's knowledge mediation characteristics (see Michaux 2002). According to Ford, 'organisations can rate the extent to which knowledge is mediated into use by measuring the extent to which they have moved from and to the following goals' (Michaux 2002: 4). These goals are depicted in Figure 12.2.

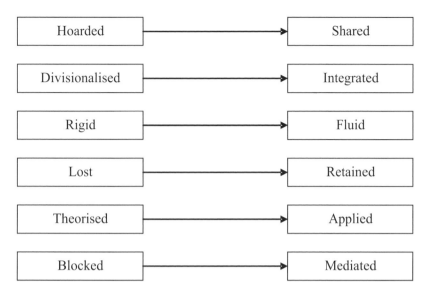

Figure 12.2 Knowledge mediation
Source: Ford (1999) in Michaux (2002)

When, in the informal survey mentioned earlier, Pathways stakeholders were asked to rate knowledge management/mediation at Pathways on a five-point scale across the bridge of Ford's table (with 1 at extreme left and 5 at extreme right of arrows), results averaged 3.5, showing a leaning towards effective knowledge mediation within the established Pathways Project. However, when stakeholders were asked to reflect on how they might have rated the early phase of the project, i.e. after its first six months, scores centred around 2. Although these results must be interpreted with caution, they suggest a perception of an improvement over time, most likely based on higher interaction and greater levels of trust between researchers and practitioners.

Regular evaluation of any knowledge management initiative is essential, and the framework described above can be used to further analyse the components, phases and types of knowledge present in the first few years of the Pathways Project to identify paths for improvement. As described in the results presented earlier (Lens 1), stakeholders have already identified types of knowledge (e.g. 'We need to find out more about how they problem-solve and the process of their interventions at the practical level') and methods for exchange and access (e.g. 'Time lags between data collection, analysis and findings are too long for a service that needs to be flexible and responsive') that would serve them better.

Lens 3: Integrated learning

Integration and Implementation Sciences (IIS) is a developing specialisation that integrates much of the theory already mentioned in this paper and applies it to the research–practice–policy interface.

As Bammer (2005) explains, IIS has the potential to respond to:

> the growing appreciation that a major deficiency in our capacity to tackle national and global problems lies in the inability to amalgamate knowledge created by different disciplines with the experience of key actors and interest groups and then to effectively use that knowledge to bring about social improvement. (2005: 6)

Bammer identifies several impediments to the implementation of integrated interventions, including:

- Disciplinary, intra- and inter-organisational, and sectoral silos, reinforced by dominant institutional structures, assumptions, and reward systems.
- Marginalisation and fragmentation of successful research approaches.
- Lack of system-wide reflection on and learning from case-studies.
- Inability to 'scale-up' successful small scale interventions.
- Lack of recognition that barriers to integrated implementation are amenable to research. Too often these barriers are greeted with resigned frustration and a view that they are too hard politically, too sensitive culturally, and too intransigent on an individual level. (Bammer 2005: 5)

According to Bammer, the central feature of the IIS approach is the changing role of the researcher, who 'must collaborate and integrate across traditional boundaries' (2005: 1) both within and outside the research sphere, as well as become 'more involved in the implementation of research in policy, product and action' (2005: 1).

IIS builds on systems thinking, complexity science, participatory methods and knowledge management, exchange, and implementation approaches to address issues and problems characterised by complexity, uncertainty, change and imperfection. The major features of the IIS model are strategies for integration and include:

- The practical application of research.
- Collaboration and partnerships between researchers and practitioners (including policy makers).
- Systems thinking – frameworks and tools for dealing with complexity and uncertainty.
- Participatory methods that value individuals, societies and cultures as aspects of complexity and encourage mutual learning and conceptual innovation.
- Valuing diverse epistemologies and recognising their impact on the conduct of research.
- Inter- and trans-disciplinarity, the former synthesising discipline specific insights and the latter aiming to produce a common conceptual framework for the disciplinary insights.

IIS is concerned with building fluid expertise, learning and practice loops across organisations, specialisations, institutions and sectors. Though the IIS label is relatively new to Pathways practitioners and researchers, the principles of IIS are a familiar part of everyday work. The 'space' inhabited by the Pathways Project – spanning the broad community of Inala, a number of disciplines at Griffith University, schools, programmes for families, children and communities – has, in some senses, provided a new location for the generation of new knowledge. Researchers inhabit the schools and programmes, practitioners meet at the university. Within the group of project 'owners', there is no dominant partner, thus removing the locus of the project from being essentially a research project first with the practice being secondary, or alternatively a practice with research tacked on. Research and practice are thoroughly integrated.

Friedlander (2001) discusses the false separation, often generated by the research and practice institutions and traditions, 'between action and research on the one hand and between practice and theory on the other' and discusses

> the interaction between these two dichotomies; that the artificial separation of practice and theory contributes to the false separation between research and action; and, finally, that participative (action) research is the most constructive response to the dysfunctional separation of practice and theory. (2001: 1)

According to Friedlander (2001), the practitioner tends to ask 'How?' The scholar tends to ask 'Why?' But it is the integration of the 'how' and the 'why', together with the other levels advocated by

261

Bammer, that will result in an enriched and useful practice-theory. To understand *how* we can reduce conflict adds to our knowledge of *why* conflict gets reduced; and to understand *why* conflict is reduced contributes to our knowledge of *how* we can reduce it. Similarly, at Pathways, though researchers and practitioners expressed frustration with each other's methods and priorities, researchers' questions about the why of prevention work have been, and continue to be, thoroughly enriched by the how of practitioners.

Lens 4: Influencing policy

If, as has been recently claimed, the policy-making process in Australia is 'generally cautious, incremental and ad hoc' (Tavan 2005: 8), how can researchers actively contribute to transforming Australian public policy into a comprehensive/integrated strategic instrument for effectively addressing complex social issues and promoting a just and equitable society?

The research–policy relationship and ways to improve its effectiveness were the focus of a recent paper published by the Academy of the Social Sciences in Australia (Edwards 2004). Edwards discusses many of the problematic aspects of the relationship between researchers and policy practitioners, especially those relating to structures, cultures and communication.

Edwards recommends greater and more regular involvement of researchers in the policy process including identifying and articulating the problem, analysing policy and conducting evaluation. This would, she argues, enable researchers to influence the policy process at various stages, as well as promote greater interaction between research and policy practitioners.

Within the political context of policy-making, researchers not only need robust, evidenced-based research; they must also be equipped with persuasive arguments. Gibson (2003) concedes that timing, communication and joint projects may assist the process of research influencing policy, but that it is knowledge invested with meaning and power that binds government to a particular view or course of action that will be most effective. Researchers also need to form advocacy coalitions to actively promote their research.

Within the Pathways Project, the link with the policy process was conscious. As Homel points out:

At the heart of the network of relationships that made Pathways possible was the practitioner–researcher links that were forged through the Development and Evaluation Group, with the assistance of the Expert Advisory Group [see Figure 12.1]. Despite the energy of these groups, however, many of their ideas could not have been tested in the real world without the willingness of senior Mission Australia staff to 'take up the cause' in terms of advocacy and fund raising. This underlines the importance of communication within a large organisation, and also illustrates how researchers and practitioners in partnership can influence policy agendas both within organisations and beyond. (Homel *et al.* 2006: 103–4)

Evidence for the influence of Pathways on the policy process is clear. At the launch of the federal government's $140 million Communities for Children programme by the Prime Minister of Australia, John Howard, in April 2004, a video of the Pathways Project was used to illustrate the model for the new national programme and the work of Pathways and its parent partners – Mission Australia and Griffith University – was acknowledged. Factors guiding the Pathways research–practice–policy interaction can be teased out:

- A direct line can be drawn, through influential actors, from the project in Inala to decision-makers in Canberra. This line weaves through Mission Australia and includes a variety of internal knowledge-brokers – people who have broadly based understanding of, and credibility with, the different sectors, to facilitate connections and support the knowledge linkage and exchange process.

- Effective advocacy, profiling and lobbying by the parent organisations and by members of the Pathways team ensured that Pathways was front-of-mind among key policy-makers. When the policy wind shifted to interest in early intervention and prevention, the Pathways Project came readily to hand, and the team provided rapid access to information.

- Key elements of the programme – strong conceptual foundation, evidence-based programmes, ongoing evaluation, economic analyses to illustrate cost-benefit ratios – were strategically highlighted during interactions with policy-makers.

- An important policy plank of the Australian government is the 'Social Coalition' and the Pathways partnership resonated as an excellent example of a project based on a strong partnership between government, community and business.

While many perceive the development of public policy as a structured and orderly process, achievements on the ground in the Pathways case have proven to be the result of a series of diverse and distributed actions undertaken by the conscious vigilance and determination of many actors in many spheres. The Pathways experience corresponds directly with the understandings of Colebatch, who has described 'policy activity as a pattern of specialised work by a range of people' (2006: 2) taking place in diverse locations, with 'many hands at the wheel' (2005: 15).

Lens 5: Partnerships and collaborative learning: Focus on engagement

Partnerships between researchers, service providers and policy-makers offer no guarantee of generating new and useful knowledge. It is the characteristics and quality of the engagement, including the degree to which all parties are aligned to the objective and challenges of generating new knowledge that makes partnerships worthwhile.

Partnerships are influenced by the organisational cultures of the various stakeholders involved and this includes their specific business and political imperatives. As representatives or agents of an organisation, each stakeholder will tend to reflect the values and ways of working of their particular organisation. These values will in turn inform their approach to problem solving, information sharing, resolving conflict and teamwork. In this sense not all organisations are well equipped to participate in partnerships. In many instances the priorities of the organisation will influence the representative's commitment to the objectives of the multi-stakeholder project. This tension can be a problem but also an opportunity for reflection and discussion (generative learning).

A high proportion of those working in non-government organisations are frequently engaged in research activities, although this fact is often under-recognised. Typical regular research functions in community organisations include needs assessments for particular clients groups, and quantitative and qualitative data analysis for submissions, community consultations and programme evaluations. These functions and skills are often undervalued and under-acknowledged, perhaps because they occur in sites other than universities.

Brown and colleagues (2003) have made an important contribution to our understanding of effective partnerships between practitioners and researchers. The Practice Research Engagement framework they have developed enables a systematic and integrated approach to the thinking and planning components of working in partnership, and makes explicit many of the often neglected challenges of interorganisational and intersectoral projects.

The four major organising elements of the Practice Research Engagement framework are:

- *Frameworks, goals and interests* that parties bring and their agreements about priorities for the engagement as a whole.
- *Relationships and organisation*, informal and formal, that shape their behaviour.
- *Strategies and methods* that the parties adopt to carry out the engagement.
- *Contextual forces and institutions* that influence engagement activities and outcomes.

One of the major strengths of this concept is its focus on the preconditions of an effective engagement or partnership: Practice Research Engagement initiatives must explicitly address how they organise their joint work. This tends to pre-empt the sorts of ambiguities, barriers and conflicts that have the potential to influence

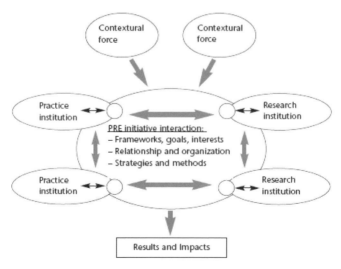

Figure 12.3   Organising 'practice research engagement'
Source: Brown *et al.* (2003)

the engagement. It also facilitates systems thinking in practical ways and can assist participants to appreciate the big picture rather than simply their part in it.

As a relational model, Practice Research Engagement acknowledges and considers the contextual factors that may impact on the work and outcomes of the project. These factors include the organisational bases of the participants, the projects' institutional 'home', as well as the broader political environment – strategically valuable considerations at many levels. The experience of Practice Research Engagement at Pathways was one that was frequently tense. However, Homel's summary of it provides insight into the core:

> Vital as they were, the partnerships at the local level could not have been as effective without the overarching relationship between Mission Australia and the researchers at Griffith University, supported financially by the Australian Research Council and a number of philanthropic foundations. From the beginning, the relationship between the university and Mission Australia has been characterised by trust and mutual respect – and the occasional robust argument about methods and directions. The terms 'trust' and 'mutual respect' sound platitudinous, but in practice the management arrangements depicted in [Figure 12.1] worked not because we relied on a formal contract or memorandum of understanding but because we shared a vision and understood that we needed each other to realise that vision. (Homel *et al.* 2006: 103)

The Pathways Project, located as it is in a range of social systems, provides a unique space for practitioners and researchers to come together on 'neutral' territory (i.e. territory not 'owned' by either practitioners or researchers). Each has had to leave their comfort zone and negotiate in an unfamiliar territory. Partners have had to commit for the long haul to an intense engagement. This removal from traditional territory is key to facilitating the ongoing and thorough iteration between practitioners and researchers. Where the Practice Research Engagement at Pathways took a step further than most was the blurring of the boundaries in terms of traditional roles. In Pathways, practitioners do research and researchers engage in practice. Stepping into the shoes of the other appears to bring an understanding that substantially enhances outcomes.

There are, of course, challenges. The experience at Pathways mirrored that described by Brown and colleagues (2003: 89):

'Practitioners are often irritated by researchers' obsession with details and the snail-like progress of "academic time", while researchers are often irritated by practitioners' indifference to important conceptual distinctions and their insistence on emphasising practical rather than theoretical significance.'

However, one of the key elements in the success of the Pathways partnerships was that potentially disruptive contextual forces from the parent and funding organisations were buffered through arrangements established by some of the leading players. This provided additional barriers to external influence – strengthening the internal partnership between practitioners and researchers.

Another key support can be found in the complex array of management structures established around the Pathways Project in its early days, which represents what we have now come to recognise as learning team structures – teams that cut vertically and horizontally across both parent organisations and beyond, including a reach into international academic spheres – enhancing cross-discipline and cross-sectoral interaction and learning, creating channels for the introduction of expertise, enabling an environment for innovation and creativity, and providing a 'light touch' in terms of administration. What appeared to some as a cumbersome and unnecessarily complex structure can be judged in hindsight as a highly sophisticated network of relationships that enhanced the development of new knowledge and created a collaborative learning environment for both practitioners and researchers.

Conclusion: Effective learning; new knowledge; improved integration; better outcomes

When we pieced together the fragments of evidence assembled as we examined Pathways through this variety of lenses, we found that Pathways *as an organisation* became a microcosm of the model of a learning organisation. By focusing on the space created by the partnership, we found many of the features that literature and experts such as Senge promote as those of learning organisations. Interviews with key players revealed that this environment emerged without a conscious knowledge and understanding of learning organisation literature and methods, but instead was an intuitive development, adopted to accommodate a complex set of systems.

This chapter has sought to illuminate some of the theoretical ideas and issues not usually part of the research focus of the innovative and ambitious Queensland Pathways to Prevention Project. What then are the most salient lessons we can derive from these theories and approaches? What are the essential features and characteristics of an effective approach to interdisciplinary and multi-stakeholder learning processes and how can new knowledge be used to improve our capacity to address complex social problems? If we want to influence the direction of the new knowledge developmental pathway, we must be conscious and active actors. Many of the approaches suggested in this paper may serve us well on this journey, including:

- More serious critiques of our current learning approach and its limitations across practice, research and policy intersections.

- The need to regard intersectoral and interdisciplinary reflection, discussion and change as a fundamental obligation of our professions.

- More active consideration of the role of advocacy in the process of integrating new evidence into policy.

- The adoption of a practical 'systems thinking' approach to interdisciplinary and intersectoral projects, acknowledging that complexity is central to our work, and that the external context is a significant factor.

- An appreciation that there are fertile opportunities for better solutions to complex problems when we are prepared to work with a range of interpretations.

- An extended and more collaborative role for researchers that spans traditional boundaries and specialisations, including the involvement of researchers in policy formulation, evaluation and implementation, as well as service delivery evaluation.

Pathways *as an organisation* was demonstrating Practice Research Engagement, integration and implementation sciences, knowledge management and organisational learning without conscious application of the theoretical frameworks of the thought leaders in the fields. In its unique way and with its particular systems, Pathways created the space/place for innovation and creativity to occur. Pathways service programs are already providing a rich field for practice and research in the areas of prevention and early intervention. Upon closer inspection, however, it is clear that there is more to be mined from this innovative initiative. Looking through lenses of organisational learning, integration, and knowledge management, the Pathways Project offers new insight into the characteristics and dynamics of thriving research–practice–policy partnerships. The impact of proven early interventions in the lives of children is obvious and powerful. But the opportunity to provide models for replicating successful interorganisational and intersectoral partnerships has its own compelling implications for a multitude of social challenges.

Acknowledgements

The authors are grateful to Professor Gabriele Bammer for providing valuable input into the revision of this paper.

References

Argyris, C. (1977) 'Double loop learning in organisations', *Harvard Business Review*, 55(5): 115.

Argyris, C. and Schön, D. (1978) *Organisational Learning: A Theory of Action Perspective*. Reading, MA: Addison-Wesley.

Bammer, G. (2005) 'Integration and implementation sciences: Building a new specialization', *Ecology and Society*, 10(2): 6. Available online at: http://www.ecologyandsociety.org/vol10/iss2/art6/ additional information can be found at: http://www.anu.edu.au/iisn/

Bateson, G. (1972) *Steps to Ecology of Mind*. New York: Ballantine Books.

Brown, D.L., Bammer, G., Batiwala, S. and Kunreuther, F. (2003) 'Framing practice-research engagement for democratizing knowledge', *Action Research*, 1(1): 81–102.

Colebatch, H. (2005) 'Policy Analysis, Policy Practice and Political Science', *Australian Journal of Public Administration*, 64(3): 14–23 (September).

Colebatch, H. (2006) *Doing Policy, Doing Analysis: Accounting for Policy in Australia*, Proceedings of Public Policy Network Conference, February, Perth, Western Australia.

Coutu, D.L. (2002) 'The anxiety of learning: The HBR interview with Edgar H. Schein', *Harvard Business Review*, 80(3): 100–7.

Dalkir, K. (2005) *Knowledge Management in Theory and Practice*. Burlington, MA: Elsevier/Butterworth Heinemann.

Davenport, T.H. and Prusak, L. (1998) *Working Knowledge: How Organizations Manage What They Know*. Boston, MA.: Harvard Business School Press.

Edwards, M. (2004) *Social Science Research and Public Policy: Narrowing the Divide*, Occasional Paper, Canberra: Academy of the Social Sciences in Australia.

Friedlander, F. (2001) *Participatory Action Research as a Means of Integrating Theory and Practice*, Proceedings of the Fielding Graduate Institute Action Research Symposium, Alexandria, VA, 2001. Available online at: http://www.fielding.edu/research/ar_papers/Friedlander.pdf

Gibson, B. (2003) 'From Transfer to Transformation: Rethinking the Relationship Between Research and Policy', PhD project, National Centre for Epidemiology and Population Health, Australian National University. Available online at: http://thesis.anu.edu.au/public/adt-ANU20040528.165124/index.html

Homel, R., Freiberg, K., Lamb, C., Leech, M., Hampshire, A., Hay, I., Elias, G., Carr, A., Manning, M., Teague, R. and Batchelor, S. (2006) *The Pathways to Prevention Project: The First Five Years, 1999–2004*. Brisbane: Griffith University and Mission Australia.

Kim D. (1993) 'The link between individual and organizational learning', *Sloan Management Review*, Fall: 37–50.

March, J.G. and Olson, J.P. (1975) 'The uncertainty of the past: organisational ambiguous learning', *European Journal of Political Research*, 3: 147–71.

Michaux, A. (2002) *The Learning Organisation: Is it Achievable in a Human Services Context?* Proceedings of the ACWA Conference, 2 September. Available at: http://www.acwa.asn.au/Conf2002/Conf_proceedings/06_A%20Michaux.doc

Senge, P. (1990) *The Fifth Discipline: The Art and Practice of the Learning Organisation*. London: Doubleday/Century Business.

Tavan, G. (2005). 'Thank Holt and Whitlam', *The Australian*, 22 August: p. 8.

Chapter 13

Leisure as a context for youth development and delinquency prevention

Linda L. Caldwell and Edward A. Smith

Abstract

This chapter highlights the importance of leisure as a context for human development as well as for prevention of risky behaviour, including crime and delinquency. We offer a brief review and synthesis of current criminology literature that examines leisure activity, and then describe leisure research that may provide additional insight into why leisure may be an important context for understanding and preventing delinquent behaviour. We end with a brief description of an intervention that teaches youth to make healthy decisions in their leisure and describe a set of *post hoc* analysis from a data set from 628 rural youth in the US used to evaluate the leisure-based intervention. Although the data we report were not collected to examine delinquent behaviour, we tentatively conclude that leisure-related variables can serve as risk and protective factors to property damage and by extension other delinquent behaviours. We suggest that helping youth become more intrinsically motivated by having goal-oriented leisure pursuits and decreasing levels of amotivation, learning to overcome peer pressure, and becoming more aware of leisure opportunities may reduce the risk of damaging property. Additionally, having parents who are aware of leisure interests, activities and friends is also a protective factor. We also found evidence to suggest that some form of leisure education intervention may be effective in preventing delinquent acts.

Introduction

This chapter highlights the importance of leisure as a context for human development as well as for prevention of risky behaviour, including crime and delinquency. We first offer a brief review of current literature that examines adolescent delinquent behaviour and leisure activity, and then describe leisure research that may provide additional insight into how leisure may be an important context for understanding and preventing delinquent behaviour. We end with a brief description of an intervention that teaches youth to make healthy decisions in their leisure and describe a set of *post hoc* analysis from a data set used to evaluate the leisure based intervention.

Activities and deviance

The relation between crime, delinquency and leisure is not new to the study of criminology. A number of theories have directly addressed the role of activity, free time, or leisure and deviant behaviour (e.g. Osgood *et al.* 1996; Wong 2005). Other theoretical perspectives certainly implicate the importance of understanding leisure as a context, even if they do not directly address it as a context (e.g. Hirschi's 1969 social control theory). A review of the criminology literature, however, suggests that although what youth do with their time, where they do it, with whom they do it, and the social controls on their time use are considered important, there is a lack of systematic attention that directly seeks to understand leisure as a context for deviance (a point alluded to by Vazsonyi *et al.* 2002). At the same time, there has been an equal lack of attention to the potential importance of leisure as a context for deviance, with some notable exceptions (e.g. Rojeck 1999a, 1999b; Stebbins 1996; Williams 2005; Williams and Walker 2006) in the leisure literature. This void, however, has recently been addressed by a special issue of *Leisure/Loisir* (2006, Vol. 30, No. 1) that was devoted to the topic of 'Deviant Leisure'. We interpret some of our findings in relation to some of the papers in that special issue. Our review of the literature suggests that from a criminology perspective, research that relates to leisure and crime among adolescents can be summarised by four related perspectives:

1 *Filled time perspective*. Time filled with prosocial activities cannot be filled with deviant activities.

2 *Association with deviant peers perspective.* Certain activities are more likely to instigate deviant behaviour or association with a deviant subculture.

3 *Activity structure perspective.* Time spent in informal and/or unsupervised activities is likely to promote deviance, while time spent in supervised activities protects against it.

4 *Person-environment interaction perspective.* Self-control and attachment to conventional norms and activities protect against deviant behaviour.

These four perspectives appear to have emanated from three main general theories that have influenced thinking on delinquency. *Social control theory* (Gottfredson and Hirschi 1990; Hirschi 1969) has been linked with the importance of social bonds, where youth with stronger attachment, commitment, involvement and belief in positive social norms, activities and institutions are less likely to be involved in delinquent behaviour. Hirschi's later work with Gottfredson (1990) suggested that association with deviant peers and delinquency is related to low self-control and consequent peer rejection. This line of reasoning is linked to *differential association theory* (Sutherland 1947), a type of social learning theory suggesting that youth learn to engage in deviant behaviour due to association with others who hold positive beliefs and values about delinquency.

Routine activity theory (e.g. Osgood *et al.* 1996; Osgood and Anderson 2004) seeks to understand the role of lifestyle and routine activities on delinquent activity. Osgood *et al.* (1996) maintained that youth are differentially motivated or tempted by situations and that youth who enact crimes do not necessarily reject conventional values but rather seek excitement, conspicuous consumption and toughness. They further suggested that unstructured activities, unlike structured ones, typically lack social control from authority figures. Thus, structured activities offer fewer opportunities to engage in deviant behaviour because one is engaged in doing something (as opposed to 'nothing' like hanging out, for example). Their research concluded that socialising with peers in unsupervised environments was closely related to deviant behaviour, but, if the unsupervised activity was associated with some type of structure (e.g. sports or dating), this relation was not present.

Some recent work has extended and combined several of these theories and perspectives. Vazsonyi *et al.* (2002) speculated that routine activity theory contains elements of social control theory via involvement, attachment to parents, and self-control in the face of situational demands of the moment. Hartjen and Priyadarsini (2003) likewise tested the theory that some combination of differential association with deviant peers, lack of social control, and lack of self-control contributes to delinquent behaviour. Interestingly, both investigations also sought to understand the cross-cultural applicability of these mainly US-based theories.

From a prevention perspective, researchers have focused on protective factors related to delinquency. These 'mitigators of deviance' include positive peer relations, good school achievement, positive response to authority, and effective use of leisure time (Hoge *et al.* 1996) and participation in extracurricular activities (McNeal 1999). McNeal concluded that participation in extracurricular activities leads to reduced levels of delinquency because participation leads to the acquisition of human capital (individual's level of skills, knowledge and educational attainment), social capital (one's network of relationships), and cultural capital (acquisition and possession of more intangible things such as art, culture, attitudes, values).

Leisure, prevention, and youth development

What can leisure theory bring to this discussion? Leisure is the 'social institution most closely associated with the world of adolescence' beyond school (Fine *et al.* 1990: 227) and is simultaneously a context of risk and protection (e.g. Caldwell *et al.* 2004; Caldwell and Smith 1995; Levin *et al.* 1995). Of all the contexts in an adolescent's life, leisure has great *potential* for personally meaningful activity, enjoyment, autonomy, self-determination, becoming connected to community, developing competence, forming durable relationships with adults, voicing opinions, being listened to, feeling a sense of belonging and mattering, and having control over one's actions (e.g. Hansen *et al.* 2003; Kleiber 1999; Witt and Caldwell 2005). On the other hand, it is also a time of activity that goes against conventional norms, such as substance misuse, crime and deviancy, excessive gambling, and so on. Thus, it is a natural context for prevention programmes.

The studies just acknowledged, however, are built on a rather undifferentiated and overly simple view of leisure engagement and behaviour. The perspectives and theories that encapsulate these studies insinuate interventions that are designed to promote positive activity in general (that is, the emphasis is typically on doing activity and keeping busy). Although a worthy goal, we advocate that a closer theoretical understanding of leisure may contribute to disentangling the pathways or mediators to delinquent behaviour. Central to our line of thinking is to appreciate that recreation is *more than just participating in an activity*, although we certainly agree that the nature of the activity itself is important.

One path to integrating leisure and criminology theories to address delinquency is to loosely disaggregate leisure behaviour into three interrelated elements: context, activity and experience. This unpacking of leisure behaviour allows a closer examination of leisure-related risk and protection factors and thus the identification of possible targets for intervention.

Structured and unstructured activity, or casual and serious leisure

Clearly a focus on activity itself has received the most attention. As evident in the criminology, developmental and leisure literatures, not all activities are equal; some are better than others at producing healthy outcomes and positive affect. Zill *et al.* (1995) cautioned that it is not the 'filling of time' that is important, but rather filling time with activities that develop skills, create challenges and provide fulfilling experiences. There is growing interest to better understand two leisure contexts, structured (or formal, organised) and unstructured (or informal, unorganised), and the types of activities and experiences afforded in these different contexts.

Much of the literature has focused on the positive aspects of structured and negative aspects of unstructured activity. Structured activities have been linked to academic achievement, lower levels of antisocial behaviour, competence, initiation and socialisation (Eccles and Barber 1999; Larson 2000; Mahoney 2000; Mahoney and Stattin 2000). A Carnegie Council on Adolescent Development (1992) report would term the 'better' activities as *high-yield activities*. These activities typically (a) are goal-oriented and/or creative and expressive in nature; (b) require discipline and focused attention; (c) offer challenges to overcome; (d) build skills and increase one's level of competence (with specific feedback given about one's performance) and (e) require persistence, commitment and continuity to participation over time. Structured activities are sometimes referred to as transitional because they help youth learn how to be self-regulated and develop internal capacities that can be transferred to other contexts as well as prepare them for future life (Larson 2000;

Larson and Kleiber 1993). Involvement in these activities develops initiative in youth, a characteristic that is linked with the successful transaction into adulthood (Larson).

The positive value of unstructured activities, however, has been largely overlooked (Kleiber 1999) and under-researched. Unstructured activities do offer adolescents the freedom to experiment with roles, behaviours, and ideas that aid in shaping identity (Caldwell and Darling 1999; Kleiber 1999) and develop personal control and autonomy (Silbereisen et al. 1986). They also help youth learn to negotiate with peers and develop co-operative behaviours. More research needs to be conducted to determine when, under what conditions, and for whom are unstructured (and structured) activities linked with protective or risk factors.

Although the leisure literature addresses the issue of activity and context using the common 'structured vs. unstructured' typology, Stebbins' (1997, 2006) work on serious leisure offers a perhaps more useful typology, although he has not applied it to adolescents. Serious leisure is undertaken by amateurs, hobbyists and volunteers, and is essentially defined as systematic pursuit of an inherently meaningfully and interesting activity that requires substantial investment. It is very similar to the construct of initiative (Larson 2000) in that it requires perseverance, overcoming constraints to participation, increasing skill development, and a continuity of participation over time. There are two additional elements that extend the concept of initiative: a strong sense of personal identity associated with the activity and a belief that one is engaged in a unique social world with its own ethos. He contrasts serious leisure with unserious and casual leisure, which are associated with immediate gratification and pleasure. The reason this typology may be more useful is that it begs the question of 'structure' and instead focuses on issues of lifestyle, social worlds, and central life interests or meanings as well as commitment, perseverance and identity, which can occur in either structured or unstructured environments as currently conceptualised.

One question to ask from the social control and routine activities perspectives is whether certain activities are better at engendering stronger attachment, commitment, involvement and belief in positive social norms, for whom, and why. The literature provides mixed support for the preventive influence of participation in both structured and unstructured activities (Mahoney and Stattin 2000). Little research, however, has examined the relation among personal characteristics as well as contextual and experiential aspects of activities and deviant behaviour in order to better understand under what conditions structured or unstructured activities are developmentally productive and preventive.

Self-determination in context

As previously discussed, it appears that the delinquency literature is heavily influenced by issues of social and self-control, particularly important in contexts where deviant peers are likely. Social and self-control are also key concepts in the leisure literature because leisure is considered the context that offers the greatest opportunity to be self-determined and intrinsically motivated to engage in activity. It is important, then, that leisure contexts offer as much opportunity as possible for youth to exercise self-determination. The relation between social and self-control in a leisure context is quite complex. For example, the amount of adult supervision and guidance may enhance or thwart the acquisition and practice of self-determined behaviour and competence (e.g. Hansen *et al.* 2003; Larson *et al.* 2005). Too much or too little adult supervision can lead to disinterest, extrinsic motivation, or amotivation (e.g. Caldwell *et al.* 1999).

To understand the tension between self- and social control, many leisure researchers use self-determination theory (SDT: e.g. Ryan and Deci 2000). SDT posits that motivation is a self-regulatory process whereby there is a natural tendency to actively engage in the world (Ryan and Deci 2000). It is a framework for investigating the social or environmental factors that promote or thwart intrinsically and extrinsically regulated forms of motivation, which exist on a continuum. At one end, intrinsic motivation signifies engagement in activity due to the inherent satisfaction derived from participation. At the other end of the continuum is amotivation, which describes behaviour that is non-intentional, non-regulated and characterised by lack of control. Between the two ends are three types of motivation that decrease in degree of external regulation: extrinsic motivation (activity compelled due to external influence), introjected motivation (activity driven by perceptions of what others might think), and identified motivation (goal-oriented activity done for a purpose). This multidimensional conceptualisation of self-control may help to overcome the criticisms of self-control theory that suggest that its dichotomous nature is not flexible enough (Boeri *et al.* 2006). Moreover, Boeri *et al.* suggested that another criticism is that the current conceptualisation of self-control does not take into account context; one may have self-control in one domain (e.g. school) but not in another (e.g. leisure).

What has not been well researched is whether the association between adult guidance and supervision and positive outcomes is moderated by person characteristics of the adolescent. For example, youth who are generally amotivated may be responsive to higher levels of adult guidance and supervision, whereas youth who are more intrinsically motivated may not need the degree of supervision or guidance (Hutchinson *et al.* 2002). Perhaps future research could address these issues in the context of delinquent behaviour.

Of particular interest to understanding delinquent behaviour are amotivation and introjected and identified motivation. Theoretically, those with high levels of amotivation would be more likely to engage in risky or negative behaviours as they would be more likely to be both disengaged and unattached to prosocial norms, or would be more influenced by peers. Those engaged in activity for a purpose (identified motivation) would be less likely to engage in risky behaviour as they would be likely engaged in personally meaningful and fulfilling leisure. In addition, they are more likely to be attached and bonded to prosocial institutions and norms (e.g. Eccles and Barber 1999).

The role of introjected motivation, which implicates peer influence, is more difficult to predict because in a leisure context, peers can exert both positive and negative influences on behaviour or experience. Peers can support another youth's attempts to try out a new activity and can promote confidence and self-efficacy (Culp 1998). They can also support each other in prosocial thinking. On the other hand, they can undermine another youth's desire to explore new activities and limit the desire to develop new interests (e.g. it wouldn't be 'cool'). In terms of risky behaviour, clearly peer pressure and the influence of deviant peers is well established (e.g. Andrews *et al.* 2002; Blackwell and Piquero 2005; Bot *et al.* 2005; Caldwell and Darling 1999; Dishion and Owen 2002; Haynie and Osgood 2005). Moore and Zaff (2002) suggested that regardless of having a negative or positive influence, peers tend to self-select groups to hang out with, and these groups are self-perpetuating.

Related to this discussion, using data from the Swedish Youth Recreation Center (YRC) Mahoney and Stattin (2000) concluded that structured activity is linked to low antisocial behaviour, while involvement at the unstructured YRC was associated with high antisocial behaviour. They reasoned that:

> the issue is not whether an individual is engaged in an activity
> – the issue appears to be *what* the individual is engaged in, and

with *whom*. In terms of antisocial behaviour, it may be better to be uninvolved than to participate in unstructured activity, particularly if it features a high number of deviant youth. (2000: 123)

Wong (2005) reported similar findings. Based on Hirschi's concept of involvement, Wong found support for the differential involvement hypothesis and concluded that some conventional activities such as playing sports do not increase conformity but rather may increase one's involvement in delinquent acts due to association with peers whose values and beliefs are consistent with delinquency.

The experience of leisure

To return to the idea of understanding leisure as context, activity and experience, the experiential element of leisure is important as various leisure experiences are linked with both positive and negative outcomes. Boredom, stress and conflict are all negative experiences that might be associated with leisure as well as risky behaviour. Perceptions of boredom have been linked with a number of problem behaviours such as alcohol and drug abuse (Brake 1997; Iso-Ahola and Crowley 1991; Orcutt 1985), higher rates of dropping out of school (Farrell *et al.* 1988), vandalism (Caldwell and Smith 1995), and obesity (Abramson and Stinson 1977; Ganley 1998; Rodin 1975). A recent study by the National Center on Addiction and Substance Abuse (2003) found that adolescents who reported being bored often are 50 per cent more likely to smoke, drink, get drunk and use illegal drugs.

On the other hand, positive leisure experiences such as joy, stress release and positive emotionality can also promote healthy development. Interest, for example, is the opposite of boredom, and is important to cognitive growth as focusing on the task at hand promotes brain activity. Interest is also associated with physical benefits such as a decreased heart rate and intrinsic motivation (Hunter and Csikszentmihalyi 2003). Being interested has been linked with joy, competence and tension release (Izard 1991). Interest and intrinsic motivation are also linked with the experience of flow (e.g. Csikszentmihalyi 1990), which contributes to positive youth development outcomes such as initiative, self-efficacy and competence.

The type and/or context of the activity can contribute to positive or negative experiences in leisure. This is one of the reasons structured activities are of such interest. With proper adult guidance and supervision, and with the opportunity for sustained engagement in high-yield activities, positive experiences are more likely to accrue. On the other hand, unstructured activities are most often linked with sub-optimal developmental experiences (Larson 2000). For example, many common forms of unstructured leisure activities do not adequately provide opportunities for adolescents to exercise concentration, face challenge, and exert effort over time, which are typical of many structured activities (Larson 2000).

Role of parents

One final point should be made in this discussion on leisure and prevention and it relates to issues of social control. The important role of parents and their influence on leisure behaviour and experience must be considered. Although it is a role that has not been well addressed in the leisure literature, fields of human development and developmental psychology have produced a rich literature to draw from (e.g. Eccles *et al.* 2003; Grolnick *et al.* 1997; Larson *et al.* 2001; Fletcher *et al.* 2000; Steinberg 2000). The little work that has been done in the leisure literature suggests that perceptions of too much parental control and lack of autonomy support are linked with boredom and negative outcomes (Caldwell and Smith 2004; Sharp *et al.* 2006; Watts and Caldwell, under review). On the other hand, perceptions of parental autonomy support and knowledge of one's activities and whereabouts is associated with positive outcomes and reduced risk for negative behaviour (Grolnick *et al.* 1997; Hutchinson *et al.* 2003). The influence of parental autonomy support on engagement in positive activities, however, may be strongest for adolescents who are amotivated and extrinsically motivated (Hutchinson *et al.* 2002; Watts and Caldwell).

Leisure education as prevention: TimeWise

Not all youth know how to construct positive leisure or take advantage of leisure opportunities for healthy development, nor are they typically aware of the various possibilities in their communities. It is particularly important in resource-restricted contexts to help youth learn to develop leisure interests and goals that are in the realm of the possible (Lerner *et al.* 2001). Adults should help youth cultivate interests that they can pursue within the parameters (limitations and opportunities) of their immediate environment. Lerner *et al.* also suggested that if interest development and activity selections are limited at an early age, acquisition of important life skills may be thwarted. The opportunity to participate in a wide range of leisure experiences is important because youth need exposure to and the ability to experiment with a wide range of activities in order to find those that they are interested in and intrinsically motivated to pursue.

Since many youth do not know how to engage in healthy leisure interests or are not aware of what exists, intervention efforts are important. The TimeWise: Taking Charge of Leisure Time (Caldwell 2004) programme was designed to help youth learn about free time, develop leisure skills, and how to take responsibility for creating positive experiences. TimeWise was developed as a substance abuse prevention programme and evaluated in a randomised control efficacy trial. It is comprised of six core and five booster lessons targeted at middle school youth. The six core lessons focus on teaching students to (a) determine personally satisfying and meaningful leisure activities and interests; (b) understand the benefits of participating in healthy leisure; (c) understand how one's motivation affects one's experience and participation in healthy behaviours; (d) alleviate boredom and increase optimal experience in leisure time; (e) learn how to take responsible action to participate in desired activities; and (f) identify and overcome constraints that get in the way of participation in desired activities. The five booster lessons include (a) educating others about leisure; (b) making decisions and taking risks; (c), achieving flow; (d) managing stress and becoming mindful; (e) friendships and leisure; and (f) leisure and change.

Although the purpose of TimeWise was to evaluate its effectiveness in preventing substance abuse it can be considered a general youth development and risk prevention programme. Given the interest in the criminology literature about leisure, we wondered whether findings from TimeWise might provide some insight into pathways to delinquent behaviour. It is an empirical question as to whether or not similar leisure variables mediate both substance use and delinquency, although we posit that there may be similar underlying protective and risk factors associated with risky behaviour (e.g. Hawkins 1999; Jessor 1991, 1994). Thus, we conducted *post hoc* analyses to illustrate some of the points made in the previous discussion.

Research questions

Two research questions guided our *post hoc* analyses: (1) What leisure-related variables predict property damage, controlling for experimental condition, gender and the previous year's levels of property damage? (2) Did TimeWise youth report lower incidences of property damage compared to the control group youth? Based on our review of the literature, we hypothesised that the following leisure-related variables would be associated with less property damage: youth perceptions that parents were knowledgeable and interested in their free time activities; high levels of identified motivation, initiative, interest (vs. being bored); awareness of opportunities in the community; and participation in sports and school or community clubs and organisations. We hypothesised that youth perceptions of too much parental control, amotivation, introjected motivation, and peer influence would be associated with higher levels of property damage. We were unable to hypothesise about the influence of going to natural public parks and other spaces. Because we did not design TimeWise to influence delinquent behaviour we also did not make predictions about this relation.

Methods

Nine middle schools were recruited to participate: four were randomly assigned to the experimental group and five to the no-treatment control group. All schools were in rural school districts in northern Appalachia in the US and were chosen to represent relatively poor, small (i.e. less than 1,000 students) school districts. In each school, approximately one-third of the students received free or reduced price lunches. About 30 per cent of the students reported living in a rural area, 29 per cent lived in a neighborhood but not 'in town', and 25.2 per cent lived in a small town. Only 6.9 per cent reported living on a farm. On average youth were about 13 years old in 2000 and 49 per cent were male. The TimeWise curriculum was pilot tested in the fall of 2000 (T1) and implemented in the springs of 2001 (T2), 2002 (T3) and 2003 (T4). After appropriate consent and assent, all students were given self-administered questionnaires in the fall of 2000, and subsequent to the implementation of TimeWise (average was post six weeks). The final number of participants at Time 4 (spring 2003) equalled 475, which represented 75 per cent of the original number.

Measures

The leisure-related measures (motivation, interest/boredom, initiative, awareness of opportunities and peer influence), and two parent variables (perceived knowledge and control) were assessed with multi-item indices using a Likert-type response format; all measures had acceptable reliability coefficients. For details on these measures see Caldwell *et al.* (2004). We only had one measure of delinquency in our data set, property damage. It was measured by asking how often the adolescent purposely damaged someone's property or belongings (the response scale was 1 = never; 2 = before but not this year; 3 = once or twice this year; 4 = once or twice a month; 5 = once or twice a week; and 6 = almost every day or daily). We also measured participation in extracurricular sports, community and school clubs, and going to public natural areas on the same response scale.

Analysis

For the purposes of this *post hoc* analysis, after examining descriptive statistics, we conducted a hierarchical linear regression to determine the leisure-related variables that predicted property damage. We then conducted a multivariate, repeated measures GLM to determine whether youth who had the TimeWise programme reported a lower incidence of property damage than youth in the control group. Ideally, we would have used multilevel modelling to analyse these data as the individuals were nested within the nine schools. Due to the limited number of schools in the study, however, this was not possible. Prior research on these same schools with the previous cohort of students, however, indicated that intraclass correlations were negligible, likely due to the fact that the schools were highly homogeneous (Smith *et al.* 2004).

Results

We predicted property damage at T4 using T4 variables since they are theoretically more salient. Before conducting the hierarchical regression analysis, we inspected the correlation matrix for high correlations. Table 13.1 displays this matrix. We concluded that despite the .640 correlation between identified motivation and initiative, we could proceed with our analysis. First we controlled for T3 incidence of property damage, condition (treatment vs. control) and gender. Next we entered the parental variables (control and knowledge), followed by the leisure variables (amotivation and extrinsic, introjected, identified and intrinsic motivation, peer influence, interest (not bored), initiative, and awareness of leisure opportunities). Finally we entered the activity participation variables. Table 13.2 displays the results of this analysis. The adjusted R^2 for the first model was .245 and for the final model was .349 (R^2 = .249 and .376, respectively). The addition of each block of variables contributed significantly (p <.05) to the explained variance.

Being male and T3 property damage both predicted T4 property damage. Positive predictors of property damage include high levels of amotivation, interest, peer influence, and going to natural public places. Identified motivation, awareness, and parental knowledge negatively predicted property damage.

To examine whether youth who got the TimeWise intervention were less likely to damage property, we conducted a multivariate, repeated measures GLM. Figure 13.1 graphically depicts this analysis. The dependent variables were property damage at T1, 2, 3 and 4 with time as the within-subjects repeated measure. Condition and gender were the between-subjects factors. Main effects for time, condition, gender and interactions were tested. Time was significant at $p = .000$, and using the Greenhouse-Geisser correction for sphericity, the time*condition interaction approached significance at $p = .058$ (F=2.56, df= 2.774). Within-subject contrasts identified that this association was cubic ($p = .007$). Cohen's d comparing treatment and comparison means at T4 (using error standard deviation) was 1.21 and the effect size was moderate at .535. Taken together, one can tentatively conclude that at T4, TimeWise youth reported significantly lower frequency of property damage than the comparison youth.

Discussion

In this chapter we made a theoretical argument for the importance of understanding leisure as a risk and protective factor for delinquent youth behaviour and used *post hoc* analysis to present empirical analysis of data from a leisure-based intervention as an example of our argument. There are clearly limitations to our analysis that prevent strong conclusions (e.g. measurement of property damage and inability to specify the model exactly as desired due to the constraints of secondary analysis), but we can tentatively conclude

Table 13.1 Bivariate correlations among leisure variables

	1	2	3	4	5	6	7	8	9	10	11	12	13
1 Parental knowledge	1	-.423 **	-.460 **	.342 **	.001	-.439 **	.378 **	.323 **	.123 **	-.419 **	.154 **	.106 **	.270 **
2 Parental control	-.423 **	1	.386 **	-.198 **	.090 *	.436 **	-.281 **	-.371 **	-.195 **	.192 **	-.120 **	-.119 **	-.012
3 Amotivation	-.460 **	.386 **	1	-.449 **	-.005	.474 **	-.504 **	-.607 **	-.178 **	.327 **	-.266 **	-.140 **	-.169 **
4 Identified motivation	.342 **	-.198 **	-.449 **	1	.417 **	-.196 **	.640 **	.443 **	.261 **	-.231 **	.244 **	.265 **	.170 **
5 Introjected motivation	.001	.090 *	-.005	.417 **	1	.292 **	.198 **	.009	.084	.017	.232 **	.136 **	.082
6 Peer influence	-.439 **	.436 **	.474 **	-.196 **	.292 **	1	-.302 **	-.451 **	-.118 **	.336 **	-.086 *	-.006	-.081
7 Initiative	.378 **	-.281 **	-.504 **	.640 **	.198 **	-.302 **	1	.588 **	.361 **	-.214 **	.319 **	.284 **	.181 **
8 Interest	.323 **	-.371 **	-.607 **	.443 **	.009	-.451 **	.588 **	1	.292 **	-.153 **	.290 **	.202 **	.157 **
9 Aware	.123 **	-.195 **	-.178 **	.261 **	.084	-.118 **	.361 **	.292 **	1	-.103 *	.190 **	.258 **	-.032
10 Damage property T4	-.419 **	.192 **	.327 **	-.231 **	.017	.336 **	-.214 **	-.153 **	-.103 *	1	-.026	.064	-.073
11 Organised sport	.154 **	-.120 **	-.266 **	.244 **	.232 **	-.086 *	.319 **	.290 **	.190 **	-.026	1	.266 **	.373 **
12 Natural public place	.106 *	-.119 **	-.140 **	.265 **	.136 **	-.006	.284 **	.202 **	.258 **	.064	.266 **	1	.152 **
13 School/community	.270 **	-.012	-.169 **	.170 **	.082	-.081	.181 **	.157 **	-.032	-.073	.373 **	.152 **	1

Note:
** Correlation is significant at the 0.01 level (2-tailed)
* Correlation is significant at the 0.05 level (2-tailed)

Table 13.2 Hierarchical linear regression predicting property damage at Time 4

Model		Unstandardised coefficients		Standardised coefficients		
		B	Std. Error	Beta	t	Sig.
1	(Constant)	1.184	.238		4.967	.000
	Condition	.163	.091	.070	1.782	.075
	Gender	−.319	.093	−.138	−3.436	.001
	Damage property T3	.469	.042	.445	11.159	.000
2	(Constant)	2.548	.373		6.837	.000
	Condition	.137	.088	.059	1.564	.119
	Gender	−.240	.090	−.104	−2.683	.008
	Damage property T3	.374	.042	.354	8.814	.000
	Parental knowledge	−.367	.060	−.269	−6.130	.000
	Parental control	.037	.055	.028	.683	.495
3	(Constant)	.809	.705		1.149	.251
	Condition	.122	.087	.052	1.399	.163
	Gender	−.247	.092	−.107	−2.679	.008
	Damage property T3	.355	.042	.336	8.485	.000
	Parental knowledge	−.253	.064	−.185	−3.938	.000
	Parental control	−.034	.057	−.026	−.591	.555
	Amotivation	.151	.069	.114	2.198	.028
	Identified motivation	−.208	.093	−.120	−2.248	.025
	Introjected motivation	.037	.070	.023	.526	.599
	Peer influence	.297	.085	.168	3.514	.000
	Initiative	.115	.102	.061	1.132	.258
	Interest	.254	.102	.129	2.490	.013
	Awareness	−.089	.052	−.069	−1.695	.091
4	(Constant)	.823	.704		1.169	.243
	Condition	.128	.086	.055	1.478	.140
	Gender	−.232	.094	−.100	−2.456	.014
	Damage property T3	.361	.042	.342	8.686	.000
	Parental knowledge	−.264	065	−.193	−4.051	.000
	Parental control	−.027	.057	−.020	−.471	.638
	Amotivation	.153	.068	.115	2.238	.026
	Identified motivation	−.222	.092	−.128	−2.405	.017
	Introjected motivation	.009	.071	.006	.133	.894
	Peer influence	.272	.084	.154	3.230	.001
	Initiative	.061	.102	.032	.594	.553
	Interest	.224	.102	.114	2.203	.028
	Awareness	−.115	.053	−.089	−2.178	.030
	Organised sport	.037	028	.056	1.312	.190
	Natural public place	.101	.034	.117	2.933	.004
	School/community club	.010	.026	.017	.404	.686

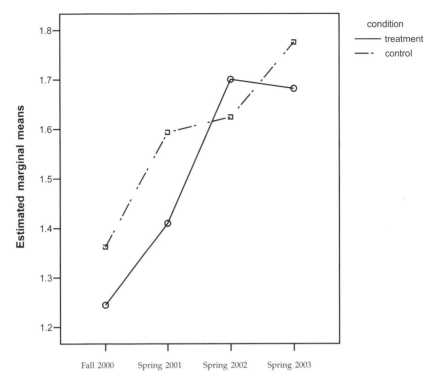

Figure 13.1 Estimated marginal means of property damage across time
Note: 1 = never, 2 = before, but not this year, 3 = once or twice this year, 4 = once or twice a month, 5 = once or twice a week, and 6 = almost every day or daily

two things: leisure-related variables can serve as risk and protective factors to property damage (and by extension perhaps other delinquent behaviours) and there is a possibility that some form of leisure education intervention may be effective in preventing delinquent acts.

The amount of variance explained in the final regression model was not trivial and represents an increase of 10 per cent explained variance by the addition of leisure-related variables. Tentatively we can suggest that helping youth become more intrinsically motivated by having goal-oriented leisure pursuits and decreasing levels of amotivation, learning to overcome peer pressure, and becoming more aware of leisure opportunities may reduce the risk of damaging property. Additionally, having parents who are aware of leisure interests, activities and friends is also a protective factor. Participating in activities that take place in natural public places (such as parks) was associated with property damage.

At first glance, it goes against theory that high levels of interest and low levels of boredom positively predicted property damage, and further investigation is warranted. Upon further reflection, however, it is possible that youth who engaged in property damage were experiencing leisure. In fact, Galloway (2006) might suggest that this is a new form of adventure recreation. Neither the criminology or leisure literatures represent perspectives that deviance and/or crime are undertaken as forms of leisure (Drozda 2006). In particular, the leisure literature usually twins leisure with 'goodness' (e.g. Drozda 2006; Rojek 1999a, 1999b; Williams and Walker 2006) and other forms of leisure have been termed 'purple recreation' (Curtis 1979, 1988) or sub-zero on the Nash pyramid (Gunn and Caissie 2006). If it is true that deviance is a form of leisure for some adolescents, it is then not surprising that high interest and low boredom are associated with enacting property damage. This discussion, however, begs the question as to just what is deviance, crime and delinquency, as well as what is leisure. This discussion is beyond the scope of this paper, but interested readers should consult the special issue on 'Deviant Leisure' of *Leisure/Loisir* (2006, Vol. 30, No. 1).

Returning to Stebbins' (2006) typology of serious, non-serious and casual leisure, property damage could be considered casual leisure for some youth. Our findings suggest that those youth who experience amotivation in leisure, and whose parents are not perceived to be knowledgeable, are highly susceptible to peer influence and are likely to be situationally motivated and engage in casual leisure. This finding seems consistent with differential association theory and routine activity theory, although in this case we are not sure if delinquency is due to positive norms to engage in property damage or due to amotivation and disengagement from 'life.' If the latter, they may be looking for some excitement or just 'something to do' (e.g. Osgood *et al.* 1996) or searching for meaning in life by trying to escape feelings of amotivation and anomie, which are both related to lack of meaning and self-control. From a sociological perspective, Durkheim (1951) suggested that anomie causes a disruption in the social fabric that is related to normlessness. Similarly, from a developmental perspective, Bronfenbrenner and Morris (1998) suggested that it is developmentally disruptive to be amotivated.

On the other hand, youth who have high levels of leisure-related initiative and identified motivation (and low amotivation), and whose parents are knowledgeable, are aware of leisure opportunities and are associated with lower levels of property damage. These findings are consistent with Hirschi and Gottfredson's (2000) definition of self-control as being concerned with long-term outcomes associated with one's actions. Presumably, these youth see a future and are purposeful in their actions so as to actively construct their futures, at least in terms of their leisure pursuits. These findings are also consistent with the notion of social bonding and attachment, although we did not directly measure these constructs. Participating in serious leisure (Stebbins 2006) by definition is characterised by social bonds to a social world associated with others who enjoy the same pursuit. This bond is forged over time and requires initiative and purposeful action. Thus, serious leisure as a context of shared personal meaning and commitment may be an important context for social bonds, as well as social control, to form. It is interesting that neither participation in sports or school/community clubs were associated with lower levels of property damage, suggesting that perhaps Stebbins' work might be useful in future research to avoid the traps inherent in classifying activity as structured (or formal) and unstructured (or informal).

Our data did not allow us to model the role of social control beyond adolescents' perceptions of parents, nor could we model the presence of social bonding or attachment. Despite that limitation, beyond engaging in property damage the previous year (β = .342), parental knowledge had the strongest association (negative) with property damage (β = −.193). Peer influence had the next strongest association (β = .154). This may suggest that the more distal influence of *perception* of social control (i.e. parents' knowledge) may be more powerful than peer influence, but again, more research is needed to better understand the tension between positive perceptions of parental knowledge, parental control, social bonding and peer influence (situationally and more generally). Research could also address whether parental knowledge and/or other social control variables work better for some youth (e.g. sensation-seekers, those who are high on impulsivity, amotivated) than others.

Because the literature is mixed with regard to the protective benefit of participating in sports and community clubs, we were not surprised that there was no association of participating in these activities with property damage. Neither was it surprising that participating in activities in public natural places was positively associated with property damage, especially with this rural sample. Upon reflection, in a way we were really looking at context versus activity with these activities, a conclusion similar to Wong's (2005). More research is needed to more appropriately study these contexts and again, perhaps research that adopts a casual versus serious leisure perspective may be more productive, or at least shed a different light on the topic, than using a structured versus unstructured approach.

Role of leisure education

Although TimeWise did not set out to reduce delinquent behaviour, property damage was lower for TimeWise youth at T4 than for the comparison group. Consistent with problem behaviour theory (e.g. Jessor 1991, 1994), our findings suggest the mediators of substance use that TimeWise was designed to influence may be relevant in interventions designed to reduce delinquency. Although more work needs to be done to strengthen the programme and determine its effectiveness in non-rural samples, results from our efficacy trial have indicated that it is a promising intervention to assist youth in making better leisure choices in their free time (Caldwell *et al.* under review). We found that TimeWise students exhibited more intrinsic motivation, less extrinsic motivation, and less amotivation. TimeWise boys' level of interest increased after the core lessons, but dissipated afterwards while the increased level of interest of TimeWise girls after the core lessons maintained across time. Finally, TimeWise appeared to affect boys' awareness of leisure activities at first follow-up, but not girls'. As we continue our work with TimeWise, we will pay closer attention to gender differences and increase the dose (i.e. more than six lessons for the core programme and stronger booster lessons).

Conclusion

We began this chapter by suggesting that a deeper, more nuanced and theoretically based perspective on leisure may be helpful to untangle the complex pathways to delinquency. Understanding leisure as interrelated elements of context, activity and experience from a socio-ecological perspective may not only help understand delinquency, but also help shape interventions designed to promote healthy youth development and prevent risk through leisure. Our brief review of the literature on delinquent behaviour in the criminology, developmental and leisure literatures suggests that there has been some excellent research already conducted that begins to understand leisure-related pathways to delinquency. Research using routine activity theory and situational motivation (Osgood *et al.* 1996) and on the role of structured and unstructured activity (e.g. Mahoney and Stattin 2002; Osgood *et al.* 1996; Osgood and Anderson 2004) has already contributed to this knowledge base. To contribute to the four perspectives on leisure and crime presented at the beginning of this chapter, we offer the following additional perspectives that require future research:

1 *Opportunity for self-determined and intrinsically motivated behaviour perspective.* Engaging in activity that is inherently interesting, self-determined and goal-oriented may protect against deviant behaviour.
   a *The right mix of parental and other adult supervision and guidance.* Parents or other adults can undermine self-determined and intrinsically motivated behaviour, or they can promote it, by providing the right amount of support and guidance.

2 *Opportunity to engage in high-yield leisure activities perspective.* It is not just 'filling time' that is important, but the activity must be personally expressive and meaningful, contain the right mix of challenge relative to skill, and provide personal benefits (both intrinsic and extrinsic).
   a *Serious versus casual leisure.* It is not necessarily whether the activity is structured or unstructured, but rather whether or not there is opportunity for sustained engagement that persists across time, provides a source of identity, and the ability to bond with a social group in a meaningful way.
   b *The need for positive experience.* High-yield, sustained activities (i.e. a leisure lifestyle) that produce positive effects such as flow, interest, joy, stress release may mitigate deviant behaviour.

3 *Deviance is leisure perspective.* Some youth participate in deviant or delinquent (or unconventional) activity for their leisure as it may give them similar short-term or long-term experiences and benefits as more conventional leisure does to the majority of youth. Much more research is needed on this perspective.

All of the preceding perspectives are primarily speculative at this point, although there is some empirical support behind each perspective. There is great potential benefit to developing effective interventions by combining disciplinary forces across criminology, and developmental, prevention, and leisure sciences to address issues of leisure and deviance or delinquency.

Acknowledgements

The authors greatly appreciate the guest editors' comments and suggestions, as well as those of the two anonymous reviewers. The chapter was greatly improved as a result.

This material is based upon work supported by the US Department of Health and Human Services under Award Nos 1R21 DA13193-01 and R01 15984. This project was totally financed by federal funds in the amount of US$420,900.

References

Abramson, E.E. and Stinson, S.G. (1977) 'Boredom and eating in obese and non-obese individuals', *Addictive Behaviours*, 2(4): 181–85.

Andrews, J.A., Tildesley, E., Hops, H. and Fuzhong, L. (2002) 'The influence of peers on young adult substance use', *Health Psychology*, 21: 349–57.

Boeri, M.W., Sterk, C.E. and Elifson, K.W. (2006) 'Baby boomer drug users: Career phases, social control, and social learning theory', *Sociological Inquiry*, 76: 264–91.

Bot, S.M., Engles, R.C.M.E., Knibb, R.A. and Meeus, W.H.J. (2005) 'Friend's drinking behaviour and adolescent alcohol consumption: The moderating role of friendship characteristics', *Addictive Behaviours*, 30: 929–47.

Blackwell, B.S. and Piquero, A.R. (2005) 'On the relationship between gender, power control, self-control, and crime', *Journal of Criminal Justice*, 33: 1–17.

Brake, S.B. (1997) 'Perspectives on Boredom for At Risk Adolescent Girls', PhD thesis, Pennsylvania State University.

Bronfenbrenner, U. and Morris, P.A. (1998) 'The Ecology of Developmental Processes', in W. Damon and R.M. Lerner (eds) *The Handbook of Child Psychology, Vol. 1: Theoretical Models of Human Development*. New York: John Wiley, pp. 993–1028.

Caldwell, L.L. (2004) *TimeWise: Taking Charge of Leisure Time*. Scotts Valley, CA: ETR Associates.

Caldwell, L.L. and Darling, N. (1999) 'Leisure context, parental control, and resistance to peer pressure as predictors of adolescent partying and substance use: An ecological perspective', *Journal of Leisure Research*, 31: 57–77.

Caldwell, L.L. and Smith, E.A. (1995) 'Health behaviours of leisure alienated youth', *Loisir and Societe/Leisure and Society*, 18: 143–56.

Caldwell, L.L. and Smith, E.A. (2004) 'Role of leisure mediators in preventing substance use among adolescents: A longitudinal analysis', *Society for Research on Adolescents*, 11–13 March.

Caldwell, L.L., Baldwin, C.K., Walls, T. and Smith, E.A. (2004) 'Preliminary effects of a leisure education program to promote healthy use of free time among middle school adolescents', *Journal of Leisure Research*, 36: 310–35.

Caldwell, L.L., Darling, N., Payne, L. and Dowdy, B. (1999) '"Why are you bored?" An examination of psychological and social control causes of boredom among adolescents', *Journal of Leisure Research*, 31: 103–21.

Caldwell, L.L., Smith, E.A., Ridenour, T. and Maldonado-Molina, M. (under review) 'Three-year effects of the TimeWise substance use prevention intervention', *Journal of Primary Prevention*.

Carnegie Council on Adolescent Development (1992) *A Matter of Time: Risk and Opportunity in the Nonschool Hours*, Report of the Task Force on Youth Development and Community Programs. New York: Carnegie Corporation of New York.

Csikszentmihalyi, M. (1990) *Flow: The Psychology of Optimal Experience*. New York: Harper and Row.

Culp, R.H. (1998) 'Adolescent girls and outdoor recreation: A case study examining constraints and effective programming', *Journal of Leisure Research*, 30: 356–79.

Curtis, J.E. (1979) *Recreation: Theory and Practice*. St Louis, MI: C. V. Mosby.

Curtis, J.E. (1988) 'Purple recreation', *Society of Park and Recreation Education National Recreation and Park Association Annual on Education*, 3: 73–7.

Dishion, T.J. and Owen, L.D. (2002) 'A longitudinal analysis of friendships and substance use: Bidirectional influence from adolescence to adulthood', *Developmental Psychology*, 38: 480–91.

Drozda, C. (2006) 'Juveniles performing auto theft: An exploratory study into a deviant leisure lifestyle', *Leisure/Loisir*, 30: 111–32.

Durkheim, E. (1951) 'Anomic Suicide', in G. Simpson (ed.), *Suicide: A Study in Sociology*. New York: Free Press, pp. 241–76 (first published 1897).

Eccles, J.S. and Barber, B.L. (1999) 'Student council, volunteering, basketball, or marching band: What kind of extracurricular involvement matters?', *Journal of Adolescent Research*, 14: 10–34.

Eccles, J.S., Barber, B.L., Stone, M. and Hunt, J. (2003) 'Extracurricular activities and adolescent development', *Journal of Social Issues*, 59: 865–89.

Farrell, E., Peguero, G., Lindsey, R. and White, R. (1988) 'Giving voice to high school students: Pressure and boredom, ya know what I mean?', *American Educational Research Journal*, 4: 489–502.

Fine, G.A., Mortimer, J.T. and Roberts, D. (1990) 'Leisure, Work, and the Mass Media', in S.S. Feldman and G.R. Elliott (eds) *At the Threshold: The Development Adolescent*. Cambridge, MA: Harvard University Press, pp. 225–54.

Fletcher, A.C., Elder, G.H. and Mekos, D. (2000) 'Parental influences on adolescent involvement in community activities', *Journal of Research on Adolescence*, 10(1): 29–48.

Galloway, S. (2006) 'Adventure recreation reconceived: Positive forms of deviant leisure', *Leisure/Loisir*, 30: 219–32.

Ganley, R.M. (1998) 'Emotion and eating in obesity: A review of the literature', *International Journal of Eating Disorders*, 8(3): 343–61.

Gottfredson, M.R. and Hirschi, T. (1990) *A General Theory of Crime*. Stanford, CA: Stanford University Press.

Grolnick, W.S., Deci, E.L. and Ryan, R.M. (1997) 'Internalization within the Family: The Self-determination Theory Perspective', in J.E. Grusec and L. Kuczynski (eds) *Parenting and Children's Internalization of Values: A Handbook of Contemporary Theory*. New York: John Wiley.

Gunn, L. and Caissie, L.T. (2006) 'Serial murder as an act of deviant leisure', *Leisure/Loisir*, 30: 27–54.

Hansen, D., Larson, R. and Dworkin, J. (2003) 'What adolescents learn in organized youth activities: A survey of self-reported developmental experiences', *Journal of Research on Adolescence*, 13: 25–56.

Hartjen, C.A. and Priyadarsini, S. (2003) 'Gender, peers, and delinquency: A study of boys and girls in rural France', *Youth and Society*, 34: 387–414.

Hawkins, J.D. (1999) 'Preventing crime and violence through Communities that Care', *European Journal on Criminal Policy and Research*, 7: 443–58.

Haynie, D.L. and Osgood, D.W. (2005) 'Reconsidering peers and delinquency: How do peers matter?', *Social Forces*, 84: 1109–30.

Hirschi, T. (1969) *Causes of Delinquency*. Berkeley, CA: University of California Press.

Hirschi, T. and Gottfredson, M.R. (2000) 'In defense of self-control', *Theoretical Criminology*, 4: 55–71.

Hoge, R.D., Andrews, D.A. and Leschied, L.W. (1996) 'An investigation of risk and protective factors in a sample of youthful offenders', *Journal of Child Psychology and Psychiatry*, 37: 419–24.

Hunter, J.P. and Csikszentmihalyi, M. (2003) 'The positive psychology of interested adolescents', *Journal of Youth and Adolescence*, 32: 27–35.

Hutchinson, S.L., Baldwin, C.K. and Caldwell, L.L. (2003) 'Differentiating parent practices related to adolescent behaviour in the free time context', *Journal of Leisure Research*, 35: 396–422.

Hutchinson, S.L., Caldwell, L.L. and Baldwin, C.K. (2002) 'That Extra Push: The Moderating Influence of Parents on Adolescent Initiative', National Recreation and Parks Annual Congress, Leisure Research Symposium, Tampa, FL.

Iso-Ahola, S.E. and Crowley, E.D. (1991) 'Adolescent substance abuse and leisure boredom', *Journal of Leisure Research*, 23(3): 260–71.

Izard, C.E. (1991) *The Psychology of Emotions*. New York, NY: Plenum.

Jessor, R. (1991) 'Risk behaviour in adolescence: A psychosocial framework for understanding and action', *Journal of Adolescent Health*, 12: 597–605.

Jessor, R. (1994) 'Problem-Behaviour Theory and the life course in adolescence: Epistemology in action', *Medicine and Mind*, 8: 57–68.

Kleiber, D.A. (1999) *Leisure Experience and Human Development: A Dialectical Interpretation*. New York: Basic Books.

Larson, R. (2000) 'Toward a psychology of positive youth development', *American Psychologist*, 55: 170–83.

Larson, R. and Kleiber, D.A. (1993) 'Free-time Activities as Factors in Adolescent adjustment', in P. Tolan and B. Cowhler (eds) *Handbook of Clinical Research and Practice with Adolescents*. New York: Wiley.

Larson, R., Walker, K. and Pearce, N. (2005) 'A comparison of youth-driven and adult-driven youth programs: Balancing inputs from youth and adults', *Journal of Community Psychology*, 33: 57–74.

Larson, R.W., Dworkin, J. and Gillman, S.A. (2001) 'Facilitating adolescents' constructive use of time in one-parent families', *Applied Developmental Science*, 5: 143–57.

Lerner, R.M., Freund, A.M., De Stefanis, I. and Habermas, T. (2001) 'Understanding developmental regulation in adolescence: The use of the selection, optimization, and compensation model', *Human Development*, 44: 29–50.

Levin, D., Smith, E.A., Caldwell, L.L. and Kimbrough, J. (1995) 'High school sports participation and violence', *Pediatric Exercise Science*, 7: 379–88.

Mahoney, J.L. (2000) 'Participation in school extracurricular activities as a moderator in the development of antisocial patterns', *Child Development*, 71: 502–16.

Mahoney, J.L. and Stattin, H. (2000) 'Leisure activities and adolescent antisocial behaviour: The role of structure and social context', *Journal of Adolescence*, 23: 113–27.

McNeal, R.B. (1999) 'Participation in high school extracurricular activities: Investigating school effects', *Social Science Quarterly*, 80: 291–309.

Moore, K.A. and Zaff, J.F. (2002) 'Building a Better Teenager: A Summary of "What Works" in Adolescent Development', Child Trends Research Brief, publication #2002–57 (www.childtrends.org).

National Center on Addiction and Substance Abuse (2003) *National Survey of American Attitudes on Substance Abuse, VIII: Teens and Parents*. Columbia University: National Center on Addiction and Substance Abuse.

Orcutt, J.D. (1985) 'Contrasting effects of two kinds of boredom on alcohol use', *Journal of Drug Issues*, 14: 161–73.

Osgood, D.W. and Anderson, A.L. (2004) 'Unstructured socializing and rates of delinquency', *Criminology*, 42: 519–50.

Osgood, W.D., Wilson, J.K., O Malley, P.M., Bachman, J.G. and Johnston, L.D. (1996) 'Routine activities and individual deviant behaviour', *Sociological Review*, 61: 635–56.

Rodin, J. (1975) 'Causes and consequences of time perception differences in overweight and normal weight people', *Journal of Personality and Social Psychology*, 31: 898–904.

Rojek, C. (1999a) 'Deviant Leisure: The Dark Side of Free-time Activity', in E.L. Jackson and T.L. Burton (eds) *Leisure Studies: Prospects for the Twenty-first Century*. State College, PA: Venture, pp. 81–96.

Rojek, C. (1999b) 'Abnormal leisure: Invasive, mephitic and wild forms', *Loisir et Societe/Society and Leisure*, 22(1): 21–37.

Ryan, R.M. and Deci, E.L. (2000) 'Self-determination theory and the facilitation of intrinsic motivation, social development, and well-being', *American Psychologist*, 55: 68–78.

Sharp, E., Caldwell, L.L., Graham, J. and Ridenour, T. (2006) 'Individual motivation and parental influence on adolescents' experiences of interest in the free time context: A longitudinal examination', *Journal of Youth and Adolescence*. Available online at: http://dx.doi.org/10.1007/s10964-006-9045-6

Silbereisen, R.K., Noack, P. and Eyferth, K. (1986) 'Place for Development: Adolescents, Leisure Settings, and Developmental Tasks', in R.K. Silbereisen, K. Eyferth and G. Rudlinger (eds) *Development as Action in Context: Problem Behaviour and Normal Youth Development*. New York: Springer-Verlag, pp. 87–107.

Smith, E.A., Swisher, J.D., Vicary, J.R., Bechtel, L.J., Minner, D., Henry, K.L. and Palmer, R. (2004) 'Evaluation of life skills training and infused life-skills training in a rural setting: Outcomes at two years', *Journal of Alcohol and Drug Education*, 48: 51–71.

Stebbins, R.A. (1996) *Tolerable Differences: Living with Deviance*, 2nd edn. Toronto: McGraw-Hill Ryerson.

Stebbins, R.A. (1997) 'Casual leisure: A conceptual statement', *Leisure Studies*, 16: 17–25.

Stebbins, R.A. (2006) *Serious Leisure: A Perspective for our Time*. New Brunswick, NJ: AldineTransaction Publishers.

Steinberg, L. (2000) 'The family at adolescence: Transition and transformation', *Journal of Adolescent Health*, 27: 170–78.

Sutherland, E.H. (1947) *Principles of Criminology*, 4th edn. Philadelphia: J. B. Lippincott (original work published 1939).

Vazsonyi, A.T., Pickering, L.E., Belliston, L.M., Hessing, D. and Junger, M. (2002) 'Routine activities and deviant behaviours: American, Dutch, Hungarian, and Swiss youth', *Journal of Quantitative Criminology*, 18: 397–422.

Watts, C.E. and Caldwell, L.L. (under review) 'Perceptions of parenting, free time activity involvement and adolescent self-determination as predictors of adolescent initiative', *Journal of Leisure Research*.

Williams, D.J. (2005) 'Forensic leisure science: A new frontier for leisure scholars', *Leisure Sciences*, 28: 91–5.

Williams, D.J. and Walker, G.J. (2006) 'Leisure, deviant leisure, and crime: "Caution: Objects may be closer than they appear"', *Leisure/Loisir*, 30: 193–218.

Witt, P.A. and Caldwell, L.L. (2005) *Recreation and Youth Development*. State College, PA: Venture Publishing.

Wong, S.K. (2005) 'The effects of adolescent activities and delinquency: A differential involvement approach', *Journal of Youth and Adolescence*, 24: 321–33.

Zill, N., Nord, C.W. and Loomis, L.S. (1995) *Adolescent Time Use, Risky Behaviour and Outcomes: An Analysis of National Data*. Department of Health and Human Services. Available online at http://aspe.os.dhhs.gov/hsp/cyp/xstimuse.htm (2001, December 10).

Chapter 14

The challenges of turning developmental theory into meaningful policy and practice

Rebecca Denning and Ross Homel

Abstract

The Youth Justice Service began in 1999 in Queensland. It embodied a new vision for the supervision, rehabilitation and reintegration of young offenders serving community-based orders. Evidence suggests that the Youth Justice Service failed to change significantly the pathways of young offenders. A random sample of 190 clients drawn from the Youth Justice Service and Area Offices that used traditional approaches was analysed to determine the effect of the new service delivery model on recidivism. Logistic regression models showed that whether clients attended a Youth Justice Service or Area Office was not a predictor of recidivism. This chapter contextualises this failure. More generally, the chapter is about the challenge of translating developmental crime prevention theory into policy and practice, particularly within a government service delivery infrastructure. It highlights a number of fundamental operational factors that can undermine the success of a developmental intervention.

The promise of developmental prevention

Developmental crime prevention programmes have demonstrated many successes and a large literature emphasises the benefits of early-in-life interventions that prevent maladaptive pathways from becoming entrenched. In disrupting the developmental pathway early in the life course, interventions can prevent the accumulation of disadvantage, as proposed by Sampson and Laub (1997) and Yoshikawa (1994). Three successful developmental interventions that have been targeted at young children and have produced favourable outcomes are the High/Scope Perry Preschool Programme (Weikart and Schweinhart 1992), the Montreal Prevention Project (Tremblay *et al.* 1995) and the Seattle Social Development Project (Hawkins *et al.* 1999).

Successes with older age groups, particularly adolescent offenders, can be far more difficult to achieve. Given that adolescence is a period that is marked by significant and continual biological and social change, the developmental life-course perspective provides a flexible lens through which to examine and interpret behaviour (Farrington 2003). Developmental prevention similarly provides a flexible framework for a range of interventions that are appropriate to the physical, social and intellectual capacities and needs of young people. In general, interventions that target young people in their teenage years concentrate heavily on educational approaches targeted towards the adolescent in isolation (Wasserman and Miller 1998: 242). Wasserman and Miller note that by age 15, individuals who are likely to manifest serious antisocial behaviour have already begun to do so and consequently interventions are often based on secondary prevention efforts aimed at altering the course of these developmental trends.

Multisystemic therapy (MST) is a treatment approach that has demonstrated long-term reductions in criminal behaviour and violence among high-risk young people. MST adopts a social-ecological approach to understanding antisocial behaviour, with criminal behaviour being viewed as influenced by a range of factors at the individual, family, peer, school and community levels (Henggeler *et al.* 1996). The approach aims to influence antisocial behaviour by altering key aspects of the young person's social context in ways that promote prosocial rather than antisocial behaviour by providing young people and their parents with the resources and skills needed to successfully navigate their social ecology.

Despite having evidence that developmental prevention can positively influence the pathways of young offenders, translating successful programme logic from the clinical, or at least researcher-controlled, environment *en masse* to the broader social context is proving particularly challenging for researchers and programme implementers (Homel 2005). In western societies like Australia, the United Kingdom and the United States, accessing large populations often means implementing programmes using the service delivery apparatus of government. For example, early intervention programmes that target young children are often operationalised through preschools and primary schools. Even those programmes that engage non-government organisations to implement local initiatives (e.g. Sure Start in the UK and Communities for Children in Australia) are often centrally co-ordinated and function in accordance with multiple reporting, accountability and regulatory mechanisms. These additional obligations make it even more difficult to implement developmental prevention successfully at the population level.

The impetus for juvenile justice reform in Queensland

The Youth Justice Service embodied a new vision for the supervision, rehabilitation and reintegration of young offenders serving community-based orders in Queensland. The policy was developed after a period in the administration of youth justice in Australia that was characterised by significant legislative and policy change. The nation had experienced the first serious challenges to the prevailing welfare orientation in the 1960s and 1970s, having gained impetus from similar trends in the United States, and a process of re-evaluation spurred a general move away from welfarism towards a more formal, neoclassical style of justice for juveniles. Like their counterparts in the United States, critics of the welfare model in Australia targeted the courts, demanding greater recognition of children's rights to formal justice and seeking abolition of indeterminate sentencing (Naffine and Wundersitz 1994).

Accompanying the increased focus on procedural justice and pressure from victim advocacy groups, the concept of restorative justice also emerged onto the criminological landscape. While traditional cultures had practised varying forms of restorative principles for centuries and, as Braithwaite (2003: 11) argues, victim reparation and victim empowerment had been occurring in the business context under the banner of Alternative Dispute Resolution for decades, the new paradigm that emerged in the 1980s was considered highly innovative. By the late 1980s, restorative justice programmes were operating in Canada, the United States, Europe and the UK (Wundersitz 1996). A more sophisticated attempt to apply principles of restorative justice occurred in New Zealand when in 1989 the Children, Young Persons and their Families Act provided the legislative framework for the introduction of family group conferencing into the system of juvenile justice. This Act embodied many restorative principles, including the central role of young people, victims and families in decision-making, the importance of group consensus as an outcome of the decision-making process and acknowledgement of the specific rights and needs of Indigenous people (Morris and Maxwell 1992). Restorative justice was first trialled in Australia by local police in Wagga Wagga, NSW. Since this time, all Australian states and territories have passed legislation providing that restorative justice principles feature in the treatment of young offenders.

The period between the 1970s and the 1990s saw the problem of youth crime entrenched firmly in the public agenda, and despite little statistical evidence to support such an allegation, claims of a youth crime wave were widespread. Government agencies also separated the provision of juvenile justice from child protection in an attempt to provide a more even-handed approach to both issues. In response to these pressures, Australian state governments individually embarked on a prolonged period of review that resulted in extensive legislative and service delivery changes.

In addition to these international and national movements, Queensland politicians were under increased pressure to deliver transparent governance. The 1987 Commission of Inquiry into Possible Illegal Activities and Associated Police Misconduct, which found extensive, systematic police corruption in a pattern that had been established since the 1950s, and the political tolerance of that corruption in return for support and favours (Key Centre for Ethics Law Justice and Governance 2001), meant that the government was in the mood for widespread reform. One of the most significant developments was the establishment of the Criminal Justice Commission (now known as the Crime and Misconduct Commission), an external oversight body which has independence from executive government and holds the power to investigate police, public servants and politicians. In response to demands for action in the area of youth justice, the Queensland government delivered the Juvenile Crime Strategy in the 1992–93 State Budget. This strategy incorporated two main types of reforms: legislative reform, and crime prevention initiatives that embraced the principles of early intervention, developmental crime prevention and positive youth development.

On 4 August 1992, the juvenile justice provisions of the Children's Services Act 1965 were repealed and were replaced with the Juvenile Justice Act 1992 and the Children's Court Act 1992. The Juvenile Justice Act 1992 in particular led the operational reform of the youth justice system. The new system was based on principles that sought to ensure fairness, divert young people from the official youth justice system, promote individual responsibility and provide increased roles for victims, families and the community.

Nearly seven years passed before service delivery in the area of community-based supervision was modified to reflect the changes made to the legislation. The juvenile justice component of the existing Area Office model was extracted and placed into a dedicated service delivery model, known as the Youth Justice Service. The new service model was first piloted in three locations in 1999, and has since replaced the traditional Area Office model in various locations throughout Queensland.

Youth Justice Services

The Youth Justice Service is a policy initiative and service delivery framework that provides supervisory, rehabilitative and reintegrative services to young offenders on community-based orders and young offenders leaving detention. The Youth Justice Service has two overriding goals. The first is to monitor the compliance of young offenders with the statutory obligations of their orders. The second focuses both on addressing risk factors associated with the offending behaviour and on assisting young people to develop skills to successfully navigate their pathways in the future. Reflecting this orientation, the case management process seeks to assist clients to gain insight into the causes and impacts of their offending, develop options for meeting their needs without offending, and develop skills, interests and networks that will better connect them to their community.

In theory, this case management process operates according to a number of key principles. Caseworkers manage 25 or fewer clients to ensure that they have sufficient time to provide a quality service to every client. A team approach, whereby case management occurs within a wider framework that includes the young person, their family and relevant community networks or agencies, is promoted in an attempt to move away from the traditional case management model where caseworker and client work in isolation. A thorough assessment, which should include the client and their family, is conducted to discuss offending behaviour and identify possible interventions that will target identified needs. Based on this assessment, the programme of needs-based interventions begins.

According to the policy documents, possible interventions

include 'counselling services, one-on-one programmes, group based programmes, rehabilitative programmes, work based programmes, community projects, education/vocation based services, cultural programmes, advocacy and support services, personal development programmes and health and living skills programmes' (Department of Families Youth and Community Care Queensland 2000). Clients are referred to existing local service providers where appropriate. Youth Justice Service program staff will develop specialised programmes where suitable community-based programmes cannot be identified.

Incorporating a developmental focus into crime prevention policy

The Youth Justice Service policy demonstrates a clear alignment with the key principles of contemporary theories of human development. First, in recognising that young people have the ability to change their behaviour from offending to less serious offending or to desistance from offending, the concept adheres to the principle of relative behavioural plasticity. Second, the aim of the Youth Justice Service policy to incorporate key stakeholders from the young person's social-relational contexts (i.e. families, extended families) and sociocultural contexts (i.e. schools, community and cultural networks) into the process acknowledges that the bases for this behavioural change lie in the individual's transactions with actors in these multiple domains (Homel 2005). Third, the policy recognises that working with young people in isolation discounts the significance of family and cultural networks, aligning with the principle that each level of human organisation functions as a consequence of its fusion or structural integration with other levels. This interdependence also means that change at any level will necessarily lead to continuity or discontinuity at another level.

It is evident that the Youth Justice Service attempted to operationalise developmental crime prevention, through a focus on:

1 the causes and correlates of offending through individualised case management;
2 rehabilitation and targeting interventions on offending behaviour;
3 age-appropriate interventions;
4 the varied contexts of risk and protective factors.

However, despite these sound principles and the Department of

Communities' commitment to the Youth Justice Service model, there is little empirical evidence to suggest that the new model delivered improved client outcomes in its first six years of operation.

Assessing the impact of Youth Justice Services on the pathways of young people

The Youth Justice Service was evaluated to ascertain its impact on offending behaviour. The evaluation incorporated a broad view of intervention that examined policy and implementation factors. In the first phase of the evaluation, an assessment was made of the quality of the Youth Justice Service policy; did it represent a 'good' policy? Key departmental documents were synthesised to determine the intention of the policy. Assessment of the quality of the policy was based on policy and implementation theory (Barrett 2004; Ham and Hill 1993; Levin 1997; Lindblom 1959; Pressman and Wildavsky 1973; Simon 1957), developmental and life-course criminology (Elder 1994; Farrington 2003; Sampson and Laub 1997) and best practice principles for crime prevention (Australian Institute of Criminology 2002; Homel 2005; Latimer *et al.* 2003; Wasserman and Miller 1998).

In the next phase of the research an attempt was made, using an in-depth case study of a single Youth Justice Service, to reconcile the intention of the Youth Justice Service policy with the reality of service delivery, and to determine the effect of the service on future offending behaviour. An embedded case study design (Yin 2003) facilitated an examination of the two key areas of service delivery and client outcomes. This study examined:

- The model of service delivery used to operationalise the Youth Justice Service concept.
- How well the model of service delivery aligned with the Youth Justice Service concept.
- The strengths and weaknesses of the model of service delivery.
- How the model of service delivery affected outcomes for clients.

Evidence was gathered from staff and client interviews, direct observations, and reviews of procedure documents and case management files. The evidence was analysed according to four key themes: (1) organisational goals; (2) organisational climate; (3) method of operation; and (4) client pathways. The *explanation building* technique (Yin 2003) was used to analyse the evidence. When using this technique the researcher stipulates a presumed set of causal links, drawing on knowledge of process and theory to arrive at critical insights about the case.

The final phase of the research sought to determine the impact of the policy. Given that a core goal of the Youth Justice Service is to reduce recidivism, the research examined the effect of the model on offending behaviour. In this study, a random sample of 190 clients was drawn from the entire six-office population of Youth Justice Service and Area Offices in South-East Queensland over a three-year period. This research design made it possible to compare the impact of the Youth Justice Service with that of the traditional Area Office model. Information on individual, familial, educational and peer risk factors, criminal careers, and intervention factors was extracted from case management files and entered into a specially developed database. After a uniform 18-month period, official rearrest data were added to the database.

Chi-square analyses indicated that the Youth Justice Service was no more effective than the traditional Area Office model at reducing recidivism. In fact, while the result was not significant, the clients of the Youth Justice Service were 1.8 times more likely to reoffend than were clients from the Area Office. Logistic regression models were used to determine the influence of different models, after controlling for risk, intervention and compliance factors.

After introducing statistical controls, whether clients attended a Youth Justice Service or Area Office was not an important predictor of recidivism, confirming that the new service delivery model was no better at preventing recidivism than the traditional Area Office model. The factors that emerged from the sample as the most important predictors of recidivism were drug use, being influenced by delinquent peers, and having family problems that were not addressed by caseworkers. Notwithstanding the failure of the Youth Justice Service model to deliver improved outcomes to young people, survival analysis did demonstrate that the Youth Justice Service prolonged the time until rearrest, perhaps highlighting the temporary deterrent impact of increased surveillance.

The remainder of this chapter attempts to situate this failure of the Youth Justice Service to facilitate positive, sustained behavioural change in clients. We focus on aspects of the Youth Justice Service policy and operational factors that underscored, and contributed to, this outcome.

Policy clarity and the importance of specifying a course for action

At their most generic level, public policies refer to decisions made by governments. One of the more precise definitions is offered by Jenkins (1978), who defines public policy as:

> a set of interrelated decisions taken by a political actor or group of actors concerning the selection of goals and the means of achieving them within a specified situation where those decisions should, in principle, be within the power of those actors to achieve. (Jenkins 1978: 15)

While policy decisions that are made within the clinical or researcher-controlled environment can develop, to some extent at least, in isolation from the broader programming environment, decisions made within the government sphere must consider a far greater number of interests and contingencies. Consequently, despite the push for policy-making that is deliberate, calculated and has clear foundations in evidence, in reality rational policy decisions are difficult to achieve in the face of competing interests, administrative structures and social and political factors. In arriving at a policy decision, bureaucrats must shape and filter these contingencies, distorting (intentionally or inadvertently) the original policy intent.

The analysis of the Youth Justice Service policy revealed six primary goals and seven goals that applied on a broader level. These, as they appeared in the policy directive, are outlined below.

Primary goals

1 Identify the issues contributing to the offending behaviour.
2 Identify the most appropriate interventions.
3 Implement an intervention strategy targeting the offending behaviour.
4 Monitor participation and compliance with order requirements.
5 Target the offending behaviour.
6 Address the support and lifestyle needs.

Broader goals

1 Divert the young person from further involvement in the juvenile justice system.
2 Reduce the extent of serious and recidivist offending.

3 Increase community confidence in the juvenile justice system.
4 Increase the target population's positive reintegration into the community.
5 Increase successful completion of juvenile justice orders and conditional bail programmes.
6 Contribute to the reduction of the over-representation of Indigenous young people in the youth justice system, particularly detention.
7 Engage community participation.

A number of observations should be made about these goals, many of which can effectively be discussed under the broad concept of *goal ambiguity* (Chun and Rainey 2005; Feldman 1989; Kelemen 2000). Defined as the extent to which an organisational goal or set of goals allows leeway for interpretation, when the organisational goal represents the desired future state of the organisation, this ambiguity results in serious dysfunctional consequences and is one of the most distinctive characteristics of public organisations (Chun and Rainey 2005: 1–2). Chun and Rainey have conceptualised goal ambiguity as consisting of four constructs: (1) mission comprehension ambiguity; (2) priority goal ambiguity; (3) evaluative goal ambiguity; and (4) directive goal ambiguity.

Mission comprehension ambiguity

This refers to the clarity of the organisation's mission; what is it that the organisation seeks to achieve? From the extensive list of goals it was difficult to formulate a succinct statement of the organisation's intent. Even when the six primary goals were synthesised into two overriding goals – to work with the offender to address their offending behaviour, and monitor the offender's compliance with court orders – staff had difficulty reconciling these two objectives.

Priority goal ambiguity

This refers to the level of interpretive leeway in deciding on priorities among multiple goals (Chun and Rainey 2005: 4). The two overriding goals of the Youth Justice Service are quite distinct: one seeks to ensure compliance with community court orders, the other to engage the clients towards addressing offending behaviour. Evidence from the case study suggested that both staff and clients had difficulty reconciling these two goals. Caseworkers indicated that their primary focus was to ensure that their statutory obligations to monitor order compliance were met. Caseworkers considered working with clients to address offending behaviour as 'extra' and noted that this work would only occur once all statutory duties had been completed. Clients, on the other hand, did not want to open up to caseworkers who were also required to monitor their compliance with their order. One client summed this position up when he said, 'Why would I want to talk about my offending with the person who can then go and breach me?'

Although not addressed in Chun and Rainey's framework, it is doubtful whether the two overriding goals of the Youth Justice Service are complementary. Is it possible for a single service (predominantly a single caseworker) to work with a young offender towards positive behavioural change while simultaneously ensuring compliance with court-imposed sanctions? Does this 'probationer' role undermine the developmental role that seeks to encourage mutual trust and respect? According to alignment theory (Semler 1997), the selection of the compliance goal as the key priority should not be unexpected. If the two overriding goals are in opposition, staff may find it difficult to effectively achieve both goals simultaneously. In this case, staff efforts will necessarily be directed towards meeting statutory obligations, thus modifying the direction of the organisation.

Evaluative goal ambiguity

Evaluative goal ambiguity refers to the level of interpretive leeway that an organisational mission allows in evaluating the progress towards the achievement of the mission (Chun and Rainey 2005: 4). The Youth Justice Service policy includes a set of key performance indicators that prescribe the way in which the policy will be evaluated. Some of these measures are quite objective and leave little room for interpretation. For example, a reduction in the number and proportion of Indigenous young people in the youth justice system and a decrease in recidivism by clients of Youth Justice Services all involve quantitative measurement of established constructs. Others, such as a high level of participant satisfaction and increased confidence in government's response to youth crime in areas with Youth Justice Services, are vulnerable to subjective interpretation.

Despite the existence of key performance indicators, staff were generally uncertain as to how best to measure the success of the Youth Justice Service. The dominant perspective was that the success of the service could not be judged against a single set of predetermined client outcomes. These staff maintained that because the service is based on an assessment of individual needs, and that the needs of each client are unique, successes for each young person will be similarly unique. Consequently, any attempt to rank client outcomes against any predetermined criteria is inappropriate, and should not be used as an indicator of success or failure of the Youth Justice Service. Staff who held this view tended to focus on very small, incremental successes, and had little regard to the broader impacts such as reoffending: 'If a child turns around and says "thank you", that's a success because they might never have said it before.'

Other staff suggested that success could be measured in terms of the creation of opportunities that, if acted upon, put clients in a better position to alter their pathway. This point of view aligns with the Youth Justice Service policy, which lists improved access for young people to programmes and services as a key performance indicator. It also aligns with the principles of developmental crime prevention. For these staff, these access routes typically involved integrating young people back into education and assisting them to gain practical work experience. A common theme here was to ensure that young people had established links with community agencies that would provide continued support once the official intervention of the Youth Justice Service had concluded.

> Really practical things, like finishing grade ten or doing a course that will help them get a job, because their current reinforcement schedule is so powerful that you really need to put them into something they are 'doing'.

Despite being a key performance indicator, staff did not consider that a reduction in offending behaviour was an appropriate measure of success. One staff member indicated that measuring a reduction in offending was not appropriate in general and should only be used to assess service effectiveness with the subset of clients who have minor offending histories: 'With the low end kids we are looking for them to not reoffend.'

Directive goal ambiguity

This refers to the amount of interpretive leeway available in translating the organisation's goals into directives and guidelines for specific actions to be taken to accomplish the goals (Chun and Rainey 2005: 3). There are a number of procedures in place that guide the process of compliance with court-imposed orders (e.g. breaching procedures). However, comparatively little guidance accompanied the goal of engaging young people to address their offending behaviour.

This kind of ambiguity, on top of the other forms discussed, helps to explain why the Youth Justice Service policy presented ample opportunity to be distorted on the ground. The remainder of the chapter examines how this ambiguous policy platform flowed through to influence service delivery in negative ways.

Commitment, capacity, communication and conflict: how operational factors can distort practice on the ground

Despite the fact that four out of the five primary goals of the Youth Justice Service policy were directed at addressing offending behaviour, caseworkers indicated that they turned their attention to issues contributing to offending behaviour only when all matters of compliance had been addressed.

> We have the statutory requirement to get them through the minimum, be it probation or the hours they have to do for community service. Anything else is of course additional, and that is something like going back to school. That's the 'extra'.

Notwithstanding the fact that caseworkers indicated that the statutory basis of the court order *legally* had to be prioritised – in essence, through no fault of their own – the research identified several other factors that also supported the prioritisation of the compliance role.

Commitment

Caseworkers generally had little faith that discussions relating to their offending behaviour would bring about positive behavioural change in their clients. They argued that their efforts were futile when a client was not 'ready to change,' and had little confidence in their ability to move clients to this point. Further, where clients demonstrated evidence of moving to a more positive pathway, caseworkers attributed this change to an external event such as getting a girlfriend or a job, not to any process related to themselves or the Youth Justice Service. In assuming this position, caseworkers evaded any personal responsibility for ensuring positive client outcomes, shifting this burden to the client. It is understandable therefore that caseworkers focused their attentions on compliance, where they could see immediate and tangible results.

In the end it is up to the young people as to whether they engage with us. Unless the kids are in the mindset to change, I don't think we have much hope.

This lack of confidence in being able to bring about positive behavioural change may also be reflected in caseworkers' opinions on appropriate measures of success. Their reluctance to subscribe to any global outcome measures can be at least partially rationalised through an adherence to an 'individualised treatment and outcomes' model.

Capacity

Another reason for prioritising the compliance goal may lie in the fact that successfully engaging clients to address their offending behaviour is very difficult to accomplish. The activity is made even more difficult when you doubt your ability in the first instance, do not fully understand developmental processes or techniques of behaviour modification, have few tools at your disposal to guide you through the process, have little experience in dealing with young people and their families, and have few opportunities for professional development.

Successfully engaging young people requires knowledge of developmental processes and significant experience in engaging with young people. Youth Justice Service clients are typically high-end offenders who have extensive offending histories and know how to negotiate the juvenile justice system and manipulate inexperienced caseworkers. The majority of Youth Justice Service caseworkers interviewed acknowledged that their understanding of techniques to successfully engage with their clients was underdeveloped. The appropriate skill base required for this role was also raised in interviews, specifically concerning whether a therapeutic or social work approach was optimal.

Most people here have a social work background, which doesn't have a therapeutic focus, and that's why people struggle to have meaningful interactions.

While caseworkers were provided with a basic needs assessment tool, there was a tendency to adopt a 'checklist approach' to intervention that inquired into needs that are typical to many young people, such as education and employment. Caseworkers indicated that their case management techniques become learned and that they didn't have sufficient time to reflect on practices towards developing new and innovative strategies for working with clients.

> If you've got a really difficult case, something you haven't come across before, I might ask someone, but often I've got this tunnel thing going on and your practices become learned. We often get caught up in doing the same thing.

Although there is a well-developed rationale that focuses on parents or family when dealing with younger children (e.g. the Montreal Longitudinal-Experimental Study, McCord *et al.* 2001), a newer body of evidence has emerged which suggests that intervention with the family is also critical in preventing the escalation of antisocial behaviour during adolescence (Chamberlain and Moore 1998; Chamberlain and Reid 1998; Latimer *et al.* 2003; Sherman *et al.* 1998). The Youth Justice Service policy embraced this concept and specified 'family' as a key social context contributing to offending behaviour. Despite this, operational factors prevented caseworkers from working proactively with families. Given that clients are minors, parents and guardians were routinely contacted regarding case management decisions. However, communication with parents and guardians rarely extended beyond contact to provide information. Caseworkers provided three major reasons for failing to work with families, despite acknowledging the role of the family in sustaining offending behaviour and being a critical target for change.

First, caseworkers argued that engaging families and working to address the family's needs fall outside the legislative ambit of the Youth Justice Service. Under the Juvenile Justice Act 1992, the Youth Justice Service is able to work with young offenders and has no legislative basis upon which to base intervention with families. This is clearly evidence of a misalignment between a policy and the underlying legislative structures upon which it is based.

> We have a responsibility to keep the parents involved until the client is 18 because they are a child. We'll keep the parents informed of what is going on but our focus is squarely on the child.

The second reason is more concerning from a developmental crime prevention perspective. Caseworkers highlighted the fact that the Youth Justice Service is not a welfare agency, so should not be concerned with the short- or long-term welfare needs of the clients or their families. While caseworkers can, and do, direct families to community agencies to seek help for problems they may be experiencing, they do not routinely follow up on these referrals or make additional efforts to intervene with family-based issues: 'We're not welfare workers. I wouldn't take on the family's issues myself.'

Finally, the caseworkers suggested that their general inexperience was a significant factor in failing to work with the families of clients. The mean age of caseworkers was 25 years, and caseworkers questioned whether they had the appropriate life experience or skills to deal effectively with the complex problems experienced by families.

> The youth of staff is a hindrance in terms of experience. All of us have limited experience just because we've only been working for a few years. So that has its limitations in not being able to draw on a vast amount of experience in what works well with clients. It is also difficult working with families.

Caseworkers were also given little opportunity for professional development. This means that all of the weaknesses that caseworkers identify, such as lack of innovative case management practices, an underdeveloped understanding of effective techniques to engage with young people and their families, poor time management skills and the inability to strike an effective balance between statutory and non-statutory demands, have little potential to be addressed.

Communication and conflict

The Youth Justice Service functions as two distinct teams: the casework team and the programme team. Caseworkers are responsible for determining the needs of the offender, setting in motion a series of interventions, and monitoring compliance. The programme work group has two major responsibilities: to develop and deliver programmes to clients, and community engagement.

This organisational structure has led to poor communication and significant underlying conflict between the two teams, both of which have negatively influenced client outcomes. A number of factors appear to contribute to the conflict between the two teams. First, there was a level of resentment over perceived unequal workloads. The work of the programme team was more elective and a significant proportion of their role was to develop relationships with service providers and the community in general. Consequently, the programme team had to work much harder to provide tangible evidence of their contribution when compared with the caseworkers whose roles are heavily regulated by the court process.

Second, caseworkers wanted to retain complete control to ensure they were accountable and protected legally. Their reluctance to refer their clients to the programme team was further reinforced by the poor communication between the two teams. Caseworkers had little confidence that the case notes made by programme staff accurately represented the reality of their interactions with clients. The resulting resentment intensified the physical and role disconnection that already existed between the two work groups.

> It is about not necessarily knowing what the programme people do with our clients and therefore a reluctance to get the programme people involved. I guess I wonder what they do.

As a result of the organisational friction that existed between the two work groups, the treatment model that evolved was focused around a single caseworker, as opposed to the collaborative, team-based model that evidence suggests is more effective with young people and was prescribed in the Youth Justice Service policy. This isolated treatment model allowed for little cross-fertilisation regarding innovative strategies to address offending behaviour. Failing to access the expertise of the programme team further reinforced the tendency of caseworkers to use learned case management practices and to treat apparently 'similar' clients in a similar fashion. While there is some degree of consistency among the general issues facing young people (for example, accessing education and employment), the way that each young person responds to intervention requires an individual treatment response, regardless of broadly similar risk factors.

Conclusion

The failure of the Youth Justice Service to help young offenders to develop prosocial pathways can be attributed to both policy and service delivery factors. The ambiguous nature of the Youth Justice Service policy meant that the goals of the policy were vulnerable to interpretation and prioritisation. Given that the responsibility of ensuring statutory compliance with court orders and addressing offending behaviour resides within a single individual, and that the competence of most staff in the areas of human development and behaviour modification was limited, prioritisation of the comparatively easier, legal goal was an obvious outcome. Staff may prefer to focus their attention on an activity where they can demonstrate clear and positive results.

The failure to manualise the treatment model also meant that caseworkers were able to manipulate the Youth Justice Service policy to adopt a case management process that centred on a single caseworker, as opposed to the collaborative, team-based model espoused in the policy directive. Such an isolated treatment approach appears to be aligned with the skills and experience of caseworkers and allows them to retain total control over case management. It is also a product of a divisive organisational structure that fostered internal conflict and mistrust.

Clearly, the developmental crime prevention focus of the Youth Justice Service policy got lost in translation. Paramount in this failure was its prioritisation of its compliance function over its goal to address offending behaviour. While this prioritisation is understandable, such an organisational focus meant that in the end there was little to differentiate the Youth Justice Service from a probation service. The pressure to effectively balance compliance and treatment could have been alleviated simply by relieving caseworkers of the compliance function. This delineation would also have helped clients to engage with caseworkers without fear of being breached.

Where genuine casework did occur, a number of failings were identified, including:

1 Case management practices became learned and were not tailored to the specific needs of young offenders.
2 Critical targets of intervention, such as families, were not included in the treatment approach, so any potential gains were likely to be eroded when the clients returned to their everyday environments.
3 In general, staff were ill-equipped to manage effectively the complex problems presented by clients.

What this research indicates is the need for increased focus on the process of implementation; how can we effectively translate developmental theory and crime prevention to the real world context? A more rigorous policy directive, manualised treatment protocols, professional development and ongoing access to expert advice and organisational structures that support rather than undermine the goals of the policy appear critical to ensuring fidelity with the intent of the original policy. The importance of these factors is further highlighted when the interventions are run by government agencies that are also responsible for ensuring compliance with court orders. In this context, legal imperatives will always win out when additional goals are not adequately provided for in policy and service delivery.

Acknowledgements

This PhD research was supported by an Australian Postgraduate Award and Queensland Department of Communities scholarships. Special thanks are due to Dr Hennessey Hayes for his guidance on data collection and analysis. We should also like to thank the Queensland Department of Communities for access to case data and to policy documents, and the Queensland Police Service for access to criminal conviction data. Special thanks to those managers and staff of the Youth Justice Service who so generously supported the fieldwork.

References

Australian Institute of Criminology (2002) *What Works in Reducing Young People's Involvement in Crime: Review of Current Literature on Youth Crime Prevention*. Canberra: Australian Institute of Criminology.

Barrett, S.M. (2004) 'Implementation studies: Time for a revival? Personal reflections on 20 years of implementation studies', *Public Administration*, 82(2): 249–62.

Braithwaite, J. (2003) 'What's wrong with the sociology of punishment', *Theoretical Criminology*, 7(1): 5–28.

Chamberlain, P. and Moore, K.J. (1998) 'Models of Community Treatment for Serious Offenders', in J. Crane (ed.) *Social Programs that Really Work*. Princeton, NJ: Russell Sage.

Chamberlain, P. and Reid, J.B. (1998) 'Comparison of two community alternatives to incarceration for chronic juvenile offenders', *Journal of Consulting and Clinical Psychology*, 6: 624–33.

Chun, Y.H. and Rainey, H.G. (2005) 'Goal ambiguity in US federal agencies', *Journal of Public Administration Research and Theory*, 15(1): 1–30.

Department of Families Youth and Community Care Queensland (2000) *Youth Justice Services: Youth justice program*. Brisbane: Queensland Government.

Elder, G.H. (1994) 'Time, human agency, and social change: Perspectives on the life course', *Social Psychology Quarterly*, 57(1): 4–15.

Farrington, D.P. (2003) 'Developmental and life-course criminology: Key theoretical and empirical issues – the 2002 Sutherland Award address', *Criminology*, 41(2): 221–55.

Feldman, M. (1989) *Order without Design: Information Production and Policy Making*. Stanford, CA: Stanford University Press.

Ham, C. and Hill, M. (1993) *The Policy Process in the Modern Capitalist State*. Hertfordshire: Harvester Wheatsheaf.

Hawkins, J.D., Catalano, R.F., Kosterman, R., Abbot, R.D. and Hill, K. (1999) 'Preventing adolescent health-risk behaviours by strengthening protection during childhood', *Archives in Pediatric and Adolescent Medicine*, 153, 226–234.

Henggeler, S.W., Cunningham, P.B., Pickrel, S.G., Schoenwald, S.K. and Brondino, M.J. (1996) 'Multisystemic therapy: An effective violence prevention approach for serious juvenile offenders', *Journal of Adolescence*, 19: 47–61.

Homel, R. (2005) 'Developmental Crime Prevention', in N. Tilley (ed.) *Handbook of Crime Prevention and Community Safety*. Cullompton: Willan Publishing.

Jenkins, W.I. (1978) *Policy Analysis: A Political and Organizational Perspective*. London: Martin Robertson.

Kelemen, M. (2000) 'Too much or too little ambiguity: The language of Total Quality Management', *Journal of Management Studies*, 37: 483–98.

Key Centre for Ethics Law Justice and Governance (2001) *Australian National Integrity Systems Assessment: Queensland Pilot*. Transparency International Australia. Available online at: http://www.transparency.org.au/documents/qnisa.pdf (retreived 22 November 2004).

Latimer, J., Dowden, C. and Moreton-Bourgon, K.E. (2003) *Treating Youth in Conflict with the Law: A New Meta-analysis*. Ottawa: Department of Justice Canada.

Levin, P. (1997) *Making Social Policy: The Mechanisms of Government and Politics, and How to Investigate Them*. Buckingham: Open University Press.

Lindblom, C.E. (1959) 'The science of "muddling through"', *Public Administration Review*, 19.

McCord, J., Satz Widon, C. and Crowell, N. A. (2001) *Juvenile Crime and Juvenile Justice – Panel on Juvenile Crime: Prevention, Treatment and Control*. Washington: National Academy Press.

Morris, A. and Maxwell, G. (1992) 'Juvenile justice in New Zealand', *Australian and New Zealand Journal of Criminology*, 26(1): 72–90.

Naffine, N. and Wundersitz, J. (1994) 'Trends in Juvenile Justice', in D. Chappell and P. Wilson (eds) *The Australian Criminal Justice System: The Mid 1990s*. North Ryde: Butterworths.

Pressman, J.L. and Wildavsky, A. (1973) *Implementation: How Great Expectations in Washington are Dashed in Oakland; or, why it's amazing that federal programs work at all, this being a saga of the Economic Development Administration as told by two sympathetic observers who seek to build morals on a foundation of ruined hopes*. Berkeley, CA: University of California Press.

Sampson, R.J. and Laub, J.H. (1997) 'A Life-course Theory of Cumulative Disadvantage and the Stability of Delinquency', in T.P. Thornberry (ed.)

Developmental Theories of Crime and Delinquency. New Jersey: Transaction Publishers.

Semler, S. W. (1997) 'Systematic agreement: A theory of organizational alignment', *Human Resource Development Quarterly*, 8(1): 23–40.

Sherman, L.W., Gottfredson, D.C., MacKenzie, D.L., Eck, J., Reuter, P. and Bushway, S.D. (1998) *Preventing Crime: What Works, What Doesn't, What's Promising: A Report to the United State Congress: Overview*, NCJ Document No: 165368. Washington, DC: US Department of Justice, National Institute of Justice.

Simon, H.A. (1957) *Administrative Behaviour*, 2nd edn. New York: Macmillan.

Tremblay, R.E., Pagani-Kurtz, L., Masse, L.C., Vitaro, F. and Pihl, R.O. (1995) 'A bimodal preventative intervention for disruptive kindergarten boys: Its impact through mid-adolescence', *Journal of Consulting and Clinical Psychology*, 63(4): 560–8.

Wasserman, G.A. and Miller, L.S. (1998) 'The Prevention of Serious and Violent Juvenile Offending', in R. Loeber and D.P. Farrington (eds) *Serious and Violent Juvenile Offenders: Risk Factors and Successful Interventions'*, Thousand Oaks, CA: Sage.

Weikart, D.P. and Schweinhart, L.J. (1992) 'High/Scope Preschool Program Outcomes', in R.E. Tremblay (ed.) *Preventing Antisocial Behaviour: Interventions from Birth Through Adolescence*. New York: Guilford Press.

Wundersitz, J. (1996) 'Juvenile Justice', in K.M. Hazelhurst (ed.) *Crime and Justice: An Australian Textbook in Criminology*. North Ryde: LBC Information Services.

Yin, R.K. (2003) *Case Study Research: Design and Methods*, 3rd edn. Thousand Oaks, CA: Sage.

Yoshikawa, H. (1994) 'Prevention as cumulative protection: Effects of early family support and education on chronic delinquency and its risks', *Psychological Bulletin*, 115(1): 28–54.

Chapter 15

Quality of childcare and its impact on children's social skills in disadvantaged areas of Australia

Karin Ishimine and David Evans

Abstract

In the past few decades, there has been increased demand for childcare, reflecting the effects of industrialisation and the changes in family structure in many developed countries. Consequently, the provision of childcare services has been of increasing interest to researchers. There is a small, but growing body of international research evidence, linking the quality of childcare to the social development of young children and to social disadvantage. This study investigated the relationship between social disadvantage, the quality of long day childcare centres, and the social skills development of the young children who attended them. Fourteen childcare centres were assessed using the *Early Childhood Environmental Rating Scale – Revised Edition* (ECERS-R) and the *Early Childhood Environmental Rating Scale – Extension* (ECERS-E). Analysis of this data was undertaken using quantitative and qualitative methods. The results showed that the long day care centres in 'disadvantaged' areas in Sydney were of lower quality than those in 'partially disadvantaged areas' in terms of personal care, activities, interactions and diversity. There were no statistically significant relationships between social skills scores and location of centres or centre quality, although qualitative analyses suggested more frequent and intense interactions (child–child, staff–child) in more advantaged areas, as well as a greater sensitivity to differences among children. Given the ubiquity of formal childcare and the importance of quality preschool programmes in moderating the effects of social disadvantage on developmental pathways, there is an urgent need for further research on the nature of the links between disadvantage, the quality of childcare, and outcomes for children.

Introduction

Over the past few decades, socio-economic factors such as economic growth, demographic balance and family structure have influenced child development in Australia and other countries. Despite an increase in economic prosperity for many Australians, social issues such as child abuse, neglect, psychiatric admissions and crime remain apparent in all socio-economic groups of society (Stanley *et al.* 2005).

Social disadvantage is often the consequence of various types of exclusion from mainstream society. The frequency of crime and juvenile delinquency is reported to be higher in disadvantaged areas than advantaged areas (Richardson and Prior 2005; Stanley *et al.* 2005). Children and families living in social disadvantage also experience inequities in education, health and well-being compared to their counterparts in more advantaged areas. Greater understanding is required of the pathways that link social disadvantage and quality developmental outcomes for young children (Karoly *et al.* 2005; Zwi and Henry 2005). In particular, the pathways for young children in the Australian context warrant examination (Vinson 2006).

The desire to promote healthy child development (and thereby have an impact on social outcomes later in life) has resulted in calls for governments to address the critical factors affecting a child's first five years of life (Karoly *et al.* 2005). Vinson (2006) called for governments to increase the number and the quality of childcare services available to families in socially disadvantaged areas in New South Wales, Australia. More recently, reports of emerging federal government policy highlight the importance being placed on supporting optimal child development outcomes:

> Mr Howard also wanted governments to agree to a strategy for 'improved childcare services ... with the aim of supporting families in improving childhood development outcomes in the first five years of a child's life, up to and including school entry'. (Colman 2006)

While there is a growing body of research about the benefits of quality early years programmes to young children and their families, analysis of its specific impact on social skills development is limited. The development of social skills and competence in the early years relies on other areas of maturation, such as physical growth and co-ordination, linguistic competence and intellectual development. It requires children to be given opportunities to interact with their peers and with adult family members, and the wider community. The longer-term impact of developing social skills and competence is a reduction in social disruption, criminal behaviour and delinquency (Karoly *et al.* 2005).

Greater understanding is required, therefore, of the pathways that young children take during these early years of development. In developing this understanding, further investigation is required into the factors that influence social development, such as the quality of childcare and the impact of the domestic environment. This chapter outlines an investigation into the relationship between the quality of childcare and the social development of children attending long day care centres in disadvantaged parts of Sydney.

The importance of quality childcare

The childcare sector in Australia has grown dramatically in the past two decades. This increase is partially a result of families striving to maintain a quality of lifestyle by both parents undertaking paid employment. It is also been driven by pressures of governments to reduce the burden on social services, and by parents moving back into the workforce at earlier stages of a child's development.

The significant expansion of childcare services in Australia has been accompanied by a stronger demand for quality and affordability (Horin 2006; Power 2005; Prior 2006). A number of childcare centres, for example, staff their early childhood programmes with unqualified childcare workers and/or teachers (Elliot 2004). Qualified early childhood teachers have been shown to be able to engage more effectively with children and to promote a range of important developmental outcomes. Further research into other aspects of childcare provision that affect its quality is required to understand the impact it has on the development pathways for young children and families (Fleer 2000; Hill *et al.* 1998; Li-Grining and Coley 2006; OECD 2000).

Longitudinal studies in the United States of America and the United Kingdom have demonstrated the impact of quality early childhood education on child development, and provide an insight into the effect it could have on young children from disadvantaged areas in Australia. These studies include the Effective Provision of Pre-school Education (EPPE) project in the United Kingdom (Sammons *et al.* 2002), the Carolina Abecedarian Project (Campbell *et al.* 2002), and the High/Scope Perry Preschool Project in the United States of America (Schweinhart *et al.* 2005). These found that young children completing these programmes had enhanced development in the areas of language, and cognitive development (Votruba-Drzal *et al.* 2004) over children who did not participate. Further, the Perry Preschool Project reported long-term benefits in relation to school completion and in avoiding trouble with the law. However, reports on the effect of these interventions on the children's social development and skills are limited.

Quality of childcare has been shown to improve children's developmental progress in the short-term, and to a lesser extent in the long term (Howes and James 2004; Karoly *et al.* 2005; Votruba-Drzal *et al.* 2004). The benefits include enhanced verbal skills, reduced anxiety and greater persistence and independence (Burchinal *et al.* 2000; Dunn *et al.* 1994). Longitudinal research into the quality of childcare in the Australian context has been limited over the decades (OECD 2000).

Defining and measuring quality

Defining the concept of 'quality' childcare is difficult, and the associated issues have been discussed and debated extensively (Burchinal and Cryer 2003; Raban 2000; Sylva *et al.* 2003). In Australia, the Quality Improvement and Accreditation System (QIAS) is used to monitor the quality of childcare. QIAS was established in the early 1990s to meet the rapid increase in demand for early childhood education and care, while maintaining quality in early childhood educational services. This system has become increasingly important in enforcing standards of quality and is often used by parents to assist in choosing a childcare centre for their child.

Discussion of quality in the research literature reveals a differing emphasis on particular components of childcare programmes. Raban (2000), for example, emphasised that quality is measured by educational and social outcomes for children and their families, while Burchinal *et al.* (2003) concluded that both cognitive and social skills were affected by childcare quality. Other approaches to defining quality focused on structural factors such as buildings and equipment, teacher–child ratio and the curriculum, while another approach focused on 'process quality' (which encompassed nurturing child–teacher relationships, harmonious peer interactions and clear communication between teachers and families) (Fleer 2000; Vandell 2004).

Examining the variables associated with structural and process quality was the basis of this study's investigation into the quality of childcare and its impact on social skills development. Figure 15.1 outlines the variables considered to be aspects of structural and process quality. The variables that have particular impact on social skills development include teacher–child interaction, peer interaction, spatial and physical environments, teacher–child interaction and quality of teaching (Burchinal and Cryer 2003; Vandell 2004).

Quality childcare, disadvantage and building social skills

Quality childcare contributes to enhanced developmental outcomes for children from socially disadvantaged backgrounds (Schweinhart *et al.* 2005; Votruba-Drzal *et al.* 2004). Results of the High/Scope project, for example, found that young children from disadvantaged background who participated in high-quality preschool programmes were more

Figure 15.1 Interrelationships between childcare quality and social skills outcomes as moderated by structural and process quality

323

likely to be prepared to participate at school, were less likely to be involved in criminal behaviour as young adults, and more likely to earn a higher income. The researchers found that an appropriate curriculum in early childhood that promoted a variety of interactions with peers and staff resulted in lasting benefits in children's learning. However, young children from socially disadvantaged backgrounds have been found to be less likely to attend early childhood programmes prior to attending formal schooling (Committee for Economic Development 2005; Vinson 2006).

In Australia, government initiatives assist and encourage access to childcare services. The Child Care Benefit (CCB) provides support for low- and middle-income families to access approved childcare services. In the state of New South Wales, the Department of Community Services (DoCS) provides opportunities for young children and their families to access early childhood services. Despite this range of government initiatives to extend access and improve affordability for families from disadvantaged areas, there remain many challenges (e.g. promoting regular attendance, maintaining quality, attracting qualified personnel to work in services). One outcome of young children not receiving quality early childhood services is the failure to develop appropriate social skills, and the awareness of society's expectations (Li-Grining and Coley 2006).

The extent and quality of social engagement fostered between children and staff is a feature of quality early childhood programmes. The ability to develop and maintain satisfactory interpersonal relationships, exhibit prosocial behaviour patterns, and be socially accepted by peers and staff reduces the chance of later behavioural and emotional difficulties in school (Gresham et al. 2004). Development of these social skills has lasting benefits, including successful completion of secondary school, and finding employment.

Young children who exhibit difficulties with appropriate social behaviour often experience peer rejection or poor peer interaction. There may be many reasons for these problems, including poor social comprehension, poor pragmatic language skills, misconception of non-verbal communication, limited interpersonal skills and low self-esteem (Elbaum and Vaughn 2003). These difficulties have been found to be influential factors in impeding quality outcomes for children from socially disadvantaged areas (Burchinal and Cryer 2003).

One strategy for addressing the impact of social disadvantage is through providing quality early childhood education (Vinson 2006) where children learn adequate social skills that enable them to socialise and communicate effectively. The specific benefits of promoting social skills within childcare centres have not been specifically examined in an Australian context, with most reference being to general social development.

Social development and development of social skills are considered most problematic in programmes located in socially disadvantaged areas (Burchinal and Cryer 2003). The impact of the level of social disadvantage on social skill development is not reported in current research; hence, this study examined this specific relationship through addressing the following research questions:

- What significant differences exist in the quality of childcare centres between socially disadvantaged and partially disadvantaged areas in Sydney?
- What is the relationship between quality of childcare and children's social skills development in disadvantaged areas in Sydney?

Method

A mixed-method design (Teddlie and Tashakkori 2003) incorporating quantitative and qualitative data was used to investigate the relationship between social skills and quality of childcare setting. The simultaneous collection of quantitative data on quality of childcare and social skills, and qualitative data on structural and process quality within childcare settings, provided a comprehensive foundation for the examination of childcare and its relationship with social skills. Similarities in findings from both kinds of data would strengthen findings, while divergent outcomes could provide insights for further research (Teddlie and Tashakkori 2003).

Sample

A proportional random sampling procedure was used to select 14 childcare centres. Seven childcare centres were selected from each of two defined domains of social disadvantage (i.e. 'disadvantaged' and 'partially disadvantaged') in the Sydney metropolitan area, using criteria established by Vinson (2004). These criteria were derived from 14 indicators: unemployment, long-term unemployment, low income, low skill employment, disability/sickness, early school leaving, non-completion of year 12 (with no further training), criminal offences, imprisonment, low birth weight, child abuse, child injuries, psychiatric hospital admissions and mortality.

Three girls and three boys from each childcare centre were selected to participate in the study. The six children were randomly chosen from those children who attended the centre on a full-time basis, and whose parents had consented to their child's participation in the study. Due to a number of centres not having six eligible children, the total number of children selected to be part of the study was reduced to 74.

Measures

Quality of childcare

The quality of each childcare centre was assessed using the *Early Childhood Environment Rating Scale – Revised Edition* or ECERS-R (Harms *et al.* 2005) and the *Early Childhood Environmental Rating Scale – Extension* or ECERS-E (Sylva *et al.* 2003) to obtain observational ratings on 11 dimensions that pertain directly to the quality of childcare. Following several hours of observation and note-taking in each centre, the trained researcher rated the centre on each of the 11 dimensions on a scale from 1 to 7, where 1 was low quality and 7 the highest measure of quality. Statistical comparison of the trained researcher's evaluations with those of a researcher highly experienced in ECERS-R produced a reliability coefficient of .86.

Social skills

The social skills measure was administered to the six children randomly chosen from each childcare centre. A childcare teacher from each centre rated each child on the two scales of the preschool level of the *Social Skills Rating System* (SSRS) (Gresham and Elliot 1990). The SSRS comprises a social skills scale (including sub-scales measuring co-operation, assertion and self-control), and a problem behaviour scale (including sub-scales measuring the tendency to externalise or internalise problems). A three-point rating scale provided a score for each student – a high score on the social skills scale indicated a high level of sociability, while a higher score on the problem behaviour scales indicated greater occurrence of problem behaviour.

Field notes and interviews

The researcher monitored each childcare centre over a period of several hours as a non-participant observer. Field notes were kept on multiple aspects of the childcare centres, based on the 11 dimensions of the ECERS-R and ECERS-E, and the two scales of the SSRS. Interviews were also conducted with teachers, other staff and the centre director about their perceptions of the children's social skills, their philosophy of childcare work, their understanding of psychosocial development, and their approach to developing these skills in the children attending the centre.

Results

Test of normality

These data were analysed to establish whether the measures were normally distributed, using the Kolmogorov-Simirnov (K-S) test. The ECERS-R and ECERS-E sub-scale data were not normally distributed ($p < .05$), and neither were the total ECERS-R ($D(14) = 0.13$, $p = .002$) and ECERS-E scores ($D (14) = 0.15$, $p < .001$). Therefore, it was necessary to apply non-parametric analyses to the ECERS-R and ECERS-E sub-scales and to both total scores. The SSRS data met the assumption of normal distribution for both subscales – social skills ($D (59) = 0.67$, $p > .05$) and problem behaviour ($D (59) = .109$, $p > .05$), indicating that a parametric analysis could validly be used.

Descriptive analysis

ECERS-R and ECERS-E were administered in 14 long day childcare centres in the Sydney metropolitan area. Data for each sub-scale and the total score of ECERS-R and ECERS-E, shown in Table 15.1, were examined for differences between disadvantaged areas and partially disadvantaged areas. The total score results for the ECERS-R and ECERS-E provide evidence that there is a small difference in the quality of childcare. Table 15.1 shows that the ECERS-R results for childcare centres in partially disadvantaged areas are 'good' (Harms *et al*. 1998), while only 'minimal' for childcare centres in disadvantaged areas. Total scores for ECERS-E (in Table 15.1) show that the quality of childcare in both areas of disadvantage was classified as 'minimal'.

Table 15.1 also shows the descriptive statistics for each sub-scale and the results of a second analysis using a Mann-Whitney test for non-parametric data. The sub-scales for personal care, activities, interaction and diversity were found to be significantly different between disadvantaged and partially disadvantaged areas, as was the total score on the ECERS-R. No statistically significant difference was found between the results from the area of disadvantage on the other sub-scales and the total score for ECERS-E.

A total of 59 completed SSRS forms were returned, including 30 from centres in partially disadvantaged areas, and 29 from centres in disadvantaged areas. As only small amounts of data were randomly missing from a range of centres the impact on the final analysis was considered to be minimal (Field 2003). The mean age of the 59 children was 51.8 months (SD = 7.8). The mean score for social skills scale across all children was 35.98 (N = 59, SD = 10.6), while for problem behaviour it was 4.53 (N = 59, SD = 3.23).

Table 15.1 Descriptive statistics on all sub-scales and total scores of the ECERS-R and ECERS-E by disadvantaged and partially disadvantaged areas

	Disadvantaged areas		Partially disadvantaged areas		Test of signifi-cances
	Mean	SD	Mean	SD	Mann-Whitney U
Space and furnishing	5.02	1.28	5.24	1.04	n.s
Personal care	4.94	1.74	5.68	1.77	S
Language-reasoning	4.49	1.21	5.01	1.79	n.s
Activities	4.27	1.39	4.79	1.33	S
Interaction	4.46	1.84	5.86	1.84	S
Programme structure	5.71	0.85	5.90	1.29	n.s
Parents and staff	5.84	1.71	6.57	0.73	n.s
Total ECERS-R	4.96	1.02	5.58	1.10	S
Literacy	4.40	1.27	4.26	1.45	n.s
Mathematics	3.19	1.61	3.33	1.62	n.s
Science and environment	4.46	1.32	4.28	2.30	n.s
Diversity	4.19	0.92	5.09	1.88	S
Total ECERS-E	4.06	0.72	4.24	1.44	n.s

An examination of SSRS scores for childcare centres in disadvantaged and partially disadvantaged areas showed small differences between the areas. The mean social skills score was slightly higher in the partially disadvantaged area (M = 37.14, SD = 11.48, range = 43) compared to the disadvantaged area (M = 35, SD = 9.83, range = 37). However, an independent t-test found the difference to be not significant (t (58) = –.82, p > .05) with a small effect size (r = .11).

A similar analysis was conducted with problem behaviour scores; the difference was found to be not significant (t (58) = –1.42, p > .05) with a small effect size (r = .18). An examination of mean scores showed that children from partially disadvantaged childcare centres scored slightly higher (M = 5.14, SD = 3.71) than the children from centres in disadvantaged areas (M = 3.97, SD = 2.64). This result indicated that children in partially disadvantaged areas demonstrated marginally more problem behaviours than the children in disadvantaged areas.

Finally, the relationship between social skills as measured by the SSRS and the quality of the centres was investigated directly. No statistically significant relationships were found between the scores from the SSRS and the subtests and total scores of the ECERS-R and ECERS-E.

Qualitative analyses

Field notes and interviews were undertaken during visits by the first author. The field notes and interviews were analysed to identify events that linked the quality of childcare to the development of social skills. The events identified were sorted to identify patterns/trends, and following a process of continual refinement a number of patterns emerged.

A recurring factor, identified from observations and interviews, was the level of interaction between children and childcare workers, and between the children themselves. It was observed that childcare centres from partially disadvantaged areas promoted social skills more through a series of semi-structured activities. Staff were observed consciously designing activities to encourage higher levels of interaction, and providing multiple opportunities for child–teacher and child–child interactions. While these kinds of interactions were also evident in childcare centres from disadvantaged areas they were not observed to be as frequent, nor to be occurring naturally. They tended to take the form of 'free play' sessions and semi-structured activities instead. The results of the ECERS-R and ECERS-E assessments, and consideration of the effects of the physical structure of childcare centres, supported this observation.

The nature and quality of interactions between children and their peers and teachers was observed to differ across childcare settings. In all childcare centres, there was evidence of positive teacher–child interactions reflected in both verbal and non-verbal engagements. The intensity of these interactions was modified by the teacher–child ratio. In one childcare centre from a disadvantaged area where the teacher–child ratio was one to seven (current NSW regulation is one to ten in this age group, Department of Community Services 2004), the teacher was observed to engage regularly with each child, promoting social skills. This observation was also made in childcare centres from partially disadvantaged areas, where the slightly smaller number of students in a class permitted more frequent interactions.

Teacher–child interaction was most obvious during the resolution of conflict between children. Teachers used these times to promote social skills, language and positive relationships, and then to refine these skills during other sessions. While this was observed to be more frequent and intense in childcare centres from partially disadvantaged areas, it was noted that children in these centres scored higher on the problem behaviour scale of the SSRS (suggesting that there were more opportunities to interact due to problematic behaviour).

While there was evidence that fewer children in centres permitted greater opportunities for interaction between children and staff, centres with more children were observed to have greater opportunities for children to interact with peers. These interactions tended to be less structured and occurred in more natural situations.

The physical sizes of the childcare centres visited during this study varied considerably. In disadvantaged areas, childcare centres tended to be larger than in the partially disadvantaged areas and they catered for more children (e.g. 70 children attending on different days throughout the week), and a wider range of ages (e.g. 12 to 60 months old). These factors appeared to place considerable stress on staffing levels, facilities and resources. In contrast, centres in partially disadvantaged areas were smaller in terms of the number of children registered to attend per week (e.g. ten children in one of the centres). This allowed them to create a more intimate environment and to foster better communication between teachers, children and parents. This kind of atmosphere appeared to create a sense of physical and emotional security in the children, providing opportunities for staff to promote social skills.

The physical environments of the centres varied according to disadvantage. Centres in partially disadvantaged areas tended to have greater natural light, and were not dominated by security fences and walls. Observations suggested that these more inviting environments were also more conducive to developing social and language skills.

The physical structures of the centres in the two areas were noticeably different. Childcare centres in disadvantaged areas, catered for more children and tended to be in larger buildings. These cluttered interiors seemed less conducive to social interaction. Inside the childcare centres in partially disadvantaged areas, however, there was an impression of greater space, and more conveniently accessible resources that facilitated interaction.

The programme and daily routine observed in each of the childcare centres was seen to vary across the areas. The routines in centres located in disadvantaged areas were more highly structured and outlined on noticeboards. They included plentiful teacher-directed activities and prescribed times for other activities. The level of divergence from these schedules was not as apparent in these centres as it was for the childcare centres of partially disadvantaged areas. This phenomenon may be explained by the demands of having to deal with larger numbers of children in one setting, or by the limited observation period, or by a combination of other variables unique to the centre.

Discussion

This study examined the quality of childcare centres in partially disadvantaged and disadvantaged areas of metropolitan Sydney, and its impact on social skills development in young children. The relationship between the two was investigated through a consideration of process and structural quality in 14 childcare centres, using a mixed-method research design. The design of this study relied primarily on the interpretation of quantitative data. Qualitative data were used to complement the findings from these analyses, and to suggest alternative explanations.

A number of significant differences in the quality of childcare were identified between centres in socially disadvantaged and partially disadvantaged area of Sydney. Statistically significant differences were found on the subtests of the ECERS-R and ECERS-E (i.e. personal care, activities, interaction, diversity) and in the total score on the ECERS-R. These results provided evidence that childcare centres in partially disadvantaged areas offered a slightly higher quality of childcare than those in disadvantaged areas.

A statistically non-significant correlation, however, was found between the scores from the SSRS, and the subtests and total scores of the ECERS-R and ECERS-E. This finding could be attributed to the small sample size (both in terms of the number of childcare centres involved, and the number of children recruited for this study). A closer examination of process and structural quality provided some qualitative insights into the relationship between the quality of childcare and the development of social skills.

The level of social interaction (e.g. child–child, staff–child) was found to be significantly different between centres in partially disadvantaged and disadvantaged areas. Observations provided evidence that interactions were more frequent and intense for children in childcare centres in partially disadvantaged areas. The level of interaction observed, and reported by centre directors, appeared to be due to smaller numbers of children attending the centres and the increased opportunities for staff to be more aware of individual differences, needs and interests. While the child–adult ratio was observed to be only slightly lower in centres in partially disadvantaged areas, this lower ratio provides greater opportunity for adults to engage with children, and to reduce stress and anxiety among staff (Li-Grining and Coley 2006; Vandell 2004). Directors also reported the level of staff qualification to be an important additional explanation for this finding, supporting evidence that formal qualifications lead to staff being better able to interact with children and to intervene constructively when appropriate. Formally qualified staff also tend to be more skilled in delivering stimulating and socially supportive programmes for young children (Burchinal *et al.* 2003; Li-Grining and Coley 2006; Vendall 2004).

There were also qualitative differences found in the activities and programmes observed between centres in partially disadvantaged and those in disadvantaged areas (supporting the results of the ECERS-R assessment). Programmes in disadvantaged areas were observed to be more structured and organised consciously around themes of relevance and interest to children. In contrast, the programmes in partially disadvantaged centres seemed to offer more scope for spontaneity and were only loosely organised around the children's interests. These observations, however, should not be interpreted as advocating one approach to programming over the other. They do, nevertheless, highlight the need for centres to purposively engage children. This engagement can lead to development across a number of areas, in particular, social skills (Li-Grining and Coley 2006; Sylva *et al.* 2006).

The results of the ECERS-E found that centres across both areas of disadvantage provided programmes of 'minimal' quality. A particular concern was the findings for literacy ($M = 4.33$) and numeracy ($M = 3.26$). Current research findings support the need for implementing quality early literacy, language and numeracy programmes to assist children from socially disadvantaged backgrounds to make a good start to their schooling (Hart and Risley 1995; Snow *et al.* 1998). This good start leads to a greater likelihood of students graduating from secondary school, obtaining employment and financial independence, and remaining out of trouble with the law. This outcome also reduces the person's likelihood of living in poverty in the future, and increases the chance that their own children will achieve greater levels of cognitive and social development than they did (Bradley and Crowyn 2002).

The diversity sub-scale from the ECERS-E indicated that the staff members in childcare centres from partially disadvantaged areas were more sensitive to differences among children than staff in childcare centres from disadvantaged areas. Childcare centres in partially disadvantaged areas tended to be smaller in physical size, had fewer children enrolled, and recorded higher levels of social interaction. These factors allow staff to be better acquainted with the individual needs and interests of children, and therefore they are more able to devise specifically tailored social skills development programmes for them.

A factor influencing the diversity variable that was noted by childcare directors was the low number of male staff working in the centres involved in the study. They believed that the employment of more male staff would offer valuable and more varied teacher–child interactions and provide more male role models for young children (Sumsion 2005).

Conclusion

The findings of this study are limited by its size (Vandell 2004), and its focus on the socially disadvantaged. The results nevertheless provide an insight into the quality of childcare in 14 centres in Sydney, and its impact on social skill development. The results highlighted a number of features of structural and process aspects that may offer promising approaches to developing social skills in children from socially disadvantaged backgrounds. The outcomes of this study suggest avenues for future interventional research that examines the relationship between the quality of childcare and social skills development.

The quality of childcare was found to be marginally different between centres in partially disadvantaged and disadvantaged areas (based on both quantitative and qualitative data). There were areas of difference that could be addressed in future research (e.g. qualifications of staff, physical size of settings, maximum number of children in a centre, factors that may affect primary and secondary school outcomes, etc.). Evidence from this further research would provide more insight into the pathways that children from socially disadvantaged background take when provided the benefits of quality early childhood programmes.

References

Bradley, R. and Corwyn, R. (2002) 'Socioeconomic status and child development', *Annual Review of Psychology*, 53: 371–99.

Burchinal, M. and Cryer, D. (2003) 'Diversity, childcare quality and developmental outcomes', *Early Childhood Research Quarterly*, 18: 401–26.

Burchinal, M., Roberts, J., Riggins, S., Zaisel, S.A., Neebe, E. and Bryant, D. (2000) 'Relating quality of centre child care to early cognitive and language development longitudinally', *Child Development*, 71: 338–57.

Campbell, F., Ramey, C., Pungello, E., Sparling, J. and Miller-Johnson, S. (2002) 'Early childhood education: Young adult outcomes from the abecedarian project', *Applied Developmental Science*, 6: 42–57.

Colman, E. (2006) 'Howard resurrects plan for preschool', *Australian*, 14 July, p.1.

Committee for Economic Development (CED) (2002) *Preschool for All: Investing in a Productive and Just Society*. New York: Committee for Economic Development. Available online at: http://www.ced.org/docs/report/report_preschool.pdf (retrieved 2 August 2006).

Department of Community Services (2004) *Children's Services Regulation*. Available online at: http://www.legislation.nsw.gov.au/fullhtml/inforce/subordleg+260+2004+FIRST+0+N (retrieved 22 May 2006).

Dunn, L., Beach, S. and Kontos, S. (1994) 'Quality of the literacy environment in day care and children's development', *Journal of Research in Childhood Education*, 9: 24–34.

Elbaum, B. and Vaughn, S. (2003) 'For which students with learning disabilities are self-concept interactions effective?', *Journal of Learning Disabilities*, 36(2): 101–8.

Elliot, A. (2004) 'Early childhood at a crossroads', *Education Review*, 7(2): 12–13.

Field, A. (2003) *How to Design and Report Experiments.* Thousand Oaks, CA: Sage.

Fleer, M. (2000) *An Early Childhood Research Agenda: Voices from the Field.* Research Fellow 2000. Canberra: Department of Education, Training and Youth Affairs.

Gresham, F. and Elliot, S. (1990) *Social Skills Rating System Manual.* Circle Pines, MN: American Guidance Service.

Gresham, F., Cook, C., Crews, S. and Kern, L. (2004) 'Social skills training for children and youth with emotional and behavioral disorders: Validity considerations and future directions', *Behavioral Disorders*, 30: 32–46.

Harms, T., Clifford, R. and Cryer, D. (2005) *Early Childhood Environmental Rating Scale – Revised Edition.* New York: Teachers College Press.

Hart, B. and Risley, T. (1995) *Meaningful Differences in the Everyday Experience of Young American Children.* Baltimore, MD: Paul H. Brookes.

Hill, S., Comber, B., Louden, W., Rivalland, J. and Reid, J. (1998) *100 Children go to School: Connection and Disconnections in Literacy Development in the Year Prior to School and the First Year of School.* Canberra: Department of Employment, Education, Training and Youth Affairs.

Horin, A. (2006) 'Even failure marked fit for child care', *Sydney Morning Herald*, 14 March, p. 1.

Howes, C. and James, J. (2004) 'Children's Social Development Within the Socialization Contexts of Childcare and Early Childhood Education', in P.K. Smith and C.H. Hart (eds). *Blackwell Handbook of Childhood Social Development.* Oxford: Blackwell.

Karoly, L., Kilburn, M. and Cannon, J. (2005) *Early Childhood Interventions: Proven Results, Future Promise.* Santa Monica, CA: Rand.

Li-Grining, C. and Coley, R. (2006) 'Child care experiences in low-income communities: Developmental quality and maternal views', *Early Childhood Research Quarterly*, 21: 125–41.

OECD (2000) *OECD Thematic Review of Early Childhood Education and Care Policy: Australian Background Report.* Available online at: http://www.oecd.org/copyr.html

Power, K. (2005) 'Parents under pressure: Childcare is the critical issue in finding a balance between work and family, say mums and dads', *About the House* (November). Available online at: www.aph.gov.au/house/house–news/magazine/ath25–Parents.pdf (retrieved 1 March 2006).

Prior, L. (2006) 'Child-care horrors kept from parents', *Sydney Morning Herald*, 13 March, p. 1.

Raban, B. (2000) *Just the Beginning ... DETYA Research Fellowship Report No. 1 1999–2000.* Canberra: Commonwealth of Australia.

Richardson, S. and Prior, M. (eds) (2005) *No Time to Lose: The Well-being of Australia's Children.* Melbourne: Melbourne University Press.

Sammons, P., Sylva, K., Melhuish, E., Siraj-Blatchford, I., Taggart, B. and Elliot, K. (2002) *Measuring the Impact of Pre-school on Children's Cognitive Programs Over the Pre-school Period,* Technical paper 8a, Institute of Education, University of London. London: Formara.

Schweinhart, L., Montie, J., Xiang, Z., Narnett, W., Belfield, C. and Nores, M. (2005) *Lifetime Effects: The High/Scope Perry Preschool Study Through Age 40.* Tpsilanti, MI: High/Scope Press.

Snow, C., Burns, S. and Griffin, P. (1998) *Preventing Reading Difficulties in Young Children.* Washington, DC: National Academy Press.

Stanley, F., Richardson, S. and Prior, M. (2005) *Children of the Lucky Country? How Australia has Turned its Back on Children and Why Children Matter.* Sydney: Pan Macmillan Australia.

Sumsion, J. (2005) 'Male teachers in early childhood education: Issues and case study', *Early Childhood Research Quarterly*, 20: 109–23.

Sylva, K., Siraj-Blatchford, I. and Taggart, B. (2003) *Assessing Quality in the Early Years: Early Childhood Environment Rating Scale – Extension (ECERS-E). Four Curricular Sub-scales.* Stoke on Trent: Trentham Books.

Sylva, K., Siraj-Blatchford, I., Taggart, B., Sammons, P., Melhuish, E., Elliot, K. and Totsika, V. (2006) 'Capturing quality on early childhood through environmental rating scales', *Early Childhood Research Quarterly*, 21: 76–92.

Teddlie, C. and Tashakkori, A. (2003) 'Major Issues and Controversies in the Use of Mixed Method in the Social and Behavioural Sciences', in A. Tashakkori and C. Teddlie (eds), *Handbook of Mixed Methods in Social and Behavioural Research.* Thousand Oaks, CA: Sage.

Vandell, D. (2004) 'Early child care: The known and the unknown', *Merrill-Palmer Quarterly*, 50: 387–414.

Vinson, T. (2004) *Community Adversity and Resilience: The Distribution of Social Disadvantage in Victoria and New South Wales and the Mediating Role of Social Cohesion.* Richmond: Jesuit Social Services.

Vinson, T. (2006) *The Education and Care of Our Children: Good Beginnings.* NSW Teachers Federation. Available online at: http://www.nswtf.org.au/media/latest_2006/20060518_Preschools.html (retrieved 21 May 2006).

Votruba-Drzal, E., Coley, R. and Chase-Lansdale, P.L. (2004) 'Child care and low-income children's development: Direct and moderated effects', *Child Development*, 75(1): 296–312.

Zwi, K. and Henry, R. (2005) 'Children in Australian society', *Medical Journal of Australia*, 183: 154–60.

Chapter 16

Policies in the UK to promote the well-being of children and young people

Gillian Pugh

Abstract

This chapter reviews the very considerable policy agenda introduced by the New Labour government in Britain since 1997, with a particular focus on prevention. Drawing on research and debate in the fields of prevention and early intervention prior to 1997, the chapter summarises the main policy areas in which the UK government is seeking to improve the lives of children and families, and examines the role that an understanding of risk and protective factors, of vulnerability and resilience, have played in promoting children and young people's overall well-being. The Green Paper *Every Child Matters*, and the subsequent 2004 Children Act and the Every Child Matters: Change for Children programme focuses on five key outcomes which aim to narrow the gap between those who do well and those who do not. The chapter considers the ambitious change agenda within this, which includes a bringing together of services around the needs of children and families, a stronger emphasis on consulting with children and young people, improvement and integration of universal services, more specialist help to promote opportunity and prevent problems, shared responsibility for safeguarding children, and a remodelling of the workforce.

Introduction

The New Labour government, elected in 1997, has put children,

337

young people and families high on its agenda. After years of neglect the twin concepts of prevention and early intervention have begun to gain acceptance. Although the 1989 Children Act required local authorities to combine child protection work with families 'at risk' with preventive services for families of children 'in need', scarce resources and lack of clarity around the definition of need led to rationing of services rather than better support. Policy decisions over the past eight years, however, have recognised that many of the problems experienced by adolescents and young adults could have been prevented or at least ameliorated had there been a greater investment in appropriate support both earlier in their lives and earlier in the course of particular difficulties. To those who work with families and young children, this seems to be so obvious as to be hardly worth arguing for, but for politicians it has taken rather longer to recognise.

Early in the life of the new government, a Treasury-led cross-departmental spending review (HM Treasury 1998) convened a number of seminars to explore the research evidence on which factors put some children and young people at risk of being socially excluded, ways in which some of these risks could be avoided or reversed, and those attributes or protective factors that can give children and young people the capacity to withstand the challenges and threats of life and 'bounce back' from potential setbacks – a concept often described as resilience. The key protective factors for a child can be summarised in four main areas (see Bynner 1998; Oliver and Smith 2000; Pugh 1998 for a detailed review). The first is the overall environment or context: an adequate standard of living. The second is the characteristics of the child: a temperament or disposition that encourages care-giving, leading to high self-esteem, sociability and autonomy, the ability to solve problems and an internal locus of control. The third relates to family characteristics: dependable care-givers, growing up in a family with one or two dependable adults, with positive and appropriate child-rearing practices. And the fourth is community or neighbourhood characteristics: networks of community support, including a prosocial peer group, and schools and children's centres where children are valued and learning encouraged. This research and the way in which it has been presented has been crucial in the development of policy since 1997 and to the seminal Green Paper *Every Child Matters* (DfES 2004a) which is discussed below.

In a review of preventive work with families in 1997, Sinclair *et al.* (1997) concluded that:

whatever the problem we are trying to prevent, there are common themes that should inform our approach to preventive work ...

- the need to work with families, to build self-esteem and to enable them to identify their needs and how these can be addressed;
- the need to achieve the right balance between universal and targeted services to ensure that those most in need can benefit from primary prevention;
- the development of interventions that are co-ordinated and which successfully interlink services delivered by all sectors and agencies and at all preventive levels;
- the essential requirement that new services or ways of working are evaluated, indicating which services are effective for which particular families or young people. (Sinclair *et al.* 1997: 40)

Looking back over the past nine years we have come a long way, but I would argue that these are still the issues that we are grappling with today.

The broad policy agenda

Early in their first term, a number of key priorities emerged from the government that have subsequently informed policy development. These are summarised briefly here as a backdrop to a more detailed look at the fairly radical changes that are under way in 2006. Driven by the huge increase in the numbers of children living in poverty during the previous administration – from one in ten in 1970 to one in three in 1997 – the overriding commitment has been the declared aim of reducing child poverty, and eradicating it in 20 years (HM Treasury 1998). The strong association between poverty and poor physical and mental health, low educational attainment, behavioural difficulties, truancy and criminal activity has been proved through numerous studies. Government policies have provided additional financial support for all families, targeted benefits for those most in need, and a drive to support parents in returning to work. Although progress has been made in reducing the number of children living in poverty, there has not been a strong emphasis on reducing inequalities and redistributing wealth, and the gap between rich and poor remains unacceptably high – leading as one recent study showed to increased level of stress, ill-health and earlier mortality among those who are worst off (Wilkinson 2005).

Improving access to employment has been a key plank in the anti-poverty strategy, and the main driver behind the very considerable expansion of childcare provision (see Sylva and Pugh 2005). The emphasis on paid employment has, however, led to many parents feeling torn between the conflicting demands of returning to work in order to come off benefits, and fulfilling the many demands of being a 'good enough' parent. Despite a seemingly integrated strategy for children's centres across the country (HM Treasury 2004) it is also leading to a continuing tension between the provision of high-quality early education and day care to support parents returning to work.

The other side of the coin has been improved support for families. The 1998 Green Paper *Supporting Families* (published by the Home Office, at that point responsible for family policy) recognised the need for a greater role for the state in supporting parents in bringing up their children. It proposed a number of developments including access to support through local Sure Start schemes (to which I will return), better financial support, a better balance between work and family life, strengthening marriage and better support for more serious problems, including support for teenage parents. More recently a £25m Parenting Fund has supported the development of a number of parenting and family support programmes. There is currently something of a vacuum in family policy, with conflicting messages coming from government departments: on the one hand an instrumentalist view of parents as the purveyors of better educated and better behaved children (and punishments for parents who do not ensure children attend school, or whose children misbehave) and on the other a strong emphasis on parental choice, or parents as consumers.

Integral to the anti-poverty agenda has been a commitment to reducing social exclusion. The focus here has been on the regeneration of inner-city areas, and reducing truancy, antisocial behaviour, homelessness and teenage pregnancy. There have been initiatives, government units and even tsars to tackle all of these. Following the Treasury spending review of 2002 there has been a much stronger emphasis on prevention with a requirement (subsequently overtaken by the Children Act) on all local authorities to establish preventive strategies. Local neighbourhood renewal strategies have been a key part of the social inclusion agenda, sometimes appearing to draw on community development initiatives from the 1970s. These have recently taken on a new urgency with the renewed emphasis on citizenship following the London bombings in July 2005.

Improving health and raising educational standards have also been central planks of the policy agenda. Following publication in 2000 of *The National Health Service Plan* (which made almost no mention of children and young people other than a recommendation about eating more fruit) a Children's Taskforce was established to create a *National Service Framework for Children* (Department of Health 2004). This lays down service standards in a number of key areas, including mental health and psychological well-being, disabled children, children in special circumstances, children in hospital and healthy children and young people. The commitment to raising educational standards is evident in a wide range of policy initiatives, including the expansion of nursery education and childcare reducing class sizes, and the focus on improving literacy and numeracy in primary schools (DfES 2004b).

There has also been a rethinking of how public services are delivered and by whom. This has included a stronger focus on what consumers want rather than what providers think they should have, as well as a renewed emphasis on the role of the private and voluntary sector providers. An important part of the consumer focus has been a recognition that children and young people should be more involved in decision-making. Building on the commitment of the 1989 Children Act to promote the best interests of the child, and the need to give children a voice in decisions that affect their lives, the importance of involving and listening to children and young people has become central at all levels of policy-making, even if it is still at times somewhat tokenistic. It has also led to the appointment – after much discussion – of a Children's Commissioner in England, following on from similar appointments in Scotland, Northern Ireland and Wales. Improved and more responsive service delivery also requires joined-up thinking and joined-up services. This has driven all policy development over the past eight years, and underpins the Every Child Matters: Change for Children agenda, which is discussed below.

Finally, there has been some attempt to base policy on the evidence of what works, with a strong emphasis on the evaluation of new initiatives. There is certainly a much greater use of research evidence in policy development – but governments are always in a hurry, and are looking for quick and easy wins, and solutions from a single bullet. Many of the major evaluation programmes under way provide evidence of the impact of shifting policy (On Track – Hine 2005), of the pressure to produce results in unrealistic timescales (Children's Fund – Mason *et al.* 2005) and of national policy developing in advance of the findings (Sure Start – Tunstill *et al.* 2005).

Sure Start local programmes – a case study

Before coming on to the broader agenda, a brief introduction to Sure Start illustrates a number of themes from the current policy agenda – the use of research evidence to establish key policies, the emphasis on prevention and early intervention, the speed of delivery, a considerable financial commitment to evaluation, the move to expansion before any findings emerged, and the model that Sure Start provided for the broader Every Child Matters agenda. Sure Start had its origins in a Treasury-led cross-departmental review of services for children under eight, established within few months of the Labour government coming into power. A number of people who were invited to contribute papers to three Treasury seminars pulled out a series of key themes related to risk and protective factors in relation to the child, the family and the community (see Pugh 1998, for example). As stated above, this is now commonplace, but in the late 1990s this was still a novel concept. Research on early brain development and the importance of the first two years was emphasised, as was research on the long-term impact of high-quality early education, on the importance of parents, of styles of parenting and of support for parents. The papers argued for the need to bring services together to respond holistically to the needs of children and families; for the importance of reaching out to vulnerable families and making services accessible; and pointed to the value of working with vulnerable families through mainstream services (Pugh 1998).

In July 1998 the government announced a £540m Sure Start programme, to fund some 250 local programmes covering 150,000 children. The senior Treasury official described it as:

> a radical cross-departmental strategy to raise the physical, social, emotional and intellectual status of young children through improved services. It is targeted at children under four and their families in areas of need. It is part of the Government's policy to prevent social exclusion and aims to improve the

life chances of younger children through better access to early education and play, health services for children and parents, family support and advice on nurturing. It will be locally led and locally delivered, but will be based on evidence from the UK and elsewhere on 'what works' in terms of improving the life chances of children and their parents. (Glass 1999: 264)

The guidance for local Sure Start schemes drew heavily on the research evidence and advice given to an initially sceptical Treasury through extensive consultation. All local schemes had to provide core services, but in response to local need as assessed by the local management board, on which parents and all relevant professionals were represented. As the Treasury spokesperson concluded:

The Sure Start programme represents a new way of doing things both in the development of the policy and in its delivery. It is an attempt to put into practice 'joined-up thinking' but it is also an outstanding example of evidence-based policy and open, consultative government. (Glass 1999: 264)

A substantial evaluation programme was commissioned, and even before the ink was dry on the contract the scheme was expanded to 500 communities. The first major evaluation report has recently been published (NESS 2005), but already the goal posts have been moved again, with further expansion of the Sure Start concept, but through the establishment of 3,500 children's centres by 2010, rather than through separate Sure Start schemes (HM Treasury 2004). This has led to some feisty articles in the national press (*Guardian*, 5 January and 16 February 2005) with Glass arguing that the original concept has been abandoned, while the head of the Sure Start Unit in government points to its expansion and 'mainstreaming'. There has also been criticism from the House of Commons Education select committee that significant changes are being made before the evidence is available (House of Commons 2005; see also Tunstill *et al.* 2005).

The Children's Fund and On Track

Brief mention should also be made of the Children's Fund, a financially much more limited initiative, but one that has been available to all local authorities to enable them to provide preventive services for children aged 5 to 13 and their families. The Children's Fund has been required to place a strong emphasis on reducing offending behaviour, and the overall programme has now incorporated some 22 'On Track' projects, initially funded by the Home Office to reduce delinquency (Hine 2005). The selection criteria for projects within the fund have included the promotion of community cohesion (with a particular emphasis on the role of the voluntary sector), multi-agency working, and consulting parents and children (Mason *et al.* 2005). The funding has been far from secure, and the Fund has not enjoyed the same level of publicity and acknowledgement as Sure Start. It remains to be seen how secure the emphasis on prevention remains when the ring-fenced grants run out in 2007/8.

Every Child Matters: Change for Children

The years since 1997 have seen a veritable blizzard of new initiatives and programmes in addition to Sure Start and the Children's Fund, including a national childcare strategy that has the aim of expanding nursery education to all three and four year olds, and the establishment of children's centres and Sure Start programmes and a 2006 Childcare Act requiring local authorities to secure childcare for working parents); a National Connexions Services, set up by the government, bringing together education, support and advice for young people; Quality Protects, in social care settings, with initiatives that ring-fenced funding intended to improve the life chances of children looked after by local authorities; and, within local areas, New Deal for Communities and Neighbourhood Renewal funding.

But it is the Green Paper *Every Child Matters* (HM Treasury 2003), described by the Prime Minister at its launch as the most important document relating to children for over 30 years, and the subsequent Children Act that are likely to have the biggest impact on changing the culture and the organisation of children's services – and hopefully outcomes for children – in the UK.

The Green Paper was initially planned as a response to the report by Lord Laming into the death of Victoria Climbié in 2000 at the hands of two people who were supposed to be caring for her. Her case was known to social services, the health service and the police in two boroughs, but on ten separate occasions they failed to protect her. The government remit was to focus on children at risk, but after discussion with many working in the field, the report took prevention as its starting point, and accepted the view that to support *all* children better through well co-ordinated mainstream services is more likely to benefit those in need and at risk than a separate child protection service. The five key themes of *Every Child Matters* are a strong foundations in the early years; a stronger focus on parenting and families; earlier interventions and effective protection; better accountability and integration locally, regionally and nationally; and reform of the workforce.

Prior to the publication of the Green Paper the government had set up a Children and Young Persons Unit, and as an adviser to that Unit, Pugh contributed to a paper that argued for a focus on entitlements for children and young people – and on better outcomes rather than inputs or outputs. Drawing on experience in the United States and to some extent in the UK, the paper described how, through better data collection and the involvement of communities, a focus on outcomes could enable local communities to be clearer about their priorities and the effectiveness of service delivery (see Utting *et al.* 2001). The publication of *Every Child Matters* took this approach as central to its recommendations. The *overall aims* are summarised as improving outcomes for all children, and narrowing the gap between those who do well and those who do not; improving and integrating universal services; more specialist help to promote opportunity and prevent problems; reconfiguring services around the child and family; and sharing responsibility for safeguarding children.

Targeted services were to be planned and delivered within a universal context, as can be seen from Figure 16.1. The five main outcomes (with a host of additional sub-outcomes) are:

- Being healthy – enjoying good physical and mental health, and living a healthy lifestyle.
- Staying safe – being protected from harm and neglect.
- Enjoying and achieving – getting the most out of life and developing the skills for adulthood.
- Making a positive contribution – being involved with the community and society and not engaging in antisocial or offending behaviour.
- Economic well-being – not being prevented by economic disadvantage from achieving their full potential in life.

The *long-term vision* emerges through the initial Green Paper and the subsequent implementation document – *Every Child Matters: Change for Children* (DfES 2004a). In terms of service provision this is seen as the development of integrated education, childcare, health and social care, including family support services for those aged up to

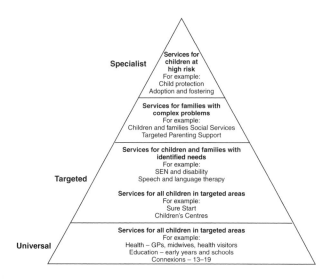

Figure 16.1 Targeted services within a universal context

19 through three main models: children's centres for children under five and their families; extended schools; and improved services for young people. There is also a focus on better support for parents, on appropriately qualified staff, and on more effective interplay between universal and specialist services.

The vision and the current implementation programme are extraordinarily ambitious, in that they require cultural and organisational change at every point of the system. At central government level most services for children and families have been brought within a Children, Young People and Families directorate, within the Department for Education and Skills, under the direction of a Minister for Children. This new department includes social care and children looked after (transferred from the Department of Health), children affected by family breakdown (transferred from the Lord Chancellor's department), family policy (transferred from the Home Office) and all early years services. But significantly it does not include schools (within the DfES but under a separate minister), children's health or the youth justice system – to which I will return.

In local areas, the existing administrative arrangements led by a director of education and a director of social services are being replaced with a single director of children's services, and an elected councillor with a brief for children and young people. The 2004 Children Act requires these changes, and also puts a duty on local authorities to promote co-operation between agencies to improve children's well-being and to work together to safeguard and protect the welfare of children; and allows for the pooling of resources. The means of delivering joined-up services that meet the needs of children, young people and families and lead to improved outcomes is through Children's Trusts. These can best be illustrated through Figure 16.2, generally referred to as the onion diagram.

Children's Trusts are seen as the main catalysts for change. The starting point is children, young people and families, living within local communities, and they are at the centre of the change programme. The next layer is integrated people – professionals working together in multi-agency teams, often co-located, with a lead professional taking responsibility for every child for whom additional support is required. There are also wide-ranging plans to ensure that the training of all staff who work with children, whether from a health, education, social welfare or youth justice background, includes a common core of skills and knowledge. The next layer is integrated processes – a single common assessment framework, and a single database of information on every child and young person.

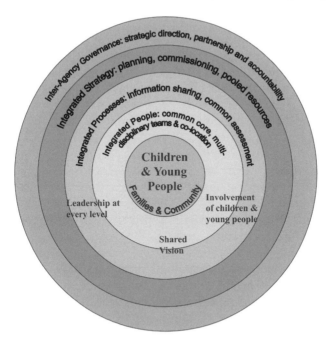

Figure 16.2 Children's Trust arrangements
Source: DfES (2004a)

Moving outwards again, though in reality this is the engine of reform, is integrated systems – a single system for assessing need, delivering a children's plan for the whole local area (through a Children and Young People's Partnership Board involving education, social care, health, police, probation, leisure and the voluntary sector), and jointly commissioning services through pooled budgets. And finally, steering the whole agenda, is inter-agency governance, led within central government by the Minister for Children, Young People and Families, and at local government level by the director of children's services, a new position integrating the previous posts of director of education and director of social services. To this must be added the integrated inspection system, whereby some ten inspectorates have come together to create a single framework for inspecting all children's services, from schools to adoption agencies to youth offending institutions, against the five outcomes, with a key question at the centre – what does it feel like to be a child or young person using this service?

The legislative underpinning for this programme of change is the 2004 Children Act, which requires the integrated inspection framework to inform inspection of all children's services, and requires local authorities and other key agencies to work together to promote children's well-being, to set up a local Safeguarding Children's Board, to devise a single children and young person's plan, and to appoint a children's services director.

The key for ensuring that prevention remains central is the concept of 'joined-up' mainstream services. For children under five, the central concept is the development of children's centres, currently numbering around 200 but with an expectation that there will be 3,500 by 2010 (DfES 2004b). Children's centres are being merged with the Sure Start local programmes where they exist, and will include early education and childcare places, in group settings, with childminders and at home; parenting and family support; health advice and information; preventative services to support additional needs, including outreach work in communities; and support for parents moving into training or employment. There are still issues about the affordability and sustainability of all-day integrated early education and care, and parents are still paying the vast majority of the cost, but free nursery education for all three and four year olds is being extended to 15 hours a week for 38 weeks of the year.

For school-age children, services are to come together around schools or clusters of schools, and by 2010 all schools are to become *extended schools*, offering a range of activities beyond the traditional school day (DfES 2005a). Primary schools are to offer 'childcare' before and after school, and secondary schools are also to open before and after school offering music, sport and holiday activities. Support for parents and health and social care are also to be based in or around schools.

Young people

When *Every Child Matters* was published, there was a strong view that while its offer for children and families was good, it neglected the needs of young people. A youth Green Paper – *Youth Matters* (DfES 2005b) – was published subsequently, which has four main strands. The main focus is on things for young people to do and places to go – a requirement on local authorities to secure positive activities for all young people, with opportunity cards, and an opportunity fund. There is also an emphasis on encouraging young people to become volunteers; a new look at information, advice and guidance, giving schools and colleges a greater role in providing advice and guidance to young people; and targeted support for young people in trouble or with serious problems, bringing together current funding and support systems.

In relation to this last point, as was noted earlier, responsibility for youth crime has remained with the Home Office, and the work of the Youth Justice Board nationally and the youth offending teams (YOTs) at local level has not dovetailed in well with the children and young people's agenda. The Home Office focus on antisocial behaviour and the introduction of and increasing use of antisocial behaviour orders (ASBOs) appears to have come from a very different stable. There is a concern that children are treated differently when they have offended – or might offend – with a strong focus on short-term behaviour change. There has also been some confusion between the respective roles of youth offending teams and mainstream children's services with regard to preventive work, with the YJB rolling out a range of programmes – Youth Inclusion Programmes, Youth Inclusion and Support Panels, mentoring, parenting programmes – that may be successful but are not always co-ordinated with other preventive measures in local areas. Although many YOTs have provided a good model of multi-agency working, the Standing Committee on Youth Justice (2005) has expressed concern that current youth justice arrangements infringe children's rights, are not congruent with children's policy and that many of the YOT programmes treat all children as potential offenders. This last point is central to the debate about targeting services. To target individual children and young people can be stigmatising and can become a self-fulfilling prophecy – but to target communities may miss some of those most at risk or in need.

Workforce strategy

The creation of the ambitious new children's agenda will only be possible through significant changes to the workforce. The *Children's Workforce Strategy* (DfES 2005c) is broad-ranging and ambitious, recognising that there need to be considerable improvements in the level of skills and qualifications within the workforce, as well as greater coherence across the many different professional groups. The newly established Children's Workforce Development Council will drive many of the proposed reforms, including improved recruitment, workforce development and retention. Among the many challenges the council faces are the creation of a single qualifications framework, and the implementation in the training of all those who work with children of a common core of skills and knowledge – effective communication with children and families, child development; safeguarding and promoting the welfare of the child, supporting transitions, multi-agency working and sharing information. There will also be an emphasis on improving leadership, management and supervision and developing local workforce strategies within every Children's Trust. Priority in the first instance will be given to the early years – the quality and stability of the workforce, improved qualifications and better leadership. The strategy has been broadly welcomed, but considerable resources are required to improve the skills of an under-qualified workforce, and there is as yet no sign that these resources will be forthcoming.

Challenges for the future

There has been very considerable investment in services for children, young people and families since 1997, and already there is substantial progress on the ground. Children are increasingly being seen within the context of their families and communities, there is a greater emphasis on consulting with children and young people, there is a continuing commitment to reducing child poverty, and at management and service delivery level there is already extensive evidence of agencies working better together and focusing on improving outcomes for children. But a number of challenges remain.

This is a very demanding agenda. It requires a paradigm shift and very considerable cultural change on the part of everyone working in children's services, and it will take a long time to work through. It requires change management skills on the part of managers and leaders at local level, and a holding of nerve on the part of ministers, who may not see outcomes improving as quickly as they would wish. In preparation for the next Comprehensive Spending Review there are already signs that both the Prime Minister and the Treasury are looking for evidence that outcomes are substantially improving.

It is also an ambitious agenda that is not cost neutral. Despite additional funding for the expansion of some services – notably early education – the overall context is one of improvements in efficiency and reductions in budgets. While making better use of existing resources by bringing agencies together will achieve some savings, further investment is required, particularly in workforce reform, if real progress is to be made. A recent report from the House of Commons Education select committee (2005) was of the view that the financial implications of the programme of reform had not been properly assessed, and expressed doubt that a policy as ambitious as this could be funded from existing budgets. Prevention requires multi-agency co-operation and is easier when funding is ring-fenced. As the Sure Start programmes begin to integrate with children's centres within a tighter funding regime, and when the Children's Fund grants come to an end, there is a very real danger that some imaginative and successful preventive work with vulnerable children, young people and families could disappear. When money is tight, experience tells us that preventive services are the first to go.

While the reforms have brought together many services, there are still some weak links in critical parts of the system. Schools and general practitioners in local communities are central to delivering 'joined-up' services, and yet many of them are not yet engaged in the change process; and the knee-jerk reaction to youth crime within central government and local communities is still driving a wedge between preventive work with vulnerable young people and policies for young offenders. The role of schools is especially critical, and yet there is no duty on them to co-operate, and the five-year DfES strategy for schools (DfES 2004b) and a controversial education White Paper *Higher Standards: Better Schools for All* (DfES 2005d) rewards successful schools with greater independence. Having focused for so

351

long on the attainment agenda, it is hard for many head teachers to understand that supporting children's overall well-being is in fact central to improving education achievement.

There is extensive evidence that policy is now much more firmly based on research evidence than was once the case. But the political imperative of quick wins and forever changing ministers mean that the young shoots of many new initiatives are pulled up before they have had time to take root. Policy is often changed in advance of evaluation findings, and evaluation studies themselves struggle as goal posts are moved. There is also an ongoing debate about 'what works' and how to make the most difference to children's lives. This is particularly lively at present in relation to Sure Start, where evaluation is showing failure to reach some of the most vulnerable families (National Evaluation of Sure Start 2005). The 'community empowerment and engagement' in the most deprived communities model on which Sure Start is based is very different from a very structured intervention targeted at specific children and families. It seems to me that we need a combination of these approaches if we are to reach those most likely to become involved in crime. We have embarked on an interesting and ambitious journey, for which there is considerable enthusiasm in the field, and already much progress has been made. It will require inspired and resolute leadership from ministers through to front-line workers and rather more funding than is currently available, if we are to achieve our goals.

References

Bynner, J. (1998) 'What are the causes of social exclusion affecting young children', in HM Treasury, *Comprehensive Spending Review: Cross Departmental Review of Provision for Young Children: Supporting papers Vols 1 and 2.* London: HMSO.

Department for Education and Skills (2004a) *Every Child Matters: Change for Children.* London: HMSO.

Department for Education and Skills (2004b) *Five-year Strategy for Children and Learners.* London: HMSO.

Department for Education and Skills (2005a) *Extended Schools: Access to Opportunities and Services for All.* London: HMSO.

Department for Education and Skills (2005b) *Youth Matters.* London: HMSO.

Department for Education and Skills (2005c) *Children's Workforce Strategy.* London: HMSO.

Department for Education and Skills (2005d) *Higher Standards: Better Schools for All.* London: HMSO.

Department of Health (2004) *National Service Framework for Children, Young People and Maternity Services*. London: HMSO.

Glass, N. (1999) 'Sure Start: The development of an early intervention programme for young children in the UK', *Children and Society*, 13(4): 257–64.

HM Treasury (1998) *Comprehensive Spending Review: Cross Departmental Review of Provision for Young Children: Supporting Papers Vols 1 and 2*. London: HMSO.

HM Treasury (2003) *Every Child Matters*. London: HMSO.

HM Treasury (2004) *Choice for Parents, the Best Start for Children: A ten-year Strategy for Childcare*. London: HMSO.

Hine, J. (2005) 'Early multiple intervention: A view from On Track', *Children and Society*, 19(2): 117–30.

Home Office (1998) *Supporting Families*. London. HMSO.

House of Commons Education and Skills Committee (2005) *Every Child Matters: 9th Report of Session 2004–5*. London: Stationery Office.

Mason, P., Morris, K. and Smith, P. (2005) 'A complex solution to a complicated problem? Early messages from the national evaluation of the Children's Fund prevention programme', *Children and Society*, 19(2): 131–43.

National Evaluation of Sure Start (NESS) (2005) *Early Impact of Sure Start Local Programmes on Children and Families*, Report 013, Department for Education and Skills. London: HMSO.

Oliver, C. and Smith, M. (2000) *Effectiveness of Early Interventions*. London: Institute of Education.

Pugh, G. (1998) 'Children at risk of becoming socially excluded: An introduction to the "problem"', in HM Treasury *Comprehensive Spending Review: Cross Departmental Review of Provision for Young Children: Supporting Papers Vols 1 and 2*. London: HMSO.

Sinclair, R., Hearn, B. and Pugh, G. (1997) *Preventive Work with Families: The Role of Mainstream Services*. London: National Children's Bureau.

Standing Committee on Youth Justice (2005) *Youth Justice: Steps in the Right Direction*. London: HMSO.

Sylva, K. and Pugh, G. (2005) 'Transforming the early years in England', *Oxford Review of Education*, 31(1): 11–27.

Tunstill, J., Allnock, D., Akhurst, S. and Garbers, C. (2005) 'Sure Start local programmes: Implications of case study data from the national evaluation of Sure Start', *Children and Society*, 19(2): 158–71.

Utting, D., Rose, W. and Pugh, G. (2001) *Better Results for Children and Families: Involving Communities in Planning Services Based on Outcomes*. London: ADSS/UKI/NCVCCO.

Wilkinson, R. (2005) *The Impact of Inequality: How to Make Sick Societies Healthier*. London: Routledge.

Index